# THE SOVIET UNION TODAY

Cover photo of the Soviet Ministry of Foreign Affairs in Moscow, decorated for the May 1 holiday, by William C. Brumfield.

Book and cover design by Lisa Grayson.

This book was set in Sabon by R&S Media Services and printed and bound by George Banta Company, Inc. in the United States of America.

Library of Congress Catalog Card No. 83-08-1916
ISBN 0-941682-06-4


Distributed by the University of Chicago Press.

Marketing Department
5801 South Ellis Avenue
Chicago, Illinois 60637
(312) 962-3510


UCP order number 03875-0


Publication of this book was supported by a grant from the J. Roderick MacArthur Foundation which we gratefully acknowledge.

# Contents

       *David E. Powell*                              317

       Further Reading Suggestions                    331

       A Note for Tourists                            339

       Authors                                        341

       Index                                          345

# Preface

Workers in the field of Russian and Soviet studies have long seen the need for a book on the Soviet Union written by experts but addressed to the general reader. This book aims to fill that need. Twenty-five experts in their respective branches of the field have contributed chapters on major aspects of Soviet life combining fact and interpretation in ways designed to attract both students and the wider lay public. This is a book for anyone wanting to understand the Soviet Union today.

Perhaps I should stress what the book is not. It is not a textbook—not in the comprehensive and mainly factual sense of the term. It is more personal than that—more interpretive, more varied in approach, concerned less with "covering" the subject than with responding to the questions most commonly asked of experts. Nor is this book a scholarly monograph, written by specialists for other specialists. The notes appended to the chapters are there only to identify the source of a particular fact or quotation, to indicate where dedicated investigators might look further in the matter at hand, or to provide a little supplementary information. Most readers, therefore, will quickly pass over the notes.

Although the chapters were written by different authors and can be read as self-contained essays, they are arranged in chronological and then thematic order, and so are perhaps better read in succession, as presented. A selection of both textbooks and more specialized works in the field of Soviet studies will be found at the book's end. These "Further Reading Suggestions," carefully prepared with the advice of the authors, are meant to assist students and others determined to know more. We hope that this may be everybody. Understanding the Union of Soviet Socialist Republics, the biggest country in the world and one of its two most powerful, is no easy task.

A note on one or two technical matters. Readers of Russian will notice inconsistencies in transliteration, and wonder what is going on. With regard to the notes to the chapters, Russian words have been transliterated in accordance with the modified Library of Congress system used by the *Slavic Review*, the journal of the American Association for the Advancement of Slavic Studies. With regard to the text of the chapters, the same system has been followed, except that soft signs have been omitted and double-"i" endings of proper names have been rendered by the letter "y." Similarly, the maps in Chapter 11 follow established geographical usage except that soft signs have been dropped and Lake Baikal is spelled thus and not "Baykal." But the case of Baykal/Baikal reminds us that many Russian names are known in the West, in the United States particularly, in some other spelling; and when that is so, the more familiar spelling has been retained. But then "Yuri" Andropov, favored by such publications as the New York Times, is, like "Gorki," an intolerable solecism; and "Yury" is employed here.

In money matters, unless otherwise noted sums given in rubles can be converted at the rate of $1.50 per ruble, which is roughly the current official rate of exchange. But this is a poor guide to the ruble's real worth, for two reasons: the official rate is far too high (on the free market one dollar will fetch three, four, even five rubles); and the operation of money within the Soviet and Western economies is quite different, with barter in goods or services and payment in kind or with coupons redeemable at special stores playing a much greater role on the Soviet side. In the Soviet Union, indeed, many if not most of the good things in life cannot be bought for cash.

The authors of this book have lived and worked in the Soviet Union for varying periods of time. Moreover, as both the chapter notes and "Further Reading Suggestions" will indicate, they have published numerous works on Russian and Soviet subjects while holding responsible positions in teaching and research. I must record my gratitude to each of them for the efficient and amicable way in which our business here was conducted despite the pressing demands on their time. Many of the authors have also been associated at one time or another with the Russian Research Center at Harvard, where much of this book was planned—indeed, written. And I must acknowledge my manifold debt to that distinguished house of higher Russian and Soviet studies, in particular to Professors Abram Bergson, Marshall I. Goldman, Edward L. Keenan and Adam B. Ulam.

This book originated in a series of articles on the Soviet Union published in the *Bulletin of the Atomic Scientists* between January 1982 and the fall of 1983. Reaction to the series was such that the *Bulletin*'s editor, Ruth Adams, and her colleagues decided to expand it into a book. As the editor of the series I was asked to assume editorial responsibility for the book, which I did gladly, thinking that apart from the project's importance working with the *Bulletin*'s staff had been a most satisfying experience. I want to thank especially, for their support in seeing the book into print, Lisa Grayson, Ruth M. Grodzins, Thomas Hazinski, Steven McGuire and, above all, Ruth Young.

J.C.
Chicago
July 1983

# HISTORY

This first section of the book does not provide a systematic history of the Soviet Union, much less of the Russian Empire that preceded it. For that, readers are encouraged to consult one or more of the textbooks listed in the corresponding section of the "Further Reading Suggestions." Rather, the following three chapters deal with major historical questions that frequently arise when discussing the Soviet Union today.

The first of these concerns the links between the Russian past and the Soviet present, a question given new urgency by Aleksandr Solzhenitsyn and his critics. Nina Tumarkin then takes up the cult of Lenin, the founder of both the Communist (originally, Bolshevik) Party and the Soviet state. And Stephen F. Cohen raises the "accursed question" of Stalin, whose shadow, more even than Lenin's, looms over so much of contemporary Soviet life.

All three essays make the basic point that free historical inquiry has been suppressed in the Soviet Union with varying, largely negative results, especially for the country's political development. At the same time, polemical or ill-informed treatments of Russian and Soviet history published in the West have contributed their share to a distorted picture of that history, a point brought out in Chapter 1. For it is true, unfortunately, that much of Soviet history remains a closed book, a set of pressing questions without firm answers, as these three essays all suggest.

# 1 HISTORY

## From the Russian Past to the Soviet Present

*James Cracraft*

What links the Soviet present with the Russian past? In one form or another the question is frequently put to historians—by their students in class, by friends at dinner, by passers-by, so to speak, on land and in the air.

One can point, in reply, to obvious linguistic and closely related cultural continuities: the Russian language, in formation for centuries, is overwhelmingly the language of the multi-national Soviet Union, just as it was of the Empire that preceded it; and language is never—cannot be—perfectly value-free.

There are basic geopolitical constants: the Russian state has been the largest territorial entity in the world since the seventeenth century, its borders the longest and most difficult to defend, its principal neighbors—China and Europe—generally hostile to its pretensions if not to its very existence. Plainly, these factors will continue to influence the policies of whoever rules in Moscow.

The natural environment in which the history of the Russian-speaking people has unfolded since the beginning of the present millennium—the generally poor soils, erratic rainfall, extreme continental climate and short growing season—has of course also helped to determine the direction of that history. It will continue to do so, technological advances notwithstanding.

Moreover, environmental, geopolitical and cultural factors continuously at work in Russian historical development have produced a tradition of centralized, authoritarian government supported by extensive armed forces. It is a tradition, precisely, that is rooted in history. And such traditions are not simply wished away—as was discovered by the revolutionary elite in Russia after 1917.

3

Or one can point to a persistent element of Russian national chauvinism, obviously pre-Soviet in origin (Lenin vigorously condemned it), in both domestic and foreign Soviet policies.[1]

But the increasingly apprehensive and strongly negative views now widely held of the Soviet Union ensure that the basic question before us readily assumes an urgent political and even moral aspect, an aspect which these professionally chaste replies fail to address. So historians are asked, in addition, to explain and even to judge contemporary Soviet political behavior in the light of the past, to predict its future course, to recommend policy. It is a trap into which many of us, amateur and professional alike, have fallen.

Aleksandr Solzhenitsyn, for one, insists that "there is no continuity in the transition from pre-revolutionary Russia to the USSR. There is instead a *fatal fracture of the spine* [italics his], a break which nearly ended in complete national destruction." He could not be more emphatic: "Soviet development is not an extension of Russia's but rather its diversion in a completely new and unnatural direction." The terms "Russian" and "Soviet," "Russia" and "USSR" not only are "not interchangeable, not equivalent, and not unilinear—they are irreconcilable polar opposites and completely exclude each other."[2]

Solzhenitsyn's motive here is to explode the "distorted and biased picture of several centuries of Russian history" he finds prevalent in the West and manifest, for example, in the "persistent and tendentious generalization about the 'perennial Russian slave mentality,' seen almost as an inherited characteristic, and about the 'Asiatic tradition.'" For Solzhenitsyn, understandably, national honor as well as the cause of historical truth is at stake.

A major implication of Solzhenitsyn's widely publicized pronouncements is that beneath the evil, alien, Marxist-inspired Soviet Union there lies the good, old, eternal Russia yearning to reassert itself. Here he definitely parts company with official Soviet publicists who, while sharing his view of the Bolshevik revolution as a decisive event in Russian, indeed in world, history and his nationalist pride, otherwise regard the pre-revolutionary past with indifference if not contempt.

In the United States, Solzhenitsyn's pronouncements, with their sweeping denunciations of Western scholarship on Russia and the Soviet Union, have provoked elaborate rebuttal. Specialists have condemned his factual errors, his "intense biases," or both.[3] Contrary to his assertions, many profound and often determinative continuities in Russian and Soviet history have been discovered, or rediscovered, by historians.[4] Indeed, an aggressive, hard-line historiography, seeking to explain the (ugly) Soviet present by reference to a more or less distant Russian past, is again in the ascendant.

In this view, the revolution of 1917 in Russia was no more of a historical turning point than was the era of Peter the Great in the early eighteenth century or that of the Great Reforms in the later nineteenth. Rather, the relentless aggression of the "hypertrophic" Russian state, against its neighbors, against its own people, is the central theme. In 1917, say the hard-liners, a Bolshevik solution to the perennial problem of Russia's rulers was as good as inevitable: the problem, that is, of maintaining as a great power such a vast, poor, backward and unfortunately situated country against the pressures of a superior West—superior in every measurable respect save, periodically, the military. And the generally successful, if essentially violent solution of this problem in earlier times decisively conditioned its solution in this century.

More particularly, there is the heritage of the so-called autocratic, patrimonial, service and/or garrison state; of Russian bureaucratism, held to be worse than others; of mass peasant culture, with its "naive monarchism" masking a basic anarchism; of a "supine" Orthodox church; of serfdom and slavery; of the nineteenth-century "intelligentsia," at once impractical and extremist. This heritage, the hard-liners say, more than the dictates of Marxism or the activities of Lenin and Stalin, or modern technology, or the world wars, or the post-war policies of other states, has made the Soviet Union and Soviet practice what they are today. In Zbigniew Brzezinski's judgment, "Because Marxist power first took root in a specific Russian environment," one "formed by an autocratic political tradition, intellectual frustration, and a strong propensity toward messianism," even Stalinism, with all its horrors, was "inevitable."[5]

And the chief casualty in the whole process, now as in the past, has been the individual—the autonomous human being, his rights secure, prospering with a clear conscience in a society made up of other such individuals or, at any rate, decisively informed by individualist values.

Reflections of this largely deterministic and negative view of Russian and Soviet history are to be found everywhere, and sometimes take an extravagant turn.

"My six and one half years' experience as the military representative on the U.S. SALT negotiating team," declares General Edward L. Rowny, "has convinced me that the Soviets have not changed their inherited traits—they are still Russians." What are these "inherited traits"? An obsession with "seemingly picayune details" and with "their security," an "extreme penchant for secrecy" and an unwillingness to compromise, both a "serious inferiority complex" and a habit of bully-

ing, duplicitous behavior in the ruthless pursuit of objectives laid down
by their Kremlin masters. And General Rowny's authority for describing
such traits as "inherited"? An old textbook on Russian history is mentioned, as are the dubious memoirs of a French aristocratic visitor to
Russia about 150 years ago and two highly idiosyncratic treatises on
Russian culture.[6]

That the Soviet people view the Soviet leadership as "dictatorially
tyrannical, nonreflective of the citizenry's political desires, just is not
so," a reader was moved to write to the New York Times (April 22,
1981). "While we would like to believe that the Communist Party of
the Soviet Union is a mere aberration of Russian history," he asserts
further, apparently on the basis of his own studies, "it is, unfortunately, totally consistent with Russian historical development."

Professor Louis Halle advises The Times of London (October 4,
1980) that "the Russian state has come to regard the outside world as
made up of deadly enemies who must be foiled by guile, by deceit, and
ultimately by as much military force as the state can generate. It is not
too much to say that the outlook of the Russian state, after a millennium of bitter experience, has become paranoiac." Like the previous
writer, if a little more circumspectly, Halle advocates a policy of militant "containment" of the Soviet Union in the name of "civilization."

A recent biography of Peter the Great by Alex de Jonge offers some
of the fairest samples to hand: "In *The Gulag Archipelago* Solzhenitsyn
is bewildered by the 'rabbits,' the millions who submitted to Stalin's terror and went to the camps quietly. Blind submission to arbitrary
authority is part of the Russian tradition—there were rabbits enough in
Peter's time, too."[7]

These lines could only have been written in willful disregard of the
widespread and violent opposition in Russia to Peter's regime, and only
after a careless reading of *The Gulag*, whose "rabbits" have far more in
common with the million-fold victims of the Nazi death camps. Yet this
book was selected for sale to its members by the editors of the History
Book Club,[8] guaranteeing it additional thousands of readers. Small
wonder that Solzhenitsyn complains of the treatment accorded his people's history in the West.

The foremost exponent of the hardline historiography is Richard
Pipes. Owing to his prominence as a contributor to journals of opinion
and as an advisor to statesmen, it is not perhaps generally appreciated
that Pipes is one of our leading historians of Russia and the Soviet
Union. Nor is it generally known that his *Russia under the Old Regime*
offers the most original (and best-written) interpretation of virtually the

whole of Russian history currently available in English.[9]

Pipes's grand theme is the rise in the later Middle Ages of a "patrimonial state" in Russia, its "partial dismantling," under Western influence, from the time of Peter the Great, and its sudden transformation, between 1878 and 1881, into the first modern "police state." His narrative largely ends in the 1880s because, as he says, by then the old regime in Russia had yielded to a "bureaucratic-police regime which in effect has been in power there ever since." It was there, and then, that the "germs of twentieth-century totalitarianism" were sown.

A "patrimonial state" is one in which "political authority is conceived and exercised as an extension of the rights of ownership, the ruler (or rulers) being both sovereigns of the realm and its proprietors." It is an ancient, and alien, type of government; for in the West, authority over people and objects has come to be split into authority exercised as sovereignty and authority exercised as ownership. "One may say that the existence of private property as a realm over which public authority normally exercises no jurisdiction is the thing which distinguishes Western political experience from all the rest." Everywhere else, "the lines separating ownership from sovereignty either do not exist, or are so vague as to be meaningless."

This is one cardinal point of Pipes's interpretation: in Russia the separation referred to occurred "very late and very imperfectly" (by comparison with Western states); thus the "essential quality of Russian politics derives from the identification of sovereignty and ownership, that is, from a 'proprietary' way of looking at political authority on the part of those who happen to be in power."

Pipes's second cardinal point is that in the later nineteenth century, owing to the survival of the "patrimonial principle" in public life, the corresponding "impotence or apathy" of the social classes with respect to state authority, and the "notorious underdevelopment in Russia of legality and personal freedom," the government was able to impose, in the midst of an apparent crisis, a quick succession of emergency measures which completed the subjection of society to the arbitrary power of the bureaucracy and police. After 1881 in Russia "the 'state' meant the tsar and his officialdom; internal politics meant protecting both from the encroachments of society." Alexander III's decree of August 14, 1881, codifying and systematizing the repressive legislation dating back at least to 1845, "has been the real constitution under which—brief interludes apart—Russia has been ruled ever since."

Yet more than this, if "all the elements of the police state" were thus present in the Russian Empire of the early 1880s, certain measures carried out experimentally by the Imperial government in the first years of the twentieth century "moved into the even more sinister realm of totalitarianism."

So the emergence of the Soviet state forms only a brief epilogue—less than two pages out of a total of more than 300—to *Russia under the Old Regime*. Here it is "not in the least surprising that almost the instant they took power, the Bolsheviks began to put together the pieces of the Imperial proto-police apparatus." Again the similarity of provisions against anti-state crimes in Soviet and Imperial legal codes is remarked on. "Then, with each passing year, the mechanism of repression was perfected until under Stalin's dictatorship it attained a level of wanton destructiveness never before experienced in human history."

And not just Stalinism: "This type of legislation, and the public institutions created to enforce it, spread after the revolution of 1917 by way of Fascist Italy and Nazi Germany to other authoritarian states in Europe and overseas. One is justified in saying, therefore, that Chapters Three and Four of the Russian Criminal Code of 1845 are to totalitarianism what the Magna Carta is to liberty."

*Russia under the Old Regime* is not in the ordinary sense a textbook.[10] It is not, more plainly still, a narrative history of the sort beloved by book clubs and the popular press, one calculated to leave the reader aglow from an access of wonder, pity, terror and nostalgia. Equally, although it sometimes quotes from documents and frequently cites its secondary sources, the book is not a work of scientific, or academic, history. It does not proceed—nor does it pretend to proceed—from an exhaustive accumulation of primary data via rigorous inference to hypothesis and tentative conclusion. It rests both on a body of accepted historical facts and on a corpus of values. It is a work of synthesis rather than analysis; its argumentation is rhetorical rather than logical. It proposes a theory of history of enormous explanatory power. No one who reads the book, expert or layman, can fail to be challenged by it.

Challenged, but perhaps not wholly persuaded. The values on which *Russia under the Old Regime* rests plainly are those once called liberal, laissez-faire or individualist but now "conservative" or "neo-conservative." Central to the book's argument (see especially Chapter 8) is the myth of the "Western middle class" as the historical bearer and protector of liberty, the rule of law, personal rights and "liberal ideas." The outlook regarding nearly everything Russian is pitiless, hostile, even xenophobic. In short, the degree to which the reader is finally persuaded by this brilliant book depends on the degree to which he shares its author's own outlook and values. And the same can be said about the hard-line historiography generally—about any history written in the venerable rhetorical tradition, committed to purposes, usually unstated, beyond itself.

Where does that leave us? Solzhenitsyn's negative response to our basic question is scarcely plausible. The proposition that there are no important links between the Russia that was and the Soviet Union that is, owing to the Bolshevik revolution and its aftermath, will not get off the ground. The debate is not over whether there are such links, but over their nature and extent.

Moreover, since much of the material needed by historians remains under lock and key, and thus much of Soviet and, in fact, earlier Russian history remains a closed book, *any* emphatic or precise generalizations emanating from this field must be viewed with intense skepticism. This is to stress the difficulties—technical, logistical, but especially political—in pursuing Russian by comparison with American, British, French, or, say, Indian history.[11]

The West suffers, if anything, from a surfeit of history, from a swelling babble of competing and even mutually exclusive claims to historical truth based on ever more esoteric sets of data. But in the Soviet Union, as in Soviet Eastern Europe, history has been suppressed. History in the sense of free, disinterested inquiry into the records of the past, and the associated right of open publication, do not exist in the Soviet Union (an important *discontinuity* between the old and the new regimes). The resulting amnesia, duplicity and manipulation of the past for immediate political ends, the painful doubts and confusion that this in turn brings, have been noted by Western observers—just as a restoration of history has been one of the principal demands of Eastern dissidents and reformers.[12] Yet we in the West, awash in history, cannot seem to grasp their sense of loss.

The loss of his history explains in large part both the course of Solzhenitsyn's literary career and the passion of his attack on Western "distortions" of the Russian past. It is as if Western historians were failing in their duty both to their own public and to the Russian people. The charge is a grave one, however obliquely, reluctantly, indeed unfairly, it is made. For the hard-line historiography invites the reflective Russian to find little or no hope in the story of his past. It asks him first to renounce his own history and then to emulate the West's (happy story that it is) in building a better world. It contemplates the evolution of another polity not with the disinterest of the scientist, but with the conviction of the crusader. It tries less to understand history than to make it.

These are not the formulas with which to break down walls of misunderstanding, allay suspicion between peoples, or further the cause of knowledge itself.

Policy-makers and others who would be informed by history should
not look for simple, all-encompassing truths. The state of the discipline,
certainly in the Russian and Soviet field, simply does not provide for
that. Yet this is not a counsel of despair. Carefully circumscribed,
thoroughly researched, detailed monographic studies of particular
historical problems can yield, for a wider audience, liberating results.

Take the case of Afghanistan. The Soviet invasion of that country in
December 1979 set off a wave of anti-Sovietism in the United States that
engulfed the Russian past in bitter condemnation. The invasion was seen
as but the latest aggression in a long history of ruthless Russian
expansionism—not simply "expansion," a matter of verifiable fact, but
"expansionism," a matter of alleged ideological imperatives. Thus viewed, the invasion was not only a concrete diplomatic and perhaps military
problem to be dealt with here and now, but a problem of immense
historic dimensions requiring a proportionate response ("historic," the
adjective favored by those who *use* history, not "historical," favored by
those who *study* it).

Patient investigation of the relevant sources leads to somewhat different, and perhaps unsettling, conclusions, however:

> Russian expansion in this part of Asia, for all its momentous
> consequences, was more the product of accident than of a
> carefully considered master plan. A series of decisions of limited
> scope designed to meet specific circumstances achieved a cumu-
> lative power that was greater than the sum of its parts. . . . [Yes,]
> there was an attitude toward expansion that affected the overall
> climate in which these decisions were made. [But] this had
> nothing to do with some legendary Russian drive to obtain
> warm-water ports or some grand design for the conquest of Asia.
> Instead, Russia, after a century of Westernization, developed a
> colonialist outlook that was consciously imitative of Western
> overseas expansion. Exotic alien lands made attractive targets for
> colonialization because it was believed that they could make their
> colonial master rich and because the colonial master could in turn
> benefit the subject peoples by introducing them to civilization.
> Furthermore, all of this would prove that Russia, too, was as
> great and civilized an empire as those of Western Europe.[13]

Similarly, an exceedingly detailed study of U.S.-Soviet conflict in the
same area after World War II makes this basic point:

> The process by which American interests in the region are
> gradually defined grows out of the traditional rivalry between

Britain and Russia; this rivalry, however, takes on a different character as new players—the United States and a powerful Soviet Union—are involved. The ideological baggage which accompanies them tends to confuse the conflict by portraying their rival national interests as a clash between two world views. . . .

[Moreover] there is an almost insurmountable difficulty in differentiating between the Soviets' aggressive and defensive actions, just as there is in distinguishing between the nationalistic and ideological elements of their policies. This problem is somewhat analogous to that of distinguishing between ideals and self-interest in American foreign policy.[14]

History at its best can indeed widen our perspectives. It can help to expose, and perhaps to eliminate, the elements of arrogance, hypocrisy and dreadful self-righteousness that still afflict the Western, perhaps particularly the American, world-view. □

1. See further Ivo J. Lederer, ed., *Russian Foreign Policy: Essays in Historical Perspective* (New Haven, Connecticut: Yale University Press, 1962) and E.J. Simmons, ed., *Continuity and Change in Russian and Soviet Thought* (Cambridge, Massachusetts: Harvard University Press, 1955).

2. "Remarks at the Hoover Institution, May 24, 1976," *The Russian Review* (April 1977), p. 188.

3. *See Foreign Affairs*, issues for Spring, Summer and Fall 1980: reprinted in book form as Aleksandr I. Solzhenitsyn, *The Mortal Danger: How Misconceptions About Russia Imperil America* (New York: Harper & Row, 1981; 2nd ed. 1983), which includes letters from six critics.

4. Discussion in *Russian History*, 1977/1, for instance.

5. Zbigniew K. Brzezinski, *Between Two Ages: America's Role in the Technetronic Era* (New York: Viking Press and the Research Institute on Communist Affairs, Columbia University, 1970), p. 126.

6. Edward L. Rowny, "The Soviets are Still Russians," *Survey: a Journal of East & West Studies* (Spring 1980), pp. 2-9. In 1981 the Reagan Administration appointed General Rowny head of the U.S. team in the SALT—renamed START—negotiations with the Soviet Union over intermediate-range nuclear forces in Europe.

7. Alex de Jonge, *Fire and Water: a Life of Peter the Great* (New York: Coward, McCann & Geoghegan, 1980), p. 16.

8. History Book Club *Review* (May 1980), pp. 1-7.

9. Richard Pipes, *Russia under the Old Regime* (New York: Scribner's, 1974). A new edition is in preparation.

10. Nicholas V. Riasanovsky, *A History of Russia*, 3rd edition (New York: Oxford University Press, 1977), is the best of the genre.

11. David H. Pinkney, "American Historians on the European Past," *American Historical Review* (Feb. 1981), pp. 1-20, reaches the same conclusion.

12. The theme of Flora Lewis's report from Warsaw, "The Cost of Lost History," New York Times (July 13, 1981).

**13.** Muriel Atkin, *Russia and Iran, 1780-1828* (Minneapolis, Minnesota: University of Minnesota Press, 1980), pp. 162-63. For a historical update, see Firuz Kazemzadeh, "Afghanistan: The Imperial Dream," *New York Review of Books*, Feb. 21, 1980, pp. 10-14; also his *Russia and Britain in Persia, 1864-1914* (New Haven, Connecticut: Yale University Press, 1968).

**14.** Bruce R. Kuniholm, *The Origins of the Cold War in the Near East: Great Power Conflict and Diplomacy in Iran, Turkey, and Greece* (Princeton, New Jersey: Princeton University Press, 1980), pp. xviii, 428.

# 2

## Lenin and His Cult

### Nina Tumarkin

An anecdote currently circulating in Moscow tells of an old man who looked high and low for an apartment, with no success. He wrote to his local Party committee and even to the Central Committee but got no reply. Finally, in desperation, he marched off to the Central Committee and asked to see Lenin. "Lenin?" exclaimed the astonished receptionist, "but Lenin died in 1924!" "How come," muttered the old man, "when *you* need him, he's alive, but when *I* need him, he's dead?"

This story shows the paradox of Lenin's historical legacy in the Soviet Union. Dead for some 60 years, he retains a reputation as the one ruler whose office door was open to his people, who cared about them enough to provide them with housing. At the same time, the Party upholds the myth of Lenin's perpetual accessibility by proclaiming his immortality. "Lenin lives!" is the watchword of an organized cult that resembles a religion. Lenin's ubiquitous portraits and busts are its icons, his writings its scripture, his idealized biography its gospel. And its central shrine is the Lenin Mausoleum in Red Square, displaying his preserved remains.[1]

The ironic twist to the story about the homeless old man turns on another widespread slogan of the Lenin cult: "Lenin is more alive than all the living." Its real meaning is that the immortal Lenin lives to provide the Party with legitimacy—not the needy with apartments. Indeed, the glorified leader is meant to symbolize a higher reality in which day-to-day popular needs give way to the generalized vision of a socialist utopia whose future realization was made certain through the heroic life, death and afterlife of Vladimir Ilyich Ulianov, also known as Lenin.[2]

Lenin himself never intended to become the object of a cult, but the

13

Party and government that created the cult bore the profound imprint of his personality and life experiences. And then the symbolic Lenin himself went through many shapes and guises: the standard cult figure of the 1920s—the martyred hero of genius—was quite distinct from the benign dimpled gentleman in soft focus who was peddled by the managers of the Lenin cult during the Khrushchev era. The real Lenin was neither hero nor gentleman, but he was a genius in revolutionary politics.

"Lenin in October": since his death countless Soviet books, articles, poems, paintings and films have celebrated this dramatic confrontation between the man and the moment. All of Lenin's talents were uniquely suited to the crisis: his extraordinary sense of timing; his uncanny ability to gauge correctly the weakness of his opponents; and something else that was a combination of rage, courage and hysteria. He did indeed play a central role in the Bolshevik seizure of power, although that event could not have happened without the escalating surge of anarchy that engulfed Russia in the summer and fall of 1917 and the political bankrupty of the Provisional Government established in February, after the abdication of the tsar.

But when it came to creating the Bolshevik system of government and directing it through the incredible trials of its first years, Lenin's contribution was extraordinary. For almost five years, until illness forced him out of the Kremlin in 1922, Lenin ruled Russia as chairman of the Council of People's Commissars, providing the country with its most dynamic leadership since the death, in 1725, of Peter I "the Great." He was the primary architect of the new government and the author of its policies.

Once in power, time and again Lenin found himself in direct conflict not only with the armed enemies of Russia and the revolution, but also with opponents from within his own Party. The first of these battles was the hardest—that of ending the futile war with Germany, begun under the tsar. Early in 1918 Lenin forced the humiliating Treaty of Brest-Litovsk on a resistant Party, summoning all his authority and talent to attain its ratification. In the end, of course, the outcome of World War I—Germany's surrender to the western Allies—nullified the treaty and Lenin's decision was vindicated. This was often the case with his policy shifts. Lenin's remarkably acute sense of timing, his feel for what at any given moment was necessary for political survival, did not fail to impress itself on his lieutenants, who helped to create his cult.

Lenin held no office that invested him with formal Party leadership; technically, he was simply another member of the ruling Central Committee and Politburo. In practice, however, he was unquestionably the Party's most authoritative voice, a role he had assumed in the years of exile before 1917 and which he retained with energy and skill. Yet as leader of both Party and government Lenin had his blind spot; he was unable to separate himself from either, and thus was unable to provide for the transition that would follow his death. It was precisely this loss of the indispensable leader in 1922 that prompted the creation of an immortalized Lenin to replace the living one, and in the process paved the way for the establishment of the basic institutions of the cult.

The only immortality Lenin had envisioned for himself was through his writings and his revolutionary transformation of Russia. Difficult as it is to speculate on any individual's sense of self, few aspects of Lenin's personality are more apparent than his confidence in his own ideas and his determination to communicate them to others with the full force of their power and clarity. He, and only he, would forge the true path to socialism by means of his teachings, his directives, his constant supervision and his personal example.

This last characteristic of Lenin was to be transformed into the most enduring aspect of the cult. Even today, he remains the ideal model of behavior for all Soviet citizens. The image of Grandpa Lenin is imprinted on the minds of schoolchildren, who are inundated with stories and poems about the leader, especially about his exemplary childhood. Emphasis is placed on his outstanding schoolwork and, even more to the point, his excellent study habits. Lenin's institutionalized persona as an embodiment of the highest socialist virtues is rooted in Lenin himself; his self-conscious and developed role as exemplar provides the strongest link between Ulianov the man and Lenin the cult figure.

Would the real Lenin have admitted into his office a petitioner looking for an apartment? Probably, yes. He liked to keep foreign dignitaries waiting as he welcomed humble workers and peasants who came with complaints, requests and often with gifts of food, which he donated to orphanages and daycare centers. Visitors frequently marvelled at the simplicity of Lenin's style of life — another characteristic that immediately entered cult literature. He was also later praised for the personal modesty that prevented him from fostering or even tolerating any manifestations of a cult during his lifetime.

In fact, Lenin *was* a man of modest tastes. His apartment was small, his salary low. He preferred to avoid photographers, sculptors, portraitists, flatterers. But his disinclination to become a cult figure is explained not by his modesty alone. Lenin's concept of the rewards of power was simply different from that offered by the frequently empty conventions of ceremonial praise. He was supremely self-confident and had no need of such vanities. As both revolutionary and statesman, he demanded from his followers submission in the form of obedience, dedication and hard work. For Lenin, ritualized praise was not an acceptable alternative expression of submission.

Yet the foundations of the Lenin cult were laid during the years of Lenin's active rule. Its builders were diverse: workers, peasants, Party agitators and the highest Party dignitaries came to laud him as a leader of genius. This development was evoked in part by Lenin's forceful leadership, but to an even greater extent by the political imperatives that called for dramatic images and symbols to legitimize the Bolshevik regime. Whatever Lenin's personal inclinations, in the end he allowed the portraits to be hung and the odes to be published. As the first Commissar of Education, Anatoly Lunacharsky, once observed: "I think that Lenin, who could not abide the personality cult, who rejected it in every possible way, in later years understood and forgave us."[3]

As an organized system of rituals and symbols, the cult of Lenin developed gradually during the five years that he ruled Russia. It acquired an institutional base in 1923, when he was incapacitated by progressive cerebral arteriosclerosis, and exploded nationwide immediately after his death—from a stroke—in January 1924. A massive campaign to mobilize the population was mounted by his heirs. The first stage was "mourning week." Every factory, every school, every conceivable organization held meetings packed with mourners and half a million people attended a three-day lying-in-state in Moscow, which culminated in a grand funeral in Red Square.

A regime that derives its legitimacy from a single ruler risks instability after his death. But if that ruler becomes the object of a cult predicated on his continuing power, the cult can serve as a stabilizing force. This is precisely what happened with Lenin. In order to retain his power and the popular emotions of solidarity his death had unleashed, Party and government propagandists followed "mourning week" with a campaign to establish the Lenin cult throughout the Soviet Union.

At this, its earliest and most vigorous period, the nationwide Lenin cult was still only partially regulated, reflecting the widest possible range of motivations and moods. From the desperate need of his successors to establish a base for their legitimacy to kindergarten teachers' assignments of poems on his death; from genuine outpourings of grief by the faithful to attempts to sell such products as cigarette packets, cups, even cookies by imprinting them with his portrait—the growing obsession with Lenin provided the emotional underpinning of the cult, and tapped the real concerns of a vast and diverse group of people.

For the Party and government leaders who were its architects, the ritualized veneration of Lenin was to serve several functions. It was to evoke in both Party and people a mood of loyalty toward the system and its values. At best it would mobilize genuine popular sentiments in a surge of political enthusiasm at a time—seven years after the revolution—when such enthusiasm had long since waned. At the very least, the organized cult was plainly a display of power by those who wielded it, a demonstration of their ability to direct political activity by fiat. From the day of his death until the end of the 1920s, Lenin was celebrated as an immortal who was accessible to his people through his writings (Leninism), his portraits, and his embalmed flesh, which was put on display in a hastily-built wooden mausoleum (replaced in November 1930 by the stone edifice which still stands).

The cult of Lenin did not survive the tenth anniversary of his death. By 1934, the idealized Lenin was relegated to the supporting role of Sacred Ancestor as the cult of Stalin took center stage in Soviet political ritual. For the next two decades Lenin remained an object of organized reverence, but only within the context of his "worthy continuer," who on revolutionary holidays stood atop the Lenin Mausoleum expressing their symbolic relationship. The dead Lenin was a pedestal for the living Stalin—until 1953, when Stalin joined his predecessor inside the mausoleum.

In 1956, in his "secret speech" delivered to the Twentieth Congress of the Communist Party, Nikita Khrushchev fulminated against the "cult of the individual," a reference, of course, to Stalin. "It is impermissible and foreign to the spirit of Marxism-Leninism to elevate one person, to transform him into a superman possessing supernatural characteristics akin to those of a god."[4] In the same breath, Khrushchev introduced a new cult of Lenin. All legitimate Party doctrine was poured back into its original Leninist vessel, a vessel that, according to Khrushchev, had been broken by Stalin in an extraordinary drive for power matched only by his overweening vanity.

The revived cult of Lenin took shape speedily and with careful orchestration. Handbooks and bibliographies told Party propagandists what to read about Lenin. Thousands of other publications—biographies, reminiscences, laudatory essays—quickly crowded the shelves of Soviet bookstores. Paintings, statues, busts, posters and little badges were produced in enormous quantities, even as the once ubiquitous Staliniana were fast disappearing from the Soviet political landscape.

Grand, sentimental and rosy-red, Khrushchev's cult of Lenin was cleansed of the funerary qualities that had characterized the cult rituals of the 1920s. The annual commemoration of Lenin was moved from his death-day to his birthday, April 22, a date which, Khrushchev explained, "better corresponds to the spirit of Leninism as an eternally alive, life-affirming teaching."[5] Pure optimism characterized all cult rituals, speeches and articles—all of which linked Lenin's immortal spirit to every achievement of the Party and Soviet government. Annual Lenin celebrations included poems, songs (usually written in a sprightly major key, even the one called "At the Mausoleum") and declamations that observed the appropriateness of the fact that Lenin's birthday comes in the spring. The cult of the 1960s was entirely standardized and regulated from above, providing the Party with a legitimacy that was unassailable. It did not skip a beat when, in 1964, Khrushchev fell from power.

Lenin of course figured prominently in the lavish celebrations of the fiftieth anniversary of the October revolution in 1967. His gargantuan face looked down on the multitudes from buildings and even from the Moscow heavens, for an illuminated portrait was suspended from a balloon. As the decade progressed the cult built to a crescendo with the Party and government preparations for observing Lenin's hundredth birthday on April 22, 1970.

The Lenin jubilee was a meticulously orchestrated extravaganza. Its main slogan was "Lenin is always with us," and indeed Lenin's spatial pervasiveness was its most striking aspect. Factories, publishing houses, looms, kilns, bakeries—everything that could produce artifacts—contributed some manner of memento for the occasion. The Soviet Union became a giant display case for busts, statues, posters, poems, banners, bric-a-brac and commemorative volumes.

The centennial had been intended to saturate political, civic and cultural life with the image and words of Lenin. But the celebration was a disaster for the credibility of communist propaganda and political ritual. The barrage of Leniniana was so vast and unrelenting that the jubilee took on the aspect of a burlesque performance. It is likely that, with the exception of a tiny group of dissidents, the population at large and Party members in particular retained their respect for Lenin's talents and a measure of admiration for his achievements. But too many slogans and busts, too many speeches, too many articles in every periodical for months and months beforehand and too many rhapsodic declamations turned an event designed to evoke enthusiasm into one that provoked disdain and even ridicule.

An awareness of the centennial's excesses is clear from the speed with which the authorities moved to diminish the frequency and pitch of the rituals. Obviously, they must have intended to ease up on the Lenin theme after April 1970, but the reduction was particularly marked and sharp. During the 1970s, even the yearly celebrations of Lenin's birthday were far more modest than those of the previous decade. The author of a Soviet book on communist ritual suggests that the modesty of the Lenin holiday is meant to reflect Vladimir Ilyich's own simplicity.[6] But it seems clear that Soviet propagandists had learned the virtues of moderation only after the 1970 fiasco. That event seems to have made it impossible to rekindle popular interest in most aspects of the Lenin cult.

Today, cult museums in the Soviet Union attract few individual visitors, and there are few buyers for Lenin's writings, phonograph records of his speeches, or the busts that come in all sizes. College students proudly boast to foreigners that they make it a point to forget promptly everything they must learn about Lenin and Leninism in their required courses. The iconographic representations of Lenin, the sacred writings, the commemorative meetings, and the grand Lenin museums appear to evoke little more than indifference.

Nonetheless, in some ways the cult still works. For example, children doubtless are impressed by curly-haired little Vladimir Ulianov who was such a fine student and grew up to emancipate Russia. And certain Lenin shrines still attract crowds of visitors. One of these is his boyhood home in Ulianovsk (formerly Simbirsk), on the Volga; another is the villa, not far from Moscow, in which he died. In both of these houses, Soviet tourists appear genuinely animated as they shuffle past the cordoned-off rooms in outsized canvas slippers tied over their shoes to protect the floors.

Surely the most successful locus of the cult is the stately Lenin Mausoleum in Moscow's Red Square. Party and government leaders gather on its tribunal on major holidays. Contemporary Soviet writings refer to it as a "sacred" place that "provides an inexhaustible supply of revolutionary energy." It is to the Mausoleum that Soviet cosmonauts come before their space flights to gather courage, and after their return to give thanks. And it is customary for newlyweds to lay flowers outside the Mausoleum right after their wedding.

The demeanor of Soviet visitors to the Lenin Mausoleum is serious and respectful. Even during the long wait in line most stand silently or chat in low tones, and admonish restless children who skip and jump to relieve the tedium. Once inside, all eyes are riveted on the body that rests, awash in light, on an ornate bier in the center of a dark gray chamber. In the more than half-century since Lenin's death, tens of millions of ordinary Soviet people have patiently waited in long queues for their permitted 80 seconds with the founder of both the Communist Party and the Soviet state. □

1. This chapter is adapted from portions of Nina Tumarkin, *Lenin Lives! The Lenin Cult in Soviet Russia* (Cambridge, Massachusetts: Harvard University Press, 1983).
2. For an introduction to Lenin's life and work, see Adam B. Ulam, *The Bolsheviks*

(New York: Macmillan, 1965); on Lenin in power, see also T.H. Rigby, *Lenin's Government* (Cambridge, England and New York: Cambridge University Press, 1979). For a general work on Soviet ritual see Christel Lane, *The Rites of Rulers: Ritual in Industrial Society—the Soviet Case* (Cambridge, England and New York: Cambridge University Press, 1981).

  3. A.V. Lunacharsky, "Shtriki," in *Lenin—tovarishch, chelovek*, 2nd ed. (Moscow: 1963), p. 179. See also Lunacharsky, "Vladimir Ilyich Lenin," in Lunacharsky, *Revolutionary Silhouettes*, trans., Michael Glenny (New York: Hill and Wang, 1968), pp. 35-56.

  4. Russian Institute, Columbia University, *The Anti-Stalin Campaign and International Communism* (New York: Columbia University Press, 1956), p. 2.

  5. *Pravda* (Jan. 11, 1955).

  6. *Nashi prazdniki* (Moscow: 1977), pp. 28-30.

# 3

## The Stalin Question

### Stephen F. Cohen

It has been called the "accursed question," like serfdom in pre-revolutionary Russia. Stalin ruled the Soviet Union for a quarter of a century, from 1929 to his death at the age of 73 in 1953. For most of these years, he ruled as an unconstrained autocrat, making the era his own—*Stalinshchina*, the time of Stalin. The nature of his rule and the enduring legacy of Stalinism have been debated in the Soviet Union for more than another quarter of a century, first in the official press and since the mid-1960s in *samizdat*—or "self-published"—writings. And yet it remains the most tenacious and divisive issue in Soviet political life—a "dreadful and bloody wound," as even the government newspaper once admitted.[1] "Tell me your opinion about our Stalinist past," goes a Moscow saying, "and I'll know who you are."

The Stalin question is intensely historical, social, political and moral. It encompasses the whole of Soviet and even Russian history. It cuts across and exacerbates contemporary political issues. It calls into question the careers of a whole ruling elite and the personal conduct of several generations of citizens. The Stalin question burns high and low, dividing leaders and influencing policy, while generating bitter quarrels in families, among friends, at social gatherings. The conflict takes various forms, from philosophical polemics to fistfights. One occurs each year on March 5, when glasses are raised in households across the Soviet Union on the anniversary of Stalin's death. Some are loving toasts to the memory of "our great leader who made the Motherland strong." Others curse "the greatest criminal our country has known."

These antithetical toasts reflect the history that inflames and perpetuates the Stalin question. Historical Stalinism was, to use a Soviet metaphor, two towering and inseparable mountains: a mountain of na-

21

tional accomplishments alongside a mountain of crimes. The accomplishments cannot be lightly dismissed. During the first decade of Stalin's leadership, memorialized officially as the period of the First and Second Five-Year Plans for collectivization and industrialization, a mostly backward, agrarian, illiterate society was transformed into a predominantly industrial, urban, literate one. For millions of people, the 1930s were a time of willingly heroic sacrifice, educational opportunity, and upward mobility. In the second decade of Stalin's rule, the Soviet Union destroyed the mighty German invader, contributing more than any other nation to the defeat of fascism; it also acquired an empire in eastern Europe and became a superpower in world affairs. All this still inspires tributes to the majesty of Stalin's rule.

But the crimes were no less mountainous. Stalin's policies caused a Soviet holocaust, from his forcible collectivization of the peasantry in 1929 to 1933, to the relentless system of mass terror by the NKVD or MGB (as the political police were variously known) that continued until his death. Millions of innocent men, women and children were arbitrarily arrested, tortured, executed, brutally deported or imprisoned in the murderous prisons and forced-labor camps of the Gulag Archipelago. No one has yet managed to calculate the exact number of deaths under Stalin. Among those who have tried, 20 million is a conservative estimate.[2] Nor does this figure include the millions of unnecessary casualties that can be blamed on Stalin's negligent leadership at the beginning of World War II, or the eight million souls (another conservative estimate) who languished in his concentration camps every year between 1939 and 1953. Judged only by the number of victims, and leaving aside important differences between the two regimes, Stalinism created a holocaust greater than Hitler's.

Most of the Stalin controversy pivots on this dual history. The pro-Stalin argument, of which there are primitive and erudite versions among Russians, builds upon the proverb "When the forest is cut, the chips fly." It insists that "Stalin was necessary." The sacrifices—they are usually termed "mistakes" or "excesses" and are said to be exaggerated—were unavoidable, it is argued. The economic advantages of collectivized agriculture made rapid industrialization possible. Repression eliminated unreliable, alien or hostile elements and united the country under Stalin's strong leadership. These events prepared the nation for the great victory over Germany and its achievement of great-power status. In this version of the past, which has again become standard in Soviet textbooks and novels, Stalin is exalted as a great builder, statesman and generalissimo.

Anti-Stalin opinion says just the opposite: "Yes, there were victories, not thanks to the cult [of Stalin], but in spite of it." The brutality of collectivization did more harm than good; there were other and better ways to industrialize. Mass represssions were both criminal and dysfunctional. They decimated the labor pool and elites essential for national defense, including the officer corps. The atmosphere of terror and corrupt Stalinist leadership caused the terrible disasters of 1941 and made the whole war effort more difficult. Soviet prestige in the world, then and now, would be far greater without the stigma of Stalin's crimes.

These arguments seem historically symmetrical, but they do not explain fully why so many, probably the great majority, of Soviet officials and ordinary citizens alike still speak mostly, or even only, good of Stalin, and thus justify crimes of this magnitude.[3] It is true that official censorship has deprived many citizens of a full, systematic account of what happened. But much of the story did appear, however elliptically, in Soviet publications by the mid-1960s. Moreover, most adult survivors must have known or sensed the magnitude of the holocaust, since virtually every family lost a relative, friend or acquaintance. Why, then, do not most people share the unequivocal judgment once pronounced, even in a censored Soviet publication, upon these "black and bitter days of the Stalin cult"—that "there is no longer any place in our soul for a justification of his evil deeds"?[4]

Two categories of Soviet citizens had an intensely personal interest in the Stalin question after 1953: victims of the terror and those who had victimized them. Most of the victims were dead, but many remained to exert pressure on high politics. Millions of people had survived—some for 20 or more years—in the camps and in remote exile. Most of these survivors, perhaps seven or eight million, were eventually freed after Stalin's death. They began to return to society, first in a trickle in 1953 and then in a mass exodus in 1956. To salvage what remained of their shattered lives, the returnees required, and demanded, many forms of rehabilitation: legal exoneration, family reunification, housing, jobs, medical care, pensions.

Their demands were shared by a kindred group of millions of relatives of people who had perished in the terror. The criminal stigma on these families, "enemy of the people," many of whom had also been persecuted, kept them from living and working as they wanted. Posthumous legal exoneration, or "rehabilitation," and restitution were therefore both a practical necessity and a deeply felt duty to the dead. These demands of so many surviving victims had enormous political implications, if only because exoneration and restitution were official admissions of colossal official crimes. Still more, some victims demanded a full public exposure of the crimes and even punishment of those responsible.

In addition to its size and passion for justice, the community of victims had direct and indirect access to the high leadership. Returnees from the camps became members and even heads of various Party commissions set up after 1953 to investigate the Gulag system, the question of rehabilitations, and specific crimes of the Stalin years. (One such commission contributed to Nikita Khrushchev's anti-Stalin speeches to the Party congresses in 1956 and 1961.) Quite a few returnees resumed prominent positions in military, economic, scientific and cultural life. (Unlike those in Czechoslovakia, however, none rose to the high Party leadership.) Some returnees had personal access to repentant Stalinists in the leadership, such as Khrushchev and Anastas Mikoyan, whom they lobbied and influenced. And other returnees, such as Aleksandr Solzhenitsyn, made their impact in different ways. As a result, by the mid-1950s victims of the terror had become a formidable source of anti-Stalinist opinion and politics.

Their adversaries were no less self-interested and far more powerful. The systematic victimization of so many people had implicated millions of other people during the 20-year terror. There were different degrees of responsibility. But criminal complicity had spread like a cancer through the system, from Politburo members who had directed the terror alongside Stalin, to Party and state officials who had participated in the repressions, to the hundreds of thousands of NKVD personnel who arrested, tortured, executed and guarded prisoners, and to the plethora of petty informers and slanderers who fed on the crimson madness. Millions of others were implicated by having profited, often inadvertently, from the misfortune of victims. They inherited the positions, apartments, possessions and sometimes even the wives of the vanished. Generations built lives upon a holocaust. The terror killed, but it also, said one returnee, "corrupted the living."[5]

The question of criminal responsibility and punishment, either by Nuremberg-style trials or by expulsion from public life, was widely discussed in the 1950s and 1960s, though public commentary usually was muted or oblique. The official and popular defense—that only Stalin and a handful of accomplices had known the number and innocence of the victims—was rudely shattered on several occasions. When the venerable writer Ilya Ehrenburg later spoke of having had "to live with clenched teeth" because he knew his arrested friends were innocent, he implied that the whole officialdom above him had also known. It may be true, as even anti-Stalinists report, that ordinary people believed the Stalinist mania about "enemies of the people." But when the poet

Yevgeny Yevtushenko wrote that the masses "had worked in a furious desperation, drowning with the thunder of machines, tractors, and bull-dozers the cries that might have reached them across the barbed wire of Siberian concentration camps," he acknowledged that the whole nation had "sensed intuitively that something was wrong."[6]

Of those who were incontrovertibly guilty, a few committed suicide, a few were ousted from their posts, a handful of high policemen were tried and executed, and some became politically repentant. But the great ma-jority remained untouched. The remote specter of retribution was enough to unite millions who had committed crimes, and also many of those who felt some unease about their lives, against any revelations about the past and the whole process of de-Stalinization. "Many people," a young researcher discovered in 1956, "will defend [the past], defending themselves." A great poet who had suffered commented, "Now they are trembling for their names, positions, apartments, dachas. The whole calculation was that no one would return."[7]

A second large dimension of the Stalin question was even more rami-fying. Proposals for change throughout the rigidified Soviet system and stubborn resistance to change became the central features of official political life after Stalin's death. The conflict between reformers and con-servatives was inseparable from the Stalin question because the status quo and its history were Stalinist. In advocating change, Soviet reformers had to criticize the legacy of Stalinism in virtually every area of policy, whether it was the priority of heavy industry in economic investment, the exploitation of collectivized agriculture, overcentralization in management, heavy-handed censorship and a galaxy of taboos in intel-lectual, cultural, and scientific life, retrograde policies in family affairs, repressive practices and theories in law, or Cold War thinking in foreign policy. And in order to defend these institutions, practices and or-thodoxies, Soviet conservatives had to defend the Stalinist past.

Unavoidably, Stalin and what he represented became political sym-bols for both the friends and foes of change. Soviet reformers developed anti-Stalinism as an ideology in the 1950s and 1960s (as did their counterparts in Eastern Europe), while Soviet conservatives embraced, no doubt reluctantly in some cases, varieties of neo-Stalinism. Khrushchev and his allies established the link in the mid-1950s, when they fused a decade of reform from above with repeated campaigns against Stalin's historical reputation. The Stalin question, they said, pitted the "new and progressive against the old and reactionary"; Stalin's defenders were "conservatives and dogmatists." Not all Soviet conserva-tives actually were Stalinists. But the relationship between attitudes to-ward Stalin and change was authentic, and it spread quickly to every policy area where reformers and conservatives were in conflict.

Popular attitudes were, and remain, an even larger dimension of the Stalin question. The expression "cult of Stalin's personality" became, after 1953, an official euphemism for Stalinism, but it had a powerful and deep-rooted historical resonance. For more than 20 years, Stalin had been officially glorified in extraordinary ways. All of the country's achievements were attributed to his singular inspiration. Virtually every idea of nation, people, patriotism and communism was made synonymous with his name, as in the wartime battle cry "For Stalin! For the Motherland!" His name, words, and alleged deeds were trumpeted incessantly to every corner of the land. His photographed, painted, bronzed, and sculpted likeness was everywhere. Stalin's original designation, "The Lenin of Today," gave way in the 1930s to titles of omnipotence and infallibility: Father of the Peoples, Genius of Mankind, Driver of the Locomotive of History, Greatest Man of All Times and Peoples. The word "man" seemed inappropriate as the cult swelled into deification: "O Great Stalin, O Leader of the Peoples, Thou who didst give birth to man, Thou who didst make fertile the earth."[8]

The cult was manipulated from above, but there is no doubt that it had deep popular roots, as did the whole Stalinist system. Many Soviet writers, though they disagree about other aspects of Stalinism, tell us that the Stalin cult was widely accepted and deeply believed by millions of Soviet people of all classes, ages and occupations, especially in the cities. Of course, many people did not believe, or they believed in more limited ways. But most of the urban populace, it seems clear, were captives of the cult. It became a religious phenomenon. And in this deeply personal, psychological and passionate sense, the nation was Stalinist.

Stalin's death, on March 5, 1953, dealt an irreparable blow to the divinity of the cult; gods do not suffer brain hemorrhages, enlargement of the heart and high blood pressure, as described graphically in the published medical bulletin and autopsy. The state funeral itself was a bizarre blend of old and new. Scores of mourners were trampled to death by a hysterical crowd gathered to view the body, adding to the death toll of Stalin's reign. But new chords were sounded in the eulogies by his successors, or the "collective leadership." They praised Stalin's "immortal name," but significantly less than while he lived. And they ascribed to the Communist Party a role it had not played, except in myth, since Stalin's great terror of the 1930s—the "great directing and guiding force of the Soviet people."[9]

Official de-Stalinization, or partial de-Stalinization, soon followed, as manifested in Khrushchev's speeches to the Party congresses of 1956 and 1961. But when the government assaulted the Stalin cult, first obliquely and then with revelations that portrayed the "Father of the Peoples" as a genocidal murderer, it caused a traumatic crisis of faith. In the words of contemporary Soviet writers, de-Stalinization "destroyed our faith, tearing out the heart of our world-view, and that heart was Stalin." Revelations about the past meant "not only the truth about Stalin, but the truth about ourselves and our illusions." Many people underwent a "spiritual revolution" and became anti-Stalinists. But because it forced a person "to reevaluate his own life," it was "hard to part with our belief in Stalin." So hard that many other people could not break with the past. They remained—and remain even today—self-professed Stalinists.

For a decade after Stalin's death, popular and official anti-Stalinism seemed to be an irresistible force in Soviet politics. But the powerful resurgence of pro-Stalinist sentiments on both levels since 1964 has seemed no less inexorable. The turnabout is reflected in the career of Aleksandr Solzhenitsyn. In 1964, he was nominated for a Lenin Prize, the Soviet Union's highest literary honor, for his prison camp story *One Day in the Life of Ivan Denisovich*; ten years later he was arrested and deported.

Khrushchev's downfall in 1964 at first encouraged both anti-Stalinists and neo-Stalinists in official circles. The former hoped that the new Brezhnev-Kosygin government would chart a more orderly course of reform and de-Stalinization, while neo-Stalinists sought a mandate to stamp out the "poison of Khrushchevism." Their struggle raged both openly and covertly in 1965 and 1966. New anti-Stalinist publications appeared, rehabilitations of Stalin's victims continued, and in October 1965 the leadership legislated a major (and ill-fated) program of economic reform. At the same time, however, influential figures, including Leonid Brezhnev, began to issue authoritative statements refurbishing Stalin's reputation as a wartime leader, eulogizing the 1930s while obscuring the terror, and suggesting that Khrushchev's revelations had "calumniated" the Soviet Union. Behind the scenes, an assertive pro-Stalin lobby, proud to call itself "Stalinist," took the offensive for the first time in several years, apparently with Brezhnev's support. Anti-Stalinists were demoted, censorship was tightened, new ideological strictures were drafted, already processed rehabilitations were challenged, and subscriptions to anti-Stalinist journals were prohibited in the armed forces.

The decisive battle in officialdom was over by early 1966. Within 18 months of Khrushchev's overthrow, official de-Stalinization was at an end; a pronounced reverse pattern had developed and anti-Stalinism was becoming the rallying cry of a small dissident movement. Two events dramatized the outcome. In February 1966, two prominent writers, Andrei Sinyavsky and Yuli Daniel, were tried and sentenced to labor camps for publishing their "slanderous" (anti-Stalinist) writings abroad. The public trial, with its self-conscious evocation of the purge trials of the 1930s, was a neo-Stalinist blast against critical-minded members of the intelligentsia. Meanwhile, a campaign began against anti-Stalinist historians. The first victim was a Party historian in good standing, Aleksandr Nekrich. He was traduced and later expelled from the Party for little more than restating the anti-Stalinist historiography, developed during the Khrushchev years, of the German invasion of 1941.[10]

These events, and the fear that Stalin would be officially rehabilitated at the Twenty-third Party Congress in March 1966, gave birth to the present-day dissident movement and *samizdat* literature as a widespread phenomenon. A flood of petitions protesting the Sinyavsky-Daniel trial and neo-Stalinism generally circulated among the intelligentsia; they gathered hundreds and then thousands of signatures, including the names of prominent representatives of official anti-Stalinism under Khrushchev. A pattern developed that has continued. The growing conservative and neo-Stalinist overtones of the Brezhnev regime drove anti-Stalinists from official to dissident ranks and gave the movement many of its best-known spokesmen, such as Andrei Sakharov, Lydiia Chukovskaia, Roy and Zhores Medvedev, Solzhenitsyn, Pyotr Yakir and Lev Kopelev. These people later went separate political ways, but the fallen banner of anti-Stalinism first turned them into dissidents. And this development transformed the Stalin question from a conflict inside the Establishment into a struggle between the Soviet government and open dissidents.

Some dissidents believe that their protests prevented a full rehabilitation of Stalin at the Twenty-third Congress, where his name was hardly mentioned. If so, it was a small victory amid a rout. The policies of the Brezhnev government grew steadily into a wide-ranging conservative reaction to Khrushchev's reforms. The defense of the status quo required a usable Stalinist past. Increasingly, only the mountain of accomplishments was remembered in rewritten history books and in the press.

By the end of the 1960s Stalin had been restored as an admirable leader. Serious criticism of his wartime leadership and of collectivization was banned; rehabilitations were ended and some even undone; and intimations that there ever had been a great terror grew scant. Indeed, people who criticized the Stalinist past (as Khrushchev had done at Party congresses) could now be prosecuted for having "slandered the Soviet social and state system." Dozens of honored anti-Stalinist writers and historians suffered persecution or were simply unable to publish. Arrests of dissidents grew apace.

If anti-Stalinist reformers in the Establishment still had any hope, it was crushed, along with the "Prague Spring," in August 1968. The Prague Spring had epitomized the anti-Stalinist cause for Soviet anti-Stalinists and neo-Stalinists alike. The language used to justify the Soviet invasion of Czechoslovakia evoked the terroristic ideology of the Stalin years. It soon crept back into domestic publications as well, along with the charge that de-Stalinization was nothing but "an anti-Communist slogan" invented by enemies of the Soviet Union.

Stalinist sentiment in Soviet officialdom has grown steadily more fulsome through the 1970s and into the 1980s. With few exceptions, critical analysis of the Stalinist experience has been banished from the official press to small circles of *samizdat* writers and readers. References to Stalin's "negative" side, to "harm" caused by his personal "mistakes," appeared in two prominent articles officially commemorating the one hundredth anniversary of his birth in December 1979. In the broader context, they seemed to be little more than carping asides. In a welter of official mass-circulation publications, Stalin's personal reputation has soared. He is no longer the subject of religious worship, but he is, once again, the great national leader and benefactor who guided the country's fortunes for 20 years. His "devotion to the working class and the selfless struggle for socialism" is unquestioned. Above all, the entire Stalinist era, now the historical centerpiece of the conservative Soviet leadership, has been wholly rehabilitated as the necessary and heroic "creation of a new order."

A coarser, more ominous form of pro-Stalinism has also emerged in official circles since the early 1970s. A variety of publications—including a spate of historical novels, some of them made into prize-winning and popular films—have justified Stalin's terror of the 1930s as a "struggle against destructive and nihilistic elements." Epithets of the terror years—"enemies of the Party and of the people," "fifth column" and "rootless cosmopolitans"—have reappeared in print. And they are popularized still more widely by Party lecturers, whose daily oral propaganda throughout the country does much to set the tone of Soviet political life. Indeed, by the mid-1970s, odious proconsuls of Stalin's terror had been resurrected as exemplars of official values. And in time for the 1979 centenary, neo-Stalinist officials seem even to have achieved, despite rulings under Khrushchev, the rehabilitation of the notorious show trials of the 1930s, which served as the juridical linchpin of Stalin's terror against the Communist Party.

Yet if this resurgence of Stalinist sentiments represents a potential base for a more despotic leadership in the Soviet Union, it does not signify a rebirth of Stalinism. As a system of personal dictatorship and mass terror, Stalinism was the product of specific historical circumstances and a special kind of autocratic personality; these factors have passed from the scene. Today, the Soviet political system is very different, however authoritarian it remains. Neo-Stalinists may press for and even achieve more hard-line policies at home and abroad. But actual "re-Stalinization" would be a radical change opposed by the great majority of Soviet officials and citizens, whose pro-Stalinist sentiments reflect something different—their own deep-rooted political and social conservatism. Indeed, the appeals of neo-Stalinism today are diverse and often contradictory.

Pro-Stalin opinion among high officials is easy to explain. For them, the generalissimo on his pedestal continues to symbolize their own power and privilege, and to guard against change. Not surprisingly, the main patrons of neo-Stalinist literature are those authorities responsible for the political attitudes of young people and the armed forces. These officials know the truth about the past and thus deserve the harshest judgment of anti-Stalinists; in the words of one of the latter, "Knowingly to restore respect for Stalin would be to establish something new—to establish respect for denunciation, torture, execution."

But as a broad popular phenomenon, today's pro-Stalin sentiment is something different, even an expression of discontent. On one level, it is part of the widespread resurgence of Russian nationalism, to which Stalin linked the fortunes of the Soviet state in the 1930s and 1940s, and which has reemerged, in various forms, as the most potent ideological factor in Soviet political life. Echoing older ideas of Russia's special destiny, most of these nationalist currents are statist and thus identify with the real or imagined grandeur of the Soviet Russian state, as opposed to the Communist Party, under Stalin. They perpetuate assorted legacies of that era, from pride in the accomplishments of the 1930s and the war years to anti-Semitism and quasi-fascist cults. In this haze of nationalist sentiment, Stalin joins a long line of great Russian rulers stretching back to the early tsars.

Such ideas are also the product of contemporary social problems. Varieties of neo-Stalinist opinion cut across classes, from workers to the petty intelligentsia, reflecting their specific discontents in Soviet society. More generally, though, liberalizing trends and other changes in the 1950s and 1960s unsettled many lives and minds; the open discussion of long-standing social problems made them seem new. By the mid-1960s, many officials and citizens saw a reformed, partially de-Stalinized Soviet Union as a country in crisis. Economic shortages, inflation, public drunkenness, escalating divorce rates, unruly children, cultural diversity, complicated international negotiations—all seemed to be evidence of a state that could no longer manage, much less control, its own society. And all cast a rosy glow on the Stalinist past as an age of efficiency, low prices, law and order, discipline, unity, stability, obedient children and international respect.

Contemporary discontents, the feeling that "we have been going downhill ever since his death," could only enhance Stalin's popular reputation. By the end of the 1970s, official portraits of a largely benevolent chief of state were reinforced by memories of Stalin as a "strong boss" under whose rule "we did not have such troubles." Little remained to counter this folk nostalgia. While anti-Stalinists have been silenced by censorship, new generations, perhaps 40 percent of the population, have grown up in the post-Stalin era. Raised on parental remnants of the cult, many think that Stalin arrested "20 or 30 people" or "maybe 2,000." When a famous anti-Stalinist told a group of young people that the arrests were "reckoned not in thousands but in millions, they did not believe me."

Outwardly, anti-Stalinism and thus the Stalin question itself appear to have lost their potency as factors in official Soviet politics. And yet, there are at least two important reasons why this is probably only a temporary condition, or even an illusion created by censorship. One is pragmatic. The reformist cause, despite its defeat in recent years, lives on in Soviet officialdom, mainly because Stalin's institutional legacy—particularly, the hypercentralized economic system—remains the source of so many serious problems. In different political circumstances, as in a time of leadership instability, another leader or faction will reach for the fallen banner of fundamental economic reform. Such a program will require not only renewed criticism of the Stalinist past but a reformist ideology to overcome widespread conservative resistance to change. And anti-Stalinism remains the only viable ideology of communist reform from above, as it was under Khrushchev and as it has been in other communist capitals, from Belgrade and Prague to Peking.

The other enduring source of anti-Stalinism is emphasized by the neo-Stalinist complaint against people who *elevate ethical-moral problems above those of the state and patriotism* [emphasis in original]. Enthralled by the apparent mountain of achievements, many Soviet citizens (and Westerners, too, it seems) will always admire Stalin as a great leader or "modernizer." But too much has become known for the mountain of crimes to vanish from view, even after all the victims of Stalinism have passed from the scene.

Historical justice is a powerful moral idea that knows no statute of limitations, especially when reinforced by a sense that the whole nation bears some responsibility for what happened. This truth is confirmed by other historical examples. But Russians need look only to the growing body of *samizdat* literature, where exposés of Stalinism and the idea of a national reckoning "in the name of the present and the future" are kept alive. The timelessness of the Stalin question and the prospect of new generations of anti-Stalinists are explained by a recent *samizdat* historian: "It is the duty of every honest person to write the truth about Stalin. A duty to those who died at his hands, to those who survived that dark night, to those who will come after us."[11] Enough anti-Stalinist themes have forced their way even into the censored Soviet press in recent years to tell us that this outlook still has adherents in the Soviet Establishment as well.

Official censorship can mute the controversy, postpone the historical reckoning, and allow another generation to come of age only dimly aware (though not fully ignorant) of what happened during the Stalin years. But it is also true, as events since Stalin's death have shown, that making the past forbidden serves only to make it more alluring, and that imposing a ban on historical controversy causes that controversy to fester, intensify, and grow politically explosive. □

1. Konstantin Simonov, "O proshlom vo imia budushchego," *Izvestiia* (Nov. 18, 1962).

2. See Robert Conquest's *The Great Terror: Stalin's Purge of the Thirties* (New York: MacMillan, 1968), pp. 525-35 and "The Great Terror Revised," *Survey*, 17, No. 1 (1971), p. 93. Several *samizdat* historians and demographers give considerably higher figures: Anton Antonov-Ovseyenko, *The Time of Stalin: Portrait of a Tyranny* (New York: Harper and Row, 1981), pt. 2, chap. 15; M. Maksudov, "Losses Suffered by the Population of the USSR 1918-1958," in Roy Medvedev, ed., *The Samizdat Register II* (New York: W.W. Norton, 1981), pp. 220-76; or the findings of Iosif Dyadkin, reported in James Ring Adams, "Revising Stalin's Legacy," Wall Street Journal (July 23, 1980); and I. Kurganov, "Tri tsifry," *Novoe russkoe slovo* (April 12, 1964).

3. Though Soviet opinion on this subject cannot be polled and quantified, all firsthand accounts suggest a majority of pro-Stalin sentiment.

4. K. Simonov, "O proshlom."

5. The cancer of responsibility is a central theme of Solzhenitsyn's two great novels of the terror years, *The First Circle* and *Cancer Ward*.

6. Yevgeny Yevtushenko, *A Precocious Autobiography* (New York: Doubleday, 1963), p. 17.

7. Anna Akhmatova, in *Pamiati A. Akhmatovoi* (Paris: YMCA Press, 1975), p. 167.

8. Quoted in Suzanne Labin, *Stalin's Russia* (London: Gollancz, 1949), p. 65; see also Antonov-Ovseyenko, *The Time of Stalin*, pt. 3, chap. 1.

9. *Pravda* (March 4-10, 1953). For the funeral, see Yevtushenko, *Autobiography*, pp. 84-87; on the death of the cult, Antonov-Ovseyenko, *The Time of Stalin*, p. 305.

10. See A.M. Nekrich, *June 22, 1941* (Columbia, South Carolina: University of South Carolina Press, 1968). Nekrich later emigrated and has since become a fellow of the Russian Research Center at Harvard University.

11. Antonov-Ovseyenko, *The Time of Stalin*, p. xviii.

# POLITICS

In the first chapter of this section Mark Beissinger directly confronts the question, who rules the Soviet Union? He suggests, in reply, that a leadership of some 15 to 20 senior Communist Party men—members of the Party's Politburo and/or central Secretariat—exercise ultimate authority through their control of extensive patronage networks within a larger political elite that is concentrated in the Party's Central Committee, at present comprising about 320 full members. The Soviet political system, in short, is both pervasive in Soviet life as a whole and thoroughly top-down in its actual functioning, at once highly centralized and highly authoritarian. Beissinger discusses the evolution of this system under Leonid Brezhnev as well as its internal dynamics, a subject that Alexander Dallin takes up, in the succeeding chapter, with regard particularly to the making of Soviet foreign policy.

The third chapter of this section deals with the question of dissent in the Soviet Union over the last 20 years. Many experts consider that the internal political significance of Soviet dissent has been exaggerated by the Western media. But there is no doubt that the plight of Soviet dissidents at home has had repercussions on Communist parties abroad, in the Third World, and in East-West relations: in sum, that it is a question of major international significance and one, therefore, that Soviet policymakers have had to take into account. And from a chapter on dissent it is one short step to the KGB.

# 4

# POLITICS

## The Political Elite

### Mark R. Beissinger

Who rules the Soviet Union? Under Stalin there was little doubt: no one—including Stalin's most intimate associates—was immune from the terror. Between 1934 and 1939 alone Stalin had 85 percent of the members of the Party Central Committee murdered; and of the 25 men who were unlucky enough to have been members of the Party's Politburo from 1924 to 1952, 11 (44 percent) were shot outright while another three (11 percent) were driven to suicide or died under suspicious circumstances. And there is ample evidence that, had Stalin himself not fallen victim to a stroke in March 1953, the ten who had survived until then through the caprice of the dictator would nearly all have been liquidated in the major purge that was being planned. Thus while particular factions in Stalin's entourage were often influential in shaping policy, none of them was able to exercise a consistent influence independent of Stalin's will.[1]

Under Nikita Khrushchev, those who lost in the political intrigues of the Kremlin no longer paid for their mistakes with their lives—only with their positions. Yet despite Khrushchev's efforts at de-Stalinization, he continued to rule by means of massive, though bloodless, replacement of personnel. From 1956 to 1961 he replaced over two-thirds of the members of the Party Presidium (Politburo), the Council of Ministers and the regional Party apparatus; and during this same period he removed half of the members of the Central Committee.[2]

Similarly, in the realm of policy Khrushchev acted as if he were unconstrained by the elite or even by the rest of the leadership. With little consultation he went about shifting investment priorities, dissolving the central ministries and sending their officials off to the provinces, dividing the Party apparatus into industrial and agricultural branches, ordering the planting of corn in regions where it could not grow, and risking nuclear confrontation with the United States by placing Soviet missiles in Cuba. Not only did these policies alienate an elite yearning for stability, but they also largely failed. By the early 1960s the growth rate of the Soviet economy was beginning to slow; the Soviet Union was forced to import grain for the first time in its history; and the embarrassing Soviet retreat from Cuba encouraged further splits within the Soviet camp. Khrushchev's removal in October 1964 was both a response to his "hare-brained" policies and a backlash against the insecurity from which the Soviet elite suffered. It was as if Khrushchev had mistakenly thought that he could enjoy Stalin's power without employing Stalin's instruments of control.

In contrast to its predecessors, the Brezhnev regime was characterized above all by stability in both policy and personnel. Unlike the situation under Khrushchev, there were few administrative shuffles. At the same time, however, many basic features of the system fathered by Stalin—the clumsy mechanism of central planning, the grossly inefficient collective farm program, the priority of military investment, the country's shackled intellectual and cultural life—were preserved. In the first years of Brezhnev's reign collective leadership prevailed; but after the early 1970s he clearly was "first among equals," enjoying his own mini-cult of personality in imitation of his predecessors.

Still, the biggest story of Brezhnev's rule was the new political contract he established between the leadership and the elite—his "trust-in-cadres" policy. This amounted to an informal promise by the leadership to forswear the massive replacements of personnel that were so characteristic of previous Soviet regimes. The increasing ages of the highest officials of every major Soviet institution were but one indicator of this new feature of the Soviet political scene. From 1966 to 1982 the average age of Politburo members rose from 55 to 68, of members of the Council of Ministers from 58 to 65, and of members of the Central Committee from 56 to 63.[3] Some members of both the elite and the leadership were replaced under Brezhnev, but only very slowly and deliberately. Of the three Central Committees elected during his years, at least four-fifths of the living members of the previous Central Committee were re-elected each time.[4] Of both the voting and non-voting members of the 1966 Central Committee elected after Khrushchev's downfall, 44 percent were still in the Central Committee 15 years later. By 1982 the average voting member of the Central Committee had been in office approximately 13 years. By contrast, in 1981 the average tenure in office of the U.S. Senate—a body also known for its longevity—was eight years.

This stability was the major legacy which Brezhnev left to his successors and it has raised new questions among students of the Soviet political system about who is really calling the shots. Is it the General Secretary, the political leadership collectively (meaning, essentially, the Politburo), the Party apparatus, a military-industrial complex, a conglomeration of bureaucratic and institutional interest groups, or a "new class" that rules the Soviet Union today? Was the new political contract over which Brezhnev presided indicative of a significant change in the distribution of power in the Soviet system? And has this contract also altered the relationship between the Soviet leadership and the society it governs?

The key element in Brezhnev's new contract, and in any discussion of the Soviet political system, is the group we refer to as the elite. Because elites occupy the top positions (outside of the leadership itself) in the most powerful institutions in society, in general they possess a potential capacity to restrain the actions of the political leaders or to serve as a conduit for popular demands to the leadership. The role which an elite tends to play depends largely on three factors: its relationship to the population at large; the extent to which it is able to combine the power resources its members possess as individuals, in order to act cohesively as a group; and the degree to which it is able to use these resources as a system of incentives for the leaders, rewarding them when they follow the desires of the elite and punishing them when they do not.[5]

The Soviet elite is representative neither of Soviet society as a whole nor of the Party from which it is drawn. Whereas workers make up 61 percent of Soviet society and 43 percent of the Party, they have less than a 6 percent representation in the Party Central Committee—the institution which virtually embodies the elite. Only 7 percent of Soviet society and 28 percent of the Communist Party have a tertiary—that is, higher—education, as against 78 percent of the Central Committee members. Although women make up approximately 56 percent of the adult population and 27 percent of the Party membership, they comprise less than 3 percent of the Central Committee.[6] Moreover, certain ethnic groups, particularly the Russians, are represented far out of proportion to their numbers in the total population, while 11 nationalities are clearly underrepresented. If the Central Committee represents anyone in the Soviet Union, it is the educated, white-collar, Russian, male Party member (Tables 1 and 2).

But the average educated, white-collar, Russian, male Party member in turn has little say in the selection of members of the elite. Personnel assignments in the Soviet political system are made according to the system of *nomenklatura*—a list of positions in state, society and the Party

Table 1. National Composition of the Soviet Union,
the Communist Party and the Central Committee

| Nationality | 1979[a] Soviet population (percent) | 1981[b] Communist Party (percent) | 1981[c] Central Committee (percent) |
|---|---|---|---|
| SLAVIC | | | |
| Russians | 52.4 | 60.0 | 67.1 |
| Ukrainians | 16.1 | 16.0 | 15.5 |
| Belorussians | 3.6 | 3.7 | 3.1 |
| MUSLIM | | | |
| Uzbeks | 4.7 | 2.3 | 1.4 |
| Kazakhs | 2.5 | 1.9 | 2.4 |
| Azeris | 2.1 | 1.6 | 0.7 |
| Kirgiz | 0.5 | 0.4 | 0.3 |
| Tadzhiks | 1.1 | 0.4 | 0.3 |
| Turkmens | 0.7 | 0.4 | 0.3 |
| BALTIC | | | |
| Estonians | 0.4 | 0.3 | 0.7 |
| Latvians | 0.5 | 0.4 | 1.4 |
| Lithuanians | 1.1 | 0.7 | 0.3 |
| OTHER | | | |
| Armenians | 1.6 | 1.5 | 1.0 |
| Georgians | 1.4 | 1.7 | 0.3 |
| Moldavians | 1.1 | 0.5 | 0.7 |
| Others | 9.9 | 8.2 | 4.1 |

[a] Figures drawn from the 1979 Soviet census, published in *Vestnik statistiki*, No. 2, 1980, pp. 24-26.

[b] Figures for total Party membership (full and candidate members) according to nationality, from *Partiinaia zhizn'*, No. 14 (July 1981), p. 18. Since the age distributions of various nationalities of the Soviet Union differ substantially, figures for Party membership according to nationality can be compared with the population levels of the nationalities only with caution. (See Ellen Jones and Fred W. Grupp, "Measuring Nationality Trends in the Soviet Union: A Research Note," *Slavic Review*, 41, Spring 1982, pp. 112-22.) In 1981, Party membership totalled 17,430,413—a figure equal to 9.7 percent of the total Soviet population above the age of 20.

[c] Percentages computed on the basis of the officially-listed national backgrounds of 289 full members of the 1981 Central Committee for whom such data were available. Of the 30 remaining full members for whom official data on nationality were not available, 23 have Russian-sounding names and have spent their entire careers in traditionally Russian geographic areas; 3 have Russian-sounding names but spent most of their careers in a Union Republic; 4 have Ukrainian- or Belorussian-sounding names; and none have Muslim-, Baltic- or Caucasian-sounding names. Thus, the figures in the table most probably underrepresent the Slavic (and in particular, the Russian) element in the Central Committee.

## Table 2. Selected Characteristics of the Soviet Elite

| | 1981 Central Committee (percent)[a] | 1982 Political Leadership (percent) |
|---|---|---|
| NATIONALITY[b] | | |
| Russian | 67 | 62 |
| Slavic | 86 | 76 |
| FAMILY ORIGIN[c] | | |
| Peasant | 45 | 48 |
| Worker | 37 | 33 |
| White-collar | 18 | 14 |
| AGE | | |
| Over 60 | 54 | 76 |
| EDUCATION | | |
| Higher | 78 | 90 |
| PARTY MEMBERSHIP | | |
| Before 1950 | 74 | 95 |
| CAREER EXPERIENCE | | |
| Some experience in the military or in defense-related industry | 55 | 53 |
| REGIONAL AFFILIATION | | |
| Member of a regional Party or governmental organization | 42 | 43 |
| OCCUPATION | | |
| Party | 44 | 71 |
| Government | 31 | 19 |
| Military | 7 | 5 |
| Diplomatic | 4 | 5 |
| Police | 2 | 0[d] |
| CENTRAL COMMITTEE | | |
| Membership before 1957 | 10 | 43 |

a Unless otherwise noted, percentages are computed on the basis of information for all 319 full members of the 1981 Central Committee and all 21 members of the Politburo.

b Information available for 289 out of 319 full members of the 1981 Central Committee.

c Information available for 136 out of 319 full members of the 1981 Central Committee and for 20 out of 21 members of the 1982 Politburo.

d In May 1982 Politburo member Yury Andropov was transferred from head of the KGB to the Central Committee Secretariat, in charge of ideology.

which can be filled only with the approval of certain Party organs. The *nomenklatura* system is shrouded in deep secrecy, and no one knows the list's exact size. But its existence guarantees to the Central Committee Secretariat (the administrative arm of the Politburo) the power to assign whomever it wants to the senior posts in the most powerful institutions in Soviet society, while the Secretariat's appointees in turn have the power either to appoint directly or to veto appointments made by others to most of the remaining important positions throughout the country. In this respect, Brezhnev's new contract altered little in the Soviet system.

Western studies have shown that the degree to which an elite can act cohesively depends largely on the establishment of "sufficient mutual trust, so that its members will, if necessary, forego short-run personal or partisan advantage in order to ensure stable rule."[7] This mutual trust is reinforced when the members of an elite have experiences and backgrounds in common and enjoy similar privileges.

The fact that the Soviet elite is drawn largely from educated, white-collar, Russian, male Party members does reinforce its potential to act as a cohesive restraint on the actions of the leadership. Moreover, members of the elite do share privileges which they could jointly defend: special stores, vacation resorts, country houses and town apartments, chauffeured limousines, special medical clinics, trips abroad, and foreign and restricted literature. Such privileges are guaranteed by one's position in the *nomenklàtura* system; therefore stability in personnel holding important posts is essential if the elite is to enjoy these privileges uninterruptedly. Indeed, the key to Brezhnev's longevity in power was his understanding of this yearning for stability and its associated benefits within the Soviet elite. It is also a major reason why the considerable differences of opinion that sometimes arise within the leadership and/or the elite rarely overflow the narrow bounds of conventional Soviet politics, thus avoiding the explosions which so often occur elsewhere in the world today and tear other political systems apart at the seams.

The Soviet elite, however, is not a class in the usual sense of the term: a socially closed group able to transfer its property and privileges from one generation to another. Relatives of government leaders, such as Brezhnev's son Yury or Dzherman Gvishiani, son-in-law of the late prime minister Aleksei Kosygin, often do occupy positions of power. Some members of the elite and of the leadership are related to each other by marriage: the late Arvid Pelshe, Politburo member and chairman of the Party Control Commission, was said to be married to a sister of the late chief Party ideologist, Mikhail Suslov; and the recently deceased first deputy chairman of the KGB, Semyon Tsvigun, was married to Brezhnev's sister-in-law.

Yet information on the class backgrounds of the fathers of the present Soviet elite — available for 136 out of 319 full members of the 1981 Central Committee — shows that only 18 percent come from white-collar families. Nor is the Soviet elite, as some have suggested, primarily composed of the descendants of the workers who carried out the Bolshevik revolution; only 37 percent of the 1981 Central Committee grew up in blue-collar families. Rather, the roots of the elite are found more often in the countryside; fully 45 percent of the members of the 1981 Central Committee were born to peasant families.

Given these origins, it would be difficult to maintain that the Soviet elite constitutes a socially closed class. On the other hand, this shared background appears to reinforce a common outlook. As "self-made men" from the lower classes they tend to feel less secure in their social status and to be less assertive about their privileges than might have been the case with an elite of less humble, more urban origins. They have always tried to hide their privileges from public view, leaving their special stores unmarked, building their vacation homes in secluded places, riding in their limousines with the curtains drawn. At the same time, they have sought to bolster their position by acquiring the highest status symbols in Soviet society: academic degrees or titles. Almost a quarter of the members of the 1981 Central Committee now bear such honorifics, even though only about two-fifths of these have actually engaged in scientific research or educational work.

Certain other factors tend to divide the Soviet elite, however, and to diminish its ability to act as a cohesive restraint on the political leadership, particularly on issues other than personnel stability. While drawn from a wide variety of institutions and organizations, each having different goals and interests, most members of the elite have spent their entire careers working within the confines of a single organization. The most numerous occupational group within the Central Committee — about 35 percent of its membership — is from the regional Party apparatus, while officials of the governmental apparatus comprise another 31 percent. The rest of the Committee membership is drawn from the central Party apparatus (9 percent); the military (7); the diplomatic service (4); the cultural and scientific community (3); the KGB (2); the trade unions (2); and others (8).[8]

Moreover, in a centrally planned economy, where each organization competes directly with every other organization for centrally allocated resources, a high degree of competition for these resources is built into the system. Typically, individual planners are pitted against individual ministers; representatives of heavy industry against representatives of light industry; and individuals within the same occupational grouping against one another. Again, although a majority of the Central Committee are concurrently employees of central Party or governmental organizations, many of these officials have worked extensively in the provinces. At the same time, 42 percent of the Central Committee are concurrently employees of regional Party and government organizations. Even the most numerous category of officials in the Central Committee—the regional Party *apparatchiki*—often find that their regional affiliations supersede their common interests.

At the Twenty-sixth Party Congress, in February 1981, a major conflict arose between Party officials from the southern regions and those from Siberia and central Russia over plans to reverse the direction of Siberian rivers—now flowing north into the Arctic Ocean—in order to deal with a vexing water shortage in the southern portion of the country. Sharp criticism of the work of central government institutions comes frequently from provincial Party officials. At the same Party Congress, the head of the Gorky regional Party organization criticized central planning organizations for not paying enough attention to the development of river transport, a major industry in his district, while the head of the Georgian Party organization (who is also a candidate member of the Politburo) attacked the Ministry of the Food Industry for its discriminatory policies against Georgian winegrowers.[9] In short, regional divisions constitute one of the most serious obstacles to any cohesive group action on the part of the Soviet elite.

Given the strength of these institutional and territorial rivalries within the elite, and its insecurity as a social group, can anything other than a desire for stability hold the elite together? Some observers hypothesize that its members are bound together by personal ties to the military or by direct participation in a military-industrial complex bent on military expansion in order to solidify its position domestically. However, as we have noted, in 1981 representatives of the military constituted only 7 percent of the Central Committee, their number having, in fact, declined during the Brezhnev era.[10] Even if we include members of the elite currently occupied in the defense industry sector, the figure would come to no more than 11 percent. In view of its numerical weakness, therefore, this group could dominate the elite only on the basis of pervasive informal ties with other powerful factions.

But less than half of the Central Committee has ever served in the Soviet armed forces, and then usually for a short tour of duty or during World War II, and only another 12 percent has worked in the defense industry. Nor would all of these officials have had contact with the current military elite during their defense-related duties, or have maintained these contacts over the years. Similarly, while informal contacts do exist between members of the leadership and members of the military and defense-industry elite, only 53 percent of the Soviet leadership has had any career experience in either the armed forces or defense-related industry. Though this is by no means an insignificant figure, it hardly speaks for the dominance of a military-industrial complex in Soviet politics.

It would seem, rather, that the Soviet military buildup of recent decades has to do with the intrinsic power of the military establishment, the schemes of the leadership, or the nature of the international situation in which the Soviet Union finds itself. In fact, the Soviet military has shown itself to be an important political resource in times of internal political crisis in the country, playing a crucial role, for instance, in Yury Andropov's accession to the position of Party leader in 1982.

Two factors appear to be especially important in giving some sort of cohesion to the Soviet political elite: its Stalinist origins and its relationship to the leadership.

While less than a fifth of present Party members joined during Stalin's rule, almost three-quarters of the Central Committee, in 1981, were recruited into the Party under Stalin. For most members of the elite, it was their first political experience and first political act; and this is also characteristic of the Soviet leadership itself, 95 percent of whom, as of 1981, had joined the Party before 1953. In this sense, the men who run the Soviet Union today are truly Stalin's heirs. And partly as a result of this experience, a high degree of consensus is apparent within both the elite and the leadership on the legitimacy of certain basic features of the Stalinist system: central planning, collectivized agriculture, expansion of national power, censorship and repression of dissent. Attempts to alter some of these features have repeatedly failed. Agreement is lacking among students of the Soviet political system as to whether the passing of this generation from the Soviet political scene will usher in a period of reform, or whether it has succeeded in transmitting its values to its heirs-apparent. But what *is* clear is that Stalin's spirit lives on in the men who run the Soviet Union today.

A second factor which keeps the Soviet elite from disintegrating into warring factions is its clearly subordinate relationship to the leadership. As we have seen, the elite and the leadership share many characteristics (Table 2). But there are important differences. For one thing, though Party *apparatchiki* constitute 44 percent of the Central Committee, they made up 66 percent of the leadership on the eve of Brezhnev's death. Most highly represented in the leadership (as in the Central Committee) are regional Party *apparatchiki* (38 percent), but the central Party apparatus, representing only 9 percent of the Central Committee member-

# How the Soviet Union Is Ruled

## Communist Party

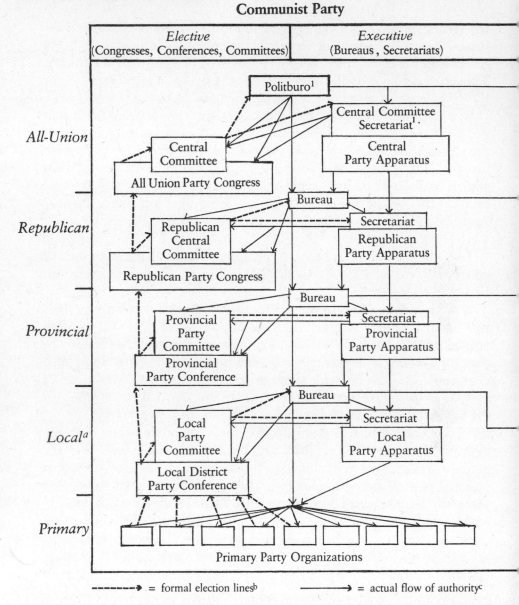

|  | *Elective*<br>(Congresses, Conferences, Committees) | *Executive*<br>(Bureaus, Secretariats) |
|---|---|---|

**All-Union** — Politburo[1], Central Committee, All Union Party Congress, Central Committee Secretariat[1], Central Party Apparatus

**Republican** — Bureau, Republican Central Committee, Republican Party Congress, Secretariat, Republican Party Apparatus

**Provincial** — Bureau, Provincial Party Committee, Provincial Party Conference, Secretariat, Provincial Party Apparatus

**Local[a]** — Bureau, Local Party Committee, Local District Party Conference, Secretariat, Local Party Apparatus

**Primary** — Primary Party Organizations

- – – – – → = formal election lines[b]     ———→ = actual flow of authority[c]

[a]Local Party organizations include the approximately 4,400 urban (*gorkom*) and rural (*raikom*) Party Committees and their executive bureaus and secretaries. The local state organizations include the approximately 44,400 village, town, district and city soviets (councils) and their executive committees. Above this local level are the comparable Party and state organizations for the 164 provinces, regions, and areas into which the Soviet Union is officially divided, and those for the 15 Union Republics, as indicated in the chart. The Party, with a total membership (1981) of about 17 million, is divided into approximately 400,000 primary organizations, each consisting of the Party members in a particular enterprise, army unit, research institute, and the like.

[b]The lines indicate formal election procedures for Party and state organizations. In actual practice, the elections are strictly controlled from the top, with single-candidate ballots the rule.

[c]These lines should not be understood to indicate a formal chain of command, since a higher Party or state organ can intervene at any level in the hierarchy below it. Also, the complex lateral relationships—consultative and/or directive—between the Party apparatus and the corresponding level of the state bureaucracy are not indicated here.

[1]Both the Politburo (21 full and candidate members) and the Central Committee Secretariat (10 secretaries) are chaired

# Soviet Government

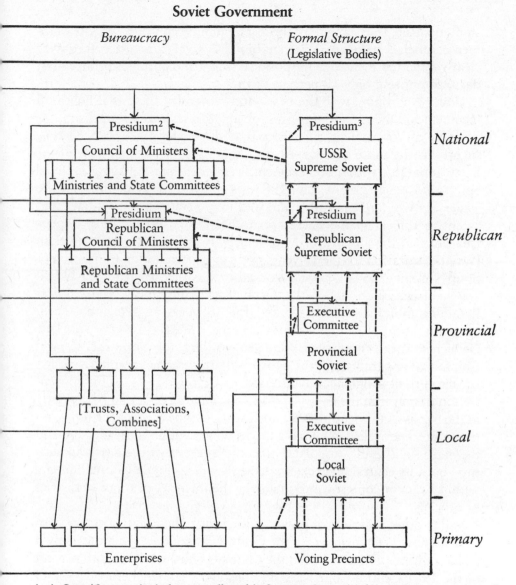

|  | Bureaucracy | Formal Structure (Legislative Bodies) |  |
|---|---|---|---|

Bureaucracy

Formal Structure
(Legislative Bodies)

Presidium[2]

Council of Ministers

Ministries and State Committees

Presidium[3]

USSR
Supreme Soviet

*National*

Presidium

Republican
Council of Ministers

Republican Ministries
and State Committees

Presidium

Republican
Supreme Soviet

*Republican*

Executive
Committee

Provincial
Soviet

*Provincial*

[Trusts, Associations,
Combines]

Executive
Committee

Local
Soviet

*Local*

Enterprises

Voting Precincts

*Primary*

by the General Secretary, the chief executive officer of the Communist Party and *de facto* the single most important official in the Soviet Union. About half of the secretaries are usually full or candidate members of the Politburo. The system of an executive "bureau" and "secretariat" presided over by a first secretary, all supposedly responsible to an elected Party conference and central committee, is replicated at every level of the Party above the primary organizations. As the chart indicates, this system provides a channel for control of the entire Party from the top down.

[2]The Presidium is the steering committee of the Council of Ministers of the Soviet Union, which has about 100 members (ministers, deputy ministers, and so forth); the Council's chairman is head (Premier) of the Soviet government. The system is replicated in each of the 15 Union Republics.

[3]The Presidium of the Supreme Soviet, sitting permanently, has 39 members; its chairman is chief of state (president of the Soviet Union). The Supreme Soviet is composed of two houses: the Soviet of the Union (one member per 300,000 voters) and the Soviet of the Nationalities (representing the Union Republics and the Autonomous Republics, Regions and Areas). The membership, currently totalling more than 1,500, is periodically adjusted to reflect population trends; and deputies to the Supreme Soviet, which usually meets twice annually for three or four days, are elected every five years, as are deputies to the Supreme Soviets of the 15 Union Republics. Deputies to the provincial and local soviets are elected every two-and-a-half years. All Soviet citizens who have reached the age of 18 are eligible to vote; well over 90 percent of eligible voters invariably turn out.

ship, made up nearly a third of the leadership. By contrast, while governmental officials make up 31 percent of the Central Committee, they were clearly underrepresented in the political leadership during Brezhnev's last days, comprising only 19 percent of that group.

Under Andropov, with the death and retirement of several Politburo members and the reshuffling of responsibilities among the survivors, the position of government officials within the leadership improved only slightly, rising to 26 percent. At the same time, the leading role of the Party apparatus within the leadership remained intact, having declined only to 63 percent as of May 1983. Moreover, many of those in the leadership who are currently employed in the state apparatus have had extensive careers in the Party apparatus. Geidar Aliev, First Deputy Chairman of the Council of Ministers, was head of the Azerbaidzhan Party organization for the 13 years prior to his promotion to his present post (November 1982), having worked even earlier in the KGB. Mikhail Solomentsev, chairman of the Council of Ministers of the Russian Republic until June 1983, worked for 18 years as a regional Party secretary before assuming his present duties (July 1971). Petr Demichev spent most of his career working for both the Central Committee apparatus and the Moscow Party organization until receiving his current assignment as Minister of Culture (1974). This concentration of power in the hands of the Party *apparatchiki*, and particularly in the hands of the central Party apparatus, is indicative of the forces on which Brezhnev relied in building up his power within the leadership and the elite. As a result, it is likely that the interests of the Party apparatus—both its central and regional cores—will continue to predominate within Kremlin conference rooms over the interests of other categories of officials.

Still another indicator of power is longevity: the longer a category of officials have been members of the Central Committee, the more likely it is that power is concentrated in their hands. Thus, while only 10 percent of the 1981 Central Committee had become members before 1957, 43 percent of the Politburo in April 1982 had been members of the Central Committee for over a quarter of a century. It is these men who have been the real power brokers in the Soviet Union in the post-Stalin era.

This concentration of power in the Party Secretariat and the Politburo —in many cases the same people—derives from the *nomenklatura* system. Because these men control the assignment of officials to the most powerful posts in the country, they have been able to build up large followings within the elite. Their extensive networks crisscross all the major institutions, providing factional cohesion to what otherwise might have been a motley collection of individuals and organizations.

Brezhnev's following in the Central Committee, for instance, nicknamed the "Dnepropetrovsk mafia" by the Western press after the region where he first rose to prominence, included at least three officials who went to college with him; two officials who worked with him at the Dzerzhinskii Metallurgical Plant in Dneprodzerzhinsk; and six other officials associated with Brezhnev in the Dnepropetrovsk Party organization in the 1930s and 1940s. Almost every other member of the Politburo has similar followings. Thus despite the great stability of personnel within the Central Committee during the Brezhnev era, the leadership has been able to dispense this type of patronage merely by expanding the size of the Central Committee itself—from 195 members in 1966 to 319 in 1981—and thereby packing it with loyal followers. Though Andropov's patron-client ties appeared to be somewhat weaker than Brezhnev's, by the spring of 1983 he had already promoted several men who had worked closely with him during his days as head of the KGB: Geidar Aliev (now a full member of the Politburo and, as mentioned, First Deputy Chairman of the Council of Ministers); Vitalii Fedorchuk (now Minister of the Interior); and Viktor Chebrikov (now chairman of the KGB).

The ability of an elite to get its way usually depends decisively on the rewards and punishments at its disposal. But in the Soviet system, as we see, most of these are in the hands of the political leadership. It controls the *nomenklatura* system, commands personal followings, and makes the decisive choices over the direction of policy and the allocation of resources. In fact, the Soviet elite has never been able to act cohesively to constrain the actions of the leadership.

One of the few cases in which the Central Committee played a more independent role was during the so-called anti-Party crisis of 1957, when certain members of the leadership attempted to overthrow Khrushchev. Outnumbered in the Politburo, Khrushchev nevertheless managed to alert his supporters in the Central Committee who, with the help of army planes, gathered in Moscow from all parts of the country to aid their beleaguered leader. But the crisis demonstrated how the power of the Central Committee depended both on the military and on the decision of higher authorities to mobilize it.

Normally, the Central Committee meets for a few days several times a year; and so long as this is the case, it will have an independent say over policy only when the political leadership is extremely polarized, as in a succession crisis. Even Khrushchev's ouster in October 1964 by a unified political leadership was presented as an accomplished fact to a passive Central Committee, although this act was no doubt popular among its members. All signs indicate that Andropov's succession to power in November 1982 was similarly decided by a small group of 15 to 20 men and then presented to the Central Committee for ratification.

Under Khrushchev, Central Committee meetings were often used to launch attacks against particular leaders or bureaucrats and political squabbles were often aired in public. But under Brezhnev the meetings of the Central Committee were more closed, less spontaneous, shorter and less frequent.[11] At the same time, the size of the Committee became unwieldy. In effect, the Brezhnev regime concluded a new political contract with the elite, providing it with greater job security while weakening the collective role of the Central Committee. In this sense, Brezhnev's political contract was not a unilateral concession by the leadership but rather an exchange between it and the elite: security for quiescence.

This does not mean that individual members of the Central Committee are not powerful in their own right. But they have not been able to combine their power to shape the system according to their collective will, and should therefore not be considered a "power elite" in the classic sense of the term.[12] As far as is known in the West, the Soviet Union is routinely governed by numerous commissions and committees dealing with specific policy areas. In defense policy, for instance, there is a Defense Council, once chaired by Brezhnev and now by Andropov, which evidently includes the nation's most powerful Party and military officials. Similarly, a commission under the Council of Ministers, chaired by an old Brezhnev protege, L. V. Smirnov, coordinates policy for the defense industry.

Through participation in the various commissions, members of the Soviet elite can have a decisive impact on decision-making. But the key to political influence is having the ear of the leadership. Moreover, the power of individual members of the elite, as opposed to the power of individual members of the leadership, is largely confined to their own narrow policy spheres. Soviet experts on Soviet-American relations have little influence over agricultural policies, for example, just as officials from the Ministry of Health have little influence over nuclear weapons policies.

The Soviet leadership is no longer the one-man band it was under Stalin—an arrangement Khrushchev attempted to imitate. But neither is it a mere collection of political equals. For one thing, as of this writing the members of the Politburo are themselves formally divided into 11 full members and seven candidate members—a difference in status thought to be connected with the voting rights of Politburo members, but whose import is not entirely clear. Moreover, some individuals have been closer to the center of power for longer than others, enabling them to build up their authority and power within the leadership.

By the spring of 1983, the full members of the Politburo had held their present positions and status an average of eight years, and six—including Andropov and Andrei Gromyko—had been full members for more than eight. While not all of these men enjoy the same degree of power, in general they constitute a senior circle within the leadership. Others in the leadership, while lacking seniority among the full members of the Politburo, are powerful figures because of the positions they occupy outside the Party, such as the Defense Minister, Dmitrii Ustinov, or Nikolai Tikhonov, the Chairman of the Council of Ministers. Still others gained power through their closeness with the late General Secretary (Brezhnev), such as Central Committee Secretary Konstantin Chernenko, who served for years as Brezhnev's aide. Since meetings of the Politburo are held in strict secrecy, we know little about the attitudes of members of the leadership on particular issues. But ultimately the Soviet political system today is run through a shifting combination of political alliances and personal factions at the top.

Some conclusions about the Soviet political system and its future now come to mind:
- The answer to the question posed at the outset—who rules the Soviet Union?—depends largely on how one envisages the process of ruling. Neither the Soviet leadership nor the Soviet elite can have its way on all issues, simply because no mortal or group of mortals can be all-powerful. And while the leadership clearly enjoys the upper hand, members of the elite can have some influence over policies within their own narrowly specialized spheres if they have the opportunity and the ability to persuade the leadership. The relationship between the elite and the most senior politicians is a subordinate one; but it is dynamic as well, and in this respect similar to the political process elsewhere in the world.
- While there are many elements in the political and social system of the Soviet Union that date back to the Stalin era, some things *have* changed. Brezhnev never manifested either Stalin's independence or his murderous tendencies, but he and his cohorts, as well as his heirs, are very much the products of Stalin's system. Although they have dismantled some of its features, such as the indiscriminate use of terror, the heirs have attempted to preserve and maintain many of its controls over the populace and the bureaucracy. Yet Brezhnev's regime demonstrated greater concern for the interests of the Soviet elite than did any previous Soviet leadership, and the new contract between the leadership and the elite, exchanging personal security for political quiescence, was the key factor in his long reign. Moreover, government by commission and rule through alliance and factions replaced the *diktat* of a single leader.

• There is no "new class," no ruling or power elite, no one amalgam of interests dominating the Soviet political system. Collective action by the elite in pursuit of its common interests has been weak, and both the elite and the policy-making process itself are sufficiently fragmented to ensure that all decisions are essentially dependent on the will of the political leadership. If any conglomeration of forces does predominate, it is the Party apparatus, although this category of officials has also exhibited a high degree of fragmentation.

Yet a crucial question remains: can Brezhnev's contract survive his death, or is it only a passing feature of the Soviet political scene? There is an inherent conservatism built into the contract, both in terms of the values it represents and the policies it presupposes. Any serious reformer of the Soviet political system must possess the capacity not only to change policies, but also to change the personnel responsible for carrying out those policies.

Brezhnev's rule was marked by a cautious, even stagnant, style of governance which left his heirs with a long list of serious social and economic problems. Given this situation, Brezhnev's contract might well become a formidable obstacle to needed reforms, if not an impediment to the effective functioning of the Soviet political system itself. Moreover, the very stability of cadres under Brezhnev eventually led to the widespread flourishing of materialistic values, careerism and corruption within the Soviet elite.

In sum, the campaign to crack down on corruption and on the privileges of the elite, inaugurated after Andropov's accession to the Party leadership, doubtless put the Brezhnev contract under some strain. But so long as it remains in place, the capacity of the system to produce needed reforms is severely limited. □

**1.** For the history of Stalin's purges, see Robert Conquest, *The Great Terror: Stalin's Purges of the Thirties* (New York: Collier Books, 1968). On Stalin's plans for a major purge immediately before his death, see Robert Conquest, *Power and Policy in the USSR: The Struggle for Stalin's Succession, 1945-1960* (New York: Harper and Row, 1961), pp. 79-191.

**2.** Jerry F. Hough, *The Soviet Union and Social Science Theory* (Cambridge, Massachusetts: Harvard University Press, 1977), p. 29.

**3.** All statistical information, unless otherwise noted, has been computed on the basis of biographical information gathered by the author from a variety of sources, among them: Alexander G. Rahr, *A Biographic Directory of 100 Leading Soviet Officials* (Munich: RFE-RL, 1981); *Deputaty Verkhovnogo Soveta SSSR* (Moscow: 1959, 1962, 1966, 1970, 1974, 1979); *Ezhegodnik Bol'shoi Sovetskoi Entsiklopedii* (Moscow: 1966-81).

**4.** Hough, *The Soviet Union*, p. 29.

**5.** For a sampling of the literature on elite studies, see Robert D. Putnam, *The*

*Comparative Study of Political Elites* (Englewood Cliffs, New Jersey: Prentice-Hall, 1976); John A. Armstrong, *The European Administrative Elite* (Princeton, New Jersey: Princeton University Press, 1973); Carl Beck and others, eds., *Comparative Communist Political Leadership* (New York: David McKay, 1973); Harold D. Lasswell and others, *The Comparative Study of Elites: An Introduction and Bibliography* (Stanford, California: Stanford University Press, 1952); C. Wright Mills, *The Power Elite* (New York: Oxford University Press, 1956).

6. This percentage is based upon information published in *Narodnoe khoziaistvo SSSR, 1922-1927* (Moscow: Statistika, 1972), p. 30; age related information from the 1979 Soviet census has not yet been published. Other data from *Vestnik statistiki*, Nos. 1-12, 1980; and *Partiinaia zhizn'*, 14 (July 1981), pp. 13-26.

7. Putnam, *Comparative Study*, p. 122.

8. Figures for occupational breakdown are from Elizabeth Teague, "The Central Committee and Central Auditing Commission Elected at the Twenty-Sixth Congress of the CPSU," *Radio Liberty Research Report*, RL 171/81 (April 28, 1981), p. 20.

9. See *Pravda* (Feb. 25, 1981); (Feb. 26, 1981); (Feb. 28, 1981); (Mar. 3, 1981).

10. Jerry F. Hough and Merle Fainsod, *How the Soviet Union Is Governed* (Cambridge, Massachusetts: Harvard University Press, 1979), pp. 456-7.

11. Hough and Fainsod, *How the Soviet Union Is Governed*, pp. 459-62.

12. Mills, *The Power Elite*.

# 5

## Policymaking and Foreign Affairs

### Alexander Dallin

Of all the major political concerns of the Soviet authorities, the conduct of foreign policy was the one the Bolsheviks had least expected when they took power. By the same token, the course of world affairs since 1917 has often challenged and belied the beliefs and expectations of Soviet analysts and decision-makers. The record of Soviet foreign policy is replete with remarkable successes and stupendous failures—both due in part to Soviet perceptions and behavior, in part to factors beyond Soviet control.

The survival of the Soviet state, between the two world wars, in a capitalist encirclement (as well as the failure of revolutions abroad sponsored or supported by Moscow) heightened the tension between conventional (state) and transformational (revolutionary) perspectives and impulses, a tension that remains alive to this day. Similarly, conflicting pressures have stemmed from the simultaneous attractions of "expansion and coexistence," to quote the title of a standard history of Soviet foreign policy.[1]

Whether the Soviet Union has more to gain from a stabilization of the international environment or from the fallout from destabilization has been a matter of further uncertainty. And these are but a few of the many areas of ambiguity and tension in the Soviet approach to public policy—foreign policy included—which Soviet secrecy and ritual reiteration of orthodox formulas have at times made to appear more single-minded, more unambiguous and more relentless than seems warranted by closer inspection of the record.

The past 65 years have seen a remarkable growth, not of Soviet communism but of the Soviet state. From an impoverished, inexperienced

53

and underdeveloped pariah in the family of nations, it has grown into a formidable superpower, able to project its power globally, to exercise effective control over a number of other polities, and to wield considerable influence in many other areas. Yet the years since Stalin's death in 1953 have seen, along with a substantial increase in Soviet power, evidence of serious strains and failures; considerably heightened professionalization and competence in the conduct of public policy, but also pockets of serious and dysfunctional rigidities and bureaucratic irrationality; international assertiveness and involvement, but also a measure of restraint in Soviet conduct abroad. Indeed, the record, with some glaring exceptions, confirms a fairly pervasive Soviet proclivity to avoid high risks in foreign affairs and, even when apparently committed to "adventurous" behavior, to back down or shy away in crisis situations, such as the Cuban missile crisis of 1962 or the Middle Eastern crises of 1973 and 1982.

The general outlook of the Khrushchev era (1955-1964), in its original and optimistic version, may retrospectively be boiled down to three sets of expectations:

• The Soviet-controlled socialist camp would grow in strength, cohesion and influence, as would the international communist movement abroad.

• The capitalist world, in the West and Japan, would be plagued by general economic and political crises that, coming on the heels of decolonization, were bound to weaken its relative weight in the "correlation of forces" with the communist bloc.

• The Third World, finally freed from imperialist fetters, would inevitably gravitate toward the Soviet camp, with which it shared common interests and common adversaries.

None of these expectations has come true. To all intents and purposes, international communism has ceased to function as a unitary, let alone Moscow-controlled, movement. In the Third World, Moscow has sustained a long series of setbacks in its extensive and expensive efforts to profit from its support of nationalist movements. (Almost the only substantial gains Moscow could point to in the Third World resulted from unanticipated circumstances over which it had no control, such as Cuba.) And while the West has had its own share of serious difficulties, these have not been such as to change the overall "correlation of forces" fundamentally. If anything, Soviet elite perceptions of continuing Soviet needs and of Soviet backwardness relative to the West in regard to advanced technology, industrial and agricultural productivity, and economic efficiency have become markedly stronger. Indeed, they provided a far-reaching rationale for stepped up interaction between the Soviet

Union and the "developed" West in the Brezhnev years.

From Moscow's perspective, this reorientation under Brezhnev presupposed approximate parity in strategic weapons, which enabled the Soviet Union to act as a coequal superpower, to demand to be treated as one, and to pursue what one observer has astutely labeled its "global vocation." But if, in Moscow's view, the 1970s witnessed the "objective" shift away from previous Soviet inferiority, Moscow apparently neither holds to, nor acts upon, the belief that the Soviet Union has gained a substantial edge in military power, let alone in other indicators of power, over its potential adversaries.

Soviet foreign policy may be seen as the pursuit of a number of interrelated objectives in the face of complex constraints and pressures, both internal and external to the Soviet Union. In recent years these objectives have ranged from self-preservation and security to others whose relative priority may depend on the expected price to be paid for their attainment: the recognized need to avoid military conflict with the United States; the commitment to promote control and integration of Eastern Europe under Soviet auspices; the desire to derive benefits from the stepped-up interaction with the West in science, technology and the economy; the attempt to stem or forestall a further rapprochement among China, Japan and the developed West that would leave the Soviet Union "encircled"; the improvement of relations with the European members of NATO; the pursuit of arms control negotiations but also a continued commitment to the buildup of the Soviet armed forces; and an inclination to exploit political crises and power vacuums in the Third World insofar as this can be done without incurring undue costs or risks.[2]

It is not surprising that at times the simultaneous pursuit of these and other policy objectives has given rise to tensions and incongruities among the component policies. These have been heightened still further by the perceived inconsistencies and ambiguities in the behavior of other powers, especially the United States.

Thus the record of Soviet foreign policy is rather mixed, as are the considerations that go into making it; and it is well to guard against oversimplification. The Soviet Union is neither a conventional imperialist state nor an old-fashioned, satiated status-quo power. It is not simply traditional Russia in new garb nor another variant of the Nazi system. And while its role abroad has often been troublesome and quarrelsome, even foolish and provocative, whenever it comes to fundamental choices in preferences, orientations and values the dominant decisionmakers in the Soviet Union have remained fundamentally wedded to the primacy of domestic over foreign affairs.[3]

Time and again basic policy orientations in Moscow have had foreign policy components and implications. In fact, the course of Soviet history suggests an inner logic in the pattern of linkages between internal and external policy choices. While no single formula will serve to explain all the instances of such linkages, the single most pervasive and persistent pattern of political cleavages and linkages has been the dichotomy between "left" and "right" within the communist sector of the political spectrum.

In essence, the left describes a syndrome centered on "transformation," whereas the right opts for "stabilization"; mobilization is found on the left, normalcy on the right; tension-management on the left, consensus-building on the right; a willingness to resort to militancy and if need be to violence is characteristic of the left, a preference for incrementalism is typical of the right. Partisanship and the priority of politics belong on the left; rationality and the priority of economics (or, more generally, science) on the right. Congruent with this cleavage is the priority of the development of heavy industry on the left, as against the more vigorous development of agriculture and/or consumer goods on the right. Voluntarism tends to be identified with the left, determinism with the right. Going it alone, autarky and self-isolation are correlates of the left, alliances and interdependence of the right. These are some of the major components of two distinct communist tempers and outlooks, at least in their extreme, polarized manifestations.

In practice, of course, political actors are not always consistent in occupying the same "space" on a range of different issue areas. Still, such a perspective helps us to understand both a "radical" approach to communist policy at home and abroad, and the logic linking divergent Soviet views of U.S. intentions with bitter arguments over resource allocation, military posture and arms control. In earlier years one could also speak of a linkage between detente and welfare priorities at one extreme, as against "vigilance," repression, preparedness and a forward foreign policy at the other.

To be sure, today such a left-right yardstick has become an inadequate tool. As the Soviet economy has grown and choices need no longer be seen in such stark terms, Soviet policy often manages to combine "left" and "right" elements. Moreover, some sources of cleavage do not fit the left-right dichotomy at all: center-periphery tensions, regional rivalries, generational alignments and, last but not least, patronage networks and cliques.

Stalin's death, it is worth emphasizing, marked a profound watershed in Soviet history. True, power to make final decisions remained and still remains normally concentrated in the hands of a very few. Yet it would be a serious distortion of Soviet reality to minimize the nature and scope of the changes that have occurred since Stalin left the scene. In particular, it may be said that beginning in the 1960s Leonid Brezhnev brought foreign policy home.

On the one hand, certain trends were "objectively" given, as economic development proceeded and as the Soviet Union underwent what it calls the "scientific-technological revolution." In this respect things were not so different from trends elsewhere in the world, including the United States, which have also been marked by the growing erosion of the boundaries between foreign and domestic policy areas. Developments in fields such as energy, weapons and communications illustrate this point.

On the other hand, the new tendency, which flowered in the policy of detente, was reinforced and promoted by "subjective" political choices made by the Party Politburo. These decisions included a departure from the Stalinist commitment to economic self-sufficiency in favor of greater interaction with the outside world, especially in trade and technology, for the benefit of the Soviet economy. In essence, these were efforts to remedy the continuing and, in some instances, chronic deficiencies of Soviet economic and technological development and to do so without embarking on economic and administrative reforms that would be apt to provoke more serious political fallout, including perhaps tacit resistance and actual disruption.

Soviet policy under Brezhnev thus sought to call on the external to help the internal environment, on condition that the political costs at home were held to a manageable minimum. Regardless of whether, in retrospect, he and his colleagues correctly gauged their ability to keep the price to a minimum—in terms of access to "alien" ideas and values—the policy commitment itself underscores the indissolubility of the domestic and foreign policy spheres.

The overall effects of developments since the 1960s may be summarized as follows:

• A spillover effect, greater than in the past, of discrete decisions in other sectors—such as dissent, weapons, research and development, energy—on foreign affairs;

• A growing complexity—technical, administrative and intellectual—in Soviet foreign policy-making;

• A growing awareness by Soviet foreign policy-makers of the domestic arena in which they function.

In this last area, too, a subtle change has occurred. Stalin could effectively ignore "public opinion" in making foreign policy decisions. But, as Adam Ulam has cogently argued, the Soviet leadership today cannot afford great political defeats abroad of the sort that Stalin could; presumably such setbacks would reflect on the perceived legitimacy of the regime. By the same token, as Ulam suggests, foreign policy successes are for the Soviet elite a "principal means of legitimizing their policy system."[4]

The Soviet Union's rather uneven record in foreign policy, especially in relation to the United States, has in all likelihood put the senior decision-makers in Moscow on the defensive. To be sure, toward the outside world the Soviet elite has continued to present a united front; and the constituency that benefits from this informal accountability remains narrowly circumscribed. Yet within these limits, one may posit, the necessity to seek continual policy legitimation will remain in force, especially for a newly installed Soviet leadership. And this imposes a new parameter of constraints on policy-making.

Moreover, there has been a marked increase in ambiguity and in unreconciled diversity of approaches and cognitions in Soviet outlook and utterance. While Soviet ideological treatments, textbooks and some mass media continued to convey the image of a crisis-ridden, declining enemy camp even at the height of detente, the presuppositions of detente included the notion of mutual benefit and a recognition that the Soviet Union stood to gain from closer ties with the West. They also presupposed that the capitalist system would *not* collapse. Nor were these entirely novel insights: some pragmatic emancipation from ideological stereotypes was a major element in the Sino-Soviet dispute of the early 1960s.

Indeed, if the process is at times slow and reluctant, there is solid evidence of Soviet willingness to learn from experience. The inclusion of a "mutual hostage" posture in the SALT I treaty marked, for the Soviet Union, a recognition of interdependence that had previously been resisted. Negotiators who have been involved with their Soviet opposite numbers in arms control talks over a number of years give various examples—along with instances of infuriating stubbornness—of the gradual adoption and absorption by the Soviet side of "American" concepts and assumptions in the field of strategic and arms-control theory.[5]

Then too, there is considerable anecdotal evidence of vastly improved familiarity with conditions abroad on the part of the Soviet public—or, at least, of that segment of the public that evinces any interest. This has resulted from improved access to Western as well as the Soviet media and from some modest improvement in opportunities both to travel abroad and to meet foreigners in the Soviet Union. While the political payoff of these transactions and opportunities remains in dispute among outside experts, one *can* point to a slow but real, cumulative impact. Consider only the striking contrast between the virtual isolation of the

Soviet citizen from the outside world a generation ago and the current state of affairs, in which channels and arenas of interaction have multiplied by the hundreds and now run the gamut from athletics to professional meetings, from blue jeans and Pepsi to Western pop music. A better informed public, it could be, imposes new constraints on Soviet policy-making.

More exactly, how are the seemingly discrete areas of Soviet policy linked? There are apparently three such sources of linkage: the structural base, elite politics, and the Soviet mindset.

The first is rooted in the very nature of the Soviet polity and economy. This structural or institutional aspect is a function of the central command system and, in particular, of the centrality of decisions regarding resource allocation. Given a pool of limited resources, options regarding, say, the procurement of weapons are bound to affect the availability of assets for agriculture, light industry and capital construction—and vice versa. Priority given to the acquisition of foreign grain or chemical fertilizer or technology implies the adoption of appropriate measures calculated to promote these objectives, along with restraint from others that might imperil them. This is not to argue that foreign policy decisions are made strictly in terms of financial cost-benefit analyses. But the alternative uses of scarce resources clearly militate for a rational coordination of domestic and foreign options consistent with an ordering of priorities.

A second source of linkages may be found in the emergence, in recent years, of tacit, informal or incipient coalitions among policy-makers and their advisors. In this case, the pursuit of a given foreign policy may be in the nature of side payments in return for a consensus or "deal" on domestic policies, or vice versa. Here the linkage is not so much substantive as political.

And last, an obvious place to focus is on the minds of the actors. In the Soviet case we encounter a special and important trait that might be called a psycho-ideological compulsion, rooted in the Leninist tradition, to provide a totalist, homogeneous, analytical framework for the entire domain of public policy. More specifically, one may speak of a special Soviet predisposition to perceive or provide linkages due to a combination of the notion of a "general line"; the claim to be engaged in "scientific" analysis and definition of political strategy and tactics; and the axiom that there are no accidents.

Both conceptually and empirically, all of these sources of linkage between domestic and foreign policy perceptions and orientations may be present in Soviet decision-making at any one time. Yet the evidence increasingly suggests that the specifically Leninist elements among the "subjective" variables sketched above are declining in operational importance, and that the other two complexes—the structural and political—must be given more weight in explaining Soviet policy in the 1970s and 1980s. In short, it appears that Soviet policy-making is becoming more pragmatic.

True, the official style requires continued adherence to the conventional formulas and jargon, although experienced Soviet officials and scholars know how to manipulate and circumvent these when necessary or possible. This fact makes for a greater gap between public pronouncements and private beliefs, of course; but given the elaborate reiteration of doctrinal formulations, something rubs off and becomes part of the diffuse body of assumptions accepted in the dominant culture.

In a system where the entire society has been systematically and repeatedly subject to the same stream of political stereotypes, many people are bound to accept their terms uncritically and unthinkingly. What, then, about the role of "ideology" in foreign policy-making today? It can be described as at most a partial guide to perception—shaping categories and expectations and often limiting the range of the permissible. But to what extent it actually functions in Soviet decision-making must be assumed to vary not only from time to time but also from individual to individual; and this cannot be deduced from a generalized, aggregated, abstract discussion of either "ideology" or "political culture."

Meanwhile, the "objective" dimensions of Soviet power include natural and human resources and the economic, scientific and technological capabilities that make up the environment in which policy decisions are made. These variables, too, impose constraints or apply pressure on the decision-makers insofar as they communicate needs or opportunities, comparative advantages or disadvantages in relation to other states. While it is often important to have a precise picture of Soviet assets and liabilities in these respects, for our purposes here it is their role as inputs into policy decisions that counts. How are these "objective" assets and liabilities perceived and made operational by the Soviet leadership?

We can accept it as a fact that the Soviet Union has been firmly and lastingly committed to maximizing its power. Under Stalin this was the overriding objective of state policy, pursued at considerable cost to other sectors of public, let alone private, life and economy. The methods and the mix of objectives have changed since his death; but the impetus toward the acquisition of power remains and has become virtually an end in itself. And while successful in this quest, the Soviet Union is very far from having solved the many problems associated with economic development, use of resources, efficient management, distributive justice or the challenges presented by rampant and seemingly ubiquitous corruption, red tape and low civic morale as well as resistance to innovation. Indeed, a combination of factors presents the current leadership with an exceptionally heavy agenda of unresolved problems and seemingly intractable difficulties, beginning with the slowing growth of the economy—a problem much aggravated by the commitment to huge defense expenditures—and the unprecedented manpower shortage.

These developments will affect Soviet behavior abroad. Yet some uncertainty is warranted insofar as the decisions will soon be made, in all likelihood, by a new generation of Soviet leaders, a generation whose values and priorities remain in dispute and are perhaps not fully crystallized. Still, it is virtually certain that—as long as policy in Moscow is made more or less rationally—a keen awareness of these domestic ills will serve to restrain, rather than promote, Soviet adventurism abroad.

Unfortunately, some credence has been given in the United States to the notion that the Kremlin seeks successes abroad—perhaps victorious little wars—as a way of compensating for shortages at home, to take its people's minds off their problems. But it is not historically true that domestic weakness has produced greater Soviet aggressiveness. Moreover, Soviet leaders today do not see their country in the throes of a systemic political or economic crisis. Nor do they advertise their involvement abroad in a fashion calculated to titillate or distract domestic audiences. The Soviet intervention in Afghanistan, for instance, could not possibly be perceived as a victorious patriotic pageant by Soviet newspaper readers or television watchers. Finally, it would scarcely make sense for Soviet policy-makers to think of expensive and hazardous operations abroad as an answer to shortages, deviance, or corruption at home.

What seems clear, in any case, is that the sum total of domestic problems and challenges—and the political jockeying they give rise to—will be much more on the minds of Soviet decision-makers in the period ahead than they have been for the past 15 years.

Once we transcend Soviet constitutional and ideological myths, we find informal political behavior that comes closer to a "conflict model" than to the stereotype of consensual authoritarianism. Members of the Soviet elite, it has been argued, "acting as individuals or as members of factions and interest groups, seek to convert inputs or . . . demands, based on often divergent interests and values, into outputs of public policy."[6] Again, in the years since Stalin "elite politics has evolved from arbitrary, personalistic rule to a competitive oligarchy. Group access to the principal policy-making arenas has become more regularized and less dangerous."[7]

Without question, the Soviet Union remains a one-party dictatorship, with a political life marked by the tradition and mystique of unity, hierarchy, discipline and centralization, and a habit of (at least formal) consensus and compliance. Yet it would be a grievous error to accept claims and pretense as reality, and to neglect the evidence of a multitude of tensions, functional and jurisdictional disputes, role conflicts, special groups, lobbies, vested interests, intellectual and perceptual differences, regional and ethnic rivalries, power struggles, technical disputes and various other antagonisms. Indeed, it is precisely the variable relationship among these elements that make it so difficult to provide simple analytical formulas for the inputs into Soviet policy-making.

Even a cursory survey of Soviet history suggests the wide range of issues over which there have been significant differences, overt or otherwise, within the Soviet elite. Some of the issues in dispute have only indirectly addressed Soviet foreign policy. The perennial tug-of-war over resource allocation, as noted above, inevitably has had implications for Soviet posture and policy abroad; conversely, the foreign and defense policies of the Soviet state set priorities in the allocation of budgetary expenses and scarce resources. Individuals and groups have developed a vested interest in a particular policy because of the role and status it confers on them, while others have perceived themselves as deprived in status and rewards because of existing allocations. At one time the linkages between domestic and foreign policies tended to align those favoring reform, de-Stalinization and welfare-consumer priorities with advocates of better relations with the capitalist West, and the traditionalists with the isolationists. But this is no longer so simply the case.

What have remained major sources of divergencies of outlook are differing perceptions of the international scene: differing judgments regarding the prospects for war and peace and therefore the size, structure and deployment of the armed forces; differing assessments of opportunities abroad; and, together with these, differing images of self, of the United States and of China. From this complex flows the central set of problems often described as "strategy and tactics" in relation to the adversary. Recent internal Soviet differences over detente are but one manifestation of a continual cleavage reflecting, at least in part, diverse communist tempers and temperaments, outlooks and mindsets. Subsidiary to such broad questions, but often congruent with the actors' orientations toward them, are divergent attitudes toward particular means of promoting or implementing policy decisions: emigration as a *quid pro quo* for a more forthcoming U.S. attitude; the risks and benefits of intellectual and cultural contacts abroad; and whether Soviet purposes are better served by tension or stabilization on the world scene. The evidence of such divergencies within the Soviet elite is growing in volume as both the elite and the larger society itself become more complex, more sophisticated and, albeit to a very limited extent, more open.

One implication of this chapter is that, whether it wants to or not, whether it knows it or not, the United States, by what it says and does—and by what it fails to say and do—inevitably contributes to the dialogue being carried on within the Soviet elite. The United States cannot hope to manipulate Soviet behavior and perspectives, of course, but at least marginally the mutual perceptions of both superpowers are shaped by each other's behavior. The United States may properly be seen as an unwitting participant in the internal debates and assessments going on in the Soviet Union, much as Soviet behavior in turn provides contending schools of U.S. political analysts with ammunition.

What we have in fact is not merely a pattern of mirror images, but something which may be called a tacit alliance between adversaries. The "moderates" on each side share an interest in agreements they deem to be mutually beneficial, and in fact cooperate to promote such agreements. Others help each other as well—in deed if not in intent. The military-industrial establishments on both sides cite the research and procurement of the other in justification of their demands for larger budgets and new programs. It has been suggested that in a number of branches Soviet and U.S. counterparts are in effect "functional bureaucratic allies" and "external pacers" for each other. The "hawks" on both sides also help validate each other's expectations. Their commitment to worst-case analysis requires the assistance of the adversary to provide support for their prophecies of doom and gloom.

If there is one lesson that suggests itself from this analysis it is, above all, the need for sensitivity to the Soviet domestic scene on the part of foreign observers and policy-makers; for greater awareness of the likely effects of U.S. behavior and pronouncements on internal Soviet dialogues and debates. This calls for a major effort at consciousness-raising in foreign affairs. □

1. Adam Ulam, *Expansion and Coexistence*, 2nd ed. (New York: Praeger, 1974).
2. On various aspects of the Soviet outlook and posture in the Brezhnev era, see Robert Legvold, "The Nature of Soviet Power," *Foreign Affairs*, 56, No. 1 (Oct. 1977), pp. 49-71; Lawrence T. Caldwell, *Soviet-American Relations in the 1980s* (New York: McGraw-Hill, 1980); Helmut Sonnenfeldt and William Hyland, "Soviet Perspectives on Security," *Adelphi Papers*, No. 150 (1979), pp. 1-24; Dimitri K. Simes, *Detente and Conflict . . . 1972-1977*, The Washington Papers 5, No. 44 (Beverly Hills, California: Sage Publishing, 1977); Robert Legvold, "The Soviet Union and Western Europe: Ex-

pansion and Detente," in William E. Griffith, ed., *The Soviet Empire* (Lexington, Massachusetts: Lexington Books, 1976), pp. 217-58; and George W. Breslauer, "Why Detente Failed: An Interpretation," in Alexander L. George, ed., *Managing U.S.-Soviet Rivalry* (Boulder, Colorado: Westview Press, 1983), pp. 319-40.

3. This essay is a condensed and revised version of my article "The Domestic Sources of Soviet Foreign Policy," in Seweryn Bialer, ed., *The Domestic Context of Soviet Foreign Policy* (Boulder, Colorado: Westview Press, 1981), pp. 335-408. In addition to the other essays in Bialer, see Vernon V. Aspaturian, "Internal Policies and Foreign Policy in the Soviet System," in Barry Farrell, ed., *Approaches to Comparative and International Politics* (Evanston, Illinois: Northwestern University Press, 1966), pp. 212-87; Sidney Ploss, "Studying the Determinants of Soviet Foreign Policy," *Canadian Slavic Studies*, I No. 1 (Spring 1967), pp. 44-59; Morton Schwartz, *The Foreign Policy of the USSR: Domestic Factors* (Encino, California: Dickenson Publishing, 1975); and Erik Hoffmann and Frederic J. Fleron, eds., *The Conduct of Soviet Foreign Policy*, 2nd ed. (New York: Aldine Publishers, 1980), which includes several relevant essays.

4. Adam Ulam, "Russian Nationalist," in Bialer, ed., *Domestic Context*, pp. 3-17.

5. Wolfgang Panofsky, "The Mutual-Hostage Relationship between America and Russia," *Foreign Affairs*, 52, No. 1 (Oct. 1978), pp. 109-18; Raymond L. Garhoff, "SALT I: An Evaluation," *World Politics*, 31 No. 1 (Oct. 1978), pp. 1-25.

6. Frederick C. Barghoorn, *Politics in the USSR*, 2nd ed. (Boston: Little, Brown, 1972), p. 200.

7. George W. Breslauer and Stanley Rothman, *Soviet Politics and Society* (St. Paul, Minnesota: West Publishing, 1978), p. 209.

# 6

## Dissent

### Joshua Rubenstein

Dissent in the Soviet Union had unexpected beginnings. Following Stalin's death in 1953 Nikita Khrushchev initiated significant reforms, as Stephen F. Cohen explains (Chapter 3). But Khrushchev was removed from power in October 1964, and within a year his successors, led by Leonid Brezhnev and Aleksei Kosygin, began to reverse the process of de-Stalinization. Among other ominous developments, the writers Andrei Sinyavsky and Yuli Daniel were arrested in Moscow in September 1965 for challenging the regime's censorship controls by sending their stories to the West.

These arrests initiated a crucial series of events. Friends and supporters of Sinyavsky and Daniel organized a petition campaign on their behalf and even held a demonstration in Moscow's Pushkin Square on December 5, 1965, Soviet Constitution Day, demanding an open trial for the two writers. This was the first demonstration since Stalin's death in defense of individual rights. Sinyavsky and Daniel were convicted of "anti-Soviet agitation and propaganda" in February 1966 and sentenced to long terms of confinement in the labor camps of Mordovia, east of Moscow. Their stories, which had been published abroad under pseudonyms, were the principal evidence against them.

The trial, however, did not intimidate their supporters. Aleksandr Ginzburg assembled a history of the case, including an account of the trial, and sent it to the West; he was arrested in January 1967.[1] Then Vladimir Bukovsky was arrested and tried for demonstrating against other arrests. Pavel Litvinov, a physics teacher and the grandson of Maxim Litvinov, the Soviet foreign minister from 1930 to 1939, was warned by the KGB not to distribute the transcript of Bukovsky's trial.[2]

Finally, in January 1968 Ginzburg was brought to trial along with three other defendants.

By this time almost two years had passed since the case of Sinyavsky and Daniel, and more than a thousand Soviet citizens had signed appeals protesting the various trials. Pavel Litvinov himself would be arrested in Red Square with six of his friends on August 25, 1968, for demonstrating against the invasion of Czechoslovakia by units of the Soviet army and other Warsaw Pact forces.[3] By then, however, Litvinov had compiled an account of Ginzburg's trial and sent it to Western Europe.[4]

As the cycle of arrests and trials unfolded between 1966 and 1968, the Soviet human rights movement developed its fundamental strategy. At the urging of Alexander Esenin-Volpin, a distinguished mathematician who took it upon himself to study Soviet law, the dissidents referred to the government's own statutes and Constitutional guarantees. The demand for legality became a fundamental theme of their activity. More and more petitions and letters were sent to international agencies and to foreign newspapers, protesting the regime's breaking of its own laws. Reliable information was passed to foreign journalists.[5]

An unofficial journal, *A Chronicle of Current Events*, was founded by the poet and translator Natalia Gorbanevskaya.[6] The *Chronicle* provided the dissidents with a vehicle for publicizing arrests, court proceedings and the conditions prisoners faced in labor camps. Using the chain-letter method, Gorbanevskaya collected reports and sent issues of the journal to readers across the country. Since 1968, it has appeared more than 60 times, although its editors have been variously harassed, imprisoned, or even forced to emigrate.

The regime has responded only cynically to repeated demands for adherence to its own laws. During psychiatric examinations, Bukovsky insisted that organizing a demonstration or expressing criticism of the government was perfectly legal. But the psychiatrists responded: "You keep talking about the Constitution and the laws, but what normal man takes Soviet laws seriously? You are living in an unreal world of your own invention; you react inadequately to the world around you."

Still, for more than a decade the human rights movement maintained a visible presence. Journalists, diplomats, and academics visiting the Soviet Union knew whom to see. The activists signed their letters of protest and their names were then carried over Russian-language radio broadcasts from abroad, making it possible for other Soviet citizens to contact them.[7]

The high point of this cooperation came in May 1976 when Yuri Orlov, a specialist in high-energy physics and the design of particle accelerators, founded the Moscow Helsinki Watch Group. Orlov was responding to the fact that in August 1975, 35 countries, including the Soviet Union and the United States, had successfully concluded a Conference on Security and Cooperation in Europe. The various governments, meeting in Helsinki, Finland, signed a Final Act which included humanitarian provisions concerning the reunification of families, greater freedom of communication and contact and a commitment to respect, in the words of the Final Act, "freedom of thought, conscience, religion or belief"; to "promote and encourage the effective exercise of civil, political . . . cultural and other rights"; to accord ethnic minorities "equality before the law"; and to "act in conformity" with international commitments on human rights.[8]

Orlov understood that the agreements made in Helsinki gave dissidents a useful opportunity to test the Soviet government's sincerity. He hoped that Western governments would monitor Soviet compliance with the Final Act's human rights provisions. In the meantime, however, he organized a group of Soviet citizens who would, on their own initiative, collect information about the government's behavior in this connection and send it to the other governments which had signed the Helsinki Final Act. With Orlov's help, allied groups were also established in Kiev, Vilnius, Erevan and Tbilisi—the capitals, respectively, of the Ukrainian, Lithuanian, Armenian and Georgian Soviet Republics. Dissident nationalists in the different republics, religious believers, Zionists and Moscow human rights activists were now adopting a common, coordinated approach.

It was the Moscow activists, however, who played the crucial role. They issued 200 documents and sent representatives to the Baltic republics and to the Far East to collect first-hand evidence of political harassment and persecution.[9] The most audacious of such projects was implemented by Alexander Podrabinek, a young paramedic who, in 1976, helped organize the Working Commission to Investigate the Use of Psychiatry for Political Purposes. Fourteen people involved in the 22 cases of political incarceration reported by the Working Commission during its first year were released within two months. Using the Helsinki Final Act, Podrabinek and his friends were able to marshal grass-roots resistance to the "cops in white coats."

Soviet Jews, too, were able to organize an effective movement. For decades they had experienced severe anti-Semitic discrimination. Like all religions in the Soviet Union, Judaism suffered official restrictions. By the 1960s, there were fewer than 100 synagogues, barely a handful of trained rabbis and no operating institutions of Jewish learning. Jews in the Soviet Union are also recognized as one of the country's nationalities and so, like the Russians or the Ukrainians, are "guaranteed" under

Soviet law the right to cultural and national expression. Yet while Yiddish is the official language of the Soviet Union's Jewish minority, only one magazine and very few books are published in Yiddish. The teaching of Hebrew, except to highly specialized university scholars, is not officially permitted. Also, Jews have faced discrimination at work and in school. The best universities enforce quotas against Jewish applicants, the foreign and security services are closed to them, and scientific institutions limit how far they can advance in their professions (see Chapter 18 below).

Inspired by the example of the human rights activists, who had begun to campaign openly for liberalizing Soviet society, large numbers of Jews petitioned the Soviet authorities for permission to emigrate to Israel. And when this approach produced little result, several activists adopted more direct and provocative methods. Determined to leave, or at least to create a scandal that neither Soviet officials nor the West could ignore, a group of Jewish activists based primarily in Riga, capital of the Latvian Republic, planned to hijack an airplane to Sweden.

The KGB learned of the plot and arrested 12 people at Leningrad's Smolny Airport on June 15, 1970. At the same time, the security policemen carried out scores of searches in Riga, Kharkiv and Leningrad, confiscating material on Israel and Jewish history. Using the hijacking plot as a pretext, the authorities tried to crush the emigration movement before it gained momentum, but the strategy failed. The hijacking trial took place in December 1970, generating international publicity. When the two principal conspirators, Edward Kuznetsov and Mark Dymshits, were sentenced to death on December 24, there were immediate protests around the world. Jews began to demonstrate in the Soviet Union, and by the end of 1971 more than 14,000 had been allowed to leave the country. In 1972 and again in 1973, more than 30,000 would emigrate.[10]

The large-scale emigration of Soviet Jews inspired other groups. Citizens of German origin—those stranded on Soviet territory after World War II, who lived in the Baltic states when they were annexed in 1940, or who are descendants of the eighteenth-century Volga German settlers—began a movement to leave. In 1972, the West German government secured an agreement with the Soviet Union that permitted between 6,000 and 8,000 people to reach West Germany every year for the rest of the decade. By the end of 1982, almost 70,000 ethnic Germans had left the Soviet Union.

Armenians also achieved a small emigration, particularly among those from Western countries who had joined their families in Soviet Armenia after World War II. By the end of 1982, over 15,000 Armenians had emigrated.

If the human rights movement did indeed influence broad sectors of Soviet society, a serious weakness has been its inability to foster contact with workers. There is little of the cooperation between non-conformist intellectuals and disaffected workers that developed, for instance, in Poland in the late 1970s.

The reasons are fairly clear. The authorities know that working and living conditions still prevalent in the Soviet Union would lead to massive labor strife in any Western country. The great majority of workers do not live well, even by Soviet standards. The right to strike is not recognized by Soviet labor legislation; trade unions are controlled by the government, and their responsibility is to maintain labor discipline and increase productivity—not to protect the rights of workers.

Further, the government has always reacted with overwhelming force to any serious demonstration of unrest. In 1962, for example, just after the announcement of drastic increases in the price of butter and meat, wages were lowered in a factory in Novocherkassk by some 30 percent. When the workers called a strike, Army units were rushed to the city. Not intimidated, about 300 strikers, including women and children, formed a procession displaying portraits of Lenin and headed for the center of town. The soldiers opened fire, leaving over 70 people dead on the street.

Thus Soviet workers know that their government is capable of violent repression. Nonetheless, attempts have been made to establish independent worker associations. Early in 1978, a group of workers, most of whom claimed that they had lost their jobs because they had protested illegal or corrupt management practices, announced the formation of the Free Trade Union Association of Workers in the Soviet Union. Its 43 founders offered membership and help to "any blue or white-collar workers whose rights and interests are being unlawfully infringed by administrative, legislative, or juridical organs."[11] News of the group was broadcast over the Voice of America, and other workers looking for help contacted its leader, Vladimir Klebanov, in Moscow.

Within a few weeks, Klebanov was arrested and relegated to a psychiatric hospital. Other worker activists suffered a similar fate. Aleksei Nikitin, a coal miner from Donetsk, gave an extensive interview to the Moscow correspondent of the Washington Post. Nikitin described the conditions workers faced in the mines and their inability to register grievances. He, too, was arrested and, as with Klebanov, the authorities avoided an embarrassing trial by declaring Nikitin mentally incompetent and placing him in a psychiatric hospital. At this writing, neither man has returned to his family.

The Soviet invasion of Afghanistan in December 1979 poisoned relations with the West to such an extent that the Kremlin had little to lose by handling dissent more callously. Andrei Sakharov, the prominent scientist and dissident, was arrested just weeks after Soviet troops arrived in Kabul. The 1980 Moscow Olympics provided another occasion to purge the capital of people who might disrupt the image of a united and orderly society. By the spring of 1980, the KGB was arresting some five to ten dissidents a week, including nearly 100 Christians, another 100 representatives of national minorities and scores of activists who had campaigned on behalf of workers' rights and political prisoners.

Many Jewish "refusniks" (persons refused permission to emigrate) were told to spend the summer away from the capital. Several dissidents who were known abroad were compelled to emigrate, among them the worker activist Vladimir Borisov, Yury Yarim-Agaev of the Moscow Helsinki Watch Group, author Vasily Aksyonov, and three feminists from Leningrad who had founded a feminist journal and called for Soviet withdrawal from Afghanistan.

The rise of Solidarity in Poland no doubt was a lesson to the Kremlin in how far dissent could go in the Soviet Union itself if it were not thoroughly suppressed. Thus on August 20, 1980, the jamming of broadcasts from the three principal Western stations—the Voice of America, the British Broadcasting Corporation, and Deutsche Welle—was resumed. (Radio Liberty has always been jammed.) These stations had not been electronically jammed since September 1973; but the success of Solidarity evidently moved the Soviet authorities to restrict the flow of news and commentary from the West.

Unless relations with the West improve, it is unlikely that the present leadership will react to dissent any more tolerantly than did Leonid Brezhnev in his last years, after detente had collapsed. In fact, the Soviet human rights movement today faces its most difficult challenge. Wholesale arrests, intimidation and the banishment of well-known activists have disrupted the familiar pattern of dissent. Sakharov's arrest and subsequent removal to Gorky in January 1980 signalled the regime's determination to prevent the flow of uncensored information from the Soviet Union to the West, for Sakharov had been a principal link between Western journalists and a broad variety of active dissidents.

Since then, the situation has grown steadily more discouraging. All members of the Working Commission against the Use of Psychiatry for Political Purposes have been arrested or forced to emigrate including Dr. Anatoly Koryagin, a psychiatrist from Kharkiv who documented the internment of healthy dissidents in mental hospitals. In 1981 Koryagin was sentenced to a total of 12 years of imprisonment and exile. Other members of the Working Commission, including Vyacheslav Bakhmin and Alexander Podrabinek, who had been imprisoned in 1978, were re-arrested at the end of their sentences and subjected to new trials on trumped-up charges in order to extend their confinement. This form of reprisal used to be rare, but since 1980 it has become commonplace.

Jewish dissidents, too, are now much more vulnerable. In contrast to Ukrainian nationalists or dissident workers, Jewish activists were formerly subjected to the KGB's cruder punishments only rarely. They constituted the most visible and perhaps most easily understood expression of dissent in Western eyes; they also had a large and vocal constituency of supporters among Jewish communities in the West. And they achieved the most tangible results: the emigration of more than a quarter million Soviet Jews since 1970 marks the most significant humanitarian concession the regime has made since the release of millions of prisoners after Stalin's death.

Now, however, the emigration movement is stalled. Only 2,670 Jews were allowed to leave the Soviet Union in 1982, the lowest number since 1970 and a drastic drop from the 51,320 who left in 1979. Moreover, a growing number of refusniks have been imprisoned, and the regime has hinted it will never allow them to emigrate. This, too, indicates a shift in policy for the worse.

Despite such adverse developments, the Soviet human rights movement continues to collect information and to alert the world to the Kremlin's abuses of power. The movement's network of informants still exists, as evidenced by the remarkably detailed USSR News Brief, edited in Munich by Cronid Lubarsky, an astrophysicist and former prisoner of conscience.[12] Lubarsky bases his reports on a bulletin called The V Papers, a collection of up-to-date news items which circulates among a tight-knit group of dissidents. A Chronicle of Current Events also continues to appear, demonstrating the dissidents' determination to maintain channels to the West.

But we can no longer expect active dissidents to expose their identities as they did in the past, to form "public groups," or to hold press conferences with foreign reporters. Writing in August 1982 for the Los Angeles Times, Robert Gillette reported "that the KGB is warning dissidents it once ignored and arresting those it once merely warned, now that virtually all the major human rights activists are in prison, labor camps, or internal exile."

As Gillete's report reminds us, for nearly 20 years the West has had to rely on correspondents in Moscow for first-hand information about dissent. The correspondents come to know individual activists, usually those who have taken on a public role, which at any given time may mean several score people. When they are arrested, the correspondents conclude that dissent has been crushed. But not all the work of the human rights movement is so public. Thousands of other people type and circulate uncensored writings, collect money for political prisoners and their families and quietly document the regime's abuses. Their identities are not known—either to Western correspondents or to the KGB.

Furthermore, just as public expression of dissent does not constitute the only activity of the human rights movement, neither is the movement the only manifestation of dissent. A dissident in the Soviet context is someone who has openly expressed disagreement with the country's official ideology or with a certain policy adopted by the authorities. As Ludmilla Alexeyeva, an early Moscow dissident and later a member of the Helsinki group, has noted: "It is important to distinguish between the *expression of disagreement* and simply *being in disagreement*."

Since the 1960s, in short, many groups have emerged in the Soviet Union who oppose by non-violent, legal means some aspect of the regime's policies. These groups have often involved far greater numbers of people than the human rights movement. In particular, movements for the preservation of national culture have arisen among Ukrainians, Lithuanians, Georgians, Armenians and Estonians. Ethnic Germans in the tens and even hundreds of thousands, as we have seen, applied for permission to emigrate. Religious believers, especially Baptists, Pentecostals, Seventh-Day Adventists and Roman or Uniate Catholics have stubbornly resisted suppression of organized religious activity. Let us look at a few instances:

• Ukrainians make up the second largest nationality in the Soviet Union, numbering over 42 million people. Possessing a proud and distinctive culture, the Ukraine has been under the political control of Russia for more than three centuries, with only brief periods of independence. One such period was in 1918, but it was terminated by the Bolsheviks and followed by a prolonged interval of resistance. Another such time of internal resistance was occasioned by events of World War II. In retaliation, since Stalin's time the Ukraine has suffered sharp cultural and linguistic repression, a policy continued by Khrushchev.

Under the Soviet Constitution the Ukrainians—like the other Soviet nations—have the right to a wide measure of sovereignty, including cultural autonomy and even the right to secede from the Union. Yet in practice they have been subjected to increasingly militant Russification. This includes reduction in the use of Ukrainian in schools and colleges, neglect or destruction of monuments of Ukrainian culture, and the arrest of hundreds of intellectuals simply for their devotion to Ukrainian literature. These arrests have often come in organized crackdowns, as in 1965 and 1972, when the KGB rounded up scores of writers, poets, historians and literary critics in order to halt their efforts to preserve their people's heritage.[13]

Ukrainian cultural figures appear to have been murdered under mysterious circumstances. Volodymyr Ivasyuk, for example, was a 25-year-old poet and composer whose arrangements of Ukrainian folk songs were performed at international festivals and competitions; he was even allowed to perform abroad. But he also had conflicts with the authorities. According to issue 53 of *A Chronicle of Current Events*, Ivasyuk refused to compose an oratorio in 1979 to commemorate the fortieth anniversary of the "reunification of the Ukraine." (In 1939, following the Hitler-Stalin pact, the Soviet Union occupied and annexed western Ukraine, hitherto part of Poland.) In April 1979, Ivasyuk disappeared. His body was found hanging from a tree about three weeks later. The authorities claimed it was a suicide.

At Ivasyuk's funeral on May 22 more than 10,000 people formed a procession behind his casket. In June, there was a pilgrimage to his grave. Two members of the Ukrainian Helsinki Watch Group, Petro Sichko and his son Vasyl, spoke to the crowd, mentioning other well-known Ukrainians, like the painters Alla Horska and Rotislav Paletsky, who had also died under mysterious circumstances. At Vasyl Sichko's suggestion, the crowd honored the memory of these people with a moment of silence. A month later, Petro and Vasyl Sichko were arrested, convicted of "anti-Soviet slander," and sentenced to three years in a labor camp.

• The struggle of the Crimean Tatars to regain their homeland has also involved large-scale dissent. In World War II, the whole nation was accused of betraying the Soviet Union, and in a single day, more than 200,000 Tatars were taken from their homes in the Crimea and resettled in Central Asia. Most able-bodied men were actually at the front, so the deportees were mainly women, children and the elderly. They were transported in closed trucks and cattle cars, with little food or water, for almost three weeks. Tens of thousands failed to survive the journey.[14]

To this day the Crimean Tatars are trying to return to their ancestral lands. Since 1964 they have maintained an unofficial delegation in Moscow which attempts to obtain hearings with government and Party leaders and circulates an information bulletin. They have collected more than three million signatures to their various petitions, meaning that each adult Tatar has affixed his name at least ten times. But to little avail. In 1967 the Crimean Tatars were officially cleared of the charge of treason, but a large-scale return to their homeland was not permitted; the matter was still "under discussion."

• The situation in the Baltic republics, particularly Lithuania and Estonia, also deserves attention. A majority of their populations harbor strong nationalist feelings and hostility against the Russians for annexing, in 1940, their once independent states. In Lithuania, nationalist expression is linked with the Roman Catholic Church. Still ethnically homogeneous, its population of over three million is 80 percent Lithuanian and overwhelmingly Catholic. People remember how convents and monasteries were closed at the time of annexation, and several bishops died in labor camps. In the same period thousands of ordinary citizens were imprisoned, executed or deported to Siberia for resisting the Soviet occupation. In 1980 and 1981, three Catholic priests were killed in questionable circumstances—in all three cases after articles denouncing them had appeared in the official press.

The Soviet government's concern over developments in Lithuania is understandable. Since the early 1970s over a dozen *samizdat*—"self-published" or underground—journals have circulated inside the republic. Catholic priests have been especially active, and *The Chronicle of the Lithuanian Catholic Church*, begun in 1972, has appeared over 50 times. Inspired by the Moscow *Chronicle of Current Events*, the Lithuanian *Chronicle* provides reliable information on religious and nationalist dissent.[15] The Lithuanian Helsinki Watch Group established personal contact with its Moscow counterpart, which helped to distribute reports of enforced Russification in Lithuania and attacks on the Catholic Church.

• Dissent in Lithuania has inspired ferment in Estonia.[16] The Estonian Soviet Republic, with a population of about 1.5 million, has witnessed some of the largest and most spontaneous incidents of protest' in the whole country, a development that has gone largely unnoticed in the West. In September 1980, the authorities banned a performance by the pop-group "Propeller" because "nationalist themes" were detected in its lyrics. In response, more than 1,000 youngsters demonstrated in a soccer stadium in Tallinn, the Estonian capital. This was followed by the expulsion of several high school seniors from their schools.

The expulsions triggered new protests. On October 1 and 3, 1980, an estimated 5,000 young people held demonstrations in four parts of the city. They carried the forbidden blue, black and white flag of independent Estonia and shouted "More meat, fewer Russians" and "Freedom for Estonia!" They also demanded better heating and food in their schools. More demonstrations soon followed in the coastal town of Parnu and the university city of Tartu, where students demanded the removal of Elsa Grechkina, the first Russian ever to be appointed to the sensitive post of Estonian Minister of Education. In addition, 1,000 workers went on strike in a farm machine factory in Tartu, protesting changes in their production quotas and bonuses as well as food shortages in the city's stores. And throughout 1981 and 1982 reports reached the West of student demonstrations in Estonia.

• Numerous cases of religious dissent have also been reported from the Soviet Union. As Paul A. Lucey makes clear (Chapter 24), believers continue to face often severe disabilities. In fact, believers comprise the largest group of Soviet prisoners of conscience known in the West. They have been harassed and arrested for printing and distributing copies of the Psalms, organizing congregations without government permission, or providing religious instruction to children. Many are conscientious objectors and refuse to serve in the armed forces, for which they also face arrest.

The Soviet human rights movement has also come to the assistance of religious believers, and *A Chronicle of Current Events* regularly carries reports of religious persecution. Fundamentalist Christian groups like the Pentecostals or Seventh-Day Adventists abhor political activity; but as their misery deepened, they came to understand the need to publicize their situation, to appeal to the West, and even to seek emigration. At the request of the Moscow Helsinki Watch Group, a young philosophy student spent two weeks with Pentecostal communities in the North Caucasus and in the Far East in December 1976. People stood in line to speak with her, anxious to relate their individual stories of persecution. It was evident that they regularly listened to Western radio broadcasts, a sure sign of social resistance. By the late 1970s, numerous Pentecostals had applied for exit visas, hoping to practice their religion elsewhere without harassment. Only a handful have, in fact, been permitted to leave, but their willingness to insist on their rights indicates how far the lessons of the human rights movement had reached.

Dissent in the Soviet Union has been concerned for the most part with internal problems. Yet several dissidents, most notably Andrei Sakharov, have made major statements on matters of foreign policy, including the Soviet occupation of Eastern Europe and the Soviet role in the Middle East. In September 1973 Sakharov also appealed to the U.S. Congress to link U.S.-Soviet trade relations to the issue of emigration.[17] Government authorities were especially furious with him for these appeals, interpreting his actions as betrayals of the Soviet national interest.

The double issue of peace and nuclear war has been revived in recent years as a prominent aspect of Soviet foreign policy. The official campaign is designed, it would seem, to improve the Soviet Union's image abroad, particularly in Western Europe. The authorities have organized rallies and set up a nationwide peace organization, using them as vehicles to oppose Western deployment of nuclear weapons and to applaud the peaceful intentions of the Kremlin.

No doubt the great majority of the Soviet population abhors the threat of war, nuclear or conventional, but the government has not permitted genuine public debate on the matter. Even Sakharov, who helped develop the Soviet hydrogen bomb and who made a significant contribution to the negotiations over the 1963 Nuclear Test Ban Treaty, has not been allowed to engage in public discussion of Soviet nuclear policy.[18]

It must therefore have been something of an embarrassment to the government when a dozen Soviet citizens announced the founding of the Group for Establishing Trust Between the U.S.S.R. and the U.S.A. on June 4, 1982. Led by Sergei Batovrin, a young artist, the group's aim was to begin a "four-sided dialogue" in which not only the governments but the general public of the two superpowers would participate. Batovrin and his group advocated an end to nuclear testing and more contact between citizens of the two countries. They suggested that Moscow be declared a nuclear-free zone. Members of the group, including several refusniks, stated that they were not dissidents, that their aims were identical to those professed by the Soviet government, and that any persecution of them "would only be the result of a misunderstanding."

The government reacted quickly, nonetheless. Within a week almost all of the group's members were threatened with arrest; several had their telephones disconnected, and visitors to their homes were barred entry by police and plainclothes agents. Despite this harassment, the group managed to gather support for its proposals. Within a month over 170 persons had signed their declaration, and still another support list of 70 Moscow students was confiscated.

Batovrin was arrested on August 6, 1982 and placed in a Moscow psychiatric hospital. Under threat of electric shock treatment, he was forced to take aminazin, a strong anti-psychotic drug, which made him feel weak and lethargic. But news of his incarceration reached the West and, in the face of protests from Western peace groups, the government released him in September. In May 1983, Batovrin was permitted to leave the Soviet Union with his wife and baby daughter.

New unofficial Soviet peace groups have been formed in Leningrad, Odessa and Novosibirsk—the last led by Mark Meleyev, a senior scientist at a prestigious research institute in nuclear physics. In Moscow a group calling itself "Independent Initiative" claims to have about 300 supporters. As part of its effort, the group held a demonstration near Moscow University on December 12, 1982, in memory of John Lennon. Police dispersed them and confiscated placards with pacifist symbols.

The government's reaction to unofficial peace groups is one example among many that it is not ready to tolerate independent political activity by its citizens. Even a group formed to defend the rights of invalids—to publicize their situation and to improve the education, training and public welfare assistance they receive—has not been allowed to operate freely. Its members, too, have seen their homes ransacked and have faced the threat of arrest. The fate of the Solzhenitsyn Fund, which has aided thousands of Soviet political prisoners and their families for nearly ten years, is another case in point.

Since the outset of the Soviet human rights movement, when people began learning more about the labor camps, dissidents have quietly raised money to help support families and provide packages of food and clothing to political prisoners—when they were permitted to receive them. In 1974, following publication of *The Gulag Archipelago*, Solzhenitsyn pledged the worldwide royalties from his three-volume account of Stalin's labor camps to the Fund. His donation soon accounted for about 70 percent of the Fund's income; the remainder was donated by Soviet citizens. Expenditures exceeded $120,000 a year.

Not surprisingly, the authorities have tried to suppress this activity. Previous managers of the Solzhenitsyn Fund, notably Tatyana Khodorovich and Cronid Lubarsky, were compelled to emigrate; others, like Aleksandr Ginzburg, the Fund's first manager, have been imprisoned. Valery Repin, a journalist who managed the Fund in Leningrad, was arrested in December 1981 but not tried until May 1983. (Under Soviet law, defendants are supposed to be tried within nine months of detention.) Repin was charged with treason, which carries a potential death penalty.

Repin apparently broke down under this threat and confessed in court that his work for the Fund made him a "thoughtless pawn" of the CIA and its efforts to obtain "military-political" secrets. He was given the minimum prison sentence of two years, and three years of internal exile.[19] Meanwhile, KGB efforts to put an end to the Fund continue. Any successful effort to help political prisoners and their families reduces, however slightly, the cost of exercising one's political conscience.

Soviet human rights activists and other dissidents face more than pressure from the government and the constant threat of arrest. They are a tiny minority in a large, complex and troubled society. The crudity of everyday Soviet life, the widespread drunkenness and general dedication to material pursuits provoke longing for a less cynical, more idealistic approach to social problems. Many dissidents are also concerned about the growth of Russian nationalism. They understand that elements of Russian nationalism reinforce resentment and suspicion of other ethnic or national groups, fear of Western influence and values, anti-Semitism and intellectual intolerance. Indeed, by many accounts the conservative, authoritarian streak in traditional Russian nationalism has a broader appeal in the Soviet Union today than does the human rights movement, with its emphasis on the rule of law and ideological toleration.

Within the dissident community itself there has been vigorous debate about the future of Soviet society, its political institutions, economic development and the role of religion. Among the dissidents, Roy Medvedev and Solzhenitsyn have long embodied the divergent attitudes of substantial segments of their fellow citizens who desire some kind of major change. From his somewhat idealized view of Russian history, Solzhenitsyn longs for a return to tradition, which would include a Russian Orthodox religious renaissance with a corresponding rejection of "the murky whirlwind of progressive ideology [Marxism] that swept in on us from the West." A genuine reactionary, he mistrusts political activity and prefers the establishment of a benevolent, authoritarian order in Russia. Sakharov, on the other hand, admires Western institutions and favors the development in the Soviet Union of a pluralistic democracy, with independent judicial institutions, full civil rights and contending political parties.

In contrast to both Solzhenitsyn and Sakharov, Roy Medvedev, who was dismissed from the Communist Party for his dissident activity, remains a socialist. He does not believe that the West can exert much influence on internal Soviet affairs, and then only during periods of detente, when East-West relations are improving. Medvedev contends that liberalization will really come only when the regime decides to institute major "reform from above," such as an attempt to develop a genuinely modern economy. This would require dismantling the heavily bureaucratic, centralized control that has prevailed since the 1930s and gradually replacing it with a more decentralized system. Medvedev believes that this kind of reform, should it ever occur, would lead to political liberalization as well.

Dissent is now part of the fabric of Soviet life. It was perhaps inevitable that in such a large country, with its strong literary and cultural traditions, sustained violations of human rights would generate protest. In any event, since their emergence in the mid-1960s the dissidents have compelled the regime to remember that the Soviet Union is not as isolated as it was under Stalin. They have provided a consistent and reliable means for both the West and their fellow citizens to see and understand the reality of Soviet life.

If the Soviet authorities, even today, would like to impose the kind of silence and secrecy that Stalin so successfully achieved, the dissidents have made it impossible. They made human rights in the Soviet Union an international issue and added such words as *samizdat* and *gulag* to the world's vocabulary. Most of all, they provide an example of courage in the struggle against fear. □

1. See Max Hayward, ed., *On Trial* (New York: Harper and Row, 1966).

2. Litvinov described his New York encounter with the KGB in a statement sent to the West; see Abraham Brumberg, ed., *In Quest of Justice* (New York: Praeger, 1970), pp. 90-92. Despite the warning Litvinov also sent the transcript of Bukovsky's trial to the West; see Pavel Litvinov, ed., *The Demonstration in Pushkin Square* (New York: Gambit, 1969).

3. Natalia Gorbanevskaya, *Red Square at Noon* (New York: Penguin, 1973), has an account of the demonstration by a participant.

4. Peter Reddaway, ed., *The Trial of the Four* (New York: Viking, 1972).

5. Vladimir Bukovsky, *To Build a Castle — My Life as a Dissenter* (New York: Viking, 1979). Involved in the human rights movement from its inception, the author provides a vivid account of its beginnings.

6. A compilation of the *Chronicle*'s first 11 issues was published in *Uncensored Russia: Protest and Dissent in the Soviet Union* (New York: American Heritage Press, 1972). Current and back issues of the *Chronicle*, translated into English by Amnesty International, are available from Routledge Journals, 9 Park St., Boston, Massachusetts 02108. Since 1974 Khronika Press, 508 Eighth Ave., New York, N.Y. 10018, has published the *Chronicle* in English. See also Joshua Rubenstein, *Soviet Dissidents, Their Struggle for Human Rights* (Boston: Beacon Press, 1980).

7. In January 1968, Pavel Litvinov and Larisa Bogoraz issued an appeal in defense of Aleksandr Ginzburg and his co-defendants after their trial had begun. The appeal was carried in Russian by the BBC. For weeks afterwards, Litvinov received letters of support for his efforts. See "Letter from Twenty-four Students to P. Litvinov" in Brumberg, *In Quest of Justice*, pp. 105-106. A collective farm chairman named Ivan Iakhimovich heard the appeal, then located Litvinov in Moscow. See *Uncensored Russia*, pp. 145-46 for an account of Iakhimovich's subsequent career as a dissident; also Brumberg, *In Quest of Justice*, pp. 129-32.

8. For more information about the Helsinki Final Act and attempts to implement its human rights provisions, contact the Commission on Security and Cooperation in Europe, Room 237, House Annex #2, U.S. House of Representatives, Washington, D.C. 20515.

9. The Helsinki Commission in Washington (see n. 8) has translated and published many of the Soviet Helsinki Watch Group's documents.

10. Kuznetsov and Dymshits were subsequently sentenced to 15 years' imprisonment. Both were sent to the West in 1979 along with three other Soviet political prisoners in exchange for two convicted Soviet spies. For a comprehensive account of the Jewish emigration movement's initial years, see Leonard Schroeter, *The Last Exodus* (Seattle, Washington: University of Washington Press, 1979).

**11.** *A Chronicle of Human Rights in the U.S.S.R.*, No. 29, Jan.-March 1978, p. 37.

**12.** The journal is available through Cahiers du Samizdat asbl, Anthony de Meeus, 48 rue du Lac, 1050, Bruxelles, Belgium.

**13.** *The Chornovil Papers* (New York: McGraw-Hill, 1968) concerns the trial of 20 Ukrainian intellectuals in 1965 and 1966. Vyacheslav Chornovil was a journalist assigned to cover some of the court sessions. Rather than produce the usual reports, he came to the defense of the prisoners, writing petitions to the authorities on their behalf. He has been under detention or in Siberian exile almost continuously since 1966.

**14.** See Alexander Nekrich, *The Punished Peoples* (New York: Norton, 1978) for an account of the events by a distinguished Soviet historian who now lives in the West.

**15.** Copies of the Lithuanian *Chronicle* are available in English from the Lithuanian Roman Catholic Priests League of America, 351 Highland Boulevard, Brooklyn, N.Y. 11207.

**16.** See Peter Reddaway, "Recent Ferment in Estonia," in *A Chronicle of Human Rights in the U.S.S.R.*, No. 40, Oct.-Dec. 1980.

**17.** See Harrison Salisbury, ed., *Sakharov Speaks* (New York: Vintage, 1974), p. 211.

**18.** Herbert F. York, "Sakharov and the Nuclear Test Ban," in Alexander Babyonyeshev, ed., *On Sakharov* (New York: Vintage Press, 1982).

**19.** For an account of Repin's trial see The New York Times (May 22, 1983).

# 7

# The KGB

*John E. Carlson*

"The KGB"—*Komitet Gosudarstvennoi Bezopastnosti*, the Committee for State Security—pops up regularly in these pages, as it does in virtually any book on the Soviet Union. Indeed, if we are to understand the Soviet system and Soviet society as they have evolved to this point it is important to understand what the KGB is. It is equally important to understand that our curiosity in this respect cannot really be satisfied.

This problem of evidence, as historians call it, must be stressed. Writing in 1957, two American scholars stated forthrightly that "ever since it was established in 1917 the Soviet secret police has followed the policy of not publishing important documents concerning its structure, functions and operations, while those documents which have been published have often been fragmentary or distorted." Thus, "scholars have been largely restricted to bare administrative announcements and accounts by former members of the secret police or its victims." But this latter source scholars have tended to distrust "because of its often sensational character and the difficulty of submitting it to adequate tests for reliability."[1] These words are as true today as they were then.

The years since 1957 have witnessed the defection to the West of a number of KGB agents as well as the arrival of rather more Soviet citizens who had suffered at the KGB's hands. To be sure, the testimony of both agents and victims—often, by its nature, unverifiable—has enhanced our appreciation of the KGB's significance particularly in two areas: Soviet covert operations abroad and the suppression of dissent at home. Yet we still lack anything like a clear picture of its overall organization and range of activities—in part because of the clandestine nature of some of those activities, obviously, and in part because of the habitual secretiveness of Soviet officialdom in matters large or small. Moreover, while

Soviet scholars have been prohibited, not surprisingly, from freely working in this field, a function of the continuing official cover-up of past
abuses of power, their Western counterparts, less understandably, "have
devoted scant attention to the KGB. . . . There have been no serious attempts to assess its impact on the Soviet political process or to examine
its role in society."[2]

There also remains the problem of the Soviet dissident or defector as
witness. Take the case of Oleg Penkovskiy, the publication of whose
"papers"—notes, diaries, late-night ruminations—in 1965 caused a sen-
sation. Penkovskiy was a colonel in Soviet military intelligence who
spied for the West (his contact was British) between April 1961 and
August 1962, when he was caught, tried in Moscow, and executed in
May 1963. At some point these papers were "received" in the West by
Peter Deriabin, a former major in the KGB who had defected in 1954. He
translated them with the help of Frank Gibney, co-author of Deriabin's
own sensational memoirs.[3] In a remarkable foreword to *The Penkovskiy
Papers* Edward Crankshaw, the longtime British observer of Soviet affairs, noted that Penkovskiy "was in some measure unbalanced (a man
who will take it upon himself to betray his government because he is
uniquely convinced that he is right and they are wrong is by definition
unbalanced, although he may also be a martyr), and, almost certainly,
this lack of balance made it impossible for him to distinguish between
government intentions and government precautions." As Crankshaw
said, "like so many others, Penkovskiy confused loose, menacing talk
with tight-lipped calculation; contingency planning with purposive
strategy. This confusion is liable to overtake all sorts of individuals in all
sorts of governments and military machines."[4]

We will return to this point. Meanwhile, Major Deriabin continues to
publish—and to excoriate what he sees as the "tendency of Western
scholars to overlook, dismiss, or downplay the role of coercion and
violence in the Soviet system. . . . The KGB is the power of their party. It
occupies the center of their regime."[5]

There can be no doubt that the KGB is an important institution in
Soviet society, one without parallel in the West. Its uniformed armed
forces alone number as many as 250,000 men, the largest component of
whom, the Border Troops (including the Maritime Border Troops, or
Coast Guard), are estimated to total from 175,000 to 200,000; their
olive drab uniforms with green flashings are seen by every visitor to the
Soviet Union, particularly at passport control. The KGB's Signal Troops,
responsible for high-level communications in the country, number
perhaps 15,000, while soldiers of its special guard units, with their
bright blue flashings, are to be seen on duty in important government

and Party buildings and at monuments such as the Lenin Mausoleum in Red Square. These uniformed KGB forces are not to be confused with the Internal Troops of the Ministry of the Interior, numbering another 250,000 or more and considered the "ultimate bulwark of the regime." The uniformed police of the Soviet Union—the "militia"—also comes under the Ministry of the Interior, which nevertheless appears to have close ties with the KGB—ties which "might be getting closer."[6]

But it is the KGB's plain-clothes forces, engaged in the work of foreign intelligence (espionage), domestic counter-intelligence and internal security, that raise the most questions. And here, numbers are yet harder to come by; even former KGB officers have said they could not make meaningful estimates because the organization is compartmentalized into so many different directorates, services and departments, each largely or wholly ignorant of the others' activities, some of which are worldwide.

John Barron reports that in 1973 two Western intelligence services estimated to him that the KGB then employed about 90,000 staff officers and another 400,000 technicians, secretaries, clerks, "security and border guards, and special troops." Since, as we have just seen, the latter total perhaps 250,000, this would leave about 150,000 technical and clerical workers, a number that has no doubt grown. Barron himself suggests that the number of people employed by the KGB as informants inside the Soviet Union and as agents (non-Soviet) outside it "doubtless runs into the hundreds of thousands."[7] Other recent estimates put the total of KGB operatives deployed abroad at over 250,000, and the total of all KGB officers, agents and informants working within the country at roughly 1.5 million.[8] Deriabin says that internal informants alone "average one in every eight to ten citizens, by my professional estimate, and one in five in sensitive areas":[9] this would mean as many as 25 million adult Soviet citizens reporting to the KGB, which scarcely seems credible.

Nor is the organization of the KGB much clearer, even at its most general level.[10] The five Main Directorates of "the Center" in Moscow are subdivided into an unknown number of directorates, services and departments. The First Main Directorate conducts KGB operations abroad through dozens of "residencies"; the Second is responsible for counter-intelligence and internal security; the Border Troops Directorate speaks for itself; the Fifth Main Directorate is charged with controlling dissent; and the Eighth monitors foreign communications. Lesser, independent directorates include the Third, which watches the Armed Forces from the General Staff down to company level; the Seventh, with more than 3,000 personnel engaged in internal surveillance; and the Ninth, which safeguards the leaders and important installations. Among the plain-clothes Main Directorates the Second appears to be the largest, but it should be noted that both the Third and the Seventh Directorates, as well as the Fifth Main Directorate, are also engaged in internal surveillance. Each of the Main Directorates and perhaps some of their subdivisions have their own intensive training programs and special schools.

We know most about the KGB's First Main Directorate—the CIA of the Soviet Union. It includes a Directorate S, whose job it is to train and plant Soviet "illegals" in countries throughout the world; a Directorate T, the second largest, responsible for collecting scientific and technological intelligence in the industrialized countries, and which works closely with the State Committee on Science and Technology and the Academy of Sciences; and a Directorate K, which tries to penetrate foreign intelligence and security services, maintains security at Soviet embassies and watches all Soviet citizens abroad.

Its Service I—the third largest division of the First Main Directorate—produces among other things a daily summary of events for the Politburo and regularly submits forecasts of world developments. Its Service A, now called the Active Measures Service but formerly the Disinformation Department, drafts plans for a wide range of covert activities abroad, including propaganda and disinformation, subversion and sabotage. Service R continuously analyzes in detail all of the KGB's foreign operations with a view to improving them. Founded in the 1970s, it was modeled on what was believed to be a special, computerized division of the CIA. Among the First Main Directorate's dozen or so Departments, organized both geographically (to deal with specific areas of the world) and functionally, one, the Eleventh, conducts liaison with and penetrates the intelligence services of the Soviet bloc countries; another, the First, runs agents in the United States and Canada. In 1983 the FBI was said to be watching roughly 450 Soviet spies operating in the United States under diplomatic or other legal cover.[11]

There is plenty of evidence, in short, that KGB operations abroad are both extensive and increasingly sophisticated. But the success of these operations is another question—whether measured by the Soviet investment of time and money or by the success of similar operations mounted by foreign governments against the Soviet Union. Study after study, often quite alarmist in tone, manages to suggest at the same time a record of KGB incompetence, bungling and plain bad luck in this regard. Between 1974 and the end of 1982 some 190 Soviet officials were expelled or withdrawn from foreign countries for their involvement in espionage or subversive activities, all of them known to be officers of the

KGB or of Soviet military intelligence (now thought to be under KGB control); and in the first six months of 1983 another 94 were caught.[12] These figures do not speak well for KGB methods.

Moreover, the very openness of Western societies, which in itself accounts for much of the success Soviet agents have had in obtaining sensitive technological information, also confuses them. As a former FBI counter-intelligence chief put it, "So much in this country is open. But if they can get it clandestinely, it's much better; it's 'proof' that they're not being duped. . . . Their country is so different from ours and so controlled that they sometimes have difficulty believing what they hear."[13]

Indeed, this may be the main point. If a KGB were to be created in the United States it would absorb the functions of numerous existing agencies: the CIA, the FBI, the National Security Agency (in charge of spy satellites, code-breaking and so on), the Secret Service, the Coast Guard and the Border Patrol. It would also absorb some of the functions of the Immigration Service, of the State Department and of various regular military units (for instance, those guarding key installations or the Army Signal Corps). The head of this new agency—this American Committee for State Security (CSS)—would also control, informally, all other U.S. intelligence and internal security organs, for example the Defense Intelligence Agency and some 250,000 special troops nominally subordinate to the Secretary of the Interior and available to quell internal disturbances like the Detroit and other riots of 1968. The one uniformed national police force (all local police forces would have to be merged), formally under the control of the Secretary of the Interior, would also be subject to CSS supervention. The point is, all of these many and varied offices and functions exist within the U.S. system but not in a single organization, directed by a top official who is subject only to the orders of the Executive Office of the President and/or his Cabinet.

Yet for the analogy really to work the head of our CSS would have to be himself a member of the Cabinet, carry the military rank of full general and, as in the case of Yury Andropov (head of the KGB from 1967 to 1982), be one of the dozen or so most senior officials of the Democratic or Republican Party. Furthermore, that Party would have to be the sole party in existence in the United States, with an absolute monopoly of political power at all levels of the U.S. government—federal, state and local. In fact, from its modest beginnings under Lenin (as the *Cheka*)[14] through its years as the instrument of Stalin's terror and its subsequent setbacks and demotion under Nikita Khrushchev, the KGB has emerged more recently as one of the main power blocs in the Soviet Union, along with the military establishment and the Party bureaucracy. Or so it would seem. And it would also seem that the KGB's present eminence is owed in considerable measure to the work of one man: Yury Andropov.

Andropov's rise in the Soviet system is as obscure as that of every Soviet leader of his generation. Born on June 15, 1914, his official biography has him joining the *Komsomol* (Communist Youth League) at the age of 16 and the Party itself in 1939, first holding office—in the *Komsomol*—in 1936. The decisive years of World War II Andropov spent in the Finnish-Soviet borderlands (Karelia), where he was "an active participant in the guerrilla movement" and then held a succession of senior Party posts. In 1951 he was transferred to the central Party apparatus in Moscow (still headed by Stalin). Between 1953 and 1957 he was Soviet envoy to Hungary, but in 1957 he rejoined the *apparat* in Moscow and in 1961 was elected a member of the Central Committee—to which he has been regularly reelected ever since. In 1962 he was appointed to the all-powerful central Party Secretariat, the executive organ (see Chapter 4) supposedly of the Central Committee but actually of the Politburo, whose membership often overlaps with that of the Secretariat. In May 1967 Andropov was appointed chairman of the KGB, and in June became a candidate member of the Politburo.[15]

What Andropov's official biography does not tell us, however, is whether he ever completed his higher education (if he did, it was at a narrowly technical institute); against whom he fought in World War II (Germans—or Finns?); what role he really played in the Party *apparat* and in the Soviet suppression of the Hungarian uprising of 1956; who his patrons were (probably both Khrushchev and Mikhail Suslov, the longtime gray eminence of the Party who died in 1982). Nor does it tell us why he was picked to head the KGB, still badly tainted from the Stalin years and mistrusted, even feared, by the leadership. It was also poorly managed and perhaps demoralized. Evidently Andropov's peers decided that as a Party man of long standing he would be both pragmatic and loyal in his new job: "an intelligent person whom everybody else in the leadership trusted," in the words of a seasoned Soviet observer of the political scene.[16]

We have at least one Western portrait of Andropov in his years at the KGB—the impressions of Hugh Hambleton, the Canadian professor who spied for the Soviet Union from 1956 to 1978 and spent an hour virtually alone with him, at supper in a Moscow apartment, in 1975:

> Expecting simply another debriefing by a senior KGB officer [Hambleton told John Barron], he did not trouble to inquire who his inquisitor might be. And he was not disposed to be particularly deferential the next evening when a tall, dignified man in his

sixties [actually, just 61] entered the apartment followed by three aides who kept a respectful distance. His thick, gray hair was brushed straight back above an ashen face that expressed deep fatigue. Behind rimless glasses, his hazel eyes seemed thoughtful and searching, but they too bespoke weariness.

Without introducing himself or being introduced, he said in halting, formal English, "Professor Hambleton, I am pleased to welcome you to Moscow. I hope you have found the arrangements here satisfactory and your work productive."

Though quite courteous, the visitor seemed rather aloof, and never identified himself. He insisted upon speaking English, and Hambleton surmised that he had once spoken it well, for his word selection and syntax were excellent. However, he frequently had to ask one of his subordinates for English words he desired and to clarify in Russian what Hambleton said in English.

A KGB housekeeper had set out a cold supper, and after a brief exchange of pleasantries the Russian [Andropov] invited Hambleton to be seated. While one aide stood behind to assist him with his English, the other two braced themselves against the wall, and Hambleton realized they were bodyguards.

As they dined, the Russian posed a series of questions: Is not military spending becoming too onerous for the United States? Are Jews persecuted in America? Do progressive American youths look upon the Soviet Union as the hope of the future? Will not the European Common Market eventually fail? When the conversation turned to China, he remarked sadly, "Our relations with them are a tragedy."

After surveying the world, the Russian discussed future KGB assignments with Hambleton. . . . Almost exactly an hour after his arrival, he rose from the table, and Hambleton stood also. Shaking hands, the Russian said, "I hope our collaboration will be even more fruitful in the future, and I wish you personally health and good fortune."

As soon as the visitor left, the KGB officer staying with Hambleton in the apartment filled two glasses with vodka, his hands trembling, and slumped into a chair.[17]

Professor Hambleton was exposed a few years later and ended up in a British jail.

As head of the KGB Andropov continued the effort to improve its image that had begun under Khrushchev and been greatly stepped up after his removal from office, possibly with KGB help, in 1964. KGB agents—often called *Chekisty*, after the original *Cheka* of Lenin's time—were given increased attention in the Soviet press and a flood of memoirs, biographies, documentaries and semi-fictional thrillers began to appear glorifying them and their exploits and projecting an image of respectability, legitimacy, even of romance. The campaign to rehabilitate the KGB enjoyed the support particularly of Leonid Brezhnev, then Party leader, who bestowed numerous awards and honors on some of its personnel in quite exceptional circumstances. KGB representation in the leading organs of Party and state grew steadily. In July 1978 its official status was changed from that of the Commitee for State Security "attached to" or "under" the Council of Ministers to that of the Committee for State Security of the Soviet Union, which meant that its head automatically became a member of the Council of Ministers. Meanwhile, in 1973, Andropov himself became a full member of the Party Politburo, thus cementing his position as one of the country's top dozen or so leaders.

Under Andropov the KGB became, by all accounts, a much more efficient and sophisticated, as well as much larger, organization. He is credited, most notably, with creating its Fifth Main Directorate—the "dissident" or "ideological" Directorate—charged with eliminating overt manifestations of dissent. Whatever Andropov's personal views, the organization's activities here reflected a fundamental policy of the Brezhnev regime: detente abroad but ever stricter security at home—the latter aimed precisely at containing what were seen as the dangerous domestic effects of the steadily greater communication with the West that detente brought with it. With the breakdown of detente in 1979 the KGB assumed an even freer hand internally; and by the end of 1982, as we have seen (Chapter 6), any independent human rights or peace movement in the Soviet Union had been largely crushed.

In connection with the suppression of Soviet dissidents it has been charged that "the KGB under Andropov institutionalized the perversion of psychiatry."[18] The reality is perhaps a little more complicated. Walter Reich, a U.S. psychiatrist, has studied Soviet psychiatry for many years, his methods including personal examination of Soviet emigres who had been diagnosed as mentally ill back in the Soviet Union. And on the basis of his studies Dr. Reich has concluded that while in some cases Soviet dissidents were hospitalized as a result of deliberate misdiagnosis (and then variously abused), in some others the subjects *were* mentally ill: "Dissent is, after all, a marginal activity in the Soviet Union, with its highly repressive political system, and the margins of any society contain a disproportionately high number of people with mental illnesses."

But more, in Dr. Reich's opinion "most hospitalized Soviet dissidents were pronounced ill not because the KGB ordered the psychiatrists to make that diagnosis, and not because they were really ill, but for other reasons." He is worth quoting at length on this point:

In the context of Soviet society . . . dissidents constitute a deviant element. They behave and speak in ways that are different from other Soviet citizens, and, for that reason, they come to be seen as strange. . . . In fact, there is good evidence, based on dissident accounts, that, upon encountering dissidents, many KGB and other Soviet officials are often struck by a sense of strangeness, a sense that is compounded when the dissidents start lecturing them about their rights under the Soviet Constitution. The sense that someone is strange is not infrequently followed by the suspicion that the strangeness may be due to mental illness. And as soon as that suspicion arises in the minds of Soviet authorities, they have powerful reasons to call upon psychiatrists to examine the dissidents.

Among these reasons Dr. Reich mentions the requirement of the Soviet criminal code that in all cases—not just political ones—psychiatrists must be consulted if there is any doubt as to the mental state of the accused; the fact that the trial of a dissident who has been pronounced ill and in need of hospitalization is usually less demanding on the prosecutor than an ordinary trial; and the obvious fact that the psychiatrists called on to give their diagnoses are themselves Soviet citizens.

They grew up in the same culture, are affected by the same political realities and develop the same social perceptions. And since the way in which a psychiatrist goes about determining whether a person is ill depends to a great extent on the psychiatrist's assumptions about what is usual and expected in his society, he may, upon coming into contact with the dissident, have the same sense of strangeness felt by the KGB agent—and may go on to suspect that the defendant may be ill.

Once that happens, Dr. Reich urges, it would not be hard for the Soviet psychiatrist to find a category of illness—particularly that of "sluggish schizophrenia," a Soviet invention—to apply to the dissident: "In other words, in many and perhaps most instances of diagnoses of mental illness in dissident cases not only the KGB and other responsible officials, but the psychiatrists themselves, really believed that the dissidents were ill."[19] We can only add that, like a study of the KGB itself (or of the laws under which dissidents are arrested), a study of Soviet psychiatry in this connection reveals how profoundly different Soviet is from Western society.

In May 1982 Andropov resigned as chairman of the KGB and rejoined the Party Secretariat, the better to position himself for the top Party job, then held by the ailing Brezhnev. Within 48 hours of Brezhnev's death, in November 1982, Andropov had been elected General Secretary; and between then and June 1983 he also became chairman of the Defense Council and ceremonial chief of state (chairman of the Presidium of the Supreme Soviet). There appears to be little doubt that in thus assuring himself of victory over the entrenched leaders of the Party bureaucracy Andropov was aided by the military establishment and backed by the KGB.

The KGB was headed in this crucial year first by Vitaly Fedorchuk, a longtime professional security official and former head of the Ukrainian KGB who had no other power base; then, on Andropov's succession as General Secretary, by Viktor Chebrikov, Andropov's longtime deputy at the KGB (Fedorchuk was made Minister of the Interior). In addition, Geidar Aliev, another old KGB official (1941-1969) and later Party chief in Azerbaidzhan, was made a full member of the Politburo as well as Deputy Prime Minister of the Soviet Union.

Never before in Soviet history had KGB men assumed, and so obviously, so much power. Would it be used to promote the status quo, further Stalinist reaction, or genuine reform? At this writing it is impossible to tell. □

1. Simon Wolin and Robert M. Slusser, eds., *The Soviet Secret Police* (New York: Praeger, 1957), p. vii.

2. Amy W. Knight, "The Powers of the Soviet KGB," *Survey: A Journal of East & West Studies* (Summer 1980), p. 138.

3. Peter Deriabin and Frank Gibney, *The Secret World* (Garden City, New York: Doubleday and Company, Inc., 1959).

4. Edward Crankshaw, Foreword to Oleg Penkovskiy, *The Penkovskiy Papers* (Garden City, New York: Doubleday and Company, Inc., 1965), p. xi.

5. Peter Deriabin and T.H. Bagley, "Fedorchuk, the KGB, and the Soviet Succession," *Orbis* (Fall 1982), pp. 622-23. Deriabin and Bagley refer here to their "forthcoming book-length study of the KGB." Other recent books include Brian Freemantle, *KGB* (New York: Holt, Rinehart & Winston, 1982)—short and superficial—and John Barron, *KGB Today: The Hidden Hand* (New York: Reader's Digest Press, 1983), which is more solid but often sensationalist and novelistic in exposition as well as thoroughly biased; it is concerned almost entirely with KGB operations abroad and is based on the revelations of three men—a KGB officer who defected to U.S. agents in Tokyo in 1979, a KGB spy in the United States who agreed to cooperate with the FBI (1977-79), and a Canadian who worked intermittently for the KGB from 1956 to 1978. Another insider's account is Aleksei Myagkov, *Inside the KGB* (New Rochelle, New York: Arlington House Publishers, 1978; also Ballantine Books, 1981); Myagkov, a KGB captain on duty with the Soviet army in East Germany, defected to the British in Berlin in 1974.

6. Knight, "KGB," pp. 145-46; David R. Jones, ed., *Soviet Armed Forces Review Annual*, vol. 6 (Gulf Breeze, Florida: Academic International Press, 1982), pp. 280-302, 304-5.

**7.** Barron, *Hidden Hand*, p. 41.

**8.** *The Economist* (Nov. 27, 1982), pp. 105-6.

**9.** Deriabin and Bagley, "Fedorchuk," p. 624.

**10.** What follows is based on Barron, *Hidden Hand*, Appendix B (pp. 443-53). Barron's sources here are former KGB Major Stanislav Levchenko, who defected to the United States in 1979, and certain "Western intelligence officers."

**11.** Washington Post (June 21, 1983).

**12.** Barron, *Hidden Hand*, pp. 437-42; Washington Post (June 21, 1983); New York Times (June 22, 1983).

**13.** Washington Post (June 21, 1983).

**14.** George Leggett, *The Cheka: Lenin's Political Police* (Oxford and New York: Oxford University Press, 1981).

**15.** See Y.V. Andropov, *Speeches and Writings*, Robert Maxwell, ed. (Oxford and New York: Pergamon Press, Inc., 1983).

**16.** Roy Medvedev, quoted by Joseph Kraft, "Letter from Moscow," *The New Yorker* (Jan. 31, 1983), p. 105.

**17.** Barron, *Hidden Hand*, pp. 13-14, 403-4.

**18.** Barron, *Hidden Hand*, p. 21.

**19.** Walter Reich, "The World of Soviet Psychiatry," The New York Times *Magazine* (Jan. 30, 1983), pp. 20-27.

# THE ARMED FORCES

The expansion and continual updating of the Soviet Armed Forces over the last 20 years or more has been justified by Soviet leaders largely in terms of national defense. The Soviet Armed Forces, they say, are designed to defend the Soviet Union if it is attacked, to hold the "socialist camp" together (the so-called Brezhnev doctrine), and to support Third World struggles of "national liberation" (when it suits Soviet purposes). In particular, the Soviet buildup in nuclear weapons has been justified (since 1977) as necessary first to achieve and then to maintain strategic parity with the United States—a relationship more often known in the West as "mutual assured destruction" or "mutual deterrence."

The authors of the three chapters that follow are concerned to study this aspect of contemporary Soviet reality, as best it can be, in a spirit of sober realism, eschewing both the alarmist hyperbole and the facile optimism that infect so much Western comment here. David R. Jones discusses the overall organization and deployment of the Soviet Armed Forces, concluding that they are sufficient for the defense of the Soviet Union but not much more—given Western, especially U.S., retaliatory power. Mikhail Tsypkin, next, warns against exaggerating either the deficiencies or the strengths of the basic "human factor" in question, the Soviet servicemen, most of whom are short-term conscripts. And Eugenia Osgood points out, in the third chapter, that Soviet strategic thought has yet to absorb the doctrine of parity. In fact, the Soviet military establishment at present has no clearly enunciated nuclear strategy, a situation fraught with both danger and hopeful possibility for all concerned.

There can be no doubt that whatever its precise nature, extent and cost (matters of considerable debate in the West), the Soviet military buildup is regarded by Western and some other governments as a threat to their security. The continual Soviet search for security has aroused insecurity around the world.

# 8 | THE ARMED FORCES

## Military Organization and Deployment

### David R. Jones

Wars and the preparation for war have always been central to Russian life. In large part this simply reflects Russia's geographical position. Situated in the midst of the great Eurasian plain, the Russians have no natural frontiers that offered either protection from attack or hindrance to their expansion east to the Pacific, south to the Black Sea and the Caucasus, or west to the Baltic and Europe. The causes of this expansion are too complex for analysis here. Yet we should note that the Russians have suffered from recurring, deep-rooted and often justified fears of invasion. These fears in turn help explain why maintenance of a military establishment capable of ensuring the security of the state has always been among the government's highest priorities.

The Soviet Armed Forces retain the essential characteristics of the national mass armies, based on conscription, which grew up in nineteenth-century Europe and took root in Russia thanks to the conscription law of 1874. In short, they depend on a skeleton of regular cadres of long-service professionals—perhaps 400,000 in 1970—fleshed out by annual conscriptions in peacetime and by a call-up of reservists in case of war. At present, conscription in the Soviet Union is carried out in accord with the Law on Universal Military Obligation, which is further discussed in the following chapter. All 18-year-old males are considered eligible to serve, and some 70 to 76 percent are conscripted annually. In 1982 the Armed Forces probably totalled some 3,705,000 uniformed personnel. At least another 560,000 served in the internal security, railroad and construction troops.[1]

Following a conscript's term of service, normally two years, he is assigned to the reserves, there to remain until age 50. Thus theoretically, the Soviet Union has some 25 million reservists. But while all are required to attend refresher courses, Western analysts generally agree that only those who have been on active service during the last five years (in 1981 to 1982 about five million) have any military value.

Apart from those in the frontier or internal formations, all other Soviet military and naval personnel come under the aegis of the Ministry of Defense. Depending on his experience and qualifications, a conscript will be assigned either to one of the five main services, or to one of the Ministry's support branches, that is, the Troops of the Rear, Civil Defense, Railroad, Construction, and so on. The latter frequently are involved in work that is not strictly military. As Marshal D.F. Ustinov, the Defense Minister, recently pointed out:

> A considerable amount of housing and large numbers of buildings used as facilities for social and cultural services are built by military construction workers. A number of important economic projects have been built with their participation as well, and they have aided in the construction of thousands of kilometers of hard-surfaced roads. Railway workers [troops] are involved in the building of a number of rail lines and are at work on the eastern section of the Baikal-Amur Railroad. Soviet military personnel make an active contribution to the harvesting of our country's crops and in performing other tasks for the economy.[2]

But while such functions have considerable value in the view of the government, the Armed Forces' primary mission nonetheless is to be ready to wage war in defense of the "Fatherland." This is the immediate task of the five regular services: the Strategic Rocket Forces, the Ground Forces, the Air Defense Forces, the Air Forces, and the Navy. Soviet sources almost always list them in this order, which reflects their importance in Soviet strategic doctrine. Before looking at them in greater detail, however, an examination of the military's command and administrative system is in order.

Soviet sources are very close-mouthed when discussing any aspect of defense, including policy-making and the institutional framework through which policy is implemented. Nevertheless, Western analysts can discern the system's general outlines, even while disagreeing on the exact competence or membership of a given agency. If, for example, Soviet accounts of developments tend to overplay the "leading role" of the Communist Party in this as in other areas of Soviet life, they do provide a useful distinction between the "leadership of the country's defense" and the "leadership of the Armed Forces."

The first form of leadership takes as its sphere the whole complex of policies which determine the Soviet Union's defense posture: those relating to arms production, the preparation of the civilian population for military service (and for mobilization, if necessary), the basic organization of the Armed Forces, and the overall focus of ideological indoctrination. Meanwhile the second type of leadership is more narrowly concerned with the practical implementation of such policies in the Armed Forces themselves: with the details of military planning, troop organization and training, weapons acquisition and so forth. It is therefore more military, and less political, in the professional sense. But if the first realm of leadership is obviously superior in authority, the input of the second on most military questions is such that it remains fully involved in the policy-making process.

Major decisions about defense almost always seem to be made by the Politburo of the Party, given executive action through the Party's Secretariat, and simply ratified by its Central Committee, the periodic Party congresses, and all other Party and state organs. So the Politburo has the final word on major matters of defense and military policy. Yet in large measure the Politburo's role consists of accepting, rejecting or modifying the proposals and recommendations of the two defense leaderships, whose agencies in turn implement the broader policies. For this reason the latter also play a vital part in determining those policies, even if the Politburo, and through it the Party, retains the final word.

More precisely, the supreme "leadership of the country's defense" today is vested in the Defense Council of the Soviet Union, about which little is known. Indeed, although rumors of its existence began circulating in the West late in the 1960s, the Soviet press confirmed the fact only in 1976, when Leonid Brezhnev was identified as the Council's chairman. Its existence was then formally sanctioned by the new Soviet Constitution of 1977. In May 1983, it was publicly confirmed—by Marshal Ustinov writing in *Pravda*—that Yury Andropov had replaced Brezhnev as the Council's chairman, presumably in his role as the new Party leader. Otherwise, in addition to the head of the KGB, the Council appears to be made up of the most important members of the Politburo and the senior military officials. The successor to such earlier bodies as Stalin's all-powerful Committee of State Defense of World War II, the Defense Council's peacetime role seems confined to examining all major military questions with the aim of making recommendations to the Politburo. Programs for developing and procuring new weapons systems seem to be of prime concern, as does the definition of each of the five services' basic mission with reference to overall strategic planning.

The more circumscribed "leadership of the Armed Forces" is vested in the highest body of the Ministry of Defense, usually known either as the

Collegium of the Ministry or as its Main Military Council. It is chaired by Marshal Ustinov, who as Defense Minister has powers roughly comparable to those of the U.S. Secretary of Defense and Chairman of the Joint Chiefs of Staff combined. Other presumed members include the head of the Main Political Administration, the commanders of the five services (each of whom is a Deputy Minister of Defense), other branch chiefs and deputy ministers, the chiefs of the General Staff, and the Commander-in-Chief of the Warsaw Pact. The Main Military Council's responsibilities include resolving most professional issues that touch on the "development of the armed forces" proper, as Soviet sources put it; the adjudication of major professional rivalries; and the settlement of inter-service disputes over the assignment of missions, funds, economic capacity and manpower. Framing as it does various proposals that will then pass through the Defense Council and on to the Politburo, it also has a major role in resolving just how the latter's decisions will be implemented.

The second agency of the Ministry of Defense intimately involved in leading the Armed Forces is the General Staff. Modeled on its Imperial Russian predecessor—and thus to some extent on the pre-1914 German General Staff—this body has no U.S. equivalent. It is responsible for basic strategic planning and for working out proper roles for each of the five services. It has ten subordinate "directorates," of which the three most important handle intelligence, organization-mobilization and operations. In the main, the General Staff is run by officers who have completed courses at its Voroshilov Academy. Since it is responsible for coordinating the work of the main staffs of the services and branches, these latter bodies can be considered subordinate to the Ministry through the General Staff. Other important directorates are concerned with "military science," that is, the further development of military theory; with the Warsaw Pact; and recently with military assistance programs abroad. Since the 1960s the General Staff has also played a major role in introducing cybernetics and automated systems of planning and command into the Soviet military.

At roughly the same administrative level as the General Staff, but outside the Ministry of Defense in the government hierarchy, is the Military Industrial Commission. Despite some opinion to the contrary, it appears unlikely that the Commission is directly connected with the Defense Council. At any rate, it is headed by a Deputy Chairman of the Council of Ministers, and other members probably include representatives from the various ministries of defense industry, from the State Planning Commission (*Gosplan*), from the Party, and from the Ministry of Defense and its General Staff. The Military-Industrial Commission deals with technical problems related to the Armed Forces' requirements for armaments and materiel; with ensuring that sufficient resources are available to meet production targets; and with coordinating the delivery of new equipment with the military's schedules for its introduction. Thus the Commission is an essential link between the military establishment and its industrial "rear."

The Ministry of Defense itself, then, includes the General Staff and its directorates, the Main Political Administration, the individual commands of the five services, and various agencies for administering support services. Of these last, the most important are the Inspectorate and those that manage the Services of the Rear, Armaments, Construction and Quarters, and Personnel. All of these agencies are headed by Deputy Ministers who are probably members of the Ministry's Collegium or Main Military Council as well. The same is true of the commanders-in-chief of the five individual services. But between the commanders and the Defense Minister stand the three more senior First Deputy Ministers: Marshal N.V. Ogarkov, chief of the General Staff; Army General A. A. Epishev, head of the Main Political Administration; and Marshal V. G. Kulikov, Commander-in-Chief of the Warsaw Pact. Below the remaining Deputy Ministers are the heads of the lesser directorates: for highways, tactical rockets and artillery, inventions, military-educational institutions, civilian military training, military bands and so on. Many of these lesser section chiefs have no seat in the Ministry's Collegium, though on occasion some may be involved in its discussions.

One major institutional component of the Ministry deserves special comment—the anachronistically labeled Main Political Administration, the chief means by which the Party Central Committee guides and controls political indoctrination within the armed forces. This agency's significance is underlined by the fact that as well as being a part of the Defense Ministry it is a department of the Central Committee, which gives it dual representation. In addition to Epishev as head, its leading officials include his assistant chief for *Komsomol* (Communist Youth League), the secretary of the Party Commission, the head of the Party-Organization Administration, and that of the Administration for Agitation and Propaganda. In addition to indoctrination through its network of political officers (or "deputy commanders for political affairs"), the Main Political Administration is responsible for troop morale and for maintaining the Armed Forces' "ideological purity." All in all, this agency is the conduit for Party control and influence over the rest of the military establishment at every level. Moreover, since 1960 it has been considered a "collegial" institution empowered to issue its own directives. These directives sometimes require the signature of the Minister of

Defense as well, but those on routine activities are signed by Epishev alone. And since all of the Defense Ministry's leading figures are Party members who frequently hold seats in both the Central Committee and the Supreme Soviet, the Party's control of the Armed Forces is assured.[3]

The central institutions just enumerated are all "collegial" in nature, which in Soviet parlance means they are "organs of collective leadership." To varying degrees this same pattern is replicated in the high commands of each of the five services, in the military and air defense districts, in the fleets, and probably in the recently created "Theaters of Military Operations." Each is headed by a commander and his "military council" of deputy commanders, the appropriate political officer and sometimes other major figures as well. Theoretically, this and the other councils "discuss and resolve" major questions by a majority vote, but in practice they are mainly deliberative, since the Commander-in-Chief's position easily allows him to achieve a consensus. Let us examine each service in their official order of ranking.

• The Strategic Rocket Forces were founded in 1959 and are still shrouded in great secrecy. This service includes all medium- and long-range ground-based nuclear-armed missiles; that is, all such systems with ranges over 1,000 kilometers. According to the late Minister of Defense Marshal A. A. Grechko, the Strategic Rocket Forces have "most fully absorbed the achievements of modern scientific-technological progress," are "the basis of combat watch," and so are "always ready to retaliate against an aggressor."[4] Commanded by Army General V. F. Tolubko since 1972, the service is staffed by some 325,000 military personnel backed by 50,000 civilians. Those assigned to this premier service constitute an elite. For example, officer recruits must be certified as suitable by the local Military Commissariat (the induction agency), a procedure not followed by the other four services. Such recruits then follow a five-year course at one of the service's four Higher Military Schools before being commissioned. Active personnel serve in six rocket armies, each of which is subdivided into divisions, regiments, battalions and batteries, with one launcher assigned to each battery.

Operational control is achieved through some 300 launch-control headquarters which normally carry out orders issued by the Rocket Forces' own command and military council. Such operational orders, however, would be passed presumably from the Defense Council to the Rocket Forces through the General Staff, and the latter can by-pass Tolubko's command center if necessary. It is possible that any operational "push of the button" would require KGB sanction as well. Otherwise, the Rocket Forces control the Soviet Union's three missile testing grounds and play a major role in the space program.

The International Institute for Strategic Studies in London estimates that in 1982 the Strategic Rocket Forces controlled 1,398 strategic ICBMs, of which 308 are the feared "heavy" SS-18s, carrying some eight to ten warheads each. The Rocket Forces also were in charge of some 606 intermediate-range and medium-range missiles, of which 500 were thought to be deployed in the western part of the country. The most significant element of these last missiles is the much discussed mobile SS-20, each carrying three warheads. In 1982 and 1983 the Strategic Rocket Forces were believed to be deploying a total of 37 SS-20 complexes with nine missiles each, for a total of 333. Of this number, about 250 were aimed at European targets, the rest at China and Japan. It is often overlooked in the West that, unlike the United States, Britain and France, who presumably have only one potential enemy, the Soviet Union has to deal with the strategic forces of all three, and counter a small but growing Chinese capability as well. Having achieved parity with the United States in strategic systems, the Soviet leaders undoubtedly expected their new SS-20s to overcome the lesser but much closer threats along their extensive frontiers.

• Although ranking second in official protocol, the Ground Forces continue, through their senior commanders, to dominate the upper echelons of the Soviet Ministry of Defense. This service, headed by Army General V.I. Petrov, is also the largest of the five. In mid-1982 his forces numbered an estimated 1,825,000, as many as 1,400,000 of whom were conscripts. They were enrolled in 46 tank, 126 motorized-rifle, eight airborne, eight air-assault (aeromobile), and 14 artillery divisions as well as in a number of smaller independent units.

Not all of these divisions are kept at anything like their full strength. In fact, three categories of readiness exist. The first, in which a unit maintains its full complement of equipment and 75 to 100 percent of its manpower, is applicable to the 31 divisions stationed in eastern Europe. About 25 percent of the 76 divisions stationed in the western Soviet Union, and 50 of those on duty in the Far East, are maintained at either this or the second level of readiness—a full complement of combat vehicles and 50 to 75 percent of required personnel. The rest of the Ground Forces, including the bulk of those deployed in the central and southern regions, are in the third category. This means that they function with only 25 percent of their manpower even if they have all of their vehicles, some of which are bound to be obsolescent. Divisions lacking personnel in peacetime would be brought up to full strength in the event of a general mobilization, which would take an estimated seven to 14 days to complete for divisions in Categories I and II and some 30 to 40 days for those in Category III.

The Soviet Ground Forces have seemingly vast stocks of equipment available: an estimated 50,000 tanks; 62,000 armored personnel carriers, scout cars and other vehicles; 7,200 mortars; 4,000 multiple-rocket launchers; numerous anti-tank weapons; and 1,300 nuclear-capable surface-to-surface tactical missile launchers, of which at least 802 face Europe. Yet in many instances these numbers reflect the Soviet habit of retaining equipment withdrawn from service during modernization programs, much of which is obsolescent if not obsolete. Thus the core of any Soviet armor thrust to the West would consist of T-64/72 main battle tanks—of which there are only some 12,000. Similarly, as the SS-21, 22 and 23 tactical missiles replace the older FROGs, Scuds and SS-12s, the latter presumably will be mothballed. This does not make them suitable for immediate use, especially given the slack standards of much Soviet maintenance. Indeed, many reports suggest that much of the equipment found in Category III divisions is out of date. The same may be true of many divisions in the other two categories (particularly the second) stationed outside of Eastern Europe (and excepting those involved in Afghanistan).

Soviet leadership continues to modernize the Ground Forces and to prepare them for all possible eventualities. For example, units are being trained to operate in an environment of nuclear-chemical-biological warfare, and equipment is being designed for such use. Changes in Soviet tank design, as well as the growing use of automated or computerized command and control systems have also been noted. Revised conceptions of the scale of combined operations have led to the formation of units of "army aviation" (helicopters and possibly light aircraft), special artillery divisions for use at the front, and other specialized units. Presumably the programs in the Ground Forces' higher schools are being altered to train officers capable of employing the new techniques.

Even so, many problems persist. Apart from uncertain morale, obsolete equipment, shortages and slack maintenance, there is concern with a lack of "initiative" among subordinate and junior commanders. These factors make any calculations regarding the Ground Forces' effectiveness difficult for Western and Soviet experts alike.

• This observation is equally applicable to the Air Defense Forces. Charged with protecting the homeland against enemy air attack, this service is also responsible for research in ballistic missile and "anti-space" defense. The commander, Marshal of Aviation A.I. Koldunov, therefore presumably has charge of the remaining 32 Galosh-B anti-ballistic missile launchers around Moscow and of the development of new

**Table 1. Relative U.S./Soviet Levels of Technology in Deployed Military Systems***

| Deployed System | U.S. Superior | U.S./Soviet Equal | Soviet Superior |
|---|---|---|---|
| **Strategic** | | | |
| Intercontinental ballistic missiles | | X | |
| Submarine-launched ballistic missiles | X→ | | |
| Bomber | X→ | | |
| Surface-to-air missiles | | | X |
| Ballistic missile defense | | | X |
| Anti-satellite | | | X |
| **Tactical** | | | |
| Land Forces | | | |
| SAMs (including naval) | | X | |
| Tanks | | | ←X |
| Artillery | | X | |
| Infantry combat vehicles | | | X |
| Anti-tank guided missiles | | X | |
| Attack helicopters | | X→ | |
| Chemical warfare | | | X |
| Theater ballistic missiles | | X→ | |
| Air Forces | | | |
| Fighter/attack aircraft | X→ | | |
| Air-to-air missiles | X | | |
| Precision guided munitions | X | | |
| Air lift | X | | |
| Naval Forces | | | |
| Nuclear propelled ballistic-missile bearing submarines | | X | |
| Anti-submarine warfare | X→ | | |
| Sea-based air | X→ | | |
| Surface combatants | | X | |
| Cruise missiles | | X | |
| Mine warfare | | | X |
| Amphibious assault | X→ | | |
| **Command, Control, Communication and Intelligence (C³I)** | | | |
| Communications | X→ | | |
| Command and control | | X | |
| Electronic countermeasures | | X | |
| Surveillance and reconnaissance | X→ | | |
| Early warning | X→ | | |

Source: U.S. Department of Defense, *The FY 1982 Department of Defense Program for Research, Development, and Acquisition* (1981), II-33.

*The arrows denote that the relative technology level is changing significantly in the direction indicated.

**Table 2. Relative U.S./Soviet Standing in Twenty Most Important Areas of Basic Technology***

| Basic Technologies | U.S. Superior | U.S./Soviet Equal | Soviet Superior |
|---|---|---|---|
| Aerodynamics/fluid dynamics | | X | |
| Automated control | X | | |
| Chemical explosives | | | X→ |
| Computer | ←X | | |
| Directed energy | | X | |
| Electrooptical sensor (including IR) | X→ | | |
| Guidance and navigation | X→ | | |
| Hydro-acoustic | X→ | | |
| Microelectronic materials and integrated circuit manufacture | ←X | | |
| Non-acoustic submarine detection | | Cannot determine | |
| Nuclear warhead | | X | |
| Optics | X→ | | |
| Power sources (weapon) | | | X→ |
| Production/manufacturing | X | | |
| Propulsion | X→ | | |
| Radar sensor | | X | |
| Signal processing | X | | |
| Software | X | | |
| Structural materials | | X | |
| Telecommunications | X | | |

*The arrows denote that the relative technology level is changing significantly in the direction indicated.

Source: U.S. Department of Defense, *The FY 1982 Department of Defense Program for Research, Development and Acquisition* (1981), II-32.

defense systems—missiles, anti-satellite interceptors, laser systems or some form of "beam weapons." His main concern, however, must be the threat posed by the enemy's aerodynamic means of delivery—aircraft, cruise missiles or a combination of the two. The importance that Moscow attaches to this mission is indicated by the CIA's assessment that from 1971 to 1980, the Soviets allocated as much as 48 percent of their strategic budget to the Air Defense Forces, 25 percent to intercontinental attack weapons (ICBMs), and 15 percent to "peripheral attack" (theater) weapons.[5]

In 1982 Koldunov's command contained an estimated 630,000 men in three main branches: the radio-electrics (radar) troops; the surface-to-

#### Table 3. Main Indicators of U.S.-Soviet Military Strength, December 1981

|  | United States | Soviet Union |
|---|---|---|
| Population | 225,300,000 | 265,500,000 |
| Total military manpower | 2,049,100 | 3,673,000 |
| Terms of service | Voluntary | Conscription 2-3 years |
| *Strategic nuclear offensive forces* | | |
| ICBMS | 1,052 | 1,398 |
| SLBMS | 576 | 989 |
| Long-range bombers | 316 | 150 |
| Warheads | 9,480 | 8,040 |
| *Strategic defense systems deployed* | | |
| SAMS | — | 12,000 |
| Interceptors | 312 | 2,500 |
| ABMS | — | 32 |
| *Ground forces* | | |
| Men | 775,000 | 1,825,000 |
| Tanks | 11,400 | 45,000 |
| *Naval forces* | | |
| Manpower (marines and naval infantry excluded) | 528,000 | 431,000 |
| Major surface combatants | 201 | 294 |
| Attack and cruise missile submarines | 84 | 259 |
| Aircraft carriers | 14 | 2 |
| Helicopter carriers | — | 2 |
| Combat aircraft | 1,450 | 755 |
| Marines and naval infantry | 188,100 | 12,000 |
| *Air forces* | | |
| Manpower | 558,000 | 475,000 |
| Combat aircraft | 3,200 | 5,300 |

*Source*: International Institute for Strategic Studies, *The Military Balance, 1981-1982* (London, 1981).

air missile (SAM) troops; and the air interceptor forces. The first branch mans the approximately 7,000 early-warning ground-controlled intercept and anti-missile radars, which in turn control the operations of both the interceptors and the SAMS. In all, the SAM forces include some 10,000 "strategic" defensive launchers at 1,400 fixed sites backed by numerous tactical launchers and anti-aircraft guns.

Major organizational changes were introduced into Koldunov's command over the last three years. Since its formation in 1948, this service has existed independently of the tactical anti-aircraft assets of the Ground Forces. With the appearance of a special commander-in-chief in 1954, it constituted a highly centralized air defense system comprised of ten air-defense districts within the Soviet Union and one each in the six Warsaw Pact nations, all under the direction of headquarters in Moscow. But in 1980 signs of the reorganization began to appear, and by January 1981 today's service had clearly emerged. Although some aspects of the restructured system remain uncertain, the Air Defense Forces have lost two flying schools to the Air Forces (see below), gained five SAM schools from the Ground Forces (for a total of 14 for training in its requisite specialties), and acquired administrative control of the army's tactical air defense units.

At the same time, all the old air defense districts, except Moscow's, have disappeared. Their establishments appear to have been merged with the appropriate military districts or commands. Thus the central headquarters in Moscow must still provide overall strategic direction, but it now exercises operational control through local authorities rather than its own separate network. And it seems unlikely that Romania's air defense assets now operate under Moscow's direct orders.

The significance of this reorganization remains unclear. Some Western experts contend that the Air Defense Forces have become mainly a SAM service, its interceptors having been transferred to a reformed tactical air service. In this view, the Soviets' aim is to increase the offensive weight of their air power for expanded combined-arms operations discussed below. But the continued development of mission-specific interceptors (Foxhound and Fulcrum) suggests that a more purely defensive air mission still exists for today's Air Defense Forces. Moreover, the new American tactic of low-level penetration by means of air-launched cruise missiles, along with the demonstrated weaknesses of Soviet strategic SAMs and interceptors at such low levels, suggests that the reorganization reflects serious concern about the Air Defense Forces' ability to meet the challenges of the 1980s.

While new weapons are under development, tactical SAM systems have been pressed into service to fill the low-level gap. Yet events in the Middle East in 1982 show that these missiles are also inadequate. Worse still from Koldunov's viewpoint, Soviet technological backwardness in general (in microcircuits and other important areas) indicates that in spite of high levels of expenditure his service would be unable successfully to counter an aerial onslaught against the Soviet Union in the foreseeable future.

• The Soviet Air Forces, under Chief Marshal of Aviation P.S. Kutakhov, also consist of three branches: Frontal (tactical) Aviation, the Long-Range Air Force and Military-Transport Aviation. Together they number about 543,000 men. Frontal Aviation's mission is to provide direct support to the Ground Forces; it is organized into 16 air armies attached to 12 of the 16 military districts and to the four Groups of Soviet Forces in Eastern Europe. It has lost some helicopters and light aircraft to the new army aviation units, but it now can count on more direct operational support from the Air Defense Forces' interceptors (and vice versa). This branch of the Air Forces nonetheless has its own, slowly modernizing inventory of 2,300 armed helicopters and 4,480 other aircraft, including an estimated 2,050 ground-attack planes and 1,750 fighters, as well as reconnaissance, electronic warfare and other special purpose equipment.

Because of the Soviet Union's poor highway system, limited railway network, and vast area, the Military Transport branch is vital in moving troops about the Eurasian land mass and in supporting clients abroad. It has only 600 aircraft, but in case of war it can count on Aeroflot's 200 light and 1,100 medium and heavy transport-passenger aircraft. Yet if its role and status are clear, those of the bomber forces are not. Long- and medium-range units still exist, and the development of a new strategic bomber, known to NATO as Blackjack or the Ram-P (perhaps officially designated the Tu-160), shows that the Soviet military value their services. Nonetheless, while Colonel General (Aviation) V.V. Reshetnikov appears in the press as a Deputy Commander-in-Chief of the Air Forces, he no longer is specified as chief of the Long-Range Air Force. Even so, he undoubtedly still commands the 809 aircraft (including 150 long-range and 535 medium-range bombers) which, according to Western analysts, remain divided into three air armies, two facing NATO in Europe (with at least 425 medium bombers), and a third stationed in the Far East. The operational command of these forces is obscure: it is just possible, in the light of some hints dropped by the Soviet press, that Moscow has decided to consolidate all its strategic weapons—missiles, bombers and ballistic missile submarines—into a single strategic command.

• Since the early 1960s the growth of the Navy under Admiral S.G. Gorshkov has been so pronounced that many in the West consider the Soviet Union a maritime superpower. Apart from the usual administrative and educational networks (five regular and five specialist officer schools), the Navy comprises 69 nuclear and 14 diesel submarines armed with ballistic missiles, 69 cruise-missile submarines (49 nuclear and 20 diesel), 202 attack submarines (56 nuclear and 146 diesel), the 755 aircraft and 300 helicopters of the Naval Aviation, 290 major and 837 minor surface combatants, 84 amphibious ships, 214 auxiliaries, 59 intelligence collection vessels and 459 oceanographic ships. Eight thousand coastal artillery and missile troops, with 100 Sepal surface-to-surface launchers, are under Naval command, as are 13,500 marines in five regiments. These forces total some 450,000 men, of whom about 75 percent are short-term conscripts. Gorshkov's fleet also has 107 attack submarines and 28 major surface combatants mothballed as reserves; and in a crisis he can press the extensive Soviet merchant marine into auxiliary service. This force soon will be upgraded further with more of the new Typhoon nuclear submarines, two further Kiev carriers, three Kirov and two "Black-Com-1" cruisers, and a number of destroyers, frigates and corvettes, as well as other vessels. Since these ships are generally more powerful and efficient than the earlier models they replace, the overall number of major surface combatants in the Soviet Navy should fall from 294 in 1981 to roughly 250 by 1990.

Apart from the smaller vessels in the Caspian Flotilla, the Navy's resources are divided among four fleets. Of the nuclear submarines, 45 are assigned to the Northern Fleet and 25 to the Pacific. Of the non-nuclear submarines, the Northern Fleet has 140, the Pacific, 95. Major surface combatants are also divided between the two fleets: 75 to the Northern; 85 to the Pacific. The Pacific Fleet has the strongest amphibious capability—25 landing craft and two (of five) regiments of marines. Moreover, the Northern and Pacific Fleets between them have slightly over half of the Navy's 390 strike and medium bombers. Numerically, the Black Sea Fleet (including the Mediterranean Squadron) ranks third, with 20 submarines, 80 major surface warships and 90 bombers. The Baltic Fleet, ranked fourth, is structured to play an important role in any European conflict. Thus while it comprises only 50 major surface vessels, it has, like the Black Sea Fleet, a greater number of amphibious craft than does the Northern. The Baltic Fleet maintains 30 submarines and 100 bombers, as well as some 35 Su-17 land-based ground-attack aircraft. And each of the three European fleets has one regiment of marines at its disposal.

Such forces are obviously sufficient to protect Soviet home waters and, if little risk is involved, to support diplomatic goals abroad. Clearly, Moscow is aware of the possible benefits accruing from the latter option. Thus while the buildup of the 1960s and 1970s was probably a response to the U.S. Polaris missile program, today's Soviet navy seeks to maintain, as Gorshkov has pointed out, other more general "state interests." By 1981 an average of 140 warships were forward-deployed on any given day.

Still, the Soviet leadership shows no willingness to commit these forces, even diplomatically, in any situation of real danger. For apart from the usual caution, considerable doubt remains as to the Navy's likely effectiveness in any future conflict with Western forces. Soviet sailors get less sea-time than do their American counterparts; their fleets are much less experienced in underway replenishment than NATO's; and a number of embarrassing incidents—a mutiny in the Baltic, the nuclear-armed submarine run aground in neutral Swedish waters—raise questions about both morale and performance. Soviet submarines are noisier than their Western counterparts and Soviet anti-submarine warfare capabilities are much less developed. These factors may help explain why Moscow maintains fewer submarines on regular station in a nuclear-response role than does the United States.

The quality of any state's armed forces depends largely on that of their equipment and training. With respect to the former, the systems used by the Soviet Armed Forces have been moving away from technically simpler but generally reliable weapons to more sophisticated ones. Yet because of complicated problems of maintenance, their new tanks, like their new aircraft, have lower readiness levels and in general remain inferior to their Western counterparts. In some ways, indeed, the Soviets have obtained the worst of both worlds.

With reference to the quality of enlisted personnel, problems of discipline were referred to above, and the training of the conscripts is dealt with in the following chapter.[6] It is worth stressing that any pre-conscription military training available in the Soviet Union is at best of very limited value, and that the military value of perhaps 80 percent of the reservists—those who have been out of service more than a few years—is even more dubious.

The Soviet Armed Forces continue to be plagued by shortages of long-service officers and non-commissioned officers, who are the backbone of the system. Yet the majority of officers have received good education and training in the extensive network of higher military schools, and senior commanders are usually graduates of at least one of the 17 military academies—of which the Voroshilov Academy of the General Staff, the Frunze Military Academy, and the Lenin Military-Political Academy are the most prestigious. It is their professors and graduates who produce most of the major Soviet works on military doctrine and science, tactics, history, and military-political themes.

One of the greatest problems facing the Soviet leadership derives from the demographic trends discussed elsewhere in this book (Chapter 23). While the army has always served as a means of indoctrinating and assimilating non-Russians and especially non-Slavs, the Russians and their Slavic neighbors have formed the overall majority. But the Kremlin currently faces the dilemma of a decreasing pool of young men for use in the military and in industry on the one hand, and a rising proportion of non-Slavs within that pool on the other. According to one U.S. estimate, the number of non-Russians among available conscripts will increase from 51.7 percent in 1980 to 74.7 percent in the year 2000. The picture is further complicated by the lower educational levels of non-Russian and especially non-Slavic recruits, who, if present force levels are maintained, must be trained to use increasingly complex equipment. Given the economy's general stagnation, there are obviously no easy solutions here.[7]

The Soviet leadership does indeed have an impressive military machine constantly at its disposal. Under a tightly centralized command, it is capable of intervening effectively in eastern Europe as well as elsewhere around the Soviet periphery. Yet, in the long view, there is nothing "unprecedented" about this fact. Historically, the Russian armed forces have usually been large, have frequently had an offensive tactical doctrine, have often required a high level of expenditure, and have commonly inspired fear in potential enemies. The deployment of a large army near the western frontier by Nicholas I (1825-1855) is but one example reflecting these trends. Similarly, the combat potential of Russia's forces has been as frequently denigrated by outsiders as it has been overestimated—a result, often, of domestic political considerations in other countries. As usual, the truth probably is to be found somewhere in between.

The Soviet Armed Forces are sufficient for the defense of the Soviet Union and for external expansion, when the latter entails little or no risk. They are hardly sufficient to launch a strike for European hegemony, let alone "world domination." As the planners of the Ministry of Defense know full well, any such course almost certainly would bring about the destruction of the very "Fatherland" they have sworn to protect. ☐

1. Figures from *The Military Balance, 1982-1983* (London: International Institute for Strategic Studies, 1982); and especially David R. Jones, ed., *The Soviet Armed Forces Review Annual*, 6 (Gulf Breeze, Florida: Academic International Press, 1982), which draws on numerous other sources.

2. D.F. Ustinov, *Sluzhim rodine, delu Kommunizma* (Moscow: 1982), p. 62; English translation, *We Serve the Homeland and the Cause of Communism* (Washington, D.C.: JPRSL/10604, 1982), p. 47.

3. KGB supervision of the Armed Forces also ensures their loyalty (see Chapter 7).

**4.** A.A. Grechko, *The Armed Forces of the Soviet State* (Washington, D.C.: USAF translation, "Soviet Military Thought Series," No. 12, 1975), pp. 79-80.

**5.** Adapted from CIA, *Soviet and U.S. Defense Activities, 1971-1980: A Dollar Cost Comparison* (Washington, D.C. 1981), Figure 6, p. 9.

**6.** See also Herbert Goldhamer, *The Soviet Soldier, Soviet Military Management at the Troop Level* (New York: Crane, Russak, 1975); Andrew Cockburn, "Ivan the Terrible Soldier," *Harper's* (March 1983), pp. 50-57.

**7.** On this problem see D.R. Jones, "Military Manpower," *Soviet Armed Forces Review Annual*, 2 (Gulf Breeze, Florida: Academic International Press, 1978), pp. 30-45.

# 9

## The Conscripts

### Mikhail Tsypkin

Relatively little attention has been paid in the West to the human dimension of the Soviet Armed Forces. Official Soviet sources emphasize that "no weapon or combat equipment can of themselves replace" the "moral, political, psychological and combat qualities" of a soldier.[1] The huge Soviet military machine is based on conscription, and providing for its smooth functioning involves special arrangements within both the Armed Forces and Soviet society as a whole. Analysis of this "human factor" is made difficult by the biases inherent in official Soviet publications, however, as well as by the extraordinary secrecy in which the Soviets cloak their military establishment. Still, by combining information contained in official Soviet publications with the accounts of eyewitnesses, recent emigres and defectors, and by evaluating the results on the basis of our general knowledge of Soviet society, we can form a picture of how the Soviet conscript army works.

In manpower, the Armed Forces are impressive: approximately 3,705,000 servicemen, plus some 560,000 internal security, railroad and construction troops.[2] Such diverse factors as long and exposed frontiers, the need to control a vast empire, relative technological backwardness, ideology, and the experiences of World War II have resulted in an emphasis on mass in manpower.[3] This has led to a reliance on conscription. Conscription is also viewed by the Soviet leadership as an instrument for political socialization, while the abundance of military manpower provides cheap and adaptable labor which can be used on such different priority projects as construction of the Baikal-Amur Railroad and of the Olympic Village in Moscow.

The 1967 Law on Universal Military Obligation, amended in 1980, not only deals with conscription but also formulates a program of "mili-

113

tary-patriotic" training from elementary school on. Since 1967 each secondary school has hired its military instructor, and millions of school children have taken part in compulsory paramilitary exercises, including trips to battlefields of the Great Patriotic War (the Soviet name for World War II), mock fighting engagements and visits to military units, where a show of modern weaponry is usually organized for the young guests. A visitor to the Soviet Union can observe uniformed teenagers with dummy submachine guns goose-stepping around the Great Patriotic War memorials erected in practically all major cities. The next stage of military education begins when all 17-year-old males have to show up at their borough military commissariats to receive their draft certificates, after which they are assigned to a local unit of the Volunteer Society for Cooperation with the Army, Aviation and Fleet for part-time training in the basics of their future military specialty.

It is not easy to measure the precise effect of this gigantic attempt at a "military-patriotic upbringing." One remains skeptical about the ability of this program to instill an enthusiasm for military service and self-sacrifice: much of the earlier exuberance, born of Stalin's great industrialization campaign and of victory in World War II, has been eroded by decades of unfulfilled economic promises, widespread petty corruption and alcoholism. One also suspects that the pre-draft training conducted by the Volunteer Society cannot provide future draftees with the necessary military skills. For the giant scale of the undertaking ensures inefficiency, good performance is virtually unenforceable, and Soviet secretiveness guarantees that Volunteer Society classrooms are equipped with obsolete military hardware.

At the same time, the "military-patriotic" program has its positive aspects. It accustoms young people to the inevitability of military service and fortifies the lessons of obedience they receive in the highly authoritarian Soviet secondary schools.

Two other factors influence young minds here. First, the massive infusion of the "military-patriotic theme" into literature, cinematography and the theater incessantly glorifies the Great Patriotic War and the sacrifices and victory of the Soviet people. Second, very few young people are exempt from military service, so almost every young man has the example of an older brother, older friends, or a father who was drafted. The result is that military duty is viewed by future conscripts as normal. It is only the offspring of the privileged strata in Soviet society who are very reluctant to be drafted, and who literally scramble for college admissions and attendant draft exemptions. Relatively few Soviet young people go to college full time; in 1979, the total was 2,932,000, of whom approximately half were women.[4]

According to the Law on Universal Military Obligation, all 18-year-old males are liable for two years of active duty (three years in the Navy). A 1980 amendment permits exemptions in several instances: when the potential draftee is the only breadwinner for dependents incapable of working; for health reasons; for "reasons of state," which implies work in a priority branch of the defense industry; and to full-time students at colleges and universities,[5] institutions which in turn have compulsory reserve officers' training programs. There is no conscientious objector status under Soviet law.

Conscripts are usually sent thousands of miles from home. Of course, geography has some bearing here. But this policy also reflects a general effort to maintain control over the conscript force by isolating soldiers from the civilian world. Proximity to family and friends might lead to drinking and going "AWOL" (absent without leave). Even more important, in case of civil unrest servicemen without local roots would be more reliable for crowd-control operations. This isolation is particularly noticeable in Soviet troops stationed in the Warsaw Pact countries, where the fear of "ideological contamination" and of conflicts between the local population and unruly soldiers keeps the conscripts virtually confined to barracks throughout their term of duty.[6]

Conscripts accept military service but usually without enthusiasm. The enlisted men's pay is negligible, usually not more than about $30 a month, and most conscripts are not interested in possible careers as non-commissioned officers. To overcome this problem, a number of formal programs and informal arrangements have been devised. Political indoctrination is an example of the former. But a necessary precondition for political indoctrination is a cutoff of unauthorized sources of information. Thus, like the great majority of Soviet citizens, servicemen have no access to non-technical Western publications. To prevent enlisted men from listening to foreign radio broadcasts they have to surrender their radios to their non-commissioned officers, who return them on Sundays and holidays.[7] The prohibition against listening to foreign radio broadcasts is such that even radio operators are afraid to receive anything but Soviet broadcasts.[8]

No precaution is considered excessive. Television sets in the barracks of the Group of Soviet Forces in East Germany are specially outfitted *not* to receive West German programs. Possession of such a non-political Western publication as *Playboy* magazine may be viewed as a serious political offense. Committee for State Security (KGB) officers are assigned to every military unit down to company level, and by developing a network of informers can acquire compromising information about servicemen and thus considerable power over them.

Yet the effect of the political indoctrination itself is problematical. Regular sessions of political indoctrination contain repetitive harangues against U.S. imperialism or lengthy discussions of the latest Party congress, and the officers conducting the sessions are frequently ill-prepared and bored themselves. Argument is excluded as "politically subversive." The audience of young conscripts, 18 to 20 years old, are tired from the heavy training schedule and their thoughts naturally gravitate to their homes or girlfriends. Most of them view the sessions as a convenient moment for writing a letter or taking a nap. Even enlisted men who see active participation in political work as a way to promotion and discharge with a good character reference can do no more than recite from their textbooks in order to satisfy the officers.

Moreover, the political indoctrination system often fails to provide plausible explanations of international crises that result or might result in the use of Soviet military might. Thus, at least some Soviet soldiers during the 1968 invasion of Czechoslovakia thought they were in West Germany or even in Israel.[9] During the 1968 crisis a Soviet infantry division was alerted and moved forward to the Sino-Soviet border, but its enlisted men were not told why. Similarly, neither enlisted men nor officers of a surface-to-air missile (SAM) battery alerted during the 1973 U.S.-Soviet showdown were offered any explanation of the international situation.[10]

Discipline, however, was not impaired, and therein lies the paradox of political indoctrination. By its sheer irrelevance to the conscripts' everyday life indoctrination anesthetizes their interest in politics. At the same time, because of its reiteration it imprints on their minds the image of an unreservedly aggressive outside world which surfaces under combat or quasi-combat conditions.

In the early 1970s, seamen on a ship in the Baltic were ordered to stay below decks when passing through the straits near Denmark. The officers explained that they were "in capitalist waters" and could be attacked at any moment by boats spraying their ship with machine-gun fire. Having no basis for thinking otherwise, the seamen obeyed.[11] More recently, we know from interviews with several Soviet prisoners held by the Afghan guerrillas that Soviet soldiers believed it when told that they had to fight "American and Chinese agents" in Afghanistan. In a system where political decisions are made by a small elite, political passivity combined with basic loyalty is, after all, a desirable quality in the conscript.

The ethnic diversity of draftees presents problems in managing the Soviet Armed Forces. In 1977, Slavs comprised about 69 percent of the draft pool, with Muslims constituting about 18 percent and other minorities about 13 percent. By the mid-1980s, the Muslim share will grow to 24 percent at the expense of the Slavic.[12] Closely related to this development is the problem of language: Russian is the official Armed Forces language, yet according to some estimates about 15 percent of the current draft pool can speak it only haltingly.[13] Other differences arise between the urban residents who now comprise more than 60 percent of the draft pool and the draftees from rural communities, whose educational and technical proficiencies are usually much lower.[14] At the same time, the urbanites have more trouble adjusting to the harsh living conditions.[15]

The military has devised ways to tackle these problems. The unofficial motto of the Armed Forces is: "If you can't do something, we'll teach you; if you don't want to do something, we'll make you." This reflects two basic realities: a very heavy training schedule and very tight discipline, enforced by various types of punishment. An important informal arrangement here is the practice of giving enlisted men in their second year (third in the Navy) very considerable power over new conscripts, or the "young ones." While officers spend only part of the day with the enlisted men, these "old men," as they are called, who are confined to barracks with the "young ones," enforce discipline and teach them necessary skills.

An "old man" is expected to train his relief before he is discharged, particularly in the Navy, with its greater technical demands.[16] In exchange for such services officers are usually ready to overlook the fact that "old men" often exploit and habitually abuse the "young ones." The abuse ranges from practical jokes and discriminatory treatment in matters of food to extortion of new uniforms and money. The arrangement works because the "old men" are a highly cohesive group ready to protect their privileges against the disunited "young ones" who find consolation in knowing that, if they behave, they will in time become "old men" themselves.

The Soviet approach to training conscripts is characterized by repetitiveness and a heavy load of classes and exercises as well as by narrow specialization and compartmentalization. Soviet military writers ritualistically call for more "initiative" on the part of servicemen, but "initiative" actually means the more precise implementation of orders and regulations—the main requirement of the Soviet enlisted man. The result of such training is well described by a former Soviet seaman: "We were drilled and drilled and drilled, relentlessly. . . . I could undoubtedly do my job, even now, five years later, in my sleep."[17]

This approach to combat training, like the Soviet military's approach to political indoctrination, is reflected in the training of enlisted men for combat under conditions of nuclear (as well as chemical and biological) warfare. Servicemen operate their equipment while wearing gas masks and protective coveralls; radioactive decontamination is practiced; officers are taught to evaluate the possible effects of nuclear blasts on their units or ships in various circumstances. But any discussion of nuclear issues is narrowed to the presumed essentials of survival and implementation of orders at a given level of the military establishment. This "need to know" approach, based on a very narrow definition of responsibilities, is another indication that questions of nuclear strategy are discussed only by those immediately involved in strategic planning. It is also typical of the compartmentalization of decision-making and of Soviet secretiveness. Servicemen go through the motions of training for nuclear war but have very little interest in matters over which they have no influence and cannot even discuss—not an unwelcome result, obviously, from the point of view of the Soviet military command.[18]

Officers and non-commissioned officers have a whole array of punishments at their disposal to enforce strict discipline. Assignment of extra duties or deprivation of Sunday leaves (these are not granted automatically) are usual for such minor transgressions as a poorly made bed, irregularity in uniform and attempting to argue with a superior. More serious offenses, such as drinking, rudeness to superiors or going AWOL for less than 24 hours can be punished by up to 15 days in the guardhouse. Conditions there are usually harsh: it is often cold; there is no stool or chair; the prisoner has to stand for 18 hours a day (his bed is folded up and bolted to the wall); his rations are reduced. Court-martial is reserved for such offenses as desertion, major negligence, assaulting a superior or mutiny. Offenders at this level are sentenced to confinement in disciplinary battalions, a punishment much feared by servicemen because of the brutality, forced labor and starvation diet characteristic of the Soviet penal system as a whole.

The two most frequent violations of military discipline are drinking and going AWOL. Enlisted men can be punished for drinking even when on Sunday leave, and sobriety in garrison cities is enforced by military patrols. The men are not allowed to carry any unauthorized bags or parcels in their hands so smuggling liquor into the barracks is very difficult. Liquor stores are under orders not to sell anything to enlisted men, who are required always to be in uniform. Drinking still persists, a fact that has affected the image of the Soviet Armed Forces in the West. One should, however, avoid hasty conclusions: for young Soviet males, becoming intoxicated is an act of bravado. It is also inextricably linked with the notion of "enjoying oneself" in a country notorious for its lack of entertainment. This does indeed frequently lead to alcoholism, but not yet in 18- to 20-year-old men. Also, drinking normally takes place when enlisted men are off duty and so does not seriously affect combat readiness. Those who return drunk to the barracks are not given leaves thereafter.

Going AWOL is another serious disciplinary problem. It is frequently related to drinking. But mostly it happens because the sexual needs of soldiers confined to barracks 24 hours a day, without regular leaves, are completely ignored. The AWOL incidence is reduced by such strong preventive measures as military patrols and the ban on wearing civilian clothes at any time. (A recent amendment to the Law on Universal Military Obligation stipulates that on arrival at the place of service, the civilian clothes of the conscripts be mailed home.)[19] Nor does the AWOL problem seriously impair combat readiness, since soldiers know that after 24 hours AWOL is viewed as desertion and punishable by court-martial.

The same factors help to make desertion exceedingly rare. But here the strongest deterrent is the unlikelihood of success in a society where police surveillance is omnipresent and the state controls everything. Lacking the basic document of every Soviet citizen, the internal passport—surrendered at the moment of induction—a deserter would simply be unable to obtain work, medical care or even shelter.

Strict discipline and intensive training are instrumental in solving many problems inherent in a multi-ethnic conscript army. Indeed, ethnic friction is often reduced by the pressure of training and the common feeling it engenders of shared and overcome hardship. At the beginning of their service members of ethnic groups tend to stick together, but friendship patterns soon cross ethnic barriers and common interests and tenure of service become more important.[20]

In top combat priority sectors of the Soviet Armed Forces—such as the Navy—the quality of officers and the educational standards of enlisted men are higher, living conditions less harsh, food more abundant and training more sophisticated. These units appear to succeed better in softening ethnic and other kinds of friction and in achieving good combat cohesion. Moreover, the sheer size of the military allows for flexibility in utilizing the diverse manpower pool: top combat priority branches —the Strategic Rocket Forces, the Paratroops, the combat-ready divisions based in Eastern Europe, the Navy—get a larger share of better educated draftees. The less combat-ready units have to make do with less qualified conscripts while non-combat branches (the construction and railroad troops) absorb such "undesirables" as soldiers not fluent in Russian, members of "politically unreliable" minorities—ethnic Germans or Crimean Tatars, for example—or even former criminals.[21]

The two most recent examples of the Soviet use of military force demonstrate that the disparity between the top combat-ready units and the rest of the Armed Forces is consistent with the functions assigned to them. In Czechoslovakia in 1968 and in Afghanistan in 1979 elite para-troops successfully secured the main military and political targets, while the massive invasion force symbolized the irreversibility of the Soviet move. (The symbolism apparently did not impress the Afghans, but it worked with the Czechs, and with the West, both in 1968 and in 1979.)

While it is too early to assess the impact on the Soviet Armed Forces of the Soviet involvement in Afghanistan, preliminary observations are possible. First, despite rather serious problems with discipline and morale, the Soviet soldier has performed adequately in the conditions of limited, anti-guerrilla warfare for which he was not trained. Second, despite the rigidity of Soviet tactical training, the troops in Afghanistan are obviously beginning to develop more flexible tactics for that par-ticular war. Third, actual combat experience will help to identify and correct various weaknesses in the combat training of Soviet troops. Just as the confrontation with the Chinese in 1969 brought home the need to improve training for conventional warfare, including such simple skills as proper organization of small-arms fire, so the Afghanistan experience will probably result in more realistic training for the Soviet conscript army.[22]

By the time of his discharge, a typical enlisted man has lost whatever youthful interest in military service he once had, but he still believes in the importance of military service.[23] Although he was often tired and homesick, he returns home physically stronger than he was two years earlier. Sporting a snugly fitting uniform with badges, he is in no hurry to change into civilian clothes. He is a center of attention, respect and curiosity for his friends and neighbors, a true man who has fulfilled his duty to his country. Nor is his connection with the Armed Forces over. He is registered in the borough military commissariat as a member of the ready reserves and can be called up for retraining, for as long as three months, at any time. Retraining can take him rather far from home, as it did many a reservist during the invasions of Czechoslovakia and Afghanistan.

Thus, the Armed Forces have a huge pool of reservists with recent ac-tive duty experience who can be easily reintegrated into military life; be-tween 1975 and 1979 the number was about 9,221,000.[24] Of some 180 divisions of the Ground Forces, 46 are combat-ready, 37 are at 50 to 75 percent of their wartime strength, and 97 are below 50 percent of their wartime strength.[25] Reservists with fresh active-duty experience would be used to "flesh out" the units in the last two groups. Still, the simultaneous reintegration of reservists on a large scale has yet to be tested, and so remains one of the major unknowns to be considered by both Soviet and Western military analysts.

Neither reservists nor present and potential soldiers in the Soviet Union are motivated by dreams of military glory, adventure and conquest: this would be incompatible with the basic thrust of their training, which inculcates obedience and duty. Rather, they perceive military service as an unavoidable part of life. For them, being a man includes putting on the uniform whenever one is told to do so by the authorities.

In this era of nuclear stalemate, with its corresponding emphasis on perceptions of readiness to apply conventional military might, the Soviet Union has a definite advantage over the West in its potential for mobilizing its forces quickly and smoothly, without disruption and protest on the part of either the conscripts themselves or the population in general. This provides the Soviet ruling elite with credible military muscle which they can flex at will. □

**1.** Andrei Grechko, *The Armed Forces of the Soviet State* (Washington, D.C.: U.S. Air Force, "Soviet Military Thought Series," No. 12, 1975), p. 157.

**2.** *The Military Balance, 1982-83* (London: International Institute for Strategic Studies, 1982), p. 13.

**3.** See Rebecca V. Strode, "Soviet Strategic Style," *Comparative Strategy*, 3, No. 4 (1982), p. 328.

**4.** *Narodnoe khoziaistvo SSSR v 1979* (Moscow: 1980), pp. 498, 503. In the United States, by contrast, with a total population some 20 percent smaller, the corresponding figure was 6,991,000 — half, again, women: see *Statistical Abstract of the United States* (Washington, D.C.: Department of Commerce, Bureau of the Census, 1980), p. 165.

**5.** "O vnesenii izmenenii i dopolnenii v zakon SSSR 'O vseobshchei voinskoi obiazannosti,'" *Vedomosti Verkhovnogo Soveta SSSR*, No. 52 (Dec. 24, 1980), pp. 1129-30.

**6.** Aleksei Myagkov, *Inside the KGB* (New York: Ballantine Books, 1981), p. 145.

**7.** Myagkov, *Inside*, p. 147.

**8.** Robert Bathurst, Michael Burger, Ellen Wolffe, *The Soviet Sailor: Combat Readiness and Morale* (Arlington, Virginia: Ketron, Inc., 1982), p. 22.

**9.** Zdenek Mylnar, *Nightfrost in Prague* (New York: Karz Publishers, 1980), p. 186.

**10.** Robert Bathurst, Michael Burger, "Controlling the Soviet Soldier: Some Eyewitness Accounts," *Occasional Papers*, No. 1, Center for Strategic Technology, Texas A&M University (1981), p. 22.

**11.** Bathurst, Burger, Wolffe, *The Soviet Sailor*, p. 24.

**12.** Ellen Jones, "Manning the Soviet Military," *International Security* (Summer 1982), p. 118.

**13.** Ellen Jones, "Minorities in the Soviet Armed Forces," *Comparative Strategy*, 3, No. 4 (1982), p. 295.

**14.** Ellen Jones, Fred W. Grupp, "Political Socialization in the Soviet Military," *Armed Forces and Society* (Spring 1982), p. 357.

**15.** Jones, "Manning the Soviet Military."

**16.** Bathurst, Burger, Wolffe, *The Soviet Sailor*, p. 48.

17. Bathurst, Burger, Wolffe, p. 49.

18. Bathurst, Burger, Wolffe, pp. 1-5.

19. "O vnesenii izmenenii i dopolnenii v zakon SSSR 'O vseobshchei voinskoi obazannosti,'" p. 1128.

20. Jones, "Minorities in the Soviet Armed Forces," p. 299.

21. Bathurst, Burger, Wolffe, pp. 16-17, 39; Jones, Grupp, "Political Socialization," p. 369.

22. For details, see David C. Isby, "Afghanistan 1982," *International Defense Review*, 15, No. 11 (1982), pp. 1523-28.

23. Jones, "Manning the Soviet Military," p. 122.

24. John M. Collins, *U.S.-Soviet Military Balance: Concepts and Capabilities, 1960-80* (New York: McGraw-Hill, 1980), p. 89.

25. John L. Scherer, ed., *USSR Facts and Figures Annual* (Gulf Breeze, Florida: Academic International Press, 1982), 6, p. 101.

# 10

## Military Strategy in the Nuclear Age

*Eugenia V. Osgood*

In the compartmentalized edifice of Marxist-Leninist military theory, military strategy occupies a very special place. Together with operational art and tactics it constitutes "military art," the most intuitive and imaginative, as well as the most important, component of military science, which is the "objective" study of warfare.

Owing to the nature of the problems it is required to solve, military strategy enjoys a certain freedom in its choice of means for the achievement of its goals. But it is both circumscribed and governed by the general principles laid down in military doctrine. While military doctrine is the ensemble of official views on the nature of war and represents the essence of the state's military policy, military strategy deals with actual plans and preparations for war, the employment of forces in combat and the strategic views of any adversaries.

Official Soviet policy has always proclaimed that the Soviet Union is a champion of peace, and its military doctrine has consistently maintained a defensive stance. But Soviet military strategy, which is a tool of policy, has always—both in the pre-nuclear and in the nuclear age—favored offensive over defensive operations. Most Western commentators view this stance as one largely determined by Soviet capabilities.

Thus, especially since the Soviet acquisition of nuclear weapons, Westerners have taken a dim view of Soviet offensive strategy. Almost inevitably they have drawn the conclusion that a doctrine calling for warfighting capabilities, when combined with an offensive strategy, translates into an aggressive stance. This, they conclude, makes the initiation of nuclear war likely, if not imminent. But such reasoning omits a very important factor in the formation of Soviet doctrine and strategy: the historical conditioning of a nation's mentality, and the convergence of this mentality with a new set of military options.

A "war mentality" has characterized the Soviet Union from the beginning, the result of a hostile international environment encapsulated in the phrase "capitalist encirclement." Yet the concept of the offensive had been emphasized by Russian strategists as far back as the eighteenth century, when the famous Russian general Suvorov extolled the primacy of the offensive and became a proponent of the strategy of annihilation. In the 1920s the Soviet commander M.V. Frunze, often considered the inventor of Soviet strategy, taught that the offensive was superior to the defensive because it was "good for the morale of the army." Frunze believed that the tactical and strategic concepts of the Red Army should be based on the offensive. Lenin, after all, had said that "the offensive and not the defense should become the slogan of the masses," and Marshal Mikhail Tukhachevsky, victorious Bolshevik commander in the Civil War, had urged that the offensive was the only strategy that could lead to victory. More recently, Stalin was convinced that only an offensive strategy could allow the Soviet army to prevail over its adversary.

So it is ironic that while the Red Army had evolved a fairly coherent and predominantly offensive military strategy prior to World War II, what saved it from defeat in that conflict was a contingency plan based on the Clausewitzian concept of defense in depth. The German thrust deep into Soviet territory, the defense mounted by the Soviet forces and the subsequent counteroffensive all seem to have been lifted from Clausewitz's book *On War*, and to have followed a pattern established by Napoleon's Russian campaign of 1812. Defense and counteroffense, with all that they entailed in terms of extensive destruction on one's own territory and millions of dead, were the Russian experience in World War II—and not the offensive initiated beyond the country's borders. But the "revolution in military affairs" that began in about 1950, with its new atomic and then thermonuclear weapons, promised to change all that. These weapons would make it possible to defend the country with offensive weapons aimed at enemy territory without having first to retreat into the Soviet interior.[1]

Indeed, this revolutionary convergence of theory and weapons meant that the familiar concept of the offensive was now to be implemented by the strategic nuclear missiles which the Soviet Union began to acquire in the 1950s. No grander scenario was ever drawn up for the delectation of military minds. In the words of a senior Soviet strategist, the future nuclear world war would encompass all continents and be waged on the ground, on the seas, in the air and in space, where the "incredible spatial expansion of combat action" would kill hundreds of millions of people and bring about the "simultaneous defeat and destruction of the enemy's economic potential and armed forces throughout its territory."[2]

Such a conflict would embody Clausewitz's dream of the "absolute war" which, "untrammelled by any conventional restraints," would break out "in all its elemental fury."[3] Militarily, it would be an unprecedented feat of arms, for it would bring about a triumph of pure strategy, accomplishing everything in one fell swoop, without "friction" and without the intermediate stages of operational art and tactics. This was heady stuff, and it undoubtedly appealed to military men, many of whom viewed nuclear weapons as simply the highest achievement in firepower and maneuverability. The firepower of the nuclear warhead, coupled with the mobility of the rocket, became the strategic factor that would determine the outcome of war.

Yet the explosive power of the nuclear missile, which seemed to make it a perfect weapon for a warfighting strategy, led other Soviet analysts to an appreciation of its tremendous deterrent value. During his years in office Nikita Khrushchev, having first rejected Georgy Malenkov's 1954 declaration that nuclear war would be "a catastrophe for all mankind," gradually came to accept this view. Realizing that the wholesale destruction resulting from the use of nuclear weapons could make a general war suicidal for both sides, and that such a war should be avoided at all costs, Khrushchev formulated a "minimum deterrence" nuclear strategy.

At the Twentieth Party Congress in 1956 he proclaimed that war between socialism and capitalism was not inevitable and that a peaceful transition to socialism would take its place. Khrushchev thus amended that well-entrenched Soviet dictum which had served to justify Stalin's massive defense effort. He also implied that deterrence of the capitalist adversary was possible, thanks mainly to Soviet possession of the new "superweapon," as the thermonuclear bomb was then called.

Then, in January 1960, in a speech before the Supreme Soviet, Khrushchev formally unveiled his new "deterrence only," one-weapon strategy—a strategy which relied in essence on the terror-inspiring might of nuclear missiles. At the same time, he advocated deep cuts in the ground forces while promising to equip them with vastly improved firepower. His bold initiative, however, did not please the Soviet military, who rejected the one-weapon strategy as unsound. For while Khrushchev thought of preventing war and believed that a stable nuclear stand-off would eliminate or at least minimize crises, the military was concerned with the contingency of having to fight a war, and viewed crises as inevitable. Soviet military strategists still doubted that the "imperialists" could be successfully deterred, or that they would give up their "aggressive designs." The strategists saw all-out nuclear exchange or surrender as the only alternatives under Khrushchev's new deterrence strategy.

Khrushchev's dictum, that "peaceful coexistence or catastrophic war" are the only choices open to humanity, has remained in force in the Soviet Union, and is proclaimed today more loudly than ever before by the leadership. But his pure deterrence stance was quickly discredited after his ouster in 1964, as were the deep troop cuts. In fact, even before Khrushchev's departure a compromise strategic solution had been worked out by a team of military strategists under Marshal V.D. Sokolovsky. Their book, *Military Strategy*, first published in 1962, went to a second edition in 1963, to allow for a critique of the new U.S. counterforce strategy made public in June 1962 by Secretary of Defense Robert S. McNamara.

Sokolovsky's team, authors of the grandiose nuclear scenario quoted above, retained Khrushchev's reliance on the mighty rocket weapons, which were to be employed in massive strikes on both military and industrial-economic targets deep in the enemy's territory. They did not, however, relinquish the traditional Russian emphasis on the role of mass armies. Because of the huge number of casualties to be expected, they argued, even larger armies would be needed in a nuclear war. And while graphically depicting the devastation that would be wrought by it, they steered clear of the notion of "mutual assured destruction." Instead, they foresaw victory for the morally and socially superior socialist camp, which would crush any "imperialist aggressor."

Meanwhile, the Soviet Union began to build up its nuclear component, and in the 1960s and 1970s land-based missiles, both intercontinental (targeted on the United States) and regional (deployed against Western Europe and China), became the mainstay of the Soviet nuclear deterrent. Even today, land-based missiles comprise 75 percent of the Soviet intercontinental nuclear forces, the remaining 25 percent being divided between relatively small fleets of long-range bombers and of submarines equipped with nuclear weapons.

In Soviet eyes deterrence—*sderzhivanie putem ustrasheniia* or "containment through intimidation"—is considered a Western concept. Yet we can speak of a Soviet nuclear deterrent since, under prevailing Soviet military doctrine, deterrence is the principal mission of their nuclear component, just as it is the principal mission of U.S. strategic forces. We should also remember that the Soviet nuclear stance has often been misinterpreted in the West because it differs from the Western notion of "deterrence through punishment." The Soviet variant, by contrast, implies denial of success to an adversary's plans. It requires massive capabilities as well as reliance on a preemptive or a launch-under-attack posture in response to a nuclear strike, rather than on riding out the attack and then inflicting unacceptable punishment on the aggressor.

Much has been written about the importance of preemption and surprise in Soviet strategy, and about the aggressive connotations of these terms. The truth is, however, that in the 1950s, when the fear of nuclear surprise attack in Europe was so acute as to lead to the convocation of the Geneva surprise attack conference (1958), *both* sides considered preemption as the only viable option for their slowly fired, vulnerable, first-generation missiles. But by the early 1960s improvements in warning technology and in missile design had already begun to make preemption both unnecessary and unfeasible. Today preemption on the intercontinental level simply is no longer a valid option. Warning systems have made it possible for either side to fire its missiles during the 30-minute flight time required by the other's missiles, and after receiving unambiguous signals that an attack has been launched.

For a while the surprise factor assumed a disproportionate importance at the strategic level, both in the U.S. strategy of massive retaliation, with its emphasis on seizing the strategic initiative, and in the Soviet option of preempting an impending attack. Strategic surprise became less of a threat during the 1960s when, in addition to improving their warning systems, the Soviets began to acquire their second generation of storable liquid-fuel missiles that could be fired at from four to eight minutes' notice. At the same time, the United States built solid-fuel systems that could be launched practically at the turn of a key. Perhaps for propaganda purposes, or to keep relations at a suitably adversarial level, the Soviets continued through the 1970s to accuse the United States of preparing a surprise attack against them while the United States kept levelling similar accusations against the Soviets, invariably viewing Soviet intentions with suspicion.

To be sure, Western mistrust of Soviet intentions has been exacerbated by the ambiguities surrounding the Soviet force posture, with its preponderance of heavy land-based missiles believed to be targeted on U.S. strategic forces with a potentially "disarming" intent, and by ambiguities in the Soviet view of nuclear war as a possible instrument of policy. Even though Soviet leaders have always assured the world that their nuclear weapons would never be used in a first strike, and Khrushchev proclaimed that nuclear war could not serve the purposes of *socialist* politics, the issue remained unsettled.

More exactly, in the middle 1960s a doctrinal debate flared up in the Soviet military centering on the challenge Khrushchev's "revision" posed to the Marxist-Leninist (originally Clausewitzian) dictum that war is a continuation of politics by other means. A nuclear war, it was argued, would be even more "political," for it would be the final confrontation between the two opposed systems from which socialism would emerge victorious to fulfill its historic mission. This "orthodox" line persisted side by side with the outright condemnation of nuclear war by the eminent Soviet strategist General M. Talensky and others. The debate continued until 1967, when an unsigned article in the January 24, 1967 issue of *Red Star*, the authoritative military journal, put an end to it. There, the orthodox position on the viability of nuclear war as an instrument of policy was repudiated with a quotation from the current Program of the Communist Party of the Soviet Union: "Nuclear war cannot and must not serve as a means towards the solution of a political conflict. All peaceloving and anti-imperialist forces oppose world war as a means for the continuation of politics."

This statement seemed to tally with the Soviet contention that no first use of nuclear weapons would ever be contemplated by the Soviet Union. But in a nuclear war the even more critical question of what victory could mean remained unanswered. Military spokesmen ritually endorsed the triumph of socialism and the final extinction of capitalism. The third edition of *Military Strategy*, published in 1968 with very few changes, again confidently affirmed that a "general victory" was possible in a nuclear war as a result of the simultaneous "application of the entire might of the state."[4] Still, the fact that its authors, like other military theoreticians, never explained how such a victory could be obtained after absorbing either a massive nuclear first strike by an aggressor or a devastating retaliatory blow, gave rise to doubt as to the seriousness of their assertions, no matter how confidently phrased. Indeed, among some analysts the Soviet belief in victory here seemed more a patriotic exhortation than a realistic forecast.

When the SALT I interim agreement on offensive arms was signed by the United States and the Soviet Union in 1972, it was based on the principle of mutual assured destruction: the belief that both sides could completely destroy each other, either in a retaliatory or in a preemptive strike. SALT I also upheld the principle of parity rather than the striving for superiority; and in place of "equal security" and mutual survival, it stressed mutual vulnerability (reinforced by the signing of a separate treaty limiting anti-ballistic missile defenses). SALT I thus ran counter to some of the most cherished Soviet beliefs in the field of nuclear strategy and contradicted much of official Soviet rhetoric. Not surprisingly, acceptance of the new relationship with the United States, and of its implications with respect to weapons acquisition and nuclear strategy, was a slow and painful process for the Soviet military.

A debate, this time between military conservatives and mostly civilian moderates, flared up in 1973, soon after the signing of SALT I. Like the earlier debate, it concerned the viability of nuclear war and the possibility of victory. The "moderates" (mostly specialists from the Institute for the Study of the United States and Canada of the Soviet Academy of Sciences) underscored the futility of further arms competition, saw victory in a nuclear war as at best Pyrrhic, and pointed to the economic benefits of arms control and of stable deterrence. Spokesmen for the military-political establishment, on the other hand, still thought victory in a nuclear war possible and advocated a warfighting capability to forestall the growing threat of "imperialist aggression." They criticized the "quantifiers" from the Institute for placing too much stress on the material damage that would result from a nuclear war, and for discounting the "moral superiority" of the communist side.

Since 1973, however, the conservatives have softened their stance considerably. A treatise produced in 1977 by members of the faculty of the Lenin Military-Political Academy attests to the shift to a pro-deterrence and pro-detente orientation, at least among the military-political elite (as distinguished from the usually more hard-line General Staff officers). The authors of the treatise take a dim view of nuclear war as an instrument of policy, since it would not be conducive to attaining the dual Soviet political objective: to "topple capitalism at any cost," and to build communism.

Statements by Soviet spokesmen on "mutual assured destruction" have been few and far between over the years, at least partly for ideological reasons. Mutual destruction is not seen as part of the Marxist-Leninist historical process, while the victory of socialism is. Yet declarations of the "catastrophic" effects of nuclear war, which imply belief in assured destruction, have become common since the later 1970s. Leonid Brezhnev in particular frequently pictured nuclear war as the ultimate tragedy for all humanity, and even expressed the fear that the final "ideological dispute," should it ever arise, would end in catastrophe for both camps since, along with millions of people, their ideas would also perish.[5]

During Brezhnev's last years in office, and now under the new Soviet leadership, high-level Soviet civilian and military spokesmen have been endorsing what amounts to the doctrine of mutual assured destruction, stressing the unacceptable damage that would result from a general nuclear war. Some Western observers have speculated that this apparent acceptance of mutual assured destruction may have come about because the Soviet military realized that continued weapons modernization and a qualitative buildup were not hampered by SALT; equally, that the numerical parity that SALT called for was not the equivalent of functional parity. Thus while adhering to the "parity" of mutual assured destruction, so the argument goes, the Soviet Union proceeded through the 1970s to acquire a lead—a strategic "edge" in some systems—which it could then exploit to gain political leverage. Whether this lead could also be translated into any militarily meaningful results, apart from a more secure deterrence against a first strike, is debatable.

In any case, the Soviet leadership appears more reluctant than ever to fight a nuclear war. Certainly, the solemn Soviet pledge at the June 1982 U.N. Special Session on Disarmament never to use nuclear weapons first must act as more of a constraint on Soviet action than all previous peace campaigns and assurances that nuclear weapons are unsuitable as an instrument of policy. While dismissed by U.S. leaders as "only words," there is every indication that this pledge carries considerable political

### The U.S./Soviet Strategic Balance in 1964 and 1982

#### July 1964

|  | United States | Soviet Union |
|---|---|---|
| ICBMS | 834 | 190 |
| SLBMS | 416 | 107 |
| Bombers | 630 | 175 |
| **Total** | 1,880 | 472 |

#### July 1982

|  |  |  |
|---|---|---|
| ICBMS | 1,052 | 1,398 |
| SLBMS | 520 | 969 |
| Bombers | 376 | 150 |
| **Total** | 1,948 | 2,517 |
| Missile warheads | 6,920 | 7,000 (approx.) |
| Missile and bomber warheads | 9,268 | 7,300 (approx.) |

ICBM = Intercontinental ballistic missile (land-based: 1982 range up to 15,000 kilometers).

SLBM = submarine-launched ballistic missile (1982 range up to 9,100 kilometers).

Bomber = long-range bomber (U.S. 1982 range up to 16,000 kilometers; Soviet up to 12,800 kilometers).

Warheads = independently targetable nuclear weapons.

*Source*: International Institute for Strategic Studies, *The Military Balance 1977-1978* (London, 1977), p. 80 (for 1964); *The Military Balance, 1982-1983* (London, 1982), pp. 114-115, 140 (for 1982).

weight in the Soviet Union itself, making the deliberate initiation of nuclear war by the Soviet leadership very unlikely.

In June 1982, again, the Soviet leadership allowed the ideas of victory and of survival in a nuclear war to be publicly questioned by a team of Soviet and U.S. doctors. Before a television audience of millions, the team discussed the incalculable consequences of a nuclear exchange and concluded that even in a limited nuclear confrontation medical help would be almost nonexistent, since doctors would be able to treat only a small fraction of the huge number of casualties. In other words, as Nikita Khrushchev once put it, "the living would envy the dead." The doctors agreed in denying the possibility of anything even approaching victory. They stressed the view that a nuclear conflict would inevitably escalate to the global level, and asserted that nuclear war could endanger the very survival of mankind.

By allowing the program to air, the Soviet leadership implicitly endorsed its findings, leaving little doubt about official Soviet attitudes in the matter of general nuclear war. This reorientation is noticeable even at the "hard core" of the military establishment. Compare Marshal N.V. Ogarkov's low-key, cautious, seemingly pro-forma formulation in 1979 of an "objective possibility" of the Soviet Union's prevailing in a protracted nuclear war[6] with the brash rhetoric describing socialism's sweeping victory and the catastrophic end of imperialism in Marshal Sokolovsky's *Military Strategy* of the 1960s.

There is a growing consensus in the West that the Soviets may really believe in mutual assured destruction at the level of general war. But many in the West still suspect that the Soviet Union would consider initiating a *limited* nuclear war, possibly against military targets alone, and with smaller, more accurate and less damage-producing weapons. The Soviet Union, so the theory goes, would then try to blackmail the leaders either of NATO or of the United States into making major concessions, if not surrendering outright, on the principle that such a course of action was preferable to an all-out nuclear exchange. Or perhaps it is thought that Soviet conventional superiority in some theaters would preclude Western resistance. At any rate, since limited nuclear war has been traditionally a taboo subject in Soviet writings on strategy and doctrine, it is almost impossible to ascertain what the Soviets really think about it—even though their capabilities are now such that limited nuclear use is theoretically feasible.

Still, Soviet military leaders have emphatically denied that limited nuclear war scenarios have ever been developed by their staffs. They have persistently rejected the Western notion of escalation control or of deterrence and bargaining in the midst of war, perhaps because such views contradict the traditional Soviet image of an apocalyptic clash between two opposed systems. Soviet military writings describe nuclear flexibility as destabilizing—because it may make the use of nuclear weapons more likely—and maintain that nuclear forces exist solely for retaliation on the attacker's homeland with massive counter-military and counter-economic strikes. Nor do the Soviets publicly contemplate a "counterforce" strike aimed at weapons alone. Many U.S. analysts, however, are convinced that selective options are well within the reach of Soviet nuclear forces and that they exist in Soviet war plans—both at the intercontinental level, in the form of a counterforce strike on the vulnerable U.S. Minuteman force, and in the European and Asian theaters, where the new mobile SS-20 intermediate-range missiles have made it possible for the Soviet Union to implement a limited strike strategy.

Nevertheless, apart from having acknowledged with some satisfaction the newly acquired accuracy of Soviet strategic and regional missiles and their ability to strike a wide variety of targets, Soviet generals have given no indication as to what changes these developments might mean for their nuclear strategy. Rather, new SS-20s, although much more accurate than their predecessors (the SS-4s and SS-5s), are said to have basically "the same mission," that is, they are aimed at European military targets. And that is as much as Soviet spokesmen will say.

One reason why they are reluctant to make public any contingency plans involving limited nuclear use may be that this would imply the existence of a first-use option, which Soviet leaders have explicitly disavowed. Moreover, it may be that the Soviet Union has less need to retain either a first-use option or plans involving limited nuclear employment than does the United States. Unlike the United States, it is not party to a nuclear contract extending a "deterrence umbrella" to distant allies; nor is it under any obligation to use nuclear weapons first, in a limited way, to prevent a conventional defeat. Even though nuclear use has been fully integrated into the Soviet battlefield posture for years, Soviet strategists are probably more interested in reliably deterring NATO's first use should a conventional conflict break out in Europe. And there is of course the possibility that, should NATO engage in a limited strike on Soviet territory, Moscow would choose an appropriately limited response rather than unleash Armageddon.

Any changes in Soviet nuclear strategy and nuclear employment must remain matters of speculation until the strategists of the Soviet General Staff come forward with a follow-up to the last edition of their *Military Strategy* (1968). So far there is no indication that this is about to happen.

Meanwhile, one can only guess that having officially admitted that meaningful victory through a massive nuclear strike is impossible in a general nuclear war, they will adopt the strategy either of mutually assured destruction or of limited retaliation and intra-war bargaining. But they might also opt for a greater conventional emphasis. Or they might decide in favor of a defensive strategy of "assured survival" by deploying new high-efficiency, anti-missile technologies, possibly together with—or in response to—a parallel U.S. move.

Whatever the Soviet General Staff might do in this field, it is to be hoped that its nuclear strategy will be compatible with arms control and will adequately provide for the security of the country without increasing the danger of war. ☐

1. For the Soviet "military revolution," as it is called by Soviet military writers, and related material, see Harriet Fast Scott and William F. Scott, *The Soviet Art of War: Doctrine, Strategy, and Tactics* (Boulder, Colorado: Westview Press, 1982).

2. See Marshal of the Soviet Union V.D. Sokolovsky, ed., *Voennaia Strategiia*, 2nd ed. (Moscow: Voenizdat, 1963), p. 19.

3. Carl von Clausewitz, *On War* (Princeton, New Jersey: Princeton University Press, 1976), pp. 593, 351-59.

4. V.D. Sokolovsky, *Voennaia Strategiia*, 3rd ed. (Moscow: Voenizdat, 1968).

5. *Aktual'nye voprosy ideologicheskoi raboty KPSS*, Vol. 2 (Moscow: Polizdat, 1978), p. 564.

6. Marshal of the Soviet Union N.V. Ogarkov, "Strategiia voennaia," *Sovetskaia voennaia entsiklopediia*, Vol. 7 (Moscow: Voenizdat, 1979), p. 564.

*The views expressed in this paper are solely those of the author and do not represent the position of the Library of Congress or of any other agency of the U.S. government.*

# THE PHYSICAL CONTEXT

We now turn to the physical context of Soviet life today, beginning with the country's basic geography. Chauncy D. Harris reminds us of the Soviet Union's vast extent, extremes of climate, variety of vegetation and ethnic diversity, and indicates some of the economic consequences of its geographical situation. John M. Kramer then discusses major environmental problems which have emerged in the Soviet Union, contrary to Communist doctrine; problems that arise from the conflicting demands—familiar enough in the West—of economic development and environmental protection.

Economic as well as technical and aesthetic issues are raised by William C. Brumfield in his discussion of developments in Soviet architecture and urban planning since World War II, when approximately one third of all Soviet housing (already inadequate by Western standards) was severely damaged or destroyed. Again we see that massive efforts to overcome critical shortages have brought in their train huge new problems, many of them peculiar to the Soviet system. And we see, in the mass construction of high-rise housing complexes, the Soviet commitment to a policy which has been largely discredited in the West. The Soviet built environment is steadily realizing the Utopian dreams—or nightmares—of certain Western planners and builders of the early twentieth century, marking another sharp divergence between the Soviet Union and the West.

# 11 THE PHYSICAL CONTEXT

## Basic Geography

*Chauncy D. Harris*

The important geographical features of the Soviet Union are its immense size, great longitudinal extent, high latitudinal position, large aggregate quantity of forest, energy, mineral and agricultural resources, and the diversity of its peoples. On a per unit area basis, however, these resources are moderate. Their location is often unfavorable. Diverse climates, vegetation and soils form great landscape zones sweeping across the country. The state has asserted ownership of land and all other resources of the country and has pursued a policy of developing an industrial and urban society.

The Soviet Union is such a large country and extends for such a long distance in an east-west direction that it is difficult to depict the country on a map without serious distortion. It is possible to show true area, shape, angle and distance of the Soviet Union only on the surface of a globe. Any map drawn on a flat piece of paper must distort one or more of these qualities.

• Figure 1 is drawn on a sinusoidal projection to make possible easy comparisons of northerly position or distances from the equator. It is also an equal area projection on which the parallels, or lines of latitude that measure distance north of the equator in degrees, are drawn as horizontal. But the angles and therefore the shapes and distances are badly distorted on the edges of the map.

• Figures 2, 4, 5 and 7 are drawn on a conic projection, commonly used in Soviet atlases to show the entire country. Its key quality is the representation of true shapes because the meridians and parallels cross each other at right angles, as on the globe. Since the parallels are circles and the meridians diverging straight lines, apparent directions change in different parts of the map. In following a horizontal line at the top of the

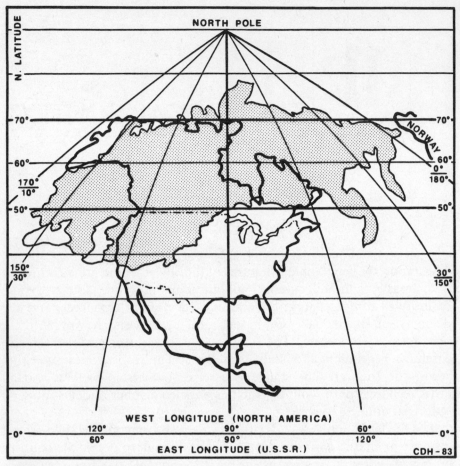

**Figure 1.** Relative size and location of the Soviet Union and North America. The Soviet Union lies in high latitudes and extends for 170° of longitude. It thus has a cool or cold, generally dry, extreme continental climate which limits agriculture. (Islands omitted.)

map from left to right one is travelling first northward (in the upper left) and then southward (in the upper right). Comparisons of latitude and all features associated with it—such as length of day, temperatures, seasons, climate and vegetation—are more difficult on this projection than on the sinusoidal, but the shapes are far superior.

• Figure 3 is drawn on Lambert's azimuthal equal-area projection in which both the meridians and parallels are curved lines. On it shapes, angles and distances are all only moderately distorted.

In looking at any map of the Soviet Union, one should bear in mind that the meridians run true north-south and the parallels true east-west. The lettering on the maps in this chapter generally follows the orientation of the parallels and thus helps the reader in sensing directions on a map. If in examining maps of the Soviet Union on a conic projection

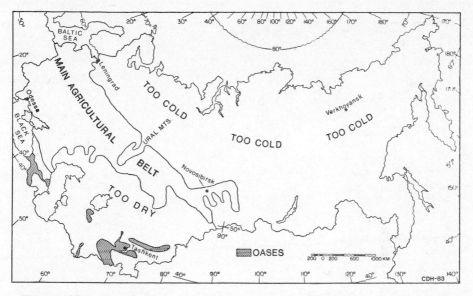

**Figure 2.** Main agricultural belt of the Soviet Union and areas generally too cold or too dry for agriculture. For climatic data of five cities named on map see table. (Generalized from distribution of state farms depicted in *Atlas SSSR*, 1st ed., pp. 112-13, and 2nd ed., pp. 114-15, and from sown area depicted in *Atlas Razvitiia Khoziaistva i Kul'tury*, pp. 62-63, and *Atlas Sel'skogo Khoziaistva SSSR*, pp. 102-3.)

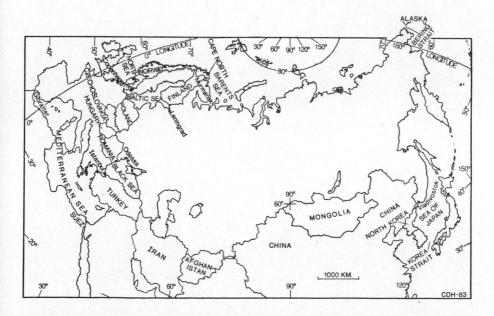

**Figure 3.** Boundaries and bordering seas of the Soviet Union. (Based on *The Times Atlas of the World*, Comprehensive edition, 5th ed., 1975, Plate 16.)

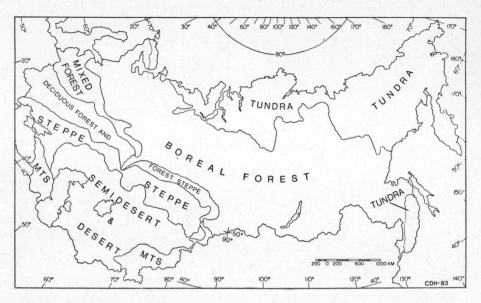

**Figure 4.** Vegetation belts of the Soviet Union. (Greatly simplified from *Atlas SSSR*, 2nd ed., pp. 90-91.)

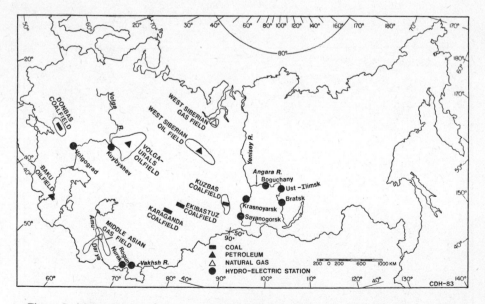

**Figure 5.** Major sources of energy in the Soviet Union. Only the largest producers are shown. (Based on *Atlas SSSR*, 2nd ed., pp. 105, 106; Leslie Dienes and Theodore Shabad, *The Soviet Energy System*, pp. 45-150; and Paul Lydolph, *Geography of the USSR: Topical Analysis*, pp. 261-301.)

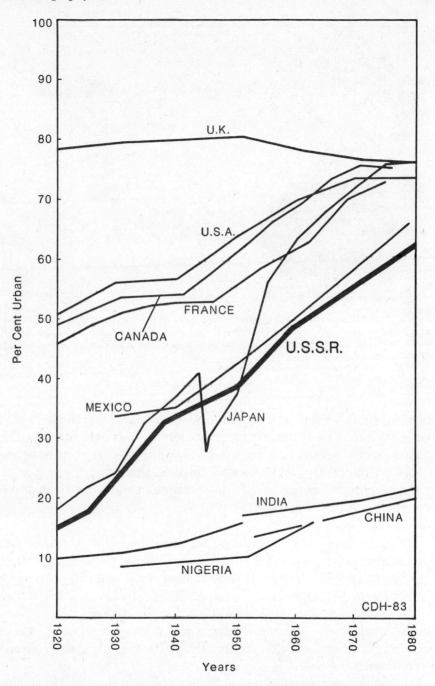

**Figure 6.** Percentage of the population urban, selected countries, 1920-1980. (Sources: *Narodnoe Khoziaistvo SSSR v 1980g.: statisticheskii ezhegodnik*, p. 7; United Nations, *Demographic Yearbook 1955*, pp. 510-73, 1960, pp. 373-95, 1972, pp. 296-327, 1973, pp. 666-85, Historical supplement, special issue, 1979, pp. 189-209, and 1980, pp. 159-96; and official statistics of individual countries, partly estimated.)

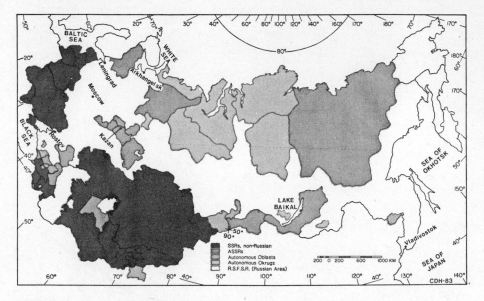

**Figure 7.** Non-Russian administrative-territorial units of the Soviet Union. (Sources: SSSR. *Administrativno-territorial'noe Delenie Soiuznykh Respublik, 1977,* p. 15 and folded map; *Atlas* SSSR, 2nd ed., pp. 2-3; and *Narodnoe Khoziaistvo* SSSR *v 1980g.: statisticheskii ezhegodnik,* pp. 12-17.)

one turns one's head so that the parallels are horizontal in the field of vision, the head is tilted to the right in looking at the western part of the country, with the result that the Baltic Sea appears to run north-south (as it does on the Earth); if the head is tilted to the left in looking at the eastern part of the country, the Bering Strait appears to run north-south, as it does in reality.

The Soviet Union is a giant among the countries of the world. Of continental dimensions, it is larger than South America, only slightly smaller than North America (Figure 1), and almost three times the size of the conterminous 48 states of the United States. It covers 22.4 million square kilometers compared with 17.8 for South America; 24.3 for North America; 7.8 for the conterminous United States. It includes about one-sixth of the land surface of the globe, excluding areas covered by continental ice sheets.

The Soviet Union extends nearly halfway around the globe in an east-west direction, or some 170 degrees of longitude (from 20 degrees east longitude eastward past 180 to 170 degrees/west longitude), through 11 time zones, or nearly 10,000 kilometers. (The east-west distance around the globe is 40,000 kilometers at the equator and 20,000 at 60 degrees north latitude). This is equivalent to stretching from the west tip of Alaska across North America and the Atlantic Ocean to Norway. As a result of this great longitudinal extent the Soviet Union has the most continental climate of any country in the world.

Most of the Soviet Union lies between 50 degrees and 70 degrees north latitude, farther north than any part of the conterminous 48 states of the United States. (The east-west segment of the United States-Canadian boundary is 49 degrees north latitude). The north-south extent of the Soviet Union is about 3,000 kilometers in the western part of the country and about 2,500 kilometers in the eastern part.

As a result of its high latitude most of the Soviet Union has a cool or cold climate. More than half of the Soviet Union lies north of the band of land which has continuous agricultural settlement. On Figure 2 this area is marked "too cold."

Because of its great longitudinal extent, most of the Soviet Union lies deep in the interior, far from the western ocean, which provides moderating influences and moisture through the "Prevailing Westerlies." The Arctic Ocean on the north is frozen much of the year. The Pacific Ocean on the east affects only a narrow band of Soviet territory. As a result, the climate is continental and generally dry. Much of the interior of the country in Soviet Central Asia consists of vast desert or semiarid stretches marked "too dry" on Figure 2; only where rivers issue from high mountains and bring life-giving waters for irrigation are there oases, agriculture and dense settlements.

The core of the Soviet Union, the main agricultural belt, occupies only about a sixth of its territory but contains most of its agriculture, people, industry and cities (Figure 2). This belt has a broad base along the western border of the Soviet Union, south from Leningrad and the Baltic Sea to Odessa and the Black Sea. It then extends eastward to the Ural Mountains, around the southern Urals and, in a narrower belt, to just beyond Novosibirsk—to the boundary of Western and Eastern Siberia and of the Soviet Union with China and Mongolia, near 90 degrees east longitude and 50 degrees north latitude.

Expansion of farming to the north and northeast of this core territory is prevented by a combination of unfavorable characteristics: short growing season, cool summer, irregular weather (with danger of unseasonable frosts), infertile podsol soils, generally poor drainage and, in the eastern part of the country, permanently frozen subsoil (permafrost). At the same time, expansion of agriculture on the dry margin to the south and southeast is discouraged by the low annual rainfall, irregularity and undependability of rainfall, and by occasional desiccating winds, called *sukhovei*.

Partly as a result of its huge size, the Soviet Union has the longest land frontier in the world. It has boundaries with 12 countries, more even than Brazil or China, which also border many countries, and far more than other large countries, such as the United States, which borders only two countries, or Australia, with no land frontier at all. Since the Soviet Union stretches across Eastern Europe, Middle Asia, and the Far East, it has boundaries with Norway, Finland, Poland, Czechoslovakia, Hungary and Romania in the west, with Turkey, Iran and Afghanistan in the south and with China, Mongolia and North Korea in the southeast. The boundary between the Soviet Union and China is comparable in length to the one between the United States and Canada, and that between the Soviet Union and Mongolia to the line between the United States and Mexico. In general, the southern boundaries of the Soviet Union lie in sparsely settled areas of deserts or mountains; but in the west the border areas are open and densely settled.

The Soviet Union has the longest coastline of any country—and the most useless. In the north the entire Arctic coastline is largely blocked by ice for most of the year. The major ports lie not on the open ocean but on seas, which can be blockaded in time of war. Ships from Leningrad in the west must go through the Baltic Sea and past Copenhagen. Ships from Odessa in the southwest must go through the Black Sea and past Istanbul to reach the Mediterranean, a closed sea except for the Strait of Gibraltar. Ships in the east from Vladivostok must go through the Sea of Japan and out through the Korea Strait, while ships from Murmansk in the extreme northwest must exit through the Barents Sea around Cape North. In peacetime these sea lanes are open; but in wartime they may become choke points controlled by a foreign power.

The extreme continentality and general low precipitation of the Soviet Union is revealed by the accompanying table.

• Odessa, on the Black Sea, in the extreme southwest of the country (Figure 2) has a climate much like Chicago (-3 degrees centigrade mean January temperature, 22 degrees centigrade mean July temperature), but with less than half as much precipitation.

• Leningrad, on the Gulf of Finland (an arm of the Baltic Sea), is among the least continental places in the Soviet Union. The city has a great temperature range from summer to winter as does Chicago, 26 degrees centigrade (between the mean January and mean July temperatures); but it is about four degrees centigrade cooler both in summer and winter. Leningrad, compared to other Soviet cities, is rainy and cloudy, but it still has only two-thirds the precipitation of Chicago.

• Novosibirsk, near the eastern tip of the main agricultural belt, has a

### Climatic Data for Selected Stations

|            | Mean Centigrade Temperature | | | Mean Precipitation in Centimeters |
|------------|--------|------|-------|------|
|            | *January* | *July* | *Range* |      |
| Odessa     | − 3    | 22   | 25    | 39   |
| Leningrad  | − 8    | 18   | 26    | 56   |
| Novosibirsk| −19    | 19   | 38    | 42   |
| Verkhoyansk| −49    | 15   | 64    | 16   |
| Tashkent   | − 1    | 27   | 28    | 42   |
| Chicago    | − 4    | 22   | 26    | 86   |

*Source*: Paul E. Lydolph, *Climates of the Soviet Union* (Amsterdam-Oxford-New York: Elsevier Scientific Publishing Co., 1977); *World Survey of Climatology*, vol. 7, climatic tables, pp. 363-427.

mean January temperature of -19 degrees centigrade (15 degrees colder than Chicago), a mean July temperature only three degrees below Chicago's, but an annual range of temperature of 38 degrees, about 50 percent greater than Chicago's. Its precipitation is less than half that of Chicago.

• Verkhoyansk in northeast Siberia, in the heart of the area too cold for successful general agriculture, has a mean January temperature of -49 degrees centigrade, some 45 degrees colder than Chicago. The difference between the January temperatures of Chicago and Verkhoyansk is almost twice as great as between January and July in Chicago. The mean July temperature of Verkhotansk is 15 degrees, about the same as May in Chicago. The annual range of temperature (between the means for January and July) is an incredible 64 degrees centigrade, or two-and-a-half times the range in Chicago. Extreme continentality, indeed! Located deep in the interior of the continent, it receives little moisture, only 16 centimeters a year; less than one-fifth that of Chicago. If it were not so dry, northeast Siberia would be covered by a continental ice sheet. Extinct mammoths from the Ice Age have been discovered with the flesh intact frozen in the permafrost of northeast Siberia.

• Tashkent, in Soviet Central Asia, in an area generally too dry for agriculture without irrigation, is warmer, with temperatures generally three to five degrees centigrade higher than in Chicago but with less than half the precipitation. Because of the high temperatures and low relative humidity, this precipitation is insufficient for agriculture, even though

Tashkent itself, at the base of the high mountains of Soviet Central Asia, receives more rainfall than the desert or semidesert regions proper.

Because of its huge size, the Soviet Union extends not only over many climatic zones, but over many vegetation belts as well. The whole northern coast, for example, is bordered by tundra, where the summer months are not warm enough to sustain the growth of trees. A low vegetation consists of mosses, lichens and dwarf willows only a few inches tall.

To the south of the tundra lies the boreal forest (taiga), occupying nearly half the Soviet Union, with a vegetation of coniferous trees such as pine, spruce, firs and larch together with broad-leafed deciduous birches and aspens. This zone, larger than all of Canada, is generally hostile to human settlement or agriculture, but it is the source of timber and locally of minerals. It covers most of the European north, Western Siberia, Eastern Siberia and the Soviet Far East. Its eastern part is underlain by permafrost, which poses difficult conditions for farming, mining and forestry and for the construction of roads, railroads or buildings.

The ancestral home of the Russian people is the mixed forest zone, with both broad-leafed deciduous trees such as oak, beech and hornbeam, familiar in Central and Western Europe, and coniferous trees typical of the taiga. This zone forms a triangle with a base along the western edge of the Soviet Union on the Baltic Sea and the land frontier with Poland, Czechoslovakia and Hungary, and extends eastward to a tip at the southern part of the Ural Mountains. It is traditionally the land of rye, potatoes and flax. It has adequate rainfall and moderately fertile soil that is improved by liming and fertilization.

To the south of the mixed forest lies a strip of deciduous forests, forest-steppe and meadow-steppe—good agricultural land with rich soils and adequate rainfall in most years. It is the land of wheat and sugar beets, extending from the western border of the Soviet Union eastward across the southern edge of Western Siberia to the base of mountains near 90 degrees east longitude and 50 degrees north latitude.

The next belt to the south is the famous steppe proper with its grassy and herbaceous vegetation, fertile black-earth soils (among the best in the world), and low and irregular rainfall with occasional catastrophic droughts. The northern margin of the steppe usually has adequate rainfall for a good crop of wheat and sunflowers but toward the south agriculture becomes increasingly precarious.

Yet farther to the south and inland lie semideserts, deserts and mountains. They are the home of non-Slavic peoples. Here are the mountains and fertile valleys of the Trans-Caucasus, with a variety of humid and dry climates, subtropical to alpine vegetation and agricultural production in favored places. Soviet Central Asia contains great deserts but also oases along rivers, at the base of the mountains or in mountain-girt valleys. Here cotton is produced.

These great vegetation belts or landscape zones formed the basis of a major contribution by Russian and Soviet scholars to the development of modern soil science. In Western Europe, with its relatively uniform climate and complicated geology, early soil scientists classified soils by their parent materials. Russian scientists noticed, however, that soils such as the fertile black-earths extended over vast stretches, regardless of parent material, and throughout areas with similar vegetation and climate, such as the steppes. Thus was born the modern field of soil geography, which emphasizes the role of climate and vegetation in the development of the major soil groups of the world.

Soviet agricultural production has regularly fallen far behind the goals of the successive Five-Year Plans. It has not kept pace with the growth in other sectors of the economy, particularly in heavy industry, and has lagged increasingly behind the improvement of agriculture in other countries. Three factors have been involved: low investments in agriculture, inefficient management and poor physical conditions. In recent years the first deficiency has been largely overcome, as D. Gale Johnson points out (Chapter 16). However, the system of overly-centralized direction of farming remains a strongly negative factor.

Yields per hectare in the Soviet Union are roughly comparable to those in climatically similar parts of North America. Within the main agricultural belt of the Soviet Union conditions are much like those in the Prairie Provinces of Canada or the northern Great Plains of the United States. Compared with areas having warmer and moister climates, average yields per hectare are lower, yields fluctuate more from year to year, possibilities of increasing yields are less favorable and the range of crops that can be grown is more limited. As a result, Soviet agriculture is heavily dominated by grains. Fruit production is hindered by the very cold winters. Vegetables are relatively less important than in the United States. The diet of the average Soviet citizen is more dominated by grains than is that of the average citizen of any other major industrial country.

The Soviet Union has an arable area about as large as the United States and Canada combined, yet total production is insufficient for Soviet needs and is much below that of the United States alone. In the Soviet Union the isotherms (lines joining points with the same mean temperature) and isohyets (lines of equal rainfall) are parallel but increase in opposite directions. As one goes northwest the rainfall increases but the temperature decreases, whereas to the southeast it becomes warmer but drier. Thus the areas warm enough for production of maize for grain are too dry, while the areas with enough moisture are too cool for the maize to mature as grain. Hence it is cut green for sileage. The Soviet Union lacks those large areas with a combination of adequate moisture, a long, warm growing season and rich soil which accounts for the high productivity of the Corn Belt of the United States, with its vast acreage of high-yielding corn and soybeans. Large areas in the production of hay or forage crops in the Soviet Union have low yields.

We know that the Soviet government has placed a high priority on the development of energy, and that the country now produces almost as much energy as the United States. The Soviet Union has some of the world's largest reserves of petroleum, natural gas and coal as well as abundant water power. But these are generally remote from centers of population and distribution. Their utilization entails high costs of long-distance overland transport. Of the energy content of fuels produced in the Soviet Union in 1980, 45 percent was accounted for by petroleum, 27 percent by natural gas and 25 percent by coal.

The Soviet Union is now the world's largest producer of petroleum. Exports of petroleum provide a significant fraction of the earnings of foreign exchange in hard currency, utilized largely to purchase imports of grain and of up-to-date technology. In recent decades, huge new oil discoveries in Western Siberia have provided a large and cheap source of energy. This energy, however, must be transported by pipeline or railroad over long distances.

Until World War II more than three-fourths of Soviet oil production came from the Baku region in the Trans-Caucasus, west of the Caspian Sea (Figure 5). With the post-war discovery of new deposits, production increased rapidly. The Volga-Ural fields, originally called the "Second Baku," generally accounted for about 60 percent of the total Soviet output from the 1950s to the 1970s, and the discovery of gigantic new fields in West Siberia in the 1970s made possible further expansion. As other fields are either declining or stagnant, Western Siberia has increasingly dominated production, now accounting for more than half the Soviet output. But in recent years no new large fields have been discovered.

Many Western experts now predict a slowing of the rate of increase and a peaking of oil production in the near future, with possible limiting effects on the growth of industrial production in the Soviet Union, on its ability to provide petroleum to the politically and strategically important countries of Eastern Europe, or on the country's capacity to maintain high levels of petroleum exports to Western Europe to earn hard currency. It is well to note, however, that geological conditions in the Soviet Union favor the possible discovery of major large new petroleum deposits. Improved technology may also make possible utilization of much deeper sources, as it has in the United States.

Natural gas has only recently come to be used in considerable quantity in the Soviet Union. As late as 1955 it produced only about half as much energy as did peat, about a third as much as firewood, and less than three percent as much as coal. Successful geological prospecting, a realization that natural gas was by far the cheapest energy to produce, and the construction of natural-gas pipelines resulted in significantly greater production. Natural gas quickly passed peat and firewood as an energy source, and in 1980, for the first time in Russian or Soviet history, oustripped coal. Production promises to increase as rapidly in the years ahead and, with the provision of capital, pipeline, compressors and other technical equipment by Western Europe, Soviet export of natural gas promises to increase substantially in the decades ahead. But again, the larger reserves and the source of rapidly increasing production lie far from the markets, either domestic or foreign. The largest known reserves lie under the cold, bleak forests and the marshes and tundra of the northern part of Western Siberia, and under the deserts of Soviet Central Asia.

In total resources of coal the Soviet Union rivals the United States. There is enough to last centuries. Coal production reached a peak in the proportion of Soviet energy supplied in 1950-1952, when it provided almost two-thirds of Soviet fuel energy. But the proportion, as already noted, has been dropping because of the increase in petroleum and natural gas. Absolute total production of coal continued to rise for many years, reaching a peak (in standard units of 7,000 kilocalories) in 1978. Since then production has been about level, even though the Five-Year Plans continued to call for substantial increases.

The Donets coal basin (Donbas) in the southwestern part of the Soviet Union has been the main coal producer for more than a century, but costs of mining in this old field have been rising. The Kuznetsk Basin (Kuzbas) in Western Siberia has easily mined, high-quality coal. Although it is far from the main markets it is increasingly supplying coal to much of the Soviet Union. Other large deposits in Kazakhstan are being developed at Karaganda and Ekibastuz, the latter producing a cheap but low-quality fuel. The enormous coal deposits in Eastern Siberia are little developed, either because of their remoteness from transportation lines or because of problems with quality.

The largest water-power potential in the Soviet Union occurs on the Yenisei River and on its eastern tributaries, which run off the Central

Siberian plateau. Here gigantic hydroelectric projects have been constructed at Bratsk and Ust-Ilimsk on the Angara River which runs from Lake Baikal to the Yenisei River, and at Krasnoyarsk and Sayanogorsk on the Yenisei River itself. These are in Eastern Siberia, far from markets. The electricity must be utilized locally, largely in power-intensive industries. Better located projects have been constructed on the Volga and other rivers, as at Volgograd and, still farther to the west, Kuybyshev. Two spectacular large projects in Soviet Central Asia on the Vakhsh River (a tributary of the Amu Darya), which flows along the edge of the Pamir Mountains, have very high dams—345 meters at Rogun and 315 meters at Nurek.

Party and government in the Soviet Union have always stressed industrialization, which has prompted geological prospecting over wide expanses of the country. As a result, the Soviet Union is now the world's largest producer of iron ore, manganese, pig iron and steel among the metals; of mineral fertilizers in the chemical industry; and of petroleum among the fuels. The Soviets have also greatly increased the production of machinery, and the country is now the largest producer of diesel locomotives and of tractors. It lags behind the United States, Western Europe and Japan, however, in many branches of light industry and in the production of consumer goods. For example, Soviet production of automobiles per capita is only about a tenth that of Japan, France or Germany, or a fifth that of the United States or the United Kingdom.

Urbanization, a phenomenon closely related to industrialization, came later to the Soviet Union than to Western Europe or the United States, and has not proceeded as far. The proportion of urban to total population rose from only 18 percent in 1926 to 64 percent in 1983 (Figure 6). Yet this figure remains substantially below that of the United Kingdom, Japan, Canada, the United States or France. In fact, the Soviet Union has closely paralleled Mexico in this respect over the last 60 years. It is, of course, far more industrialized and urbanized than countries such as India, China or Nigeria, where the proportion of population living in cities still remains very low.

Finally, there is the matter of "human geography." The Soviet Union is a multinational entity, the product of outward expansion over the centuries. Recognition is given to the various peoples by a series of ethnic-political administrative units, the most important being the 15 Union Republics which together constitute the Union of Soviet Socialist Republics. These are in turn subdivided into 20 autonomous republics, eight autonomous "oblasts" and 10 autonomous "okrugs" (Figure 7).

The western, southern and northern margins of the country are largely non-Russian in population.

The Russian is by far the largest of the Union Republics, extending from the ancient home of the Russian people in the mixed forest lands around Moscow northwest to Leningrad on the Gulf of Finland; northward to Arkhangelsk and the White Sea; southeastward to Rostov, the coast of the Black Sea and the Caucasus; and eastward across the Urals to the Soviet Far East and Vladivostok. But there are notable clusters of other peoples concentrated at the bend of the Volga around Kazan or scattered across Siberia, particularly near Lake Baikal and along the southern boundary of the Republic.

In 1979, 137 million Russians constituted 52 percent of the overall Soviet population of 262 million. Other Slavs made up 20 percent, or 52 million; Turkic and other peoples of largely Moslem tradition, 16 percent, or 41 million; and a great variety of yet other peoples, 12 percent or 32 million. (For a more detailed discussion of ethnicity in the Soviet Union, see Chapter 23.)

The major ethnic groups, those recognized at the level of a Union Republic, are being maintained with only moderate assimilation. Ethnic groups of lesser political units are showing higher rates of assimilation. Individuals retain the right to use their national languages only within the political unit which recognizes that group. When members of ethnic minorities migrate to other parts of the Soviet Union, they typically must use Russian. Among the groups that are relatively resistant to assimilation are the peoples of the Baltic (Estonians, Latvians and Lithuanians), who retain the Latin alphabet in their languages; the ancient Christian peoples of the Caucasus (Georgians and Armenians), who also have their own scripts; the peoples of Moslem heritage, especially the Turkic-speaking peoples of the Trans-Caucasus (Azerbaidzhanis) and of Soviet Central Asia (Uzbeks, Kazakhs, Kirgiz and Turkmen), and the Tadzhiks. Peoples speaking other Slavic languages and those with Christian backgrounds assimilate to the dominant Russian culture much more readily than those with Moslem backgrounds and speaking non-Slavic languages. Moreover, urban inhabitants assimilate more rapidly than do rural dwellers.

Even in areas that give political-administrative recognition to non-Russian groups, the Russians form a very significant element, typically as a minority in the rural population but forming a large fraction, often a majority, of the population in the cities. The cities thus represent Russian points in non-Russian rural expanses. The Russians are particularly important in administration and industry, as, for example, in Soviet Central Asia.

Nevertheless, owing to the demographic trends discussed in Chapter 23, the non-Russian peoples of Soviet Central Asia will furnish a disproportionate share of births, entrants into the labor force and recruits into the army in the years ahead. In the industrial core of the Soviet Union, as a result of reduced birth rates, an acute labor shortage is developing, while in the rapidly growing population of Soviet Central Asia there is a large surplus with rural underemployment. The 1979 census indicates negligible outmigration of Turkic people from Soviet Central Asia between 1970 and 1979. (In 1979 less than one percent of Uzbeks, Kirgiz, Turkmen and Tadzhiks lived outside their republics.) Thus, because of labor shortages in Russian areas and a labor surplus in Soviet Central Asia, Russians may well begin leaving the latter area to return to their homelands, vacating jobs that can be filled by the indigenous Turkic peoples. And such a trend would only work to enhance ethnic diversity in the Soviet Union. □

# 12

## Environmental Problems

### John M. Kramer

> As long as private ownership of the means of production exists, there can be no conservation and efficient utilization of natural resources. Capitalism is pushing society towards an ecological catastrophe and is threatening many important aspects of the lives of the people. True harmony between nature and society can be achieved only under conditions of socialism with its integral humane social relations. —*Kommunist Ukrainy*, No. 4, 1979.

Only since the mid-1960s has environmental protection drawn considerable attention from the Soviet authorities. Friedrich Engels once warned that man should not be "very hopeful about our human conquest over nature," since "for each such victory nature manages to take her revenge."[1] But in general, Marxism has imbued the Soviet elite with optimism concerning man's ability to transform the physical environment and create a communist society. Political and economic considerations have also impelled the elite, until fairly recently, to view economic development as sacrosanct.

Nevertheless, in its early years the Soviet regime did initiate some measures to protect the environment.[2] By 1920, it had passed laws regulating the use of land, timber, wildlife, fish and water resources; several of these laws contained provisions to control pollution. In February 1919, the regime established the Central Committee of Water Protection whose duties included combatting water pollution. But since the Soviet state faced acute political and economic problems during these early years, the implementation of conservation laws was often sadly inadequate.

The environment received even less attention during the Stalin years.

The Council of Ministers did issue a decree in 1947 outlining measures to reduce water pollution, and in 1949 it established the Sanitary-Epidemiological Service, creating at the same time a commission to elaborate norms for the permissible concentration of pollutants in the atmosphere. Yet these were isolated acts. With the initiation of the Five-Year Plans in the late 1920s, the regime repeatedly stressed the need to surpass economically the developed capitalist countries as quickly as possible. Propaganda extolled the achievements of Soviet industry, and smoke-belching factory chimneys became the symbol of Soviet industrialization. Such priorities did not facilitate the pursuit of sound conservation policies.

Concern for the environment has become more evident since Stalin's death. On June 7, 1957, the Estonian Republic passed a law "for the Protection of the Environment," and by 1963 all of the Union Republics had promulgated similar legislation. The mid-1960s also witnessed the Soviet Union's first public controversy over the status of the environment. A campaign was waged to protect Lake Baikal—the world's largest repository of fresh water—and its environs from the industrial development that threatened the unique ecology of the region.[3]

More recently, environmental protection became an issue of national concern. Numerous publications dealing with the environment have appeared, and threats to the ecology of the Caspian Sea and of the Volga-Ural Basin have received extensive press coverage while generating considerable public debate. The government has demonstrated its concern by promulgating an impressive body of environmental protection laws.

Presumably, the Soviet leadership recognizes that past policies have engendered substantial environmental disruption and that it must now strike a better balance between the exigencies of the environment and the imperatives of economic development. Several factors, however, prevent a precise determination of the overall extent of, and costs associated with, environmental pollution.

In part, the problem arises from the nature of pollution itself, since levels may fluctuate rapidly as other factors, such as the weather, also fluctuate. Further, the Soviets have only begun to establish a nationwide system for gathering data on levels and sources of environmental pollution. It is said that current measurements yield only "the most general idea about the condition of the environment" and provide no data for a whole series of air pollutants, including copper, lead and zinc.[4]

Finally, the Soviet government is not completely forthcoming in disseminating available data on environmental conditions, presumably because these may prove politically embarrassing or may undermine ideological claims regarding the superiority of socialism to capitalism in protecting the environment. Commenting on this situation, one Soviet dissident has compared "socialist nature" to a lady of the "very highest principles"; in both cases "she never exposes herself to strangers."[5]

Yet available evidence makes it clear that high levels of environmental pollution exist in the Soviet Union, which have entailed considerable costs for the society. One estimate, purportedly based on suppressed official data, reports that air and water pollution inflict upwards of 20 billion rubles (nearly $30 billion at official rates) annually in damages to the economy; unofficial sources place these damages even higher. These costs include the many valuable resources lost through emissions, massive fish kills, accelerated corrosion and decay of buildings and other structures, higher labor turnover in intensely polluted areas, and the economic and public health costs associated with the increased incidence of pollution-related afflictions such as respiratory diseases.[6]

One Western expert concludes that water pollution in the Soviet industrial heartland is already as "pervasive and serious" as in the continental United States. A 1969 study by the Soviet Academy of Sciences estimates that polluters yearly dump 36 cubic kilometers of contaminated sewage into Soviet waters. The impact of these emissions on water quality is staggering, since they pollute from 12 to 15 times their volume of pure water. According to a "conservative" Soviet estimate, more than half of the country's annual total water runoff is polluted to some degree. Overall, the "absolute amount" of water pollutants is "constantly increasing" and their presence "frequently approaches the assimilative capacity of the water sources." On the other hand, some success in controlling water pollution has been noted. Water quality in the Moscow River, which runs through the capital, has improved dramatically in recent years. The river's soluble oxygen content has increased substantially, and fish have appeared in the river "for the first time in a long time."[7]

Air pollution has only begun to assume the critical levels that water pollution has already reached in many regions of the Soviet Union. Two factors have traditionally limited air pollution—a minuscule number of motor vehicles and an energy balance that relies heavily on liquid fuels, which are less polluting than solid fuels such as coal. Official data, however, reportedly show that air pollution levels in the next few years may approach those found in the United States.

The rapid expansion in the number of automobiles is a primary cause. While the figure is still small by U.S. standards—approximately 18 to 20 million in 1980 compared to over 100 million in the United States—these cars are almost entirely concentrated in a few urban centers. Further, poor maintenance and the absence of pollution-control devices make Soviet automobiles far more intensively polluting than their current U.S. counterparts. Consequently, automobiles are already responsible for 25 percent of the air pollution in large cities, and in Moscow the figure is 50 percent.

Predictions are that air pollution levels in the Soviet Union may double in the 1980s, with the automobile responsible for almost 70 percent of total emissions. Atmospheric quality will probably diminish even further if ambitious plans to increase reliance on heavily polluting coal for generating electricity are realized. It is planned that in the year 2000 coal will constitute over 50 percent of the primary energy consumed in thermal power stations, which are already the nation's heaviest industrial polluters. The figure for 1975 was under 30 percent.[8]

In one sense, of course, the same processes of modernization and economic development that disrupt the environment in all industrialized countries account for the now considerable pollution in the Soviet Union. Befouled air and polluted water seem to be among the inevitable, if undesirable, concomitants of modern societies, whether socialist or capitalist. For example, that ubiquitous symbol of modern society—the private automobile—respects no political system as it undermines environmental quality. Yet political, economic and technological factors peculiar to the Soviet Union also contribute to its pollution problems.

First, the government has not committed the political and economic resources necessary to undo past neglect. Like many of its capitalist counterparts, the regime has made rhetorical commitments to enhance environmental quality, but it has not made the difficult and costly decisions necessary to implement these commitments. Thus, the Eleventh Five-Year Plan (1981-1985) actually allocates less for environmental protection than did the Tenth—10 billion rubles versus 11 billion rubles. In reality, inflation in the 1981-1985 period will make the real investment in environmental protection even less. Further, the funds allocated to pollution control comprise only a relatively small segment of the total funds for environmental protection, which are dispersed among many projects, such as land improvement.

Second, industrialists exhibit little interest in controlling pollution. Their attitude derives from the emphasis in Soviet economic planning on the production of goods, which leads to bonuses, premiums and other perquisites for production personnel. Thus, a low priority is assigned to any activity, including pollution control, that detracts from this pursuit. The typical view among Soviet industrialists toward environmental protection is found in the comment of the enterprise manager who admitted that "there really is a lot of smoke from our work but the plans must be fulfilled. The plan and the rates—these are the main things. The rest can wait."[9]

Such attitudes help explain why many enterprises, despite explicit legal regulations to the contrary, operate without—or with inadequate—waste treatment facilities. In Riga, the capital of Soviet Latvia, air pollution control is still an "untouched area."And even in Moscow, where the authorities with some success have pursued well-publicized campaigns to control pollution, a 1979 study found that a "large number of pollution sources are still not equipped with treatment facilities."[10]

Part of the problem, as we have seen, lies in the inadequate funds available for pollution control. Annual appropriations to control air pollution between 1976 and 1980 averaged only 260 million rubles, with Moscow receiving almost half of this amount. Nor are all of these funds actually utilized for this purpose, because industrialists divert some of the money to production activities.

Moreover, many existing treatment facilities are technologically backward and are poorly operated and maintained. A recent survey of treatment facilities in the Republic of Armenia found that "none of these facilities is highly efficient—all of them are being poorly built and poorly operated." A similar survey in the Republic of Belorussia reported that over half of the enterprises had no treatment facilities whatsoever and "about 60 percent of the existing facilities are out of commission or are operating inefficiently." To be sure, one can also find examples in the Soviet press of enterprises successfully controlling their pollution, but careful reading suggests that these accounts are exceptions.[11]

Indeed, the behavior of industrialists has prompted numerous criticisms in the Soviet press, and at times even a grim humor. Industrialists are accused of a narrow "departmental" attitude that subordinates society's interest in a clean environment to the pursuit of immediate economic gain. While this criticism has merit, it ignores the circumstance that impels polluters to behave as they do. So long as industrialists find it more profitable to pollute than not to pollute, they will continue to do so. As one source colorfully explained it, forcing enterprises without economic incentives to control pollution is like "getting a cat to eat cucumbers by giving it a lecture on the benefits of vegetarianism."[12]

The legal system has also failed to deter polluters. Most environmental legislation is hortatory, containing general principles but lacking detailed provisions. The Soviet Union still lacks a nationwide law on nature conservation, despite repeated calls by environmentalists for such an act, and it was not until 1980 that national air pollution legislation was promulgated.

The absence of such legislation permits many enterprises to pollute with legal impunity, since they are attached to All-Union ministries and not subject to local legislation. Criminal liability for water pollution exists in all 15 Union Republics, but in only eight for air pollution; fines imposed for such crimes rarely exceed 300 rubles. Administrative penalties—the most common sanction imposed on polluters—are even more lenient. For example, public health physicians, the officials most directly involved in regulating polluters, may levy fines of up to 10 rubles for violation of air pollution regulations. The chief public health physician of the Soviet Union may impose fines of no more than 50 rubles for similar violations. Such fines are even less of a deterrent than these modest sums suggest, since enterprises simply budget for them in their operating expenses.[13]

Deficiencies also exist among the numerous agencies responsible for monitoring adherence to environmental regulations. Coordinating their activities is difficult since they are attached to various ministries at the national and republic levels. As an editorial in *Pravda* explained, this situation stimulates "interdepartmental skirmishes" that engender "unhealthy competition." Then, too, these agencies typically cannot identify those guilty of a particular pollution discharge since they lack the necessary measuring equipment.

Even more serious, environmental agencies in the Soviet Union have little incentive to pursue their duties vigorously. Not only do they lack political power, but they are usually attached to the very production ministries whose activities most pollute the environment. Consequently, as articles in the press complain, polluters are rarely punished, and when "somewhere, somebody, somehow" is convicted "it is found that the punishment is purely symbolic and no more annoying than a mosquito bite."[14]

The Soviet Union has responded to its pollution problems primarily through legal and organizational measures. There is All-Union legislation on land use (1968), public health (1969), water (1970) and air (1980). In both 1973 and 1978 the Council of Ministers and the Party Central Committee issued joint decrees to control pollution and protect the environment of specific waterways, including Lake Baikal, the Baltic Sea, the Black and Azov Seas, the Caspian Sea and the Volga-Ural Basin.

Yet legal measures, as we have seen, have done little to deter polluters. Many Soviet sources, particularly in the academic world, now acknowledge this, and argue (as Western economists have long done) that enterprises will control their emissions only when given sufficient economic incentives to do so. The major impediment to the creation of these incentives is the fact that the Soviet Union does not place a price on such natural resources as water and land. This circumstance derives from the Marxist law of value, which considers "free" any goods—such as natural resources—not created by human labor. Unless the regime can overcome its ideological scruples and impose a price on natural resources, enterprises will continue to lack economic incentive to conserve "free" goods.[15]

Soviet authorities have taken several steps to enhance urban environments. They are establishing an automated network in 350 cities to monitor atmospheric quality. Cities have planted vast areas of greenery, in part to purify the air by absorbing carbon monoxide while giving off oxygen. Measures to combat motor vehicle emissions include the development of computerized traffic control systems, pedestrian underpasses and limited access super-highways to facilitate vehicular movement and reduce air pollution, since motor vehicles markedly increase their emissions when braking and accelerating. The substitution of liquid for solid fuels as a source of power for industrial and residential units has noticeably reduced air pollution in many urban centers, particularly Moscow. However, the current plans calling for a substantial increase in the utilization of solid fuels may reverse this trend.

Finally, the Soviet Union has participated in international efforts to protect the environment. Soviet and American cooperation in this field dates from agreements reached during President Nixon's trips to Moscow in 1972 and 1974. The 1972 agreement included projects devoted to air and water pollution control, urban environmental problems and scientific research on environmental issues of mutual interest. The 1974 agreement provided for the establishment of "biosphere preserves" in each country as part of a worldwide UNESCO project, wherein Soviet and U.S. scientists could jointly study the impact of man's activity on the biosphere.

The Soviet Union was also an active participant in preparations for the 1972 U.N. Conference on the Human Environment held in Stockholm, Sweden. Although boycotting the conference itself (to protest East Germany's inclusion only as a non-voting participant), the Soviet Union does support the resulting program and is represented on the governing board designed to coordinate its activities.

Other Soviet positions have not been as helpful for international cooperation. The Soviet Union consistently opposed—as have most countries, including the United States—any international regulation of domestic sources of pollution as an infringement on national sovereignty. Again like the United States, it has demanded exemptions for its warships from the provisions of international conventions to regulate pollution. On balance, its record of international environmental cooperation is probably as good (or as bad) as that of most other industrial nations.

An examination of Soviet environmental pollution must evoke *déjà vu* among Westerners. Not only are the problems themselves similar, but so too are many of the factors promoting them. *Homo economicus*, whether socialist or capitalist, seems far more concerned with maximizing production and profit than with minimizing environmental damage. And the same factor in each system—that it is cheaper to continue than to abate pollution—impels *Homo economicus* to behave as he does.

*Homo politicus*, like his economic counterpart, also manifests seemingly universal traits, including an unwillingness to implement a rhetorical commitment with the requisite political and economic resources. Americans can readily empathize with another trait of the Soviet political system: the problem of coordinating policy among numerous bureaucracies subordinated to different administrative and political jurisdictions.

To be sure, there are important differences between the Soviet and Western systems. Ideological strictures against putting prices on natural resources are an obvious example. The Soviet system also creates a collusive relationship between polluters and the nominal protectors of the environment, because both are government agencies. This circumstance is not unknown in private-ownership systems, but would U.S. environmentalists willingly emulate the common Soviet practice of having both the polluters and protectors of the environment in the same agency?

Conversely, Soviet environmentalists must envy the numerous opportunities that a democratic political system affords Western environmentalists to pursue their goals. Many tactics of U.S. or West European environmentalists, such as the mobilization of political and fiscal resources to elect favored candidates, are simply unavailable to their Soviet counterparts.

The extent to which the Soviet political and economic system can respond to environmental pollution is arguable. Yet the Soviet experience in combating pollution, like the Western, confirms an observation that Thomas Jefferson once made about political corruption: "It is better to keep the wolf out of the fold than to trust to drawing his teeth and talons after he shall have entered." □

1. Friedrich Engels, *Dialectics of Nature* (New York: International Publishers, 1940), pp. 291-92.

2. *Sovetskoe gosudarstvo i pravo* (Sept. 1967), pp. 41-49.

3. For a discussion of the controversy, see Marshall Goldman, *The Spoils of Progress: Environmental Pollution in the Soviet Union* (Cambridge, Massachusetts: MIT Press, 1972), pp. 177-210.

4. *Kommunist* (Erevan), Oct. 10, 1982.

**5.** Boris Komarov, *The Destruction of Nature in the Soviet Union* (White Plains, New York: M. E. Sharpe, Inc., 1980), p. 44.

**6.** For detailed accounts of the costs of environmental pollution, see *Gorodskoe khozaistvo Moskvy* (May 1979); *Literaturnaia gazeta* (June 18, 1980); Komarov, *Destruction*, p. 26.

**7.** W. Douglas Jackson, ed., *Soviet Resource Management and the Environment* (Washington, D.C.: American Association for the Advancement of Slavic Studies, 1978), p. 103; *Priroda* (Dec. 1969); *Materialno — tekhnicheskoe snabzhenie* (Dec. 1978); *Gorodskoe khoziaistvo Moskvy* (Aug. 1978).

**8.** Komarov, *Destruction*, p. 30. Among numerous accounts of the impact of the automobile on environmental quality see *Gorodskoe khoziaistvo Moskvy* (Aug. 1978); and *Literaturnaia gazeta* (Nov. 1, 1978).

**9.** *Zaria vostoka* (Jan. 9, 1980).

**10.** *Kommunist sovetskoi: Latvii* (Feb. 1969); *Moskovskaia pravda* (Feb. 16, 1979).

**11.** *Kommunist* (Erevan) (Nov. 14, 1978); *Sovetskaia Belorussia* (Feb. 1, 1980). For examples of successful effort at pollution control, see *Pravda* (July 15, 1979).

**12.** Komarov, *Destruction*, p. 95. John M. Kramer, "Environmental Problems in the U.S.S.R.: The Divergence of Theory and Practice," *Journal of Politics* (Nov. 1974), pp. 886-99, provides a detailed discussion of "departmentalism" and the environment.

**13.** A recent analysis of problems in Soviet environmental law is found in *Sovetskaia iustitsiia*, No. 5 (March 1979).

**14.** *Pravda* (Oct. 29, 1980; June 22, 1981); *Sotsialisticheskaia industriia* (July 12, 1980).

**15.** *Izvestia* (Oct. 30, 1979) carries an article advocating economic incentives to deter polluters. See also John M. Kramer, "Prices and the Conservation of Natural Resources in the Soviet Union," *Soviet Studies* (Jan. 1973), pp. 364-73.

# 13

## Architecture and Urban Planning

*William C. Brumfield*

"Soviet architecture" is a slippery designation, not only because of zig-zags in official policy concerning permissible styles—constructivist, functionalist, neoclassical, bureaucratic-pompous—but also because the Soviet Union is such a diverse aggregation of nationalities and cultures.

If one speaks of the architecture of Soviet Estonia or of Soviet Uzbekistan, does this imply a sub-division within a larger category known as Soviet architecture, or a distinctly national architecture? In fact, for reasons of cultural policies, the Soviets have tried to have it both ways: public buildings and housing developments in Tashkent and Dushanbe are likely to have "Islamic" decorative motifs incorporated into the design; recent architecture in Estonia shows the influence of neighboring Finland; and in the Caucasus the rough terrain has been exploited to achieve striking forms unknown in other parts of the Soviet Union. Climatic differences, geographical features, and distinctive cultural legacies unquestionably contribute to variations in architectural practice in the 15 Union Republics.[1]

Yet there can be little doubt that overall architectural policy is directed from Moscow. Moscow's influence extends to the setting of construction goals and the allocation of budgetary resources in the Five-Year Plans, as well as to more specific questions of design and construction technology. The capital contains the headquarters of all major institutions concerned with architecture, planning and construction—including the state construction agencies (*Gosstroy* and *Gosgrazhdanstroy*), the Union of Architects (with over 13,000 members), and numerous research institutes, such as the Central Scientific Research Institute of Experimental Projects. Local autonomy may be tolerated, and even encouraged; but most large projects, be they in Tallinn or in

Tashkent, utilize similar construction techniques and frequently the same basic designs.

The centralization of architectural planning—expected in a highly centralized state—has been intensified by the top priority assigned to rapid construction according to standarized plans and materials. In explaining this "industrialization" of construction, Soviet writers have noted the pressing need to rebuild the enormous amount of housing and industrial space destroyed during World War II. Yet the large-scale application of rationalized construction methods actually began some ten years after the war's end. The immediate post-war decade was characterized by a number of grandiose projects (such as the seven "Stalinist Gothic" towers that still dominate the Moscow skyline); but the larger needs of society, particularly in housing, were being addressed by construction methods of pre-revolutionary origins. Furthermore, economic considerations received inadequate attention, so that large sums were expended on prestige buildings, while the majority of the population lived in overcrowded communal apartments or in hastily-built barracks.

In 1955 the Central Committee of the Communist Party and the Council of Ministers responded to the housing crisis by adopting a series of measures aimed at transforming the Soviet construction industry. Its thrust involved the implementation of industrialized construction methods based on the prefabrication of standardized parts and modules for assembly on site. In a process called *tipifikatsiia* (typification), architects and designers produced a catalog of building types and interior arrangements that could easily be adapted to large-scale, multi-storied housing projects in a variety of settings. Such a system provided an effective means for constructing millions of square meters of housing and factory space quickly, at low cost, and without need of sophisticated technology. With a crane for lifting reinforced-concrete beams and panels into place, and a welder's torch to fasten the sections, the shell of an apartment building could be completed within a few months.

The results of two and a half decades of industrialized construction on a broad scale have been impressive—at least in quantitative terms. For example, during the Ninth Five-Year Plan (1971 to 1975) some 544 million square meters of housing space were constructed, thus providing new apartments for 56,000,000 people (the rule of thumb is roughly ten square meters per person). During the same period, around 100 new towns were founded, many of them in the Far East. More recently, from 1975 to 1979 Moscow added 17.7 million square meters of living space (for 1.7 million people, most of whom were resettled from older parts of the city), completed four million square meters of industrial space, and built 82 schools and over 1,000 stores and restaurants. The same tempo of construction is planned for the future.

These and other figures spew forth from the planning agencies, and are announced with a boosterism that would do credit to any U.S. Chamber of Commerce. To appreciate the results, however, one must wander among row after row of buildings—newly completed or still under construction—on the outskirts of Moscow, Leningrad, Kiev or Vilnius. Any of these cities provide excellent examples of industrialized construction, and the Lazdinay region of Vilnius combines efficiency with a concern for aesthetic planning.

But Moscow's projects, by virtue of their scale and use of innovative building methods, are the most impressive. The names of old country estates, formerly on the outskirts of the city, now designate gargantuan new developments within the city limits—an area of 878 square kilometers defined by the Moscow Ring Road. These projects (Chertanovo, Troparyova, Konkovo, Strogino) are called "living massifs," and they are indeed massive: Strogino, nearing completion, will be home to over 150,000 people, many of whom have been moving in during the past two years despite the area's lack of adequate transportation and services. (This is a minor shortcoming for people who have been on a waiting list for years.)

The extent of new construction poses a number of problems for planners and architects as again Moscow provides the best example, although its problems are shared by Leningrad, Kiev and other major urban areas. In the early 1970s, there were thoughts of limiting the city's population to seven million, but it is now over eight, and will continue to increase. To accommodate this number, planners have adopted a radial plan, with eight super zones extending from the city's core. Parks and green areas are interspersed among the zones; and beyond the ring expressway is a green belt, within which are located satellite communities.

This General Plan, the formulation of which began in 1961, was approved by the Council of Ministers of the Soviet Union in 1971 with the express purpose of transforming Moscow into a "model communist city." In its second phase, 1976 to 1990, particular attention is to be devoted to the formation of ensembles both in the central city and in the surrounding zones. In specific terms this will mean the integration of "microregions" into a comprehensive plan for land use within the eight major zones. Each planning region is alloted space for social and commercial centers, while other areas of the city have been designated as general, "city-wide" centers (for educational, administrative and research complexes). In addition, the plan projects 46 "production zones" to regulate and contain the city's industrial apparatus (in most cases this will mean the improvement of existing developments).

Essential to the functioning of such large-scale projects is Moscow's rapid transit system, planned to reach some 220 kilometers in length by 1985. Other Soviet cities with subway trains include Leningrad, Kiev, Tbilisi, Tashkent, Kharkiv and Baku. Most regions of Moscow are already efficiently served by a subway system with several radial lines and a ring line connecting them; but the pace of subway construction is not sufficient to meet the needs of a city overwhelmingly dependent on public transportation. Tram lines and an overloaded and frequently dilapidated bus system must fill the gap for hundreds of thousands of residents in the outlying areas. The growth of the number of private automobiles, modest by Western standards, has only served to create new problems by overloading the street network, particularly in the central city.

Moscow's demand for new housing and services is therefore restricted to an area sufficiently compact to be served by public transportation: suburban sprawl is not an option for Soviet developers. The available building space is further restricted by the need to provide open space, all the more essential as population density increases. The solution has been to design taller apartment buildings. At the beginning of the 1960s, the greater part of Moscow's living space consisted of buildings of five stories or less. With improved techniques of construction, the heights of mass-produced buildings increased: 10, 12, 14 stories. By the late 1970s apartment rows of 16 to 20 stories were not uncommon; and during the next Five-Year Plan such buildings are expected to comprise 65 to 70 percent of all new housing construction in Moscow. A similar trend has occurred in Leningrad: apartment towers in both cities now frequently exceed 20 stories.

The increase in height has required an increase in technological sophistication, extending from such basic matters as structural integrity to such details as the design of efficient, reliable elevators. More care must now be given to the siting of buildings, in order to achieve the required minimum levels of sunlight exposure and open space. In fact, such requirements are not always faithfully maintained, and in some cases land allocated for open space by the planner has been taken by the builder to meet construction quotas.

The disparity between plan and implementation has created a number of deficiencies, particularly in the area of services to the new regions. With an overriding concern to provide housing space, builders often lag in completing basic service facilities such as schools, clinics, stores and restaurants. For example, by June 1982 at the Iasenevo project—one of the city's more innovative—the percentages of completion were: housing, 94 percent; schools, 58 percent; stores, 31 percent; restaurants and cafes, 5 percent. The problem has been attributed not only to the lack of integration among planning organizations, but also to the lack of penalties against builders who neglect even the insufficient amounts allotted to service facilities in the rush to fulfill construction targets for housing space.

If the lack of coordination within housing projects has elicited complaints from citizens and Party officials, its absence on a broader, interregional level has raised questions among city planners concerned about the "seams" between microregions. In their view, individual developments have been planned with too little concern for the nature of their relation to adjoining developments. As one architect noted: "The basic problem of such projects is that these territories are built up as isolated fragments, developed only in and of themselves. As a result, the city's appearance is formed haphazardly, and the creative architect is pushed into the background."[2] The lack of coordination on this scale can produce an aesthetic disaster, particularly at major points of intersection where no attempt has been made to effect a transition between two (or more) developments.

The very success of Soviet industrialized construction—above all in the area of housing—has created a momentum which does not always respond to redirection or modification. For example, some planners in Moscow have suggested that the ground floor of new apartment buildings be adapted for commercial use, thus alleviating the lack of service facilities mentioned above. But builders with standardized plans for towers are reluctant to introduce modifications for which they are not equipped and which would slow the all-important tempo of construction. Furthermore, the momentum of standardization encourages uniformity in building height, particularly in housing developments, where a frequent pattern has been 12-story rows of blocks with 16-story towers. These figures are now moving to 16 and 22 stories, respectively, and it has been suggested that a less monotonous effect would be obtained by varying the height, with the standard figures used as an average for construction goals. One current adaptation of standardized models to relieve the monotony of the building silhouette is the "block-section" method, a form of horizontal variation consisting of a series of attached towers, or sections, which can be bent as the terrain or planner dictates. This "curtain" effect has been impressively demonstrated in Moscow's Iasenevo region.

Whatever the variations in placement and height, new projects must make some effort to address the problem of design monotony in industrialized construction. Architectural publications frequently contain discussions of this problem in regard to both outward appearance and interior design. Partial solutions include the use of colored ceramic panels on the exterior, structural modification in the basic box design, and greater variety in the arrangement of interior space. Most new projects are still characterized by ranks of buildings stamped from a few standard models, but the goals of construction can no longer be defined by the speed with which a certain number of square meters are enclosed. New approaches are developed primarily in "experimental housing regions" which display greater creativity in the design of large housing masses.

One such region is Chertanovo-North, designed for 22,000 inhabitants and located in south Moscow. In terms of innovative design and land use, and of such conveniences as underground parking complexes and shopping malls, this project offers a view of the latest concepts in Soviet urban planning. The project is dominated by a complex 30-story tower overlooking a small lake. The area around the tower leads to an esplanade and central plaza containing buildings for educational, social and commercial use. Beyond the plaza are three tower clusters (21 to 25 stories) visually linked by three additional apartment blocks, whose greatly extended horizontal facades are bent at oblique angles. Interior traffic arteries are underground. The development has a subway station and such futuristic technological services as a central waste compacting station attached to collection points in the various buildings by underground pneumatic pipes.

Whatever the project—be it for housing, administration, education, entertainment or trade—Soviet architects are usually constrained by rather limited technological and financial resources, and by the narrow range of options presented by industrialized, mass construction methods. These limitations can, however, serve as a spur to the architect's ingenuity—as in the Children's Music Theater, one of the best of Moscow's recent buildings.

In a booklet devoted to the new theater, the project's designers—V. Krasilnikov and A. Velikanov—comment on the problems of working with prefabricated materials: "Architects are forced to use methods and construction materials worked out by construction and architectural practice, and this places its mark on the architecture of a building, especially under conditions of industrialized construction."[3] A close inspection of the theater's exterior gives one example of what the architects are talking about. Wishing to create a monolithic structure of simple geometric contrasts, but unable to use the techniques of poured, textured concrete that characterize Western "brutalism," the architects have sheathed the facade in textured stone and concrete panels. The seams that mark so much of contemporary prefabricated Soviet architecture are here integrated into the rough surface, thus adapting standardized components to a boldly-sculpted design.

The pervasiveness of prefabricated materials in Soviet building does not imply that the architects are locked into patterns of industrialized conformity. New techniques are being introduced, particularly in the development of poured ferro-concrete structures. As of 1980, poured concrete was projected to comprise almost half of the concrete used in the Soviet Union; and while much of this can be accounted for in foundations, dams, and certain industrial structures, poured concrete (or "monolithic" concrete, as the Russians call it) is being used with increasing sophistication and with some awareness of its aesthetic properties. The most notable structure in this material is the Moscow television tower at Ostankino. In recent years, a number of high-rise buildings have been constructed by raising a central concrete shaft from which the rest of the structure is draped. Space frame construction is also increasingly in use.

Other innovations in design and materials have appeared in cantilevered structures, covered stadiums, and buildings composed of complex geometric forms. A new bio-chemical institute in the south of Moscow, for example, resembles a diagram of a compound molecule (the return of *architecture parlante*). Furthermore, the legacy of Russian architecture's great experiment in modernism during the 1920s is being cautiously resurrected, as architectural journals include sketches and quotations from Lissitzky, Melnikov and the Vesnin brothers.[4] Yet the results of the attempt to create, or revive, a modernist aesthetic in Soviet architecture are mixed. There is no clearly discernible movement or school; and while buildings of distinction have risen in Moscow, Leningrad, and in the Caucasus during the past decade or so, much of what passes for "modernist" architecture is overbearing and awkward. (A quite notable exception to this is Moscow's Oncological Research Center, a large research and clinical complex dominated by a starkly molded hospital tower.)

The problem is compounded by the fact that even showcase buildings in the Soviet Union do not achieve the luster of, say, the best American corporate headquarters. On this point a telling contrast is provided by Moscow's new center for international trade, designed and constructed under the supervision of Western firms. Although not particularly remarkable in conception, the building's sleek gray frame and large window panels of tinted glass stand out in its Soviet context.[5] Indeed, when Soviet planners wish to build a structure intended to accommodate—and impress—capitalists, they will often hire a capitalist firm. The Finns have built a hotel tower in downtown Tallinn, the Swedes have built a large hotel on Vasilevsky Island in Leningrad, the French have built the grand Hotel Cosmos in Moscow, and in 1980 the West Germans finished the new (second) international terminal at Sheremetevo Airport. In some cases the entire work force has been imported, as have the materials.

In the future, Soviet leaders may also decide to buy abroad rather than depend on the local product. Yet there is little of the interchange between Soviet and Western architects that characterized the vital period of the 1920s, when Le Corbusier, Frank Lloyd Wright and the architects of the Bauhaus and of *de Stijl* knew their Soviet colleagues and occasionally collaborated with them. Perhaps this will change. In architecture, as in so much else, Russia has frequently assimilated ideas from the West and recast them in remarkable form. If the past decade in Soviet architecture has produced little that is remarkable, its accomplishments in mass planning and construction are impressive and warrant our close attention. □

1. This essay draws on the author's personal observations of building in the Soviet Union as well as various Soviet sources, particularly articles published in the journals *Znanie* (architectural series) and *Stroitel'stvo i arkhitektura Moskvy*. For a helpful introductory guide to the literature, see Paul M. White, *Soviet Urban and Regional Planning* (New York: St. Martin's Press, 1980.)

2. M. Shapiro, in a round-table discussion reported in *Stroitel'stvo i arkhitektura Moskvy*, 1982 no. 11. The central city has its own problems of aesthetic and design integration, particularly in the wake of devastating urban renewal projects of the 1960s and 1970s. This problem and some solutions are discussed in *Stroitel'stvo i arkhitektura Moskvy*, 1982 no. 6. One discussant speaks of the danger of creating "dead zones" by moving people out of the center city, which becomes a purely administrative center.

3. *Moskovskii gosudarstvenii detskii muzykalnii teatr* (Moscow: 1979). The theater is also analyzed, very favorably, by V. Khait in *Stroitel'stvo i arkhitektura Moskvy*, 1982 no. 10.

4. See S. Frederick Starr, *Melnikov: Solo Architect in a Mass Society* (Princeton, New Jersey: Princeton University Press, 1978), for a well-illustrated study of this early leader in Soviet architecture whose work was later repudiated.

5. The building's innovative features—in the Soviet context—include an I-beam steel skeleton, exterior panels bolted to the frame (eliminating unsightly cement seams), use of sprayed polyurethane insulation behind the panels, and light metal frame interior walls covered with plaster board (*Stroitel'stvo i arkhitektura Moskvy*, 1982 no. 4).

# THE ECONOMY

Soviet economic growth since World War II has been steady, and Soviet economic performance has frequently been impressive. But in the last two decades the rate of growth has declined, difficulties have multiplied (in part the result of earlier successes), and a kind of stagnation has set in. The Soviet economy is not on the verge of collapsing. Yet by all indications it is in serious trouble—more serious, in several critical respects, than is the case in Western Europe or the United States.

James R. Millar surveys the current situation in the light both of developments since the 1950s and of the economy's future prospects, highlighting in the process the many dilemmas and hard choices facing the leadership. Marshall I. Goldman focuses on the plight of Soviet consumers, with money enough to spend but little that is desirable to buy. And D. Gale Johnson, again going back to the 1950s, discusses the difficulties of Soviet agriculture. He points out, as does Goldman, that food is now officially recognized as the central problem of Soviet economic planning, and suggests why, despite the enormous investment in agricuture, this should be so. (The answer is not the weather.)

# 14 THE ECONOMY

## An Economic Overview

### James R. Millar

> Comrades, the Communist Party is advancing a great task—to achieve in the coming 20 years a living standard higher than that of any capitalist country and to create the necessary conditions for achieving an abundance of material and cultural values.
>
> —Nikita Khrushchev[1]

> In the 1980s the Soviet Union may pass through the worst period since the death of Stalin. Growth rates will be the lowest ever, and the population can expect a stagnating or even declining standard of living. The very stability of the social system may be in question.
>
> —Seweryn Bialer[2]

Three years after announcing the heady goals quoted above at the Twenty-second Party Congress, Nikita Khrushchev was deposed. That same year, 1964, the Soviet Union imported a large volume of grain on a net basis for the first time since World War II, a policy that was continued in ever-increasing volume throughout the Brezhnev years. The high rates of growth in gross national product and of per capita consumption achieved during the 1950s began to decline immediately following the Congress, and they have continued in systematic decline ever since. Seweryn Bialer's prediction for the 1980s, quoted above, is based on projections into the next decade of recent declining and/or stagnant rates of economic growth.

What has happened to undermine Khrushchev's confident, sunny forecast of 1961? Is the current picture as gloomy as Bialer suggests? What are the leadership's economic alternatives? My purpose here is to describe and evaluate briefly the principal structural and performance

173

changes that have taken place in the Soviet economy since Stalin's death in 1953. I will then examine the policy options currently available to Soviet policy-makers and speculate about the course of the economy in the next decade.

Soviet history is replete with abrupt, traumatic changes in social and economic conditions. World War I, the revolution of 1917, the Civil War, collectivization and rapid industrialization, the great purges, World War II and postwar reconstruction all demanded considerable personal sacrifices and caused significant structural changes in the economy. Change has been more gradual since Stalin's death, but the cumulative effect of reform and policy revision during the 30 years of Khrushchev and Leonid Brezhnev is greater than may be generally realized. The leadership in 1983 confronts an economy that is quite different in both structure and performance from the one that faced Khrushchev in 1953.

Structurally, between 1928 and 1953 Soviet economic development represented a variant of the "classical" model. Growth was achieved by mobilizing under- and unemployed labor and by shifting labor from low (or zero) productivity sectors into sectors where productivity was relatively higher (or positive), or increasing at a relatively high rate. A large share of the resulting increase in final product was reinvested in the growth sectors, thereby providing still more employment opportunities in high productivity sectors. In general, labor moved out of rural non-agricultural as well as agricultural employment into industrial occupations. About 15 million people migrated from the countryside between 1928 and 1940. Labor also moved from activities not valued in the measurement of gross national product into those that are "counted." The largest single component of the latter flow was made up of women moving mainly into the lower productivity jobs abandoned by men — that is, into agriculture, light industry and retail sales.

The Soviet model differs from other "classical" cases of economic development, such as that of Japan, chiefly by the degree to which heavy industry was accorded priority. World War II and the Cold War that followed accentuated this priority in the Soviet Union, for conventional warfare requires a heavy industrial base above all else. Autarkic development of domestic raw materials and natural resources was another response to the Soviet Union's international situation. Thus, unlike Japan, it did not develop a comparative advantage in exportable consumer goods. It did so in energy, raw materials and armaments.

The principal structural changes in the Soviet economy *since* Stalin's time have been modifications designed to accommodate a higher priority for consumer goods and, perforce, higher priority for agriculture, light industry and residential construction. This has required changes in the leadership's long-standing preferences for industry over agriculture, for the urban worker over the rural—for, in short, the hammer over the sickle.

Khrushchev and Brezhnev were favored by several circumstances in seeking to revise priorities. Khrushchev obtained relatively quick, if somewhat transitory, returns by bringing 36 million hectares of "virgin land" under the plow and by improving incentives in agricultural production. Brezhnev benefitted from the surge in employable population resulting from the country's postwar baby boom. The rural sector also provided a substantial flow of labor. Thus, although resources were gradually shifted away from previously preferred sectors, the availability of new supplies of land and labor helped to cushion both a decline in the rate of growth of total investment and the shift of an increased share of total net investment to agriculture and related industries.

Even so, the trend in the growth rate of the gross national product declined in the early 1960s (Table 1).[3] The sectors into which resources were rechanneled were those of relatively lower productivity, while the increase in total factor productivity—that is, the increase in output not attributable to quantitative increases in inputs of capital and labor—also declined after 1970. Agricultural output after 1958 grew at a healthy, although slackening, rate. Unfortunately, the real resource cost of agricultural output rose continuously.

Table 1. Average Annual Growth of Soviet Gross National Product

|  | 1951-55 | 1956-60 | 1961-65 | 1966-70 | 1971-75 | 1976-80 |
|---|---|---|---|---|---|---|
| Average annual growth (percent) | 5.5 | 5.9 | 5.0 | 5.2 | 3.7 | 2.7 |

The chapters that follow deal with the problems of the Soviet consumers and of Soviet agriculture. But here a few generalizations are in order. Consumption per capita increased at an impressive rate during the post-Stalin period taken as a whole, averaging in excess of 3 percent per year for 1951-1980. This performance was better than that of the United States, Canada, Sweden, Switzerland and the United Kingdom. France, Italy and West Germany performed somewhat better, averaging 3.9, 4.0 and 4.6 percent over the same period, and Japan attained a phenomenal annual rate of 6.6 percent.

At the same time, the composition of Soviet personal consumption expenditures changed in accordance with the profile typical of industrialized countries, if at a more gradual rate than in most other developing economies. Food declined as a proportion of total personal consumption, from 60 percent in 1951-1955 to 45 percent in 1976-1980, and durables increased from 2 to 11 percent. But services remained essentially constant at about 23 percent.

Thus Khrushchev and then Brezhnev did succeed in raising the priority of the consumer sector in the Soviet economy. But three serious and related problems remained:

• Attainment of a relatively high rate of growth of consumption per capita was more costly in real resources than had been anticipated.

• The rates of growth in all consumption subseries began high but have been declining since. Although the Brezhnev government succeeded in reversing the downward trend in 1966-1970, immediately after assuming power, the downward trend reasserted itself thereafter.

• Khrushchev committed himself to a policy of retail price stability, which Brezhnev followed. As agricultural production costs and money payments to farmers increased, nominal retail prices on a multitude of products, especially foodstuffs, came to bear little relationship either to cost of production or to each other.

Competition among increasingly affluent consumers for underpriced goods has perpetuated queuing as a major activity of adult Soviet citizens and fostered a wide range of illegal and quasi-legal private dealings (sometimes called the "second economy"). As rates of growth in output decline, or stagnate at low levels, the hope of meeting effective demand at existing consumer prices in state retail outlets is clearly doomed. Elimination of queues and of black and gray market opportunities will unavoidably require price adjustments—all upward. To raise prices, however, has been considered risky from a political standpoint. Scattered evidence of food riots in the Soviet Union suggests that this is not an idle consideration, as does the experience of the Polish leadership in recent years.

Irrationally low prices create consumer expectations that are certain to be frustrated, and these frustrations are blamed on the government. Raising prices generates immediate protest. This is a dilemma no Soviet government since Stalin has been prepared to resolve. Thus, the annual state subsidy of consumer goods continues to grow, increasing from 35 billion rubles in 1981 to an estimated 50 billion in 1983.

During the rapid industrialization of the 1930s, procurement of adequate food grains to provision urban workers was the primary index of the success of Bolshevik agricultural policy. Since Stalin, the index has increasingly been the provision of animal husbandry products, particularly red meat. This was presaged by Khrushchev's earliest statement on agricultural policy: "Really, comrades, in the communist society you will not tell people to go and eat a potato without butter."[4]

The high priority assigned red meat supplies was demonstrated by the Brezhnev government's willingness to use hard currency to purchase large quantities of grain in the West. These purchases were not made to supply food grains for Soviet dinner tables. Rather they were needed in order to meet the goals set for livestock herd expansion, for which domestic grain and fodder production was inadequate. With the help of imports, animal husbandry expanded substantially. Between 1951 and 1979 total meat production rose by approximately 4 percent per year, and milk output by about 3.5 percent. Success in this endeavor may also be measured indirectly, by an increasing incidence of coronary-artery disease, with attendant morbidity.

The Brezhnev government benefitted from two windfalls which helped to finance the shift in priorities. The price of gold soared as a result of floating the dollar and other "hard" currencies in the 1970s; and the formation of OPEC drove petroleum prices up beyond any expectation. As a major producer and exporter of both gold and petroleum products, the Soviet Union enjoyed a substantially improved foreign position.

These windfalls were not sufficient, however, to offset completely a growing conflict of priorities during the 1970s and early 1980s. Sometime in the late Khrushchev period a decision was made to increase the share of gross national product devoted to defense expenditures, most probably as a response to Khrushchev's humiliation in the Cuban missile crisis. During Brezhnev's time, the Soviet Union achieved parity with the United States in military strength for the first time. This has absorbed about 12 to 14 percent of Soviet gross national product, and it is assumed that the share cannot be reduced if parity is to be maintained. According to an estimate by Abram Bergson, Soviet military expenditures will grow at a rate of 4 to 5 percent per year during the Eleventh Five-Year Plan, 1981-1985. The implication is that an increased share of final product will be required for military purposes, since net material product is to grow at a planned rate of only 3.4 to 3.7 percent per year. Bergson believes that the gradual shift against investment volume that has been underway since the 1950s "will have exhausted its possibilities" by 1985.[5]

The post-Brezhnev government therefore faces direct competition between the goal of increasing per capita consumption and that of maintaining—let alone expanding—the Soviet military establishment. Unless a breakthrough is achieved that will accelerate technological innovation in Soviet industry and agriculture, or unless augmented supplies of labor and capital are obtained to continue the traditional pattern of growth, the regime will face a direct trade-off between producing red meat and maintaining, so to speak, the red menace. The Soviet leadership cannot determine defense policy unilaterally. It is determined by reactions to perceived external threats as well as by domestic considerations. Thus continuation of the arms race may lead to a degree of disappointment of consumer expectation that could threaten "the very stability of the social system," as Bialer, quoted above, suggests. The alternative is to seek arms limitation, or better, arms reduction.

No help can be expected from the growth of employment, which has declined from 2 percent per annum during 1965-1970 to about 0.05 percent per annum currently. Projections suggest a constant labor force through the year 2000. As labor participation rates are already high for women as well as men, when compared to other developed economies, there is no obvious "reserve" to tap. Agriculture still employs a great deal of manpower, but outmigration is being discouraged for the sake of agricultural output. Only a sharp reduction in the large standing army would supply a significant new source of manpower.

Meanwhile, gross national investment was one-third of gross national product in 1980, up from one-fourth in 1960. This share is already high, cross-nationally, and is unlikely to increase further. The rate of growth of investment has slowed to less than 3 percent per year, down from 7.6 percent in 1965-1970. Further sources of investment capital, in short, are not likely to appear.

Imports of capital embodying new technology represent a potential source of growth, but imports have not composed a large share of total Soviet investment in machinery and equipment (only about 3 percent recently), and expansion is constrained by limits on hard currency earnings. Recent declines in the prices of gold and oil do not help. Imports of grains, meat and other consumer-related items compete directly for foreign exchange with imports of investment goods.

Innovation by Soviet enterprises has been slow and uncertain, and this has inhibited economic growth. Moreover, costs of most raw materials have been rising because of quality decline in mined-out regions and because of the increased cost of locating, recovering and transporting resources from sites that are increasingly remote from traditional population centers.

To top it all off, maintaining control in Eastern Europe is increasingly costly. Intervention in Afghanistan is proving an expensive exercise, and relations with China are unlikely to improve sufficiently to permit reduction of military power designated to protect the long common border.

The economic situation looks difficult indeed for the current Soviet leadership. A number of hard choices must be confronted, and soon.

While the troubles and constraints enumerated above are real and serious, it does not follow that Soviet policy-makers consider the situation to be as bleak as do most Western analysts. It is easy to exaggerate the long-term consequences of today's ills; most of us in the West feel this way about Soviet doomsday projections of current economic problems in the United States. Much that is completely unexpected can happen between now and the end of the century. Besides, the fundamental strength of the Soviet economy, like the American, resides in its size, in the skills of its population, in the extraordinary richness of its natural resources and in the proven ability of the leadership to respond effectively to problems new and old.

The present generation of top Soviet leaders has witnessed victory in the most ferocious and devastating war in history; a rise to military parity with the largest economy in the world; a doubling of the living standards of the population as a whole over a quarter-century; and the transformation of the Soviet Union into a modern industrial state, surrounded by a large, relatively prosperous empire. Why should its leaders conclude that the problems they face today are fatal?

Western observers of the Soviet Union have a history of misreading events. They tend to swing from predicting its imminent collapse to foreseeing a destructive onslaught against "civilization as we know it" by a horde of fanatic, semi-Asiatic barbarians. Emphasis on the weaknesses and failures of the Soviet economy has recently, in fact, alarmed certain observers. Senator William Proxmire of Wisconsin, for example, felt compelled to request a "balanced assessment of the Soviet economy" from the CIA in the fall of 1982 in order to offset a growing sense in Washington that the Soviet Union was on the point of collapse. Proxmire's preface to the resulting report stressed that Soviet economic growth would probably remain positive; that the Soviet economy is not "losing its viability or dynamism"; and that "an economic collapse in the USSR is not considered even a remote possibility."[6]

It is wise, I would agree, to discount predictions of imminent Soviet economic collapse. But what are the factors that might improve the performance of the Soviet economy significantly over the next decade or two? It is fairly safe to predict a surge in the provision of consumer goods, at least over the next few years. Such a surge accompanied the political transitions following Stalin's death in 1953 and Khrushchev's ouster in 1964. The question is whether acceptable rates of growth in the non-defense components of the gross national product can be re-established for a decade or more. For the problem is at base one of stagnation, and its solution requires searching for ways to increase the supply of final products and/or to reduce final demand. Let us consider demand management first.

The most obvious solution is a reduction in the share of gross national product absorbed by defense expenditures. As we have seen, this share is currently estimated at 12 to 14 percent. A slowdown in the rate of increase in military expenditures from 4 to 5 percent per annum to, say, 1 to 2 percent would allow for increased rates of growth for both investment and consumption. Observers of Soviet affairs agree that the leadership is ripe for serious arms talks for this reason, but successful negotiation requires readiness on the part of the United States and its allies, which is what makes this alternative problematic from the Soviet standpoint.

There are two broad schools of thought in the West about the potential usefulness of arms limitation agreements with the Soviet Union. One holds that fundamental change in the nature of the Soviet political system must precede any significant agreement. Otherwise, the Soviet leadership would merely exploit the agreement to its own advantage, one way or another. The other school operates on the assumption that the leadership is willing and able to conduct, and to adhere to, an arms-limiting agreement. Favorable change in the nature of the Soviet system would, in this view, be fostered by the agreement itself. Meanwhile, careful verification and vigilance would be required to ensure against cheating.

Appraisal of these two views is beyond the scope of this essay. What is significant is that from the end of 1979 or so, the United States apparently favored the first view. In fact, some members of the Reagan Administration suggested that acceleration of the arms race by the United States would foster favorable change in Soviet domestic and foreign policies by increasing the competition for domestic resources, as defense absorbs an ever-increasing share of Soviet output.

But from the Soviet point of view, as we have seen, the constraint on a policy aimed at deceleration of the arms race is its dependence on the other side. And insofar as Soviet leaders sense that U.S. disarmament policy is aimed at forcing change in Soviet domestic policies, they are certain to move slowly and with extreme caution. Deceleration of the arms race does not offer them, attractive as it must seem, a reliable way to free resources to support a new economic policy. A reasonable goal would be to attempt to contain their military spending at current levels, so that the crunch does not get worse.

All other economic policy options involve finding ways to increase the growth rate of the Soviet gross national product and thus the supply of final product. There remains, to be sure, the possibility of improving the way in which consumer demand is managed centrally. Many Western analysts claim that in the Soviet Union aggregate demand for consumer goods exceeds the aggregate supply. But this is not an easy proposition to test empirically, and it is elusive in theory as well. What is clear is that such a state of affairs would have a deleterious effect on total employment and on incentives to work hard and advance professionally. Time would be better spent in queues or at leisure. Elimination of any such gap between supply and demand would have a beneficial effect on productivity.

There can be no doubt that demand exceeds supply for certain quality commodities and services in state-operated retail outlets. This is because many of the most desirable goods and services, such as red meat, vegetables and fruits, quality apparel and state-of-the-art durables are underpriced by very large margins. Underpricing leads not only to queuing, but to "scarcity-mindedness." Runs on periodically scarce commodities in retail outlets tend to make these items scarce all the time. Underpricing must, in addition, tempt many Soviet citizens into illegal middle-man activities in black and grey markets in order to collect the difference between actual and equilibrium prices.[7]

Consumer demand management could be greatly improved — and illegal, petty private enterprise diminished — if flexible prices were used to a greater extent. But this would require raising prices on many goods — a process which would, in turn, redistribute income among Soviet citizens in a significant but not entirely predictable way. People with more time than money would surely lose out. And if prices were also raised in the special stores open to privileged groups, those outlets would be effectively closed. Better demand management alone, then, might do as much political harm as economic good, and so is unlikely to be seen by itself as a way of making friends or encouraging productivity. Yet some realignment of retail prices and a consequent reduction in the huge subsidies that now support many commodities represent essential first steps toward any fundamental reform of the Soviet economy.

Soviet leaders and economists have been considering and implementing structural reforms in planning and management since the early 1960s. But if periodic reform has become institutionalized by now, thoroughgoing reform has yet to be undertaken.[8] Nor are radical changes likely to be introduced by Brezhnev's immediate successors. The degree of centralization of the economy is not likely ever to be be reduced sufficiently to permit a significant exercise of discretion at the enterprise level. The tendency to write tight plans has been curbed somewhat

Table 2. Comparative Size and Allocation of U.S. and Soviet Economies

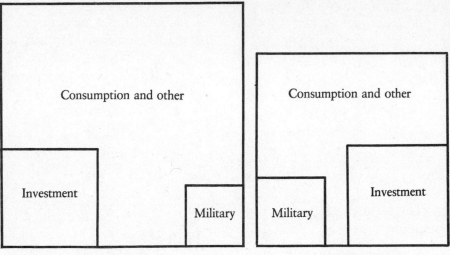

Consumption and other

Investment

Military

*U.S. Economy*

Consumption and other

Investment

Military

*Soviet Economy*

Source: Franklyn D. Holzman, *The Soviet Economy: Past, Present and Future* (New York: Foreign Policy Association, 1982), p. 4.

recently, but it remains a standard central management tool. The amount of detail in Soviet plans is also likely to be reduced only gradually and marginally. A wholesale reform of central planning and of managerial incentives—a prospect which has excited the attention of many Western observers for almost two decades—does not appear to be in the making. Rather, the fundamental paradigm of Soviet central planning remains intact and, like other paradigms, will not disappear until replaced by a new conception of planning. Market socialism has, by implication, been rejected by dominant Soviet economists and policy-makers. And while much has been written in the West about the possible applicability of the "Hungarian model" to the Soviet economy, what is often overlooked is the fact that since its introduction in Hungary itself, the rate of increase in gross national product in that country has not risen significantly. Besides, Hungary is too small and too export-oriented to serve as a model.

This does not mean that serious economic reform in the Soviet Union is out of the question; but it is more likely to happen somewhere other than the central planning and management institutions. If the reform movement of the last two decades has produced any consensus, it is that policy on consumer prices in state retail outlets must be changed before any other reforms can be expected to work properly. In sum, the present price system is perceived by all concerned as capricious and inequitable and as an invitation to citizens to participate in black, gray and other illegal marketeering.

Soviet leaders had hoped that with increased output economies of scale would eventually permit satisfaction of demand at 1953 prices. This expectation has clearly and unambiguously failed for all agricultural products. But how are anxious Soviet consumers to be persuaded, after repeated promises of stable prices, that they cannot have their cake and eat it too? Consumers complain about queues, but they complain even more loudly about price increases.

Nonetheless, Soviet authorities may seriously consider retail price reform as a component of a major economic reform program. It would not suffice by itself, but would have to be part of a package that would not only make more palatable the bitter pill of income redistribution, but would also lead to a sustained period of improved growth performance. The appeal of price reform to Soviet leaders is obvious: it would decrease queuing and complaints about special privileges and it would help stamp out economic crime. The danger is that consumers would not stand for it.

Price reform could be accompanied by the large-scale, but short-term, import of consumer goods. This policy would minimize the price increases required to eliminate queues in individual markets, and at the same time increase total satisfaction, offsetting somewhat the impact of redistribution on the "losers." Price reform would also require some wage adjustments. My guess is that the result would be greater inequality in income distribution, which might in turn have a favorable impact on incentives. Moreover, unfavorable comparison with imported consumer goods might help to improve the quality of Soviet goods.

Once retail prices were better adjusted, wholesale prices could be adjusted also, and managerial incentive reform experiments would thus have a better chance of success. But, as I have said, I do not believe that the weight of reform will be borne at the enterprise managerial level.

A minor but potentially significant component of reform might be to facilitate small-scale private enterprise in urban areas, especially in services. This is a region dominated by "second-economy" activities today. Fostering private repairs of durable goods, auto repairs, hairdressing and similar economic activities, accompanied by provision of the necessary tools, parts and other supplies through state outlets, would reduce economic crime and improve the efficiency of these activities for the benefit of all. The state need not fear such private enterprise today as it did three or four decades ago. Willingness to tolerate it would be a victory of economic rationality over hidebound ideology. The odds are, however, that the latter will prevail.

With better management of demand and three to five years of increased imports of consumer goods, the government could buy time to focus
on ways of regaining some of the dynamism of earlier growth. One
possibility would be to find a way to offset the decline in the rate of
growth of both manpower and capital stock. A second would be to
achieve a reasonable rate of growth of total factor productivity—perhaps of 1.5 to 2 percent per annum.

Restructuring prices and wages ought to make material incentives
work better all 'round, but even this would not be sufficient to achieve
what is needed. Relatively unproductive labor does exist in the Soviet
Union, labor which could be shifted to better uses, but it is located far
from the more industrialized regions. Restructuring of wages could be
done in such a way as to attract workers from Central Asia and
elsewhere to the industrial regions or to resource-rich Siberia.

Many Western specialists believe that cultural barriers limit voluntary
outmigration from these areas.[9] There is considerable countervailing
evidence from elsewhere, however: in the movement of Pakistanis to
England, for example, of Turks to West Germany, or of Algerians to
France in the 1950s and 1960s. In the Soviet Union such a policy has
never been tried with comparable incentives. The barriers may reflect
racism more than cultural preference.

Internal migration is not the only possibility. The Soviet Union might
decide to use foreign workers on a greater scale, adopting one of the
tools of successful postwar growth in Western Europe. There are,
however, two main constraints on such a policy: obtaining, or creating,
currency that is "hard" enough to be an incentive; and policing a large
number of foreign workers.

Another component of a possible reform package would be to encourage foreign investment in the Soviet Union and to rely more heavily
on foreign borrowing to finance inputs of capital. The Soviet Union has
always been a very conservative debtor country, and its current debt-
service ratio is relatively low. A more aggressive policy of risk-taking
would find lenders.[10] Careful choice of capital imports designed to max-
imize desirable technological features would help generate growth of factor productivity.

Japan, for example, represents an ideal trading and venture-capital
partner for the Soviet Union. Japan's technology is well developed in
many of the areas where the Soviet Union is particularly weak: high
technology, the production of high-quality consumer durables, and the
use of robots to minimize the demand for labor in the modern industrial
sector. The Soviet Union, on the other hand, has the vast resources
Japan lacks. There are similar possibilities with other countries, and

European nations appear prepared to continue to expand economic relations with their Soviet neighbor.

Some combination of the policies described above could alleviate the resource crunch the current Soviet leaders face. But there are other factors which could make these alternatives easier or harder to implement, factors over which they have no real control. A recurrence of better weather conditions for a decade or more could greatly ease things; two or three good harvests per Five-Year Plan would raise the rate of growth a percentage point or two and reduce competition for foreign exchange between investment and consumption.

Economic recovery in the West would also be helpful. Rising world production and a growth in international trade would help firm the prices of petroleum and natural gas. It would also help Eastern European economies, which depend heavily on exports to the West for prosperity. Greater prosperity in Eastern Europe might dampen political discontent therein and thus reduce demands for Soviet economic assistance and for Soviet forces to cope with social unrest.

Speeches by Soviet leaders over the last several decades often featured calls to Party members to return to the ideological dedication of the halcyon days of the 1930s, and to the populace as a whole for a return to the moral commitment of wartime Russia. Thus far, they have generated little more than nostalgia among senior citizens. There is no evidence that the Soviet leadership or the Party it speaks for knows how to rekindle these emotions, but there is little doubt that doing so would work miracles in the economy. What seems to be needed is a "moral rearmament" movement, the creation, somehow, of "born-again communists." Although it seems an unlikely prospect, we should not overlook the possibility of a rededication to Marxist goals among Party members or a resurgence of long-standing popular ambitions.

The best of all possible worlds for the Soviet leadership would include a series of excellent harvests, a deceleration of the arms race, quietude in Eastern Europe, and economic recovery in the West. Were it to adopt policies leading to an end of the war in Afghanistan, increased rationality in setting retail and wholesale prices, and the mobilization of new and/or more productive labor and capital, the Soviet gross national product could grow at a rate that would satisfy most members of society and help foster ideological and spiritual commitment to the regime and its goals.

Of course, the worst may happen instead. Climatic change may contribute to more poor harvests; the arms race may accelerate; Eastern Europe, Afghanistan and other parts of the Soviet Union's empire may become even more unstable and costly to discipline and police. Price reform may backfire, causing domestic unrest. Both labor and capital productivity may decline further because of the resulting economic disarray, leading to general political instability.

.    Usually, in history, neither the worst nor the best happens. The prospects for success in stabilizing Soviet economic growth at a level tolerable to the leadership are quite good. The big question is whether it has the power, the courage and the foresight to develop and implement a well-wrought, rational policy; or whether, instead, the leadership will hesitate before the risks such a course of action poses and decide instead to follow the example set by Brezhnev at the end of his career, which was to coast, leaving the hard choices to his successors. Failure to establish strong political leadership would make this course even more attractive and likely. □

1. *Report on the Program of the Communist Party of the Soviet Union* (Oct. 17, 1961), 2, p. 85.

2. Seweryn Bialer in *Time*, Nov. 22, 1982, p. 26.

3. The performance data cited here and elsewhere in this essay are based on the following computations and estimates: USSR: *Measures of Economic Growth and Development, 1950-1980* (Washington, D.C.: Joint Economic Committee, U.S. Congress, Government Printing Office, 1982); *Soviet Economy in a Time of Change* (Washington, D.C.: Joint Economic Committee, U.S. Congress, Government Printing Office, 1979); *Economic Survey of Europe in 1981* (New York: Secretariat of the U.N. Economic Commission for Europe, 1982).

4. Quoted in Sidney T. Ploss, *Conflict and Decision-Making in Soviet Russia* (Princeton, New Jersey: Princeton University Press, 1965), p. 85.

5. Abram Bergson, "Soviet Economic Slowdown and the 1981-85 Plan," *Problems of Communism* (May-June 1981).

6. "Central Intelligence Agency Briefing on the Soviet Economy," Henry Rowen, chairman, National Intelligence Council, CIA, before the Joint Economic Committee (Dec. 1, 1982, mimeo), p. i-ii.

7. See further James R. Millar, *The ABCs of Soviet Socialism* (Urbana, Illinois: University of Illinois Press, 1981), Chap. 4.

8. Joseph S. Berliner, "Managing the USSR Economy: Alternative Models," *Problems of Communism* (Jan.-Feb. 1983) for discussion of alternative paths to reforming central planning and management.

9. For a detailed evaluation and statement of the majority view, see Murray Feshbach, "Prospects for Outmigration from Central Asia and Kazakhstan in the Next Decade," *Soviet Economy in a Time of Change, 1.*

10. Franklyn D. Holzman, *The Soviet Economy: Past, Present and Future*, Headline Series, Foreign Policy Association, No. 260 (Sept.-Oct. 1982), pp. 44-48.

# 15

## The Economy and the Consumer

### Marshall I. Goldman

In the Stalinist model of economic development, the consumer generally comes last. The highest priority is placed on heavy industry. The hope is that by initially giving priority to heavy industry and capital accumulation, overall economic growth in the long run will be faster than if light industry had been stressed. Then, once the economic foundation has been created, the expectation is that economic planners will be able to switch their priorities and pay more attention to consumption. Because the economic base is larger than it otherwise would have been, the planners promise to increase the production of consumer goods rapidly. Thus, before too long, consumers will be better off than they would have been if a more traditional strategy had been followed.

Pacified by the promise of an abundant tomorrow, Soviet consumers for decades have patiently endured the diversion of the country's resources into the building of industrial and military might. But after so many years of such promises, more and more Soviet citizens are beginning to wonder if tomorrow will ever come. Indeed, to coin a phrase, in the Soviet Union "tomorrow" has become the "opiate of the people." Unfortunately for Soviet leaders, there is evidence that, just as in Eastern Europe, the impact of the drug may be wearing off. Signs of protest have begun to increase, and friction has occasionally given way to violence.

Soviet leaders are not insensitive to popular discontent. At a meeting of the Central Committee of the Communist Party in November 1981, Leonid Brezhnev, the late Party leader, acknowledged that "food is economically and politically" the central problem of the Eleventh Five-Year Plan (1981 to 1985). As we shall see, he had cause to be concerned. But it will take more than acknowledging it to remedy the problem. For that matter, merely increasing the allocation of resources to food and

187

consumer goods production is not enough. As it is, the share of the country's national investment going to agriculture has grown to 27 percent of the total.[1] The difficulty is that this new-found concern for agricultural investment has come too late to produce a quick improvement.

Until the mid-1950s, agriculture in the Soviet Union was treated as the economic sector from which resources were to be taken. Under Stalin, investment in agriculture was held to as low as 13 percent.[2] Moreover, procurement prices paid to the peasants were more often than not inadequate to cover operating costs, so that an unusually large number of farms operated at a loss. On top of everything else, a very large turnover tax of about 86 percent was added to the price of bread.[3] Agriculture had become a source of primitive accumulation.

The situation improved markedly under Nikita Khrushchev, when investment in agriculture was increased from 13 percent to 17 percent of the country's total investment package.[4] However, resources invested later are not the equivalent of resources that might have been invested at the beginning of the process. It is not just a matter of making up for lost time by providing compensatory funds. A ruble's worth of investment at the early stage of Soviet development would have been much more critical to increased production than an equal investment 50 years later. In fact, agricultural and consumer goods production suffered so during the Stalinist days of stringency that the shortages have had lasting impact on incentives and morale. Eventually workers in both industry and agriculture discovered that the money they earned for their work had little real meaning, since there were seldom enough high quality goods in the stores to buy with that money. What was the sense of working hard once it was discovered that there was no real compensation beyond the money facade? A partial demonitarization of the economy ensued. Workers became much more responsive to in-kind or barter transactions than to payments in money. Thus the system of salary incentives broke down, at least in part.

Once such a breakdown occurs, the system is not easily reconstituted. It is not enough to announce that more resources will be devoted to producing consumer goods. It is also necessary for the planning authorities to regain their credibility and to convince the workers that they mean what they say. This is very hard to do. Efforts at increasing investment generally turn out to be less effective than originally anticipated because the population has become so skeptical that it usually fails to respond properly even when the authorities are sincere. The danger is that in time the whole system will become demonetarized and demoralized and thus unresponsive to official incentives.

While there is no denying that consumption has lagged in the Soviet

Union and that Soviet workers and peasants have become dispirited, it is also true that living conditions have improved markedly from what they were in the 1940s and early 1950s. One indication of how far the authorities had neglected urban housing during the period of industrialization is reflected in statistics showing that the amount of such space per capita fell from 5.7 square meters in 1926 to 4.5 square meters in 1940.[5] To be sure, the wholesale destruction of World War II did not help the situation. By 1950, the per capita figure had increased only minimally, to 4.9 square meters.[6] But by 1958, the average had increased to 5.8 square meters, which was equal to the 1926 level. There were further improvements throughout the 1960s and 1970s, so that by 1977 the comparable figure was 8.2 square meters—which was still below the legal norm of 9 square meters per person, the equivalent of a room measuring 10 feet by 10 feet.

Nonetheless, as much as housing has improved for the majority of the population, there remain serious complaints. Perhaps the most telling reflection of the problem is that in 1980, 20 percent of the Soviet urban population still lived in communal apartments.[7] This means that one or more families each have a room in what would normally be a one-family apartment, and that toilets and kitchens are shared. Certainly the reduction in the number of communal apartments is an improvement over conditions that prevailed as recently as 1971, when as much as 40 percent of Moscow's population lived in such apartments. Yet the move to a private apartment does not always mean that housing worries are over. Even new apartments often appear to be in poor condition as well as poorly equipped. In short, by Western standards the quality of housing in the Soviet Union leaves much to be desired.

The availability of consumer goods reflects much the same pattern. While there has been a very marked increase in the production and sale of most goods, supplies are still generally inadequate. At the same time, the quality of goods is generally poor. This is seen not only in the relatively short service life of many items, but in a lack of innovation and style. Naturally, the size of Soviet apartments puts a limit on how much the Soviet family can use. Even so, Soviet workers find few desirable goods to buy.

The food situation reflects a different set of problems. The generally poor supplies are not so much a question of storage (the majority of Soviet homes now have refrigerators),[8] or of quality, but of low levels of production. Beginning in 1979, as will be seen in the following chapter, the Soviet Union had several bad harvests in a row. This inevitably has affected the country's ability to feed itself. Fortunately, the Soviet Union

Table 1.  Meat and Meat Product Imports (thousands of tons)

| Year | 1971 | 1972 | 1973 | 1974 | 1975 | 1976 | 1977 | 1978 | 1979 | 1980 | 1981 |
|------|------|------|------|------|------|------|------|------|------|------|------|
| Imports | 225 | 134 | 129 | 515 | 515 | 361 | 617 | 183 | 386 | 576 | 651 |

Source: Ministerstvo Vneishnei Torgovli, *Vneshnaia torgovlia SSSR: Statisticheskii sbornik* (Moscow), vols. 1971-1981.

has been able to supplement much of its harvest shortfall with grain imports from the United States, Canada, Australia and Argentina.

Yet in spite of poor harvests, for the last two decades the Soviets have always had enough bread. The impact of the poor harvests has primarily affected meat supplies. Never over-abundant, meat commonly becomes extremely difficult to find after the slaughter that follows a bad harvest. Feed for livestock is almost always cut back first. This is reflected in Table 1, which shows that following the bad harvests of 1976 and 1980, for example, meat imports rose to more than 600,000 tons.

Nor have meat imports been high enough to satisfy the appetites of most Soviet consumers. This is evident from the length of shopping lines after even the best of harvests. After the poorer harvests, especially when they come two or three in a row, the lines become ubiquitous, and waiting in them the chore of everyone lacking access to the special shops set aside primarily for Party functionaries. All too often, morever, supplies run out before everyone in line has had a chance. In Moscow, normally better provided than elsewhere in the Soviet Union, shopper frustration is compounded by the fact that shoppers from as far as 150 miles away come early in the morning to buy meat and other products that are almost never available in their own communities. Not surprisingly, there is not much left for Muscovites unable to go shopping until after work.

Similar experiences plague most large Soviet cities. In several instances, the local authorities have limited the purchases any one customer may make.[9] In more extreme cases, rationing has been instituted. Volodga, Irkutsk, Kazan, Naberezhnye Chelny, and Tbilisi are among the cities in which rationing was reported in late 1981 and early 1982.[10] That the authorities should find it necessary to institute rationing 35 years after ending it, in 1947, is a serious indictment of Soviet agriculture and marketing.

The supplies of other consumer goods are usually more dependable. Still, there are occasions when such basic products as matches and toilet paper will simply disappear from store shelves. The more typical complaint about non-food goods, however, is that both quality and distribution facilities are almost always poor. In part the dearth of stores and marketing facilities is a reflection of Marxist ideology, which regards marketing as a non-productive, even parasitic activity. More basically, the low priority assigned to distribution is usually predicated on the rationalization that capital investment allocated to production and construction will result in a higher overall output in the long run than if those resources were devoted to activities like services. An underlying assumption is that holding back on investment in the distribution sector will not significantly affect the ultimate supply of goods. If anything, it will eliminate the waste of unutilized capacities so often found in the West. Admittedly, there will be longer lines and the consumer will have to spend several hours more each week in line, but presumably the consumer would rather have more money spent on production than on building more stores where the clerks would stand idle a portion of the day. Or so the planners have reasoned. Yet even if the state's costs are reduced by not having to build so many stores and warehouses, the cost to the consumer of standing in line, or of running around town in search of goods, is very real—and expensive as well as demoralizing.

The downgrading of service activities affects not only capital, but also human allocation. The personnel working in the service sector of the economy are thought of as less able and honest. The Soviet press is filled with stories of store and warehouse clerks who have been arrested for diverting state supplies of goods to their friends for sale on the black market. "Why else," asked a Soviet official, "does a qualified worker making 250 rubles a month seek the job of a sales clerk who makes only 90 rubles a month?"[11] Economists call the Soviet case a classic "seller's market."

Seller's markets, particularly those of long duration, are seldom if ever noted for their solicitous treatment of customers. The customer comes to be regarded as a nuisance, and service, in the fuller or better sense, all but disappears. An attitude of "take it or leave it" is almost inevitable. We discovered this ourselves, in the United States, during the gasoline shortages of 1973 and 1979. Thus not only are there complaints about the availability and quality of the goods being sold in Soviet stores; there are also complaints about *how* the goods are sold.

In view of what has been said, it will be understandable that Soviet consumers frequently find it difficult to spend all their money. Just how serious the problem has become in recent years is reflected in Table 2. Unlike consumers elsewhere in the world, Soviet consumers frequently increase the money value of their savings faster than they increase the money value of their retail purchases. Thus savings bank deposits increased by 15.1 billion rubles from 1978 to 1979 while retail sales increased by only 12.9 billion rubles. Since the savings figures presented in Table 2 reflect only savings flowing into Soviet savings banks, actual

**Table 2.  Changes in Savings Bank Deposits and Retail Sales**
(billions of rubles)

| Year | Total savings | Increase | Retail trade volume | Increase |
|------|---------------|----------|---------------------|----------|
| 1981 | 165.7 |      | 294.1 |      |
|      |       | 9.2  |       | 16.1 |
| 1980 | 156.5 |      | 278.0 |      |
|      |       | 10.3 |       | 17.3 |
| 1979 | 146.2 |      | 260.7 |      |
|      |       | 15.1 |       | 12.9 |
| 1978 | 131.1 |      | 247.8 |      |
|      |       | 14.4 |       | 11.4 |
| 1977 | 116.7 |      | 236.4 |      |
|      |       | 13.7 |       | 10.5 |
| 1976 | 103.0 |      | 225.9 |      |
|      |       | 12.0 |       | 10.3 |
| 1975 | 91.0  |      | 215.6 |      |

savings including those held in liquid form were undoubtedly considerably higher. For that matter, even in 1981, when the ruble increase in
savings bank accounts appears to be lower than the ruble increase in retail sales, the percentage increase in savings still exceeded the percentage
increase in retail sales. This increase in the disposable income of Soviet
consumers not only reflects a lack of satisfaction with the goods that are
available, it also measures how much Soviet consumers have come to
downgrade the purchasing capabilities of the ruble. No wonder more
and more transactions are  made through barter.

Satisfying consumers in the Soviet Union has become a very serious
concern to the authorities. Nonetheless, there is little to indicate that
Soviet leaders are even contemplating any measures which will
significantly alter the situation. Initially, the Eleventh Five-Year Plan
called for a faster rate of growth for the production of consumer as compared to capital goods, but whenever similar promises have been made
in the past they have almost always been revised downward. True to
form, such a revision was made in the final version of the Eleventh Five-
Year Plan when the target for the increase in consumer goods production
was set at an average of 4 percent a year, instead of the 4.9 to 5.2 percent first projected.[12] And even if the target is not further diminished,
merely increasing the physical output of consumer goods would not, in
and of itself, solve the problem. The goods would have to be of a higher
quality than has been the case in the past, and they would have to be
properly distributed. More than that, something has to be done to stimulate industry to be more innovative and service personnel to provide
better service.

There is no doubt that the Soviet economic system is today particularly vulnerable. That should be reassuring for those in the West who worry which system is doing better. But given that economic conditions in the West are not all that good, we should not become smug. Nor should we forget that the Soviet Union seems to have solved the problem of unemployment and held inflation below what we have seen in the West. Yet its other problems are monumental. This apparent paradox brings to mind an article written by an American who had emigrated to Eastern Europe in search of a fuller life. Dismayed by some of the things he saw in Czechoslovakia in 1966, he wrote: "It is remarkable how often some of the greatest achievements of socialism, such as equality, low rents, greater security, absence of unemployment, bring with them other problems."[13] To which another disillusioned Marxist responded, "What is the strength of the communist system?" and answered, "It seeks solutions to problems that don't exist in other societies." □

**1.** Tsentral'noe statisticheskoe upravelenie SSSR, *Narodnoe khoziastvo SSSR v 1979g.* (Moscow: Statistika, 1980), p. 370 (hereafter abbreviated as *Nar. Khoz.* with the appropriate year).

**2.** *Nar. khoz.*, 1966, p. 44.

**3.** Franklyn Holzman, *Soviet Taxation* (Cambridge, Massachusetts: Harvard University Press, 1955), p. 153.

**4.** *Nar. khoz.*, 1976, p. 44.

**5.** Henry W. Morton, "The Soviet Quest for Better Housing—An Impossible Dream?" Joint Economic Committee, *Soviet Economy in a Time of Change* (Washington, D.C.: U.S. Government Printing Office, Oct. 10, 1979), p. 794.

**6.** Morton, p. 794.

**7.** *Pravda* (Feb. 24, 1981).

**8.** M. Elizabeth Denton, "Soviet Consumer Policy: Trends and Prospects," Joint Economic Committee, *Soviet Economy in a Time of Change*, p. 772.

**9.** The New York Times (Jan. 15, 1982).

**10.** *Zaria Vostoka* (Nov. 26, 1981); *Radio Free Europe-Radio Liberty Research Report*, RFE-RL, 498/81 (Dec. 14, 1981), p. 2; The New York Times (Jan. 15, 1982); The New York Times (Dec. 28, 1981).

**11.** The Boston Globe (Jan. 16, 1982); *Pravda* (Dec. 15, 1981).

**12.** RFE-RL, 496/81 (Dec. 11, 1981), p. 2.

**13.** George Shaw Wheeler, "Economic Reform in Czechoslovakia," *The Monthly Review*, 17 (Jan. 1966), p. 46.

# 16

## Agriculture

### D. Gale Johnson

The performance of Soviet agriculture for the past several years has been dismal. Since 1970 total agricultural production has barely kept up with the slow growth in population. Over the past decade, numerous food products have disappeared from the shelves of the state stores. During this period the Soviet Union changed from being a significant net exporter to the world's largest importer of grains. Starting from a rough balance between the value of its exports and imports of agricultural products in 1970 the Soviet Union, as of 1981, had imports exceeding the value of exports by $16 billion.

Before looking ahead, however, it would be useful to compare recent performance with the past record. By 1950 Soviet agriculture had recovered from World War II except for the greatly reduced farm labor force—a result of the enormous wartime casualties. During the 1950s the farm labor force consisted very largely of women, older men, young boys and girls. Given this composition, agricultural production in that period was quite remarkable. Output grew by about 4 percent annually, nearly double the rate of growth in Western Europe or North America.

As was indicated in the preceding chapter, with the death of Stalin in 1953 the rapacious exploitation of rural people by their government was largely brought to an end. Prices paid to farms in 1958, compared to 1952, were increased severalfold—the grains by six times, livestock by eleven, and sunflowers by eight. Sugar beet prices doubled, and milk prices in 1958 were four times those of 1952.

Between 1953 and 1964, Nikita Khrushchev undertook several bold and risky agricultural ventures. His New (or Virgin) Lands Program brought 36 million hectares of marginal land under cultivation. The corn program increased the planted area of corn from four million to 37

195

million hectares in 1962 (although the maximum area harvested for grain was just seven million hectares). The Machine Tractor Stations were abolished. And a single procurement price for each product was introduced. While Soviet agriculture in general responded positively, it may have been success that undid Khrushchev.

In part because of the measures adopted and in part as the result of favorable growing conditions, 1958 was a bumper-crop year. It was then that Khrushchev abolished the Machine Tractor Stations, in the expectation, widely shared outside the Soviet Union, that this would significantly improve productivity by making the collective farms more responsible for the use of their resources and by providing greater incentives. Like all too many agricultural reforms, this one was poorly planned and executed. Repair services were inadequate and the machinery was transferred to the farms under unfavorable terms for them. A new burden replaced an old one, and farm incomes declined after what could have been a constructive move.

Agriculture performed far below Khrushchev's bellicose claim that the Soviet Union would catch up with and overtake the United States in meat and milk production by 1965. Several of the goals for 1965, announced in 1958, still have not been met, including the critically important one for meat. Farm output grew by 43 percent between 1952 and 1958, but for the next six years the output increased by just 17 percent. At least in part as a result of the poor performance of agriculture and the need to import 10 million tons of grain in 1963-1964, Khrushchev was replaced by Aleksei Kosygin and Leonid Brezhnev in 1964.

The new administration instituted important agricultural reforms. Farm prices were increased, an enormous fertilizer production program was inaugurated, investment in agriculture was increased sharply, wages were introduced for farm workers, and a pension system for members of collective farms was introduced. These were clearly sensible measures and were expected to result in a revitalization of agriculture. But hardly any other aspect of the agricultural policy inherited from Khrushchev was changed. Moscow still maintained tight control over the minutest details of farm operations: extent of crop areas, plowing dates, seeding dates and rates of seeding, harvesting, delivery quotas, and the annual and Five-Year Plans for each farm. Nothing was done to gain the respect of the farm people for the planners or other governmental officials. Indeed, confidence in those officials remained minimal.

Still, given the material resources devoted to agriculture, it would have been reasonable to expect a rapid and continuing increase in production. And for a time, from 1964 to 1970, it appeared that the program was succeeding, since agricultural output grew at an annual rate of

3.9 percent. But the 1970s saw an annual growth rate of only 1.2 percent, with an even lower rate after the mid-1970s; and the 1980 output was the same as in 1973 and 1976.

The shift in resources to agriculture under Kosygin and Brezhnev can only be described as enormous. From 1961 to 1965 some 19 percent of national investment was allocated to agriculture; between 1976 and 1980 this figure increased to 27 percent. If the investment in agriculturally related industries is included, the allocation increases to 33 percent for 1976-1980. Annual rates of investment increased from nine billion rubles in 1961-1965 to 34 billion in 1976-1980. There were significant increases in the delivery of farm machines, but due to high scrappage rates inventories rose slowly during the 1970s. Yet, for all the high investment in agriculture, returns by the end of the decade were disappointing, to say the least.

Some of the recent output performance of Soviet agriculture can be attributed to poor weather: thus grain production from 1979 to 1981 may have been 13 percent less than it would have been with normal or average weather. But the effect of the relatively low production of grain and other feed supplies was partially, if not wholly, offset by grain imports averaging 36 million tons for those three years. The level of grain imports was greater than the shortfall in grain production from trend levels for that period. Thus the fact that per capita meat output in 1981 was the same as in 1975 cannot be attributed wholly or even primarily to poor climatic conditions.

Milk production in 1981 was below the absolute level in 1974. Milk production per cow in 1981 was 2,040 kilograms, compared to 2,260 kilograms in 1977 and 2,110 in 1970. This remarkable decline in milk output is difficult to account for; current production per cow is among the lowest in Europe.

Nor have the very high rate of investment in agriculture and the increase in food imports over the past two decades resulted in a marked decrease in the use of labor. Between 1965 and 1980 employment in agriculture declined by just 15 percent to an annual level of about 27 million workers. Quite remarkably, even this enormous number of farm workers has not been sufficient. In 1979 some 15.6 million non-agricultural workers were sent from city to countryside to help with various farm operations, primarily harvesting. This is approximately double the number of such non-farm workers sent to the farms in 1960 and some 40 percent more than in 1970.

One reason for the great pressure to expand Soviet livestock production, and thus to import large quantities of grain, has been the policy over the past two decades of constant nominal prices for food, including livestock products. (The same policy has applied to home energy, public transportation and housing.) While money income has continued to increase in recent years, the supplies of livestock products have risen slowly, if at all. As a result, demand exceeds supply at the stable and relatively low prices. In fact, except in Moscow, meat seems to have disappeared from the state stores; elsewhere it is available either in the collective farm markets at two or three times the official prices (so much for stable prices!) or in newly devised distribution systems at places of employment.

The costs of livestock production have increased sharply since the consumer price policy was adopted in 1962. Thus in 1965 the Soviet government inaugurated a policy of increasing prices paid to farms, making up the difference by subsidies. In 1981 the cost of food subsidies, primarily for meat and milk, came to about 35 billion rubles. Further increases in prices of agricultural products, taking effect in January 1983, will increase subsidies by 16 billion rubles. The 1983 subsidy bill exceeds 50 billion rubles; the 1982 subsidy bill already exceeded the total retail value of all meat, milk, potatoes and grain products sold in the state stores.

The relatively poor performance of agriculture in recent years and its low aggregate level (approximately 80 percent of U.S. output) is often attributed to the poor climate that prevails over most of the agricultural areas of the country. It is true, as noted above, that climatic factors have had an adverse effect on grain production from 1979 on. Yet the impact of the weather on grain production is often exaggerated: the output levels for the past few years appear very low at least partly because climatic conditions from 1969 to 1978 were *favorable*.

The effect of climatic conditions on farm production in a single year, or over a short period of years, is one thing; more important is their effect in the long run. A relatively small area of the Soviet Union is similar in climate to the American corn and cotton belts. But it is an enormous country with a huge arable area—as much as Canada and the United States combined. Regions in North America with climatic conditions similar to those in the Soviet Union include the Great Plains, the Lake States of Minnesota, Wisconsin and Michigan, and the southwestern states of Arizona, New Mexico and Utah.

Comparing grain yields in climatically similar areas, then, one finds that yields in the Soviet Union are nearly the same as in North America. To be sure, the yield relationship depends upon the method used to calculate yields. When calculated per harvested hectare, Soviet yields averaged 84 percent of the yields in five U.S. states plus the Prairie Provinces of Canada; when calculations were based on harvested area plus land in fallow, the Soviet yields were 114 percent of those of North America for 1975 to 1979. These comparisons exclude corn for the North American area. If corn is included, the relative Soviet grain yields on a harvested area basis were 68 percent; and on a harvested plus fallow area basis, 88 percent. Also, the figures for the Soviet Union are on a bunker weight basis and need to be discounted by 10 to 15 percent. Thus, where fallow is considered, corn is excluded, and the Soviet yields are discounted appropriately, yields in the Soviet and North American areas are approximately equal.

Excluding corn in the North American data, we find that grain yields over the past 25 years have increased at a slightly higher rate in the Soviet Union: 0.3 centners (300 kilograms) per hectare compared to 0.26 centners for North America. When the fallow area is included in the calculation of yields, the annual yield increase in North America is reduced to 0.18 centners per hectare. Since the amount of fallow actually declined in the Soviet Union, both absolutely and as a percentage of the grain area, its inclusion actually results in a small increase in the Soviet yield trend.

Similarly, cotton yields in the Soviet Union are higher than in the American southwest and the trend has been positive. By contrast, in two of the three American states that grow similar cotton, average yields for 1976 to 1980 were below those for 1961 to 1965.

Sunflower seeds were for a time one of the few agricultural success stories in the Soviet Union. Plant breeding resulted in a marked increase in the oil content and in relatively high yields. But in recent years yields have fallen far below expectations. During the late 1960s sunflower yields in the Soviet Union were about 25 percent higher than in the United States; from 1976 to 1980, U.S. yields were 15 percent higher. In addition to unfavorable weather, factors such as disease, poor quality seeds, inadequate supplies of fertilizer, herbicides and defoliants, and faulty rotation practices have been identified as causes of recent yield declines. Certainly, the Soviets have failed to follow through on their earlier successes in breeding improved varieties by means of hybridization. At the same time, sugar beet yields have increased very little over the past 15 years, losing ground relative to comparable areas in the United States. Yields are now two-thirds or less than those of Minnesota or North Dakota. In the late 1960s, the difference was a little less than one-fifth.

Grains, cotton, sunflowers and sugar beets have enjoyed high priority in Soviet agricultural policies. Consequently, it is not too surprising that in at least some instances yield levels compare favorably with those in

North American areas having similar natural conditions. There are, however, large—even enormous—yield differences for crops that have not had high priority, namely forage crops such as hay and silage.

Forage crops are important to plans for achieving a significant increase in livestock output. For the past decade, the Soviets have depended primarily on the increased use of grain for feed to achieve their livestock goals. Between 1966 and 1981, livestock production increased by about 32 percent while the use of grain for feed increased by about 80 percent. This means that other sources of feed supply increased relatively little during these 15 years.

What are the forage yield differences between North America and the Soviet Union? Hay yields in the latter averaged 2.04 tons per hectare between 1975 and 1979. This is a little more than half the average yield in the Canadian Prairie Provinces, about 60 percent of the average for three U.S. Northern Plains States, and a third of the average for three Great Lakes States. Thus, on average, Soviet hay yields have been only 45 to 50 percent of those achieved in climatically similar North American states.

The Soviet yields were so starkly low, in fact, that further analysis was called for. Since it is reasonable to assume that hay and grain yields are correlated, hay yields were related to wheat and corn yields in the United States. Thus figuring I found that based on the average Soviet wheat yield of 1.64 tons per hectare for 1976 to 1980, the expected hay yield would be 3.6 tons per hectare; instead, the actual yield was 2.04 tons. For the Ukraine, with its average wheat yield of three tons per hectare and a hay yield of three tons as well, the predicted yield was six tons per hectare, exactly double the actual yield. In Estonia, recent hay yields have been 3.8 tons per hectare with a grain yield of 2.5 tons; the predicted hay yield was five tons, or just one-third above the actual. For Latvia, the difference between the actual and predicted hay yields was about the same: predicted at 4.9 tons, actual at 3.5 tons. For the Russian Republic, the predicted yield was more than double the actual hay yield of 1.6 tons.

Silage yields were also significantly below the comparable North American areas: 15 tons per hectare compared to 30 to 35 tons in the Lake States and 20 tons in the Northern Plains States.

Thus the low levels of Soviet hay and silage yields must be attributed to policy factors rather than to climatic or soil differences. The yield comparisons for climatically similar areas establish this beyond any doubt. But if more evidence is required, one need only look at forage yields in other areas of Europe with similar or no more satisfactory conditions for the production of forage crops.

Let me explain some of the important policy factors which, as my research indicates, have reduced the level of agricultural production in the Soviet Union while increasing its costs. One such policy factor, as we have seen, is the low priority given to the production of forage crops, resulting in abysmally low yields. If hay yields could be brought up to the level indicated by the American comparison—an increase of 1.5 tons per hectare—the feed value would be equal to 25 to 30 million tons of grain, or more than the average annual grain imports of 20.5 million tons for 1975 through 1980. If the quality of the hay were·significantly improved, as it could be, the feed gain would be even greater.

Grain production varies substantially from year to year. In such circumstances North American farmers seed most of their wheat and other grains on land that has been fallowed. In the Soviet Union, instead of fal-

Table 1. Planned and Actual Grain Production in the Soviet Union

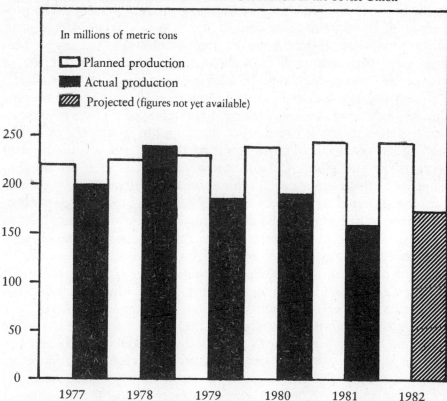

*Source*: U.S. Department of Agriculture

lowing a third to half of the land devoted to grain, the clean fallow land has been reduced both absolutely and relatively. In 1940 the clean fallow area was 26 percent of the grain-sown area of 111 million hectares. By 1975 the sown area had increased to about 128 million hectares, but the fallow area had been cut back to 11 million hectares, or just 9 percent of the sown area. Since then fallow land has increased slightly, to 11 percent.

The Soviet practice of reducing the fallow area has had two important effects. It has increased both the variability of production and costs of producing grain. North American farmers use a lot of fallow primarily because it lowers costs per unit of output. Soviet planners impose little fallow on the farms in the mistaken notion that the result will be increased output, even though some Soviet experimental data support the contrary view. And this is not counting the savings of seed, which could be significant.

Soviet farms use more than twice as much seed per hectare of land seeded to wheat and other small grains as do farms in the United States. In the Soviet Union grain used as seed is about 16.5 percent of the production of clean grain; in the United States, seed wheat is 4 percent of wheat production. If the current seeding rate of 200 kilograms per hectare were reduced by half (still above the U.S. rate for comparable areas), the grain saving would be 12.5 million tons.

Not only grains have high seeding rates. In one important potato-producing province of the Soviet Union it was reported that the amount of seed potatoes used was one-third of the output in an average year. The seeding rate on socialized farms was three times what it was on the farm workers' private plots: 4.7 tons compared to 1.6 tons per hectare. Climatic factors cannot explain this enormous difference; only policies can. In the United States, approximately 2.3 tons of seed is used per hectare; because of higher yields, this is only 7 percent of output.

Why are Soviet seeding rates so high? Primarily because the rates are established officially and not by the farms. Evidence of meddling by planning officials is overwhelming. Of course, there are some reasons for setting seeding rates at such high levels: low rates of germination, seed stock that includes a substantial fraction of extraneous material, late planting, or replanting. But whatever the problems, they could all be corrected by modifying policies and improving farming practices.

Two kinds of waste in Soviet agriculture are conspicuous, one in the handling of farm inputs and the other in the harvesting, transporting, processing and selling of farm output. A recent Soviet article estimates that nine million tons of fertilizer—some 10 percent of fertilizer production—is wasted between the factory and the field. If each ton of fertilizer properly applied increased grain output by just one ton (the Soviet author argues that the increase would be 1.5 to two tons), grain production could be increased by nearly 10 million tons. And further, "We lost approximately one-fifth of the gross harvest of grain, vegetables, fruits and berries during the harvesting itself, in transportation and storage, and during industrial processing." So wrote V. Tikhonov, a prominent agricultural scientist, early in 1982.

Due to the poor quality of farm machinery and inadequate maintenance, the average service life of a machine in the Soviet Union is significantly less than in the United States. The annual scrappage rate for grain combines was 15 percent for 1976 to 1980, compared to 8 percent in the United States; for tractors it was between 12 and 13 percent, compared to 4 percent in the United States. Between 1971 and 1975, the scrappage rate for such a simple machine as a windrower was 18 percent, an average life of little more than five years, while a farm truck has a life expectancy of less than six years. This is not only because of the poor quality of the trucks, but also because of poor maintenance, the abysmal state of rural roads, or a combination of these factors.

Still other factors are important in explaining the recent relatively poor performance of Soviet agriculture. Soviet agricultural price policies, for instance, suffer from two main deficiencies. First, prices paid to farms are used as a means of equalizing incomes within agriculture by differentiating prices regionally. In the process, they encourage production in high-cost areas and on high-cost farms, while discouraging production under low-cost conditions. Second, the relative price structure favors grain and field crops at the expense of livestock products. This seems nonsensical, since officially, priority is given to increasing per capita meat production.

Perhaps the major adverse policy factor affecting Soviet agricultural performance is that farm managers and workers are not given the opportunity to direct their skills, knowledge and capacities to efficient farming. In part, this is due to a price system that does not provide the appropriate signals. But perhaps more importantly, the Soviet bureaucracy does not trust farmers; it does not believe that farmers have either intelligence or initiative. Farmers are told what to plant, when to plant, how much seed to plant, when to cultivate, when to harvest, how many livestock to maintain (even if there is not enough feed), and when and how much fertilizer to apply. For example, in the socialized sector milk production per cow in 1980 was even less than in 1970, when it was nearly the lowest in Europe. Why is output so low and declining? One reason may be that the number of cows is imposed on farms by the central planners.

In 1965 Brezhnev himself declared: "We must put an end to the practice of command and administration by fiat, to petty tutelage, to the usurping of the function of the leaders and specialists of the collective and state farms; [we] must eradicate any manifestation of ostentation and ballyhoo." And in 1982:

> It is necessary resolutely to get rid of administrative fiat and petty tutelage with respect to collective farms and state farms, which can rightfully be called the foundation of all agricultural production. No one should be permitted to demand that farms fulfill any assignments not envisaged by the state plan or to ask them for any information except as established by state reporting requirements. This rule should be observed strictly at all levels and with no exceptions. I hope, comrades, that we are unanimous on how important and how necessary this is.

There is not the slightest evidence that the bureaucrats will modify their behavior following Brezhnev's statement of 1982 any more than they did after 1965.

In October 1981 Brezhnev called attention to the central role of food in Soviet planning; it was both "economically and politically the central problem of the whole Five-Year Plan" (1981-1985). But in May 1982, in announcing the much-heralded new Food Program, scarcely anything was said about transferring authority to the farms.

The Food Program was, in fact, shockingly unimaginative. It appears that general agreement could not be reached on what was required to improve agriculture. Instead, what emerged was the creation of two new levels of bureaucracy, a further sharp increase in prices paid to farms and, given the policy of fixed retail prices, an increase in food price subsidies of almost 50 percent. Hardly a word was spoken about the initiative or independence of the collective and state farms themselves. Yet, recalling that in all of the Soviet Union there are only 46,000 such farms, with a total of about 24 million members and employees, it would seem reasonable to assume that organizations of such large average size could well manage their own affairs.[1]

In a typical year, the United States and the Soviet Union produce about one-third of the world's grain. The United States is the world's largest grain exporter and the Soviet Union—a significant net exporter of grain in the early 1970s—is now the world's largest grain importer.

Soviet grain imports for 1983 through 1985 are likely to be no less than 30 to 35 million tons per year—totals approximate in weight to the combined annual automobile production of the United States and Japan! If annual Soviet meat production from 1986 to 1990 reaches 18 million tons instead of the planned goal of more than 20 million tons, grain imports during the period might be a little below those from 1981 through 1985, or some 25 to 30 million tons a year. However, if an effort is made to increase annual meat production to the 20-million-ton level for 1986-1990, annual grain imports could average as much as 40 million tons in those years.

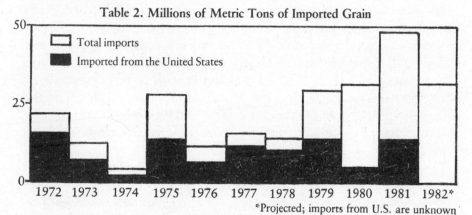

Table 2. Millions of Metric Tons of Imported Grain

*Projected; imports from U.S. are unknown

I have followed Soviet agricultural developments for somewhat more than three decades. And while there is much that continues to puzzle me, I am firmly convinced that Soviet agriculture could be much more productive than it is, and that it could be so as a socialized enterprise. With appropriate policy-setting, good performance by those sectors of the economy that furnish the products needed for agriculture, and the necessary marketing, processing and transportation services, socialist agriculture could be highly productive. After all, private agriculture cannot succeed without supportive governmental policies and an assured supply of appropriate inputs and marketing services. If one needs convincing on this point, one need only look at the sad performance of Polish agriculture—80 percent of which is private—over the last several years.

All of this is not to suggest that minor changes in policy can make Soviet agriculture much more productive. But it is to say that policy changes are possible that would retain the critical features of socialist agriculture—including either collective or state ownership of the land and even some significant elements of central planning—yet would result in substantially greater productivity. The crucial change would be to give the farms much greater authority to make their own decisions, not only with respect to what to produce and how to produce it, but also with respect to relating reward to effort. But even major changes in agricultural policy will not be enough unless the rest of the economy functions much better than it now does.

The price system, in particular, has largely lost its ability to guide producers, workers or consumers. No outsider could have been more precise or eloquent in criticizing the ineffectiveness of the Soviet price system than the drafters of the 1982 Food Program. One of the measures announced there, and anticipated by Brezhnev in his speech of May 1982, was "to increase the amounts of payments in kind to collective and state farm workers, above all in grain, fruits, vegetables, and feed." This measure was designed to improve work incentives. What it also signifies is that the ruble has lost much of its value as a reward for effort because goods and services of a kind people wish to buy, especially in rural areas, are not available at the official prices. Most such goods and services *are* available in the collective farm markets, but at two to three times the official state store prices, or in the growing black markets, where barter and foreign currency prevail.

A lesson historians and economists thought they had learned was that as economic growth occurs—as real per capita incomes increase over time—wages in kind decline in importance and eventually disappear (except as a means of tax avoidance). But the Soviet Union has demonstrated that this principle is not universally valid. There, the bureaucracy has proven that you can so mismanage a productive economy that it becomes desirable to resort to measures that you had long since tried to eliminate or minimize.

One goal of the 1965 Soviet agricultural program was to increase the role of cash payments, and so substantially to replace payments in kind. And at various times the hope was that money wages would increase to levels that would make private plot production unprofitable, thus leading to the substantial abandonment of such activities in favor of stepped-up efforts in the socialist sector. Now, however, the increase of payments in kind to collective and state farm workers is evidently viewed as a necessary evil, as a kind of bribe calculated to offset some of the advantages of those personal plots assigned to farm workers which currently account for a quarter of all Soviet agricultural production.[2] □

1. In the spring of 1983 it was reported from Moscow that Brezhnev's successor as Party leader, Yury Andropov, "has put the Food Program at the head of his list of goals." Measures were being undertaken "to provide greater autonomy and greater incentives for the farm workers, and to give them greater responsibility for organizing the entire productive enterprise." It was, in short, "a major effort by the state to get farm labor to work better and harder." New York Times (May 30, 1983), Business Day.

2. See further, on the various issues raised in this chapter, D. Gale Johnson and Karen

McConnell Brooks, *Prospects for Soviet Agriculture in the 1980s* (Bloomington, Indiana: Indiana University Press, 1983).

# SCIENCE & TECHNOLOGY

Soviet achievements in science and technology since World War II have been on occasion spectacular, have in general generated widespread alarm in the West, particularly in the United States, and have fundamentally influenced Western perceptions of the Soviet Union as well as Western policies. To illustrate the point, we need think only of Western reactions to the Soviet development of nuclear weapons and to the achievements of the Soviet space program, beginning with the launching of the world's first orbiting satellite—Sputnik—in 1957. Indeed, no aspect of Soviet life in recent years, apart from foreign policy and military matters, has given rise to more comment in the West.

But how good are Soviet science and technology? How effective is Soviet education in this respect? How is Soviet science organized? What can be said of its future prospects? And what of the prospects for Soviet-Western, especially Soviet-American, scientific cooperation? These and other questions are discussed in the following three chapters, which also refer to political and economic issues raised in earlier sections of the book.

It might be emphasized that Harley D. Balzer's assessment of Soviet technical education is based in part on interviews with 200 emigre scientists and engineers, and that Vladimir Z. Kresin was a senior physicist in Moscow before leaving the Soviet Union in 1979. Loren R. Graham's discussion of Soviet science policy and organization, like most of the contributions to this book, draws on information gained in repeated visits to the Soviet Union—most recently, in Graham's case, in the spring of 1983.

210

# 17 SCIENCE & TECHNOLOGY

## Science Policy and Organization

*Loren R. Graham*

During the last 20 years the Soviet research and development community became, in number of personnel, the largest in the world. The moment when the Soviet Union quantitatively surpassed the United States in number of research personnel is debatable, since the relevant Soviet statistics are not compiled by the same criteria as the American ones. But in a careful analysis Murray Feshbach and Louvan Nolting have concluded that the "numerical crossover occurred toward the end of the 1960s," and that by 1978 the Soviet total was "nearly 60 percent greater than the U.S. total."[1]

Further study of the statistics soon demonstrates, however, that the disparity between the sizes of the two research establishments is not quite as large as this figure suggests. If only researchers with the doctoral equivalent are included, the sizes of the two groups are almost identical. On the other hand, if one substracts from these totals the degrees in the social sciences and humanities (included as scientific degrees in Soviet statistics), the Soviet Union jumps ahead again by about a third. In other words, the Soviet Union is comfortably ahead of the United States in the number of advanced researchers in the engineering and natural sciences, but the greater U.S. effort in the humanities and social sciences brings the total sizes of the two research communities closer together.

More recently, the impressive expansion of Soviet science and technology has slowed markedly, and it would seem that the heroic period in the building of the Soviet science establishment has ended. Between 1963 and 1968 the average annual rate of increase of scientific workers in the Soviet Union was 7.8 percent; from 1968 to 1973 the average rate was 6.1 percent; and from 1973 to 1978 the rate was 3.2 percent. In recent years, too, the number of graduate students in the Soviet

Union has remained approximately stable. In the late 1970s there were actually several years in which the U.S. growth rate in the number of scientists and engineers employed in research and development slightly exceeded the Soviet rate, reversing a 20-year trend.

Statistics on the financing of Soviet research present a roughly similar picture. In the late 1950s and early 1960s the annual figures in the Soviet budget allocated to science grew at phenomenal rates, in excess of 15 percent a year. By the mid-1960s the annual increases were around 8 percent. In the late 1960s the increases grew again, but soon resumed their decline, reaching a low point of 1.7 percent in 1976. In the last few years the rate of increase for science has once again picked up, but no one expects a return to the rates of the late 1950s and early 1960s.[2]

What about quality? How good are Soviet scientists and engineers? In recent years we have had a number of high-level studies of this issue, including two official reports of the National Academy of Sciences in Washington, D.C.[3] Overall, the U.S. analysts—leaders in their fields— judged U.S. science and technology to be superior to Soviet science and technology, but they found that in certain fields, such as theoretical physics and mathematics, Soviet specialists were among the very best in the world. Soviet strength tends to be in fundamental fields rather than applied areas, but there are some exceptions, such as metallurgy. On the commercial level, U.S. industrialists do not worry about Soviet technology (they have enough anxiety about Japan); but in military technology the received opinion in Washington is that the Soviets will be able to do anything that the Americans can do, albeit with a considerable time lag.

Finally, under the general rubric of recent achievements of Soviet science, we should remember that it was only in 1965 that the scandal of Soviet biology, Lysenkoism, was eliminated. Nikita Khrushchev, who was in power until 1964, was a strong supporter of T.D. Lysenko. The prominent Soviet emigre scientist, Zhores Medvedev, has written that Khrushchev's support of Lysenko was a major reason for the Premier's ouster.[4] While that may be somewhat exaggerated, Khrushchev's successor, Leonid Brezhnev, followed a very different policy by sharply reducing ideological interference in the content of scientific work.

This relaxation of philosophical restrictions was more than matched, however, by a tightening of political controls over the extra-scientific activity of scientsts. While scientists under Brezhnev (with a few exceptions) did not have to worry about the interference of ideologists in their technical work, their concerns about orthodoxy in the political and social realm increased. Under Brezhnev and then under his successor, Yury Andropov, a scientist could easily get into trouble because of his political views and activities, as the persecution of the eminent Soviet physicist Andrei Sakharov illustrates.

The traditional organization of Soviet science and technology, as it developed under Stalin, was in three administrative pyramids: the Academy of Sciences of the Soviet Union and the regional and specialized academies; the industrial ministries with their associated institutes for research and development; and the higher educational system. In number of researchers involved, the Academy of Sciences was the smallest of these pyramids but it had the greatest authority and prestige. The industrial ministries had the most research and development personnel but usually they did not challenge the authority of the Academy as the court of last resort in scientific and technical questions. Research in the university system was, under Stalin, markedly undeveloped, although there were a few fields, such as mathematics, where the universities were strong.

During the last 20 years this pattern has changed in a number of ways. Research in the universities and in the industrial ministries has become stronger. Regional associations of industrial research and production facilities have developed. The most important event, in terms of the organization of science and technology, was the rise to power of the State Committee on Science and Technology, established in 1965. At present, the State Committee is still relatively small compared to the Academy of Sciences, but it is already a major competitor of the Academy in influence and prestige. In its system of scientific councils (*nauchnye sovety*) the State Committee obtains the assistance of thousands of Soviet scientists, including almost all the members of the Academy of Sciences.

The advisory role of these scientific councils resembles that of the committees of the U.S. National Research Council, but there is an important distinction. In the Soviet Union, the State Committee has executive authority above this advisory function, particularly when a jurisdictional conflict over technology arises among several industrial ministries. The State Committee has a unique responsibility for planning applied research. Moreover, it approves the entire research and development budget, including the gross figures for the Academy of Sciences' budget, the internal structure of which is left to the Academy. Finally, the political strength of the State Committee is revealed by the fact that its chairman, G. Marchuk, is deputy chairman of the Council of Industrial Ministries, outranking the president of the Academy of Sciences, A.P. Aleksandrov, who is only a member of the Council.

A major question in Soviet science policy is whether the State Committee will add to its present small set of research institutes—most of which are informational or policy-oriented—that actually do research and development in hard science and technology. If that happens, the Academy will face the greatest challenge in 50 years to its authority as the supreme scientific institution of the Soviet Union. Proposals for such a change have already been made but we do not yet know if they will be accepted.

Before describing those proposals, I shall review briefly the history of the Academy in the last two or three decades in order to see how it reached its present dilemma.

Under Stalin the Academy was the seat not only of fundamental research but also of a great deal of applied research, centered in its Department of Engineering Sciences. Emphasis on applied work in those years was seen by many Soviet scientists as regrettable but unavoidable, an integral part of the Stalinist dogma of "the unity of theory and practice." After Stalin's death the ideological thaw in science was equated by many scientists with the freedom to give much more attention to pure science. These fundamental scientists thought that by the late 1950s the most strenuous period of Soviet industrialization was over and that, as a result, they would be permitted to free themselves from narrow industrial concerns.

A few years after Stalin's death an influential group of scientists in the Academy of Sciences mounted a large effort to change the orientation of the Academy by putting much more emphasis on fundamental research.[5] They managed to get Khrushchev's support during one of his moments of zeal for administrative reform, and were successful in their campaign. The most important result was the elimination of the Department of Engineering Sciences from the Academy and the transfer of many of the institutes working on applied sciences from the Academy to the industrial ministries.

These changes in the Academy's priorities, which occurred 20 years ago, are in part responsible for the major problem in the present organization of Soviet science and technology. It soon became clear that if the Academy was not going to take major responsibility for coordinating applied research, then some other body would have to do so. It is no accident that only a few years after the Academy divested itself of much of its responsibility for applied research the State Committee assumed the responsibilities the Academy had spurned, and it is now powerful enough to be in direct competition with the Academy.

During the last 20 years it has also become clear that those fundamental scientists of the Academy who thought that in the post-Stalin era they could devote their time to pure science, without much concern about governmental priorities or industrial needs, were mistaken. In the last decade, the need of the Soviet economy to increase productivity through technological innovation has grown tremendously; so have the pressures on the Soviet Union to keep up with the West in high technology. The result has been that Soviet political leaders have become more and more insistent that research efforts have practical effects. The Academy of Sciences has, in fact, often been accused by economic planners of lacking interest in industrial technology.

As these challenges multiplied, the Academy's own leaders were divided in their response. Some of them, particularly a few influential physicists and chemists, continued to insist that the Academy concentrate on what it does best, fundamental research. Others, concerned that the Academy was being bypassed by the State Committee and the industrial ministries, called for the Academy to move back into industrial research. The latter camp has had some significant successes in the last ten years.[6] The share of the Academy's research devoted to industrial applications has grown appreciably Many of the Academy's institutes now have contracts with industrial ministries to do applied research. The Siberian division of the Academy of Sciences and the Ukrainian Academy have been leaders in the creation of centers of research with strong industrial connections. These two parts of the Academy system are often cited as models for the integration of fundamental and applied research. Still, the problem of how to improve applied research in the Soviet Union remains the major worry of managers of the Soviet research and development community.

Soviet journals and books published in recent years describe the problem of coordinating research and development in increasingly urgent terms. In July 1979, the Central Committee and the Council of Ministers issued a directive calling for improvements in production efficiency and quality of work. And the Soviet Academy of Sciences in 1980 devoted its annual meeting to discussions of how this directive could be carried out. Speakers emphasized that there seemed to be an essential incompatibility between the existing organization of research and development and the requirements of technological innovation.

The Academy of Sciences had the necessary talent, but few pilot plant production facilities. Furthermore, it was not clear that the Academy wanted the responsibility for all high technology research and development. The State Committee for Science and Technology had great political authority but did not possess institutes of its own working on these problems. Meanwhile, the industrial ministries had demonstrated that they usually paid attention only to their own narrow interests, placing more emphasis on short-term production goals than on long-term innovation. What seemed to be needed was a drastic reorganization of Soviet science and technology—one that would either give much greater authority to one of the existing bodies, or would create an entirely new body with the necessary authority to transcend the rivalries of existing organizations.

A number of proposals for such reforms have been published. M. L. Bashin has suggested that the Academy of Sciences be given much greater authority, and that experimental-production bases be subordinated to it. This would enable the Academy to do the original research behind an innovation and also to test it in production.[7] Such a reform would represent a great change in the role of the Academy and would put it in the middle of industrial concerns to a much greater degree than it was even in the days of Stalin.

A sharply different proposal by V. P. Rassokhin calls for a "fourth system of research and development organizations" (in addition to the Academy, the universities, and the ministries) which would be subordinated to the State Committee for Science and Technology.[8] This new system would include most of the applied research institutes removed from the Academy in the early 1960s. For the first time, the State Committee would have its own research base, and it would be directly challenging the Academy of Sciences as the leader of Soviet science.

It is not clear which (if either) of these two paths will be adopted. But the urgency of the reform was stressed by Brezhnev himself, who spoke about it during his speech at the Twenty-sixth Party Congress in February 1981. He decried the fact that the Soviet Union sometimes lost its lead even in those technical fields where it had earlier been ahead, and lamented the fact that it was often necessary for the country to buy, at great cost, technology from abroad. He called for a "regrouping" of scientific forces, but did not commit himself to any one of the reform proposals that had been advanced. To the extent that he showed a preference between the Academy of Sciences and the State Committee, he seemed to favor the Academy, calling for an increase in its "role and responsibility."

The unanswered question is whether the Academy wishes to take on greater responsibility for high technology research. Will the fundamental scientists who called for the expulsion of engineering institutes in the early 1960s still carry the day? Or has the Academy learned that if it does not fulfill the functions that the government and Party expect of it, it will be replaced in prestige and authority by a competitor? This question will surely be answered in the next few years.

Many of the pressures on science and technology that occur in the Soviet Union are also present in the United States. To be sure, there is no single U.S. equivalent of the Soviet Academy of Sciences, but the National Science Foundation is currently under great pressure to put less emphasis on fundamental science and more on research promoting industrial innovation. There have even been proposals to create a National Engineering Foundation that would support applied research. The National Science Foundation, seeing such proposals as a threat to its own authority, has assured Congress that it will give more attention to applied research. Thus, U.S. and Soviet leaders in science policy questions have some common worries which stem from the increasingly intense worldwide competition in high technology.

The Soviet economy faces major problems (see Chapters 14, 15 and 16). Industrial growth rates have dropped dramatically, and the demographic statistics show that growth cannot be invigorated in the old way, simply by bringing in more workers. The single most important means by which the Soviet Union can hope to energize its economy is by improvements in productivity, boosting the capacity per worker..

Improvements in productivity come from scientific and technological innovation. Soviet economic planners are currently putting more pressure on the scientific establishment to speed innovation than at any time in recent Soviet history. The chairman of the State Planning Committee, N. K. Baibakov, has emphasized to the Academy of Sciences that economic growth can no longer depend on extensive factors, but now must rely on intensive development. He stressed that this situation puts a heavy responsibility on Soviet scientists and engineers. He was also critical of both the Academy of Sciences and the State Committee for Science and Technology for their inattention to specific details in planning scientific-technical progress, and for being more interested in clever ideas and machines than in economic effectiveness.[9]

In a similar view, Academy president A. P. Aleksandrov has focused on energy issues, problems in computer technology, the rapid pace of genetic engineering and the need for scientific aid to agriculture. His recent speeches have been remarkable in their emphasis on industrial and agricultural applications rather than those areas of the Academy's work which in the past were so important: fundamental research in physics, astronomy, mathematics and chemistry.

At a special joint meeting of the Academy of Sciences and the Academy of Agricultural Sciences in September 1982, the leaders of both institutions underscored the need for science to improve Soviet nutrition.[10] And in an article published in April 1983, Aleksandrov asked Soviet scientists to find and eliminate "the bottlenecks" that hold back technical progress in the Soviet Union.[11] Aleksandrov has thus served the Academy notice that over the next few years industrial and agricultural problems will have top priority throughout Soviet science.

The problem of increasing industrial productivity is only one of the serious issues facing Soviet scientists today. Other increasingly sharp issues concern the adverse effects of science and technology, particularly on the environment (see Chapter 12). The days of undiluted optimism about scientific progress are over in the Soviet Union. More and more articles are being published, often written by biologists, which describe the effects of pollution on the biosphere and even on human beings in alarming terms.

The "scientific-technical revolution," so often praised in Soviet publications, is now getting its share of criticism. Biologists point out that this revolution is creating a new environment, in which radiation from nuclear power stations and mutagens from the chemical industry are having a deleterious effect on people. Some Soviet scientists have begun to criticize nuclear power. A 1979 article in the influential Party journal *Kommunist* called for future nuclear power stations to be built in the sparsely populated regions of the Soviet Union. Academician N. P. Dubinin, one of the Soviet Union's senior geneticists, has even indicated that a dramatic increase in genetic defects in children may be due to higher radiation levels.[12]

This comment relates to yet another problem in science and technology that the Soviet Union faces. And it is perhaps the most serious of all, since it suggests a major decline in the quality of Soviet life. According to published Soviet statistics, between 1971 and 1974 infant mortality rates rose by over 20 percent; between 1960 and 1974 death rates for people in their fifties rose by almost 20 percent; and death rates for people in their forties rose by more than 30 percent.[13] Although attempts have been made, in both the West and the Soviet Union, to explain these alarming statistics, there is still no persuasive hypothesis. Even if better reporting of relevant statistics is partially responsible—as several Soviet officials have suggested—the fact would still remain that the Soviet Union's current infant mortality rate ranks it near the bottom compared with other developed nations. Soviet medical health specialists regard this as an urgent problem.

A final problem concerns international science exchanges and technology transfers. Under Stalin, Soviet leaders expressed confidence that their country would soon surpass the United States in achievements in science and technology. In the 1960s and 1970s, as the research and development communities of Japan, Western Europe and the United States continued to display impressive vitality, Soviet confidence in quickly becoming the dominant research and development force in the world diminished, and Soviet leaders began to put more and more emphasis on cooperation and trade in technical areas.[14]

The ebbing of detente at the end of the 1970s, however, impeded Soviet access abroad to high technology and cooperative projects in science. Science contacts between the United States and the Soviet Union have recently reached a low point, declining from a high around 1975. American disapproval of Soviet treatment of dissidents and Jews has been one of the reasons for the cooling of scientific relations. In future, the U.S. scientific community as well as U.S. political leaders will have to determine how much and what kinds of scientific exchange with the Soviet Union is desirable. The Soviet Union would clearly prefer to have more rather than fewer contacts, but if this path does not seem to be open, they will once again take a more independent path.

I have no crystal ball for reading the future, but I would like to venture a few observations about probable developments in several of the areas I have discussed: the growth of Soviet science and technology, the organization of Soviet science, and particular problems which the leaders of Soviet science and technology face.

It seems clear that the period of tremendous expansion of Soviet research and development has ended. The emphasis in the near future will be on qualitative improvement. A vice-president of the Academy of Sciences, V. A. Kotelnikov, recently observed that now that the Soviet Union has as many scientific workers as the United States, there are no plans to increase the number rapidly.[15] In the area of science and technology, the Soviet Union measures itself by reference to the United States. Nonetheless, science budgets are likely to continue to grow by several percentage points a year.

Tremendous pressure will continue to mount for improvements in Soviet industrial productivity through more technical innovation. It is difficult to imagine great breakthroughs here, since the major obstacles seem to be systemic, but it would be a mistake to underrate the ability of Soviet scientists and engineers. They are getting better and better in important areas like computer technology and genetic engineering, where truly enormous efforts are being made. The creation of a new ministry devoted entirely to genetic engineering is currently being discussed.

In the organization of Soviet science, the Academy of Sciences continues to face major competition from the State Committee on Science and Technology and, as we have seen, there are proposals to give the State Committee even greater advantages. In the short run, however, it seems very unlikely that the State Committee will be able to supplant the Academy, and there are even some trends in the Academy's favor. So long as detente was in force and the Soviet Union was able to buy large amounts of technology from the West, the State Committee was able to improve its stature steadily, since it had responsibility for technology transfer from the West. Such men as V. A. Kirillin, head of the State Committee for the first 14 years of its existence, and G. M. Gvishiani, deputy chairman, made their reputations by promoting good relations with the West and trade in technology.

Kirillin often talked of "complementary development" in science and technology, concluding that no one nation could be autonomous in these areas, and that therefore the leading nations should trade with each other to their mutual benefit. That viewpoint no longer seems as persuasive to Soviet leaders as it once did. The State Committee, headed now by Marchuk, also known as a proponent of trade and exchange with the West, is suffering a slight diminution in its status with the decline of scientific exchanges and technology transfer.

Academy of Sciences President Aleksandrov took advantage of these developments in his speech at the Twenty-sixth Party Congress (1981). Without naming the State Committee he accused those who favored buying Western technology of placing the Soviet Union in a dangerously dependent relationship on the West. After describing the current "embargo" of the Soviet Union by the United States, Aleksandrov asserted that it was now clear that the Soviet Union must develop its own technology. He pointedly observed that "it is not correct to create, through our own efforts, areas of technological backwardness by using foreign technology on an unjustifiedly broad scale."[16] I take that statement to mean, when rephrased: "The State Committee on Science and Technology has been leading us into a dangerous dependence on foreign science and technology, but now we see that we must rely on our own resources. The Academy of Sciences can help us to be independent in science and technology because it has the talent and the resources, but the State Committee cannot." This is an argument with considerable force, and it may well help the Academy to buttress its position in the current debates.

The problems of improving industrial productivity and public health are the most serious ones facing Soviet science and technology. It seems doubtful that productivity and health can be radically improved in the near future. Both reorganization and major investment would be required, and at a time when the arms race is increasing such investment funds are very scarce. Therefore, I expect the Soviet research and development community to be burdened for a considerable period of time with these difficulties.

One can conclude that while Soviet science and technology are now stronger than at any time in the history of the Soviet Union, the problems they face are also more intractable. One of these problems—trying to increase productivity—is common to both the Soviet Union and the United States. The other—health—is one where the Soviet dilemma is more difficult. We should notice, however, that the Soviet Union can serve as an object lesson in what may happen to a nation's health if funds are taken from medicine and health care over a long period of time and devoted to the military. Indeed, if the United States and the Soviet Union continue to engage in a strenuous arms race over a long enough time it is likely that their internal problems will become more similar. □

1. Louvan E. Nolting and Murray Feshbach, "R&D Employment in the U.S.S.R.," *Science*, 207 (Feb. 1, 1980), pp. 493-503.

2. See Louvan E. Nolting, *Sources of Financing the Stages of the Research, Development, and Innovation Cycle in the U.S.S.R.*, Foreign Economics Report, No. 3 (Washington, D.C.: U.S. Department of Commerce, 1973). I am also grateful to Paul Cocks for calling my attention to several of these quantitative trends.

3. Loren R. Graham, "How Valuable Are Scientific Exchanges with the Soviet Union?" *Science*, 202 (Oct. 27, 1978), pp. 383-90. See also Thane Gustafson, "Why Doesn't Soviet Science Do Better Than It Does?" in Linda L. Lubrano and Susan Grosse Solomon, eds., *The Social Context of Soviet Science* (Boulder, Colorado: Westview Press, 1980), pp. 31-67.

4. Zhores Medvedev, *The Rise and Fall of T. D. Lysenko* (New York: Columbia University Press, 1969).

5. Loren R. Graham, "The Reorganization of the Soviet Academy of Sciences," in Peter Juviler and Henry Morton, eds., *Soviet Policy-Making* (New York: Frederick J. Praeger, 1967), pp. 133-61.

6. Simon Kassel and Cathleen Campbell, *The Soviet Academy of Sciences and Technological Development* (Santa Monica, California: Rand Corporation [R-2533-ARPA] 1980).

7. M. Bashin, "Priblizit effekt otdachi," *Khoziaistvo i pravo*, No. 4 (1980), pp. 63-67.

8. V. P. Rassokhin, "Nuzhna chetvertaia sistema nauchnykh uchrezhdenii," *Ekonomika i organizatsiia promyshlennogo proizvodstva*, No. 1 (1980), pp. 13-22.

9. N. K. Baibakov, "O sovershenstvovanii planirovaniia i upravleniia ekonomikoi," *Vestnik akademii nauk*, No. 5 (1980), pp. 13-22.

10. See "Zadachi nauk v realizatsii prodovol'stvennoi programmy SSSR," and Iu. A. Ovchinnikov, "Prodovol'stvennaia programma i zadachi sovetskoi nauki," *Vestnik akademii nauk*, No. 2 (1983), pp. 3-26.

11. A. P. Aleksandrov, "Vstupitel'noe slovo," *Vestnik akademii nauk*, No. 4 (1983), p. 8.

12. See Loren R. Graham, "Biomedicine and the Politics of Science in the USSR," *Soviet Union*, Vol. 8 Pt. 2 (1981), pp. 147-58; also, N. P. Dubinin, "Genetika i ee znachenie dlia chelovechestva," *Vestnik akademii nauk*, No. 6 (1980), pp. 73-81.

13. Christopher Davis and Murray Feshbach, *Rising Infant Mortality in the USSR in the 1970s*, Series P-95, No. 74, (Washington, D.C.: U.S. Bureau of the Census, 1980).

14. Bruce Parrot, *Politics and Technology in the Soviet Union* (Cambridge, Massachusetts: MIT Press, 1983).

15. V. A. Kotel'nikov, "Razrabotka kompleksnoi programmy nauchno-tekhnicheskogo progressa na 20 let," *Vestnik akademii nauk*, No. 5 (1980), pp. 37-43.

16. "Rech' tovarishcha A. P. Aleksandrova," *Izvestia* (Feb. 26, 1981).

# 18

## Soviet Science in Practice: An Insider's View

*Vladimir Z. Kresin*

The number of scientists in the Soviet Union is enormous—approximately 1,300,000—and to direct this army a peculiarly Soviet scientific system has evolved. Research is carried out primarily in the approximately 1,500 state-supported institutes run by the Soviet Academy of Sciences and by the affiliated Academies of Sciences of the individual Soviet republics: the Ukrainian, Lithuanian, Georgian and so forth. Many state agencies—the Committee on Atomic Science and Technology, the Committee on Chemistry, the Ministry of Electrical Industry and others—also maintain scientific institutes. The Kurchatov Institute of Atomic Energy, for instance, comes under the state's Committee on Atomic Energy; the Karpov Institute of Physical Chemistry is responsible to the Committee on Chemistry. Scientific research is conducted in the universities and higher technical schools as well. Moscow University maintains very large laboratories, as do the Moscow Institute of Physics and Engineering, the University of Gorky, and the Moscow Institute of Steel and Alloys, among others. But on the whole, as Loren Graham has already pointed out (Chapter 17), fundamental scientific research in the Soviet Union is carried out under the auspices of the Academy of Sciences and its affiliates.

Basically, there are two kinds of Soviet research institute. Some are wide-profile, such as the Lebedev Institute of Physics in Moscow, the Kurchatov Institute of Atomic Energy, the Leningrad Physics and Technology Institute and the Institute of Physics of the Georgian Academy of Sciences. Others, by contrast, concentrate in one scientific area. Examples include the Acoustics Institute of the Academy of Sciences, the Solid State Physics Institute, the Physics and Technology Institute of Low Temperatures of the Ukrainian Academy of Sciences and the Institute of Crystallography.

Thus a fundamental difference between the organization of scientific research in the Soviet Union and in the United States is immediately apparent. In the latter, basic research is carried out mostly in universities, often by scientists administering Federal or other outside grants; and scientific work is combined with education. In the Soviet Union, on the other hand, such work is done principally in institutes which are entirely state-supported, and by people occupied solely with research.

The achievements of Soviet scientists—the level of their research and the value of its results—should not be underestimated. I have often encountered such a tendency in the United States, be it a direct underrating of Soviet science or an insufficient knowledge of its activities, which is, in fact, another form of underrating. I will return to the causes of this tendency, but first let me describe the strengths of Soviet science.

The work of many Soviet scientists is up to the latest standards of research. A number of excellent scientists are employed at the Physics and Technology Institute of Low Temperatures in Kharkiv, for example, while the Institute of Physical Problems of the Academy of Sciences in Moscow, headed by Nobel laureate P.L. Kapitsa, is indisputably one of the leading such centers in the world.

More specifically, scientists at the Kharkiv Institute experimentally discovered the Non-Stationary Josephson Effect. Their work led to the creation of a new field of scientific and technical research and to the development of a wide range of equipment used in electronics, computer science, and military technology. Organizationally, too, this Institute is unusual in the Soviet Union in that it contains shops in which various kinds of industrial equipment are manufactured, as well as laboratories for the pursuit of basic research. In this respect, it is patterned after such Western companies as IBM Research or Bell Laboratories.

The method of colliding beams developed at the Nuclear Physics Institute of the Siberian Division of the Academy of Sciences under Academician G.I. Budker is now widely used in high-energy physics and other accelerator-related research. In the field of experimental optics, a special effect discovered by E.V. Shpolsky (and named after him) led to the development of a process now widely used in optical laboratories for studying complex molecules. Investigations led by V.L. Ginzburg, L.D. Landau, A.A. Abrikosov and L.P. Gorkov gave birth to a theory (now called, after them, the GLAG theory) that permitted the creation of superstrong magnetic fields. Today magnets based on this principle are in laboratories throughout the world.

It is generally agreed that Lev Davidovich Landau (1908-1968), who was awarded a Nobel Prize in 1962, was one of the greatest theoretical physicists of the twentieth century. To a great extent the high level of Soviet physics today, especially of theoretical physics, is due, I believe, to that unique phenomenon known as "Landau's School." For Landau spared no effort in the creation and strengthening of his School, at whose core was "Landau's Minimum," a series of nine examinations. The first was Math I, which was always given by Landau himself. He considered it necessary to get to know everyone who started the Minimum — some 300 students all told — and any student, whatever institution he attended and wherever he lived in the Soviet Union, could telephone Landau in Moscow, express his wish to begin taking the Minimum, and arrange a day for the first exam.

In the fall of 1955, trembling with excitement, I myself dialed Landau's number and asked him to let me begin. He was very friendly, saying that unfortunately he was busy the next day but that at two o'clock the following afternoon he would be happy to meet me in his office. When I came he led me to the adjacent room, where I spent the next three hours on the mathemtical problems he gave me. During this time Landau came into the room several times to see how I was doing. Finally, after the closing conversation, I went home in a semi-conscious state, infinitely happy for having successfully passed Math I.

After Math I the Minimum was structured to include Classical Mechanics, Classical Electrodynamics and the Theory of Relativity, Math II, Quantum Mechanics, Statistical Physics, Quantum Electrodynamics, Hydrodynamics and the Theory of Elasticity, and Macroscopic Physics and Solid State Theory.  Except for Math I, the exams were also given by Landau's closest colleagues, E.M. Lifshitz and I.M. Khalatnikov. But Landau alone gave one other, the seventh in the series, on Quantum Electrodynamics, which was therefore a kind of milestone. To the student who passed it Landau became a kind of scientific father, and there was no limit to his willingness to discuss scientific problems with his newest "son." One of his closest collaborators would be appointed the young man's research director, Landau would think about his future employment, and so on. And having passed the entire Minimum, the student was allowed to study the notebook in which Landau listed what he considered the most interesting unsolved problems in physics and his own ideas about them.

Landau was probably the last universal theoretical physicist. For him physics was a single science with general principles, and more than once he demonstrated the effectiveness of using methods from one field for solving problems in other, seemingly unrelated fields. His ten-volume *Course in Theoretical Physics*, written with E.M. Liftshitz, is famous the world over, and for many years his Thursday morning seminar at the

Academy's Institute of Physical Problems was the leading one of its kind in the Soviet Union. His students include many distinguished scientists who today occupy key posts in Soviet physics. The Landau Institute of Theoretical Physics near Moscow is now the foremost Soviet center in this field.

The Soviet system allows scientists to study highly problematic questions—those about which it is difficult if not impossible to say how long it will take to solve them, or indeed whether any solution even exists. The system of research grants, so dominant in the United States, does not operate in the Soviet Union. And in spite of its positive features, the grant system sometimes restricts opportunities for pursuing fundamental research, especially in these problematic fields. A ready example is the search for high-temperature (that is, room-temperature) super-conductors.

Electrical current flowing in a wire conductor experiences resistance, which leads to a heating of the wire and therefore to a loss of energy. But when cooled to a very low temperature (-500 degrees Fahrenheit), many metals cease to offer resistance and no energy is lost. About 20 years ago William Little of Stanford University first suggested that it might be possible to produce a substance which would remain a super-conductor up to room temperature. Obviously, if this could be done it would lead to a revolution in technology. Making power lines out of such a substance, for instance, would eliminate enormous losses of energy.

It is equally clear, however, that the task of finding high-temperature super-conducting materials is both complicated and problematic, since it is unclear in principle whether such materials could even exist. In the Soviet Union, a special session of the Presidium of the Academy of Sciences declared this problem *second* in importance after the problem of regulated nuclear fusion, and many Soviet scientists are working intensively in this field. The Institute of Steel and Alloys in Moscow alone maintains a laboratory employing some 80 people in this connection. Yet in the United States, as far as I know, only Little and his group, supported by a grant, are working on the problem. Nor do the Soviet scientists work under the pressure of deadlines. Perhaps a high temperature super-conductor will never be found, but if it is, it will most likely happen in the Soviet Union.

Or take the case of metallic hydrogen. If hydrogen, the lightest element, could be transformed into a metal, we would possess the lightest metal possible. Numerous practical applications would follow. Yet this is also a very problematic question. In the Soviet Union it is under intensive investigation, with large groups of scientists working at the Institute of High Pressure Physics near Moscow and at the Institute of Physics and Technology of the Ukrainian Academy of Sciences in Donetsk. In the United States, to the best of my knowledge, this field is not being experimentally developed.

Scientists working in the Soviet Union enjoy a well-developed system of contacts. All-Union scientific conferences take place frequently and, more importantly, there is a wide network of regular seminars. In Moscow, every Wednesday, scientists from many institutes come to the seminar chaired by Academician Kapitsa at the Institute of Physical Problems. Regular seminars in theoretical physics include the Thursday seminar at the same Institute and Academician Ginzburg's Wednesday seminar at the Lebedev Institute. Such regular meetings promote that interchange of ideas necessary for productive scientific work.

There is, to be sure, a lot of deadwood in Soviet science, a point to which I shall return. But many research groups work very hard and are highly productive—a matter of both personal devotion and a very effective system of incentives. For many scientists in the Soviet Union science is their whole life. I think especially of A. Larkin at the Landau Institute, I.K. Ianson in Kharkiv and N.E. Alekseevsky at the Institute of Physical Problems, among others; they come to their laboratories early in the morning and often do not leave until after midnight. Moreover, Soviet scientists earn relatively high incomes and benefit from a series of academic degrees and ranks, each of which corresponds to a higher degree of financial well-being. The most important degrees are Candidate of Sciences, roughly equivalent to the American PhD, and Doctor of Sciences. The salary of the former is approximately twice the average wage; that of the latter, three times or more. From being a Corresponding Member of the Academy of Sciences (about 480 in 1981) one advances to the rank of full Member (about 260 in 1981), to enjoy a standard of living considerably higher than that of the other professions. The Academy of Sciences pays its members simply for being members, and its prestige in the Soviet Union is unmatched by any single scientific body in the United States.

It is true that Soviet industry has not been equal to the task of producing adequate scientific equipment, especially vital in the experimental fields. But a number of Soviet institutes have been able to acquire excellent equipment in the West. For example, the Academy's Institutes of Solid State Physics and of Bio-Organic Chemistry are two centers which are thus able to pursue high-quality scientific work, and do not suffer from the lack of adequate domestically produced equipment.

Among the weaknesses of Soviet science, the first involves certain moral or personal failings. A recent book on the state of Soviet science argued, correctly, that many heads of Soviet scientific organizations are manipulative, venal or otherwise morally objectionable.[1] Yet, as Lidiia Chukovskaia remarked when Dmitry Shostakovich signed a widely publicized letter against Andrei Sakharov, "villainy and genius" are quite compatible. A number of leading Soviet scientists are known to be anti-Semitic, for example, or crassly political in their careerism. But a scientist's moral qualities should not be confused with the quality of his work, and the fact is that major moral failings and high scientific productivity often go together.

A related weakness of Soviet science is the reverse of one of its strengths. Compared with their Western counterparts, Soviet scientists enjoy relatively greater prestige and material rewards. Moreover, the non-political nature of science attracts many able people who find scientific work compatible with their moral, and possibly anti-communist, convictions. By the same token, however, science attracts bureaucrats who zealously believe in Marxism-Leninism—supposedly *the* scientific theory—and in the Soviet system. These bureaucrats enjoy the aura of respectability and infallibility conferred by academic degrees and memberships. The prestige and material rewards of Soviet science also attract cynical careerists, of course.

The weaknesses of Soviet science are often a direct consequence of its bureaucratization. An obvious case in point involves the movement from basic to applied science, and the implementation of their findings in industry. Here the Soviet Union is very backward. The introduction of new methods or technologies is usually an agonizingly slow procedure, one complicated by an enormous amount of red tape. (The Institute at Kharkiv, described above, is only an outstanding exception to this rule.) The problem of implementing the results of basic and applied research in industry is one of the weakest links in the whole Soviet system.

Another fundamental factor impairing scientific development in the Soviet Union is the low level of computerization. In the United States the ability to use computers in everyday work is as normal to a scientist as driving a car, while for Soviet scientists it is far from common. Undoubtedly this will soon change, given the Soviet Union's proven capacity for producing major advances in selected fields of endeavor—the space program, for example. But meanwhile computers are not adequately used, and this slows down progress in theoretical chemistry, solid state physics and other fields.

In addition to the poor quality of Soviet scientific equipment, and to the problem of insufficient contact with the outside scientific world (which I shall deal with below), another difficulty lies in the large size of

Soviet scientific organizations. Laboratories are often staffed by dozens, and institutes employ hundreds, or even thousands, of scientific workers. As a result, the heads of these organizations become so enmeshed in administration that they lose touch with their science and are gradually disqualified. This does not prevent them from claiming authorship of scientific papers, however. By the age of 45 the current vice-president of the Academy of Sciences and director of its Institute of Bio-Organic Chemistry, for example, was the ostensible author of more than 300 publications, most of which, in all probability, he had not even read. By the end of his life another academician had published more than 1,200 papers—an average of one every two weeks from the time he was 20 years old!

The large number of poorly qualified scientists attracted by the profession's prestige and material rewards, combined with Party interference in scientific appointments, constitutes a major weakness of Soviet science. With the partial exception of the Ukrainian Academy of Sciences, the Academies of the individual Soviet republics are mostly staffed by such people, and their productivity is practically nil. The current heads of the Solid State Physics Department of Moscow University and of the Institute of Atomic Energy owe their appointments to Party politics. Nor does the system, for various of the reasons already noted, give adequate attention to university teaching in science, where unqualified teachers are but one of its grave shortcomings.

For many years I taught at Moscow University and other institutions of higher education in the Soviet capital, and was a member of committees on physics curricula for schools and colleges. Soviet secondary schools, in my opinion, give a better technical-scientific education than do their U.S. counterparts, although recently they have begun to deteriorate in this area. But at the university level, as I have observed here at the University of California at Berkeley, the U.S. system takes a giant step forward. For one thing, the Soviet Union does not have a system of computerized testing in the selection of students comparable to the Scholastic Aptitude Tests and various other standardized examinations—a system remarkable for its objectivity. Instead, every Soviet university conducts its own entrance examinations, which are mostly oral. Given the intense competition for admission, especially to the top universities, this leads to arbitrary decisions based on subjective criteria—in short, to corruption.

Another reason for the comparative inferiority of Soviet higher education lies in its excessively structured nature. Students have practically no freedom of choice in their programs, and must attend many strictly required lectures. Little attention is paid to developing creative skills. At

Berkeley, students are given a great deal of work intended to do just that, whereas at Soviet universities great emphasis is placed on mechanically stuffing the memory.

It is well known that talented Jewish men and women are now, in practice, precluded from entering the leading Soviet universities. The system of oral entrance examinations works to this end.[2] Moreover, Jews are being eliminated from the scientific community as actively as they are from student life. One example is my friend Michael Reyzer, the author of many excellent works in theoretical physics, who looked for a job for over a year. At dozens of laboratories he was met with enthusiasm and told that positions were available, only to be turned down when it became clear from his application (which requires a declaration of one's official "nationality") that he was Jewish. In 1979 he gave up the ordeal and applied to emigrate. He is now a "refusnik." Another young man I knew was among the winners of the All-Union Mathematical Olympiad but later, because he is Jewish, was not admitted to Moscow University. After much difficulty he entered the Institute of Oil Engineering. He will probably become a good engineer, but his remarkable scientific talents are clearly being wasted.

Today it is possible to encounter Jews only among older and middle-aged physicists, and it would seem that in the future Soviet science is to be "cleared" of all Jews. Such policies can only lower the scientific potential of the Soviet Union.

Why is Soviet science underrated in the West, particularly in the United States? Two reasons seem to me the most important. The first is the infrequency, even the complete absence, of contacts between Soviet and Western scientists, a situation that has worsened in recent years. Today, only a few Soviet scientists are permitted to visit foreign countries regularly, to attend international conferences or visit universities. I took part, in 1981, in the International Conference on Low Temperature Physics held in Los Angeles; more than 40 papers had been submitted by Soviet scientists but only three of the authors could come and only two made presentations. In this way, the Soviet authorities drastically curtail opportunities for Soviet scientists to present their work to Western colleagues and to establish contacts which could prove useful to both sides. At the same time, there has been a big drop in the number of Western scientists visiting the Soviet Union; and this, too, has contributed to a breakdown in scientific communication.[3]

My second reason is more specific. Many scientific journals are published in the Soviet Union and a number of these are translated into English; but some U.S. scientists have told me that they are often difficult to read. It is clear, they say, that an interesting result has been obtained—but not how or why; all the intermediate equations have been left out. This happens owing to an acute shortage of paper in the Soviet Union, and leading scientific publications impose strict limits on the length of their articles. The *Journal of Experimental and Theoretical Physics*, for example, requires that submitted papers be no longer than 15 typed pages. It specifies that the account of the experiment must be very concise and that descriptions of intermediate calculations or other details may be omitted. Hence the difficulty in reading such articles.

In the United States, however, the situation is quite different. When I first submitted a paper to a U.S. journal, it was in the Soviet style; but the editor asked me to write in more detail, not to worry about its length, and to give all my attention to making the paper readily comprehensible. At the same time, Soviet scientists who might want to publish in a Western journal find the way impeded by so much Soviet red tape that only a very few are able to overcome it. Practical difficulties like these contribute further to a breakdown in scientific communication.

My general conclusions will be obvious. Soviet science has great strengths as well as weaknesses. Unimpeded scientific communication between the Soviet Union and the West, particularly the United States, could only benefit both sides. □

**1.** Mark Popovsky, *Manipulated Science* (New York: Doubleday, 1979).

**2.** Grigori Freiman, *It Seems I Am a Jew* (Carbondale, Illinois: Southern Illinois University Press, 1980.) This book contains, among other things, examples of special "Jewish problems" given to Jewish applicants in entrance examinations to universities.

**3.** See Loren R. Graham, "Scientific Exchanges with the Soviet Union," *Bulletin of the Atomic Scientists* (May 1983), pp. 2-3. Graham points out that in 1975, at the height of detente, over 2,000 U.S. and Soviet scholars and officials participated in scientific exchanges under 13 different agreements; by 1982 this number had dropped to about 300 under eight agreements.

*This paper is a revised version of V.Z. Kresin, "The State of Natural Science in the USSR," a report sponsored by Harvard University and MIT and issued by the Russian Research Center, Harvard, as Report No. 5 in the Series "Soviet Science and Technology: Eyewitness Accounts" edited by Loren R. Graham and Mark Kuchment.*

# 19

## Education, Science and Technology

### Harley D. Balzer

When the Soviet Union launched the world's first orbiting satellite in 1957, Americans undertook a major reevaluation of both nations' educational and technical capabilities. The United States responded to the challenge sufficiently to maintain a commanding lead in most areas of scientific research and technical application. Yet in retrospect, it can be seen that continued American pre-eminence results only in part from any actions taken after Sputnik. Sputnik was, in fact, an impressive piece of showmanship rather than a major scientific breakthrough.[1]

Early in the 1980s we again heard warnings about competition from Soviet achievements in science and technology.[2] In contrast with the glowing descriptions produced by educational officials, however, the Soviet press and specialized journals are replete with accounts of serious difficulties. As George Kennan put it: "All those who have lived long in Russia have had occasion to observe that when the question is placed as to which of two contrary and seemingly irreconcilable phenomena in Russian life is the true one, the answer is invariably: both."[3] An assessment of the strengths and weaknesses in Soviet technical education highlights this dilemma.

Many major characteristics of contemporary Soviet life were forged during the reign of Joseph Stalin. Yet we often fail to appreciate the degree to which the Stalinist system reinforced attributes of pre-revolutionary Russian society. This was certainly the case in education.

Russia's educational system was built from the top down. An Academy of Sciences was created before the first permanent university was established, and the university preceded the creation of a system of public schools. Institutions at the upper levels remained qualitatively superior to schools on the lower rungs of the educational ladder. Money and attention were lavished on elite institutions while other schools led a precarious existence. Moreover, in the best institutions prestige accrued to theoretical investigations; applied research occupied a distinctly secondary position.

The "orphan" of Russian education was the non-classical secondary school, especially the technical school. While managing to train a certain number of scientists, engineers and workers, educators never resolved the problem of generating middle-level personnel. Secondary specialized schools manifested the most serious drawbacks of Russian education: shortages of staff and equipment, poorly prepared entering students, a high drop-out rate and the failure of many graduates to seek employment in the geographic locations and particular specialties intended by government planners.

Specific social policy goals sought by education officials in tsarist times were, of course, very different from those of Soviet bureaucrats. Pre-revolutionary education ministers wished to reserve higher education for children from the privileged social strata. Soviet leaders have sought to use the schools as mechanisms of social mobility for politically "correct" social groups, mainly workers and peasants. In both cases the need to train skilled cadres necessitated compromise.

Today, demographic trends are perhaps the strongest influence moving Soviet education officials to adjust their policies. In the past, economic growth was achieved in large part by adding to the labor force. Now, the pools of potential workers are being depleted, overall population growth is declining, and the Soviet Union faces critical labor shortages. This is not a new phenomenon in the Soviet economy. Managers have frequently "hoarded" workers, maintaining large staffs so as to have personnel available if needed. The negative impact of such practices can no longer be ameliorated simply by adding new groups to the labor force. In the absence of a thoroughgoing economic reform, Soviet planners will have to resort to piecemeal solutions to manpower and training problems.

One solution to the labor problem that appeals strongly to Soviet planners is to increase labor productivity by improving the education and performance of workers. But the era of relatively inexpensive gains derived from quantitative improvements is past. Almost everyone who can receive a basic secondary education already does. Additional returns from education will have to come from qualitative improvements which are not only expensive but also require proficiency in areas where the Soviets have traditionally done least well—planning and fine tuning.

Each solution they might attempt involves a trade-off. One remedy might be to encourage young people to enter the labor force at an earlier age. But with the "scientific-technical revolution," workers need both a higher level of general education and advanced vocational training, which means more time in school. Another course might be to reduce enrollment in secondary and higher education, but again, the demand for educated personnel—not to mention the interests of students, parents and the institutions themselves—makes this unlikely.

Before surveying Soviet specialized education, it is important to look at the system of secondary education that prepares students for advanced study. Universal secondary education has been a major goal of Soviet educators for decades, and at the Twenty-sixth Party Congress, in 1981, it was announced that the goal would be realized during the current Five-Year Plan—an impressive accomplishment. Yet the Nineteenth Party Congress, in 1952, predicted that universal secondary education would be achieved by 1960. Which is more significant: that the Soviets are approaching the goal 20 years late, or that they are now on the verge of doing so?

The Soviet Union presents a somewhat confusing array of secondary educational institutions. Most students now spend eight years in general education secondary school. They may then choose from among a number of options in completing their secondary education:

• two additional years of general secondary education, preparing them for the intensely competitive examinations to enter higher educational institutions;

• three to four years in a specialized secondary school (technicum) providing additional general education along with technical training for a middle-level job;

• two to four years at a vocational-technical school offering practical training preliminary to entering the labor force;

• entering the labor force and completing one's education in an evening or correspondence division of a secondary school.

Officially, the system is "unified," with access to higher education open to graduates of any secondary institution. In practice, however, most of those entering higher education do so after completing a ten-year general secondary school. A "core" curriculum of general education for all types of secondary schools has been promised for the near future.

American visitors who place their children in Soviet schools generally return with stories of mathematics classes far more advanced than those in U.S. schools. The official Soviet mathematics curriculum does indeed go beyond what most U.S. schools offer. But how does the reality of Soviet education nationwide compare both with the schemes of the planners and with the achievements of the best Moscow schools?

Outside the major urban centers secondary schools do not always conform to the standards set in the capital. There are shortages of supplies, equipment and, most notably, of qualified teachers. Many secondary school teachers do not have a higher degree, and in some cases have received no specialized pedagogical training. Even the vaunted mathematics curriculum has been subject to criticism, some educators arguing that the "new math" overtaxes students and confuses teachers. The mathematics curriculum is currently being revised again.[4]

The Soviet system excels at identifying talented individuals and channeling them to the best schools. An extensive system of "mathematical olympiads" and science competitions works to this end. But while many students receive excellent grounding in mathematics and basic science, overall the system does not appear to be meeting the demands of economic and education planners.

Soviet educational officials have not resolved the basic question of whether secondary schools should provide general education or produce skilled workers. Post-Stalin reforms have alternatively stressed labor training for production (1956), science-oriented basic education (1966), and labor training again (1977). Each strategy has its costs. Nikita Khrushchev's program of production education in the 1950s and the early 1960s caused serious disruptions. In the late 1960s and early 1970s a stress on mathematics and science increased the demand for higher education while discouraging young people from seeking jobs in production. At the same time, the curriculum proved too demanding for many students and even for some teachers. Emphasis on labor training since 1977 has failed to deliver immediate economic benefits, since, according to accounts in the Soviet press, 80 to 90 percent of students receiving such training do not use it on the job.[5]

The most recent answer to the question of whether to have general education or labor training appears to be, "both." The 1981 Twenty-sixth Party Congress proposed improving the quality of general education while reducing the number of hours devoted to it, thus permitting more time for labor training.

The inability to solve the labor problem by general education secondary schools has led to a renewed emphasis on specialized secondary schools, historically the weakest rung on Russia's education ladder. Recent Soviet writings on the subject suggest that educators have failed to eliminate the long-standing problems while encountering new ones created by the economic system.

Specialized secondary schools have difficulty attracting and retaining qualified teachers and administrators. In some instances these schools are affiliated with industrial enterprises and become a dumping ground for undesirable personnel. While planners in Moscow discuss the "computerized classroom" of the future, local school officials complain about shortages of such basic supplies as chalk. Annual plans for textbook publishing are only two-thirds fulfilled, due in part to a paper shortage. There is also a dearth of basic teaching materials, such as syllabi, maps and other visual aids.

Organizational difficulties are endemic. Like workers in other enterprises, students are withdrawn from school to perform "voluntary" social labor, such as helping with sowing and harvesting in agricultural areas. Practical work experience, which constitutes an important element of the curriculum, also presents problems. Industrial managers are frequently tempted to exploit unsalaried helpers rather than to focus on purely educational goals. A 1977 reform calls for improving the quality of such on-the-job training while simultaneously decreasing the amount of time allotted to it.

Local organizational problems are in part a reflection of central administrative disorder. The delineation of responsibility for these schools between branch industrial ministries and the Ministry of Education has never been clear, and cooperation is still problematical. There remains a welter of competing administrative entities, some operating only two or three schools. In the Ukraine, for example, as of 1978 there were 71 different government departments and ministries administering 725 technicums!

Problems in secondary schools are reflected in students' poor performance on annual state examinations and a high drop-out rate. Educational quality in these institutions is also undermined by a heavy burden of paperwork and other administrative pressures. The performance of school administrators is measured by the number of students enrolled and graduated. This can create situations where school and students become partners in fraud, the school certifying skills and the students happily accepting sham diplomas. There are also instances of outright corruption.[6]

The poor quality of specialized secondary education may be one of the reasons for the surprisingly low ratio of technicians to professional workers in Soviet enterprises. The trouble is exacerbated by the fact that large numbers of individuals with specialized education do not work in the fields for which they were trained. Despite much discussion about scientific planning in manpower allocation, effective correlation of students' specialties with the needs of the economy has remained elusive.

Recently, Soviet educators have called for a massive program of guidance at all levels of the system to reduce labor turnover and the consequent "waste" of educational resources. But to provide even one guidance counsellor for every 1,500 students in grades five through ten by 1985 would require training over 33,000 specialists—a task for which neither the financial nor the human resources appear to be available.

A persistent difficulty in secondary specialized education has been the. quality of students. Since Soviet youth evince a strong preference for higher education, secondary technical schools are left with those who fail to gain admission to the more desirable institutions.

Every survey conducted in the Soviet Union has shown that a great majority of children hope to attend college. Increasing enrollments at general-education secondary schools have exacerbated this problem. In 1960, over 41 percent of secondary school graduates were able to enter higher education. In 1978, although there was an increase of nearly two-thirds in the number of students entering higher education, the total represented less than 21 percent of secondary school graduates. That the situation may be changing is indicated by recent reports that some colleges, particularly in engineering, are not filling their entering classes. Still, the pyramids of official social needs and student preferences are almost exactly inverse, suggesting continued intense competition for places in higher education.

Increased competition could result in improvements derived from increased selectivity, but not without putting great pressure on those aspiring to higher education. Students often hire tutors to prepare for entrance examinations, seek to exploit personal connections and even engage in fraud. Recently cases have been reported of young people faking careers as workers to gain admission to college under special programs for outstanding workers.

Soviet higher education, like any large system, is characterized by enormous diversity and unevenness. The system numbers about 65 universities and over 800 *vtuzy* (higher technical education institutions), which include technical and polytechnical institutes as well as factory-affiliated programs conferring institute degrees. There are likely to be significant differences between an engineer trained at Leningrad Polytechnical Institute, however, and one with a diploma from the Kurgan Machine-Building Institute. Universities manifest a similar range. In 1977 ten large universities each had more than ten independent research laboratories while more than 30 others had no such affiliated facilities.[7]

The great number of Soviet institutions of higher education has permitted the Soviet Union to develop the largest scientific-technical intelligentsia in the world. A recent careful study comparing research and development personnel in the Soviet Union and the United States found the Soviets ahead in the total number of scientific personnel, largely because of the enormous body of engineers trained in the past three decades.[8] But once again, we must question the quality of the Soviet achievement.

Beyond doubt, many Soviet institutions conduct world-class research while training first-rate specialists. However, Soviet strength is concentrated in specific fields, especially but not exclusively those in which theoretical ability is most important, as both Loren Graham and Vladimir Kresin point out (Chapters 17 and 18). Work in many applied fields is of lower quality. While this may reflect shortcomings in the economic system rather than in education, it appears that the weaknesses have been mutually reinforcing. The best students often prefer to specialize in fields where neither a lack of laboratory equipment nor the pressures of restrictive censorship will hinder their scientific work.

Shortages of supplies and equipment, plus a dropout problem, affect virtually all higher educational establishments. One striking point to emerge from interviews with recent Soviet emigres is the extent of such drawbacks even at the best institutions.[9] Conditions at less prestigious institutions and especially in evening and correspondence divisions are generally worse, athough the latter still confer about 40 percent of higher degrees.

In short, marked success in increasing the number of students in higher education has been accompanied by a dilution of quality. Interviews revealed major differences between generations in evaluating their educational experiences. Emigres educated before World War II have much higher opinions of their teachers than those who attended college after 1960. The younger group is less likely to state that they were taught by leading specialists, and more of them believe that religious and ethnic prejudice influenced admissions and grading. Clearly, among those who have left the Soviet Union there is a perception of declining educational quality. At the same time, most of the emigres interviewed retain a healthy respect for the Soviet Union's achievement in science.

The most vexing problem in Soviet higher education today, as in secondary specialized education, is that after students receive their diplomas a significant percentage do not work in their specialities. Graduates of higher educational institutions are required to serve three years in jobs assigned by the state, usually in less desirable parts of the country. However, interviews with emigres and accounts in the Soviet press indicate that the young have become adept at manipulating the job assignment process. Increasingly, they simply ignore their obligation and fail to report.

Excess demand for higher education affects career choices. The desire for higher education and the upward social mobility it can bring outweigh the attraction of a particular subject or field. The huge number of engineers in the Soviet Union—40 percent of higher education graduates—may be explained in part by the ease with which students are admitted to engineering institutes compared to other higher institutions. Yet young people who choose institutions and specialties based on admission prospects rather than aptitude are less likely to make careers in those fields after graduation. Instead, they swell the statistics on labor turnover that are so disturbing to Soviet economists.

The large number of graduates working at jobs below their officially defined "skill level" suggests that at least in some cases the quality of their education fails to meet standards set by employers. The idiosyncracies of Soviet economic planning and individual preferences for geographic locations or particular types of work may also account for some of this variety of underemployment.

Thus Soviet claims about scientific manpower planning under socialism are dubious. Estimates of future needs are produced by enterprises which often grossly overstate their requirements. This is rational behavior by industrial managers in a system that does not penalize for inflated estimates but does punish for failure to fulfill production plans. Should central planners allow for overestimates when developing national requirements? Scholarly journals are full of discussions of the relative merits of various forecasting methods. Complaints in the Soviet popular press, however, suggest that a practical resolution of this fundamental problem of manpower allocation is still in the future.

An enormous percentage of people with higher education in the Soviet Union are trained, as mentioned, as engineers. Western analysts characterize Soviet engineering education as narrowly specialized. Emigre engineers, on the other hand, have frequently stated that they received broad training preparing them for diverse technical responsibilities. Which is the correct interpretation?

Description of Soviet engineers as narrow specialists has been based in part on official Soviet lists of specialties, with technical fields divided into very detailed sub-categories. These categories are important, but it must be noted that Soviet higher education normally consists of a five-year course, with specialization beginning only after intensive grounding in basic science, particularly mathematics and physics. Engineers graduating from good Soviet schools may well receive a broader education than do typical U.S. engineers. The success of many emigre engineers in finding jobs in the United States supports this conclusion. At the same time, students of some industry-administered specialized institutes in the Soviet Union and those in many evening and correspondence institutions receive less basic science education, and may well represent the underemployed or underutilized group.

The character of individual institutions and their degrees is particularly important in graduate education. Soviet advanced degrees are organized differently from U.S. masters and doctorates. The basic Soviet postgraduate degree is the *Kandidat Nauk* (Candidate of Sciences), conferred on the basis of graduate study and/or a dissertation. The Soviet Doctor of Sciences degree, which resembles the doctorate in European academic systems, is awarded to established scholars well along in their careers. Many observers equate the *kandidat* degree with the U.S. PhD, and emigres have an obvious interest in establishing such equivalence. In many cases this appears to be fully justified; but again, questions must be asked about the type of institution conferring the degree.

In sum, training enormous numbers of engineers and other specialists has not alleviated the chronic impediments to innovation in the Soviet economy. Even when Soviet scientists achieve breakthroughs in fundamental research, applications are likely to be developed elsewhere. In the past decade a solution has been sought in establishing science-production associations responsible for managing the entire research-to-production cycle. More recently an attempt has been made to experiment similarly in higher education institutions, building on the growing amount of research done by these institutions under contracts from industrial enterprises. In 1980 a group of 73 higher schools in the Moscow region was organized as a Contractual Science Association, officially described as a "joint scientific research, experimental construction and economic complex."[10]

Extension of the association reform to higher education may bring significant improvements, but only if the difficulties impeding such projects in the past are avoided. (A previous "association" reform in the Stalin era was unsuccessful.) Creating quasi-independent administrative entities could sever institutions from their traditional sources of supplies, and can complicate the tasks of central planners. Research incentives may divert attention from teaching. There is also a real danger that too-close ties between schools and economic enterprises will result in an emphasis on meeting immediate production needs; school administrators may find it difficult to protect fundamental research from demands for direct application.

At least in the short run, there will probably be a major program to expand the system of contract associations. But even if the experiment is successful in Moscow, there are serious questions about its viability in regions where the schools, rather than representing a valuable resource, might be seen as a drain on the funds and equipment allotted to industrial enterprises.

The association reform may be the most significant recent innovation in the Soviet education system. What other changes can be expected in Soviet technical education in the near future? One likely innovation would be the emergence of a distinct intermediate school for technicians above the level of existing secondary specialized schools but below the higher institutes. The Soviet Union is the only Eastern-bloc country without such a school, and Soviet educators have recently been examining the success of such institutions in Eastern Europe.

It is also probable that a recent shift of students away from engineering to economics and the social sciences will continue. Changes in the salary scales for various occupations during the Brezhnev years made the financial advantages of engineering much less attractive. Yet gradual shifts are much more likely than drastic changes, since one of the hardest things to do in the heavily bureaucratic Soviet system is to close down an existing institution. This difficulty is already apparent in Soviet professional journals. Alongside continuing discussion of the need to reduce the percentage of evening and correspondence degrees in higher education, there are articles stressing the advantages of training specialists without their having to leave the job ("without separation from production" in the Soviet jargon). At a time of labor shortages this is a compelling argument.[11]

At the secondary level, the debate over the place of general education versus labor training could become heated; but again, in a system where there are few big losers, it is doubtful that any drastic action will be taken here.

The Soviet Union, of course, is not the only country experiencing problems in technical education. Many of the difficulties are familiar enough to Americans, and may be characteristic of advanced industrial societies. Nor should the United States take too great comfort in the difficulties of the centralized Soviet system as against America's diverse educational network. A young person with scientific aptitude in the Soviet Union is more likely to make science a career than is a young American so endowed. Such a student will receive a complete scientific education at state expense, and is thereafter guaranteed a job. But such students are likely to study theory, to repeat, rather than its practical applications. Enormous quantitative gains in Soviet education have not brought the anticipated qualitative improvements on the technical side.

The Soviet system excels at concentrating resources on priority projects and providing opportunities for large-scale research in important areas, particularly in military-related fields. Yet even in the military sphere new technology is often acquired from the West, implying a built-in time lag before others' achievements can be duplicated.

The strengths of Soviet education may offer only limited lessons for America, given the differences in the two social systems. Soviet weaknesses show what can happen when centralized bureaucracy and political controls become excessive. While no responsible observer would discount the Soviet challenge, the evidence considered here suggests that the United States should be less concerned with scientific and technical competition from the Soviet Union and more intent on ensuring that its own educational system is not allowed to decay from within. □

1. See Nicholas De Witt, *Education and Professional Employment in the* USSR (Washington, D.C.: National Science Foundation, 1961); Alexander G. Korol, *Soviet Education for Science and Technology* (Cambridge, Massachusetts: MIT Press, 1957); Robert G. Kaiser, *Russia: The People and the Power* (New York: Atheneum, 1976), Chap. 8.

2. For example, Richard B. Foster's Introduction to Catherine P. Ailes and Francis W. Rushing, *The Science Race: Training and Utilization of Scientists and Engineers, U.S. and USSR* (New York: Crane Russak, 1982).

3. George F. Kennan, "Foreword," to George P. Tschebotarioff, *Russia, My Native Land: A U.S. Engineer Reminisces and Looks at the Present* (New York: McGraw-Hill, 1964), p. xi.

4. Oskar Anweiler, "Das sowjetische Schulwesen am Beginn der achtziger Jahre," *Osteuropa*, 9/10 (Sept.-Oct. 1981), pp. 791-811. For "self-criticism" in this regard, see interview with Soviet Education Minister M. A. Prokof'ev, *Izvestiia* (April 11, 1982). The most extensive criticism by an authoritative Soviet source appeared in *Kommunist*, No. 14 (1980), pp. 99-112.

5. There have been a number of reports on this problem in the Soviet press, for example *Pravda* (June 28, 1982).

6. See, for example, *Pravda* (April 27, 1982) and *Komsomol'skaia Pravda* (Oct. 23, 1982).

7. V. O. Miller, "Prospects for the Development of University Education," *Soviet Education*, XX, 6 (April 1978), p. 38: translation of *Nauchno-teknicheskaia revoliutsiia i razvitievysshego obrazovaniia* (Moscow: 1974).

8. Louvan E. Nolting and Murray Feshbach, "R&D Employment in the U.S.S.R.," *Science*, 207 (Feb. 1, 1980), pp. 493-503; also Ailes and Rushing, *The Science Race*.

9. Interviews with 200 scientists and engineers who worked in Soviet research and development institutions were conducted by a team directed by Harley Balzer and Mark Kuchment at the Harvard University Russian Research Center under a grant from the National Council for Soviet and East European Research. The report, "Soviet R&D: Information and Insights from the Third Emigration," is forthcoming.

10. E.K. Kalinin, "Khozraschetnoe nauchnoe ob'edinenie deistvuet," *Vestnik vysshei shkoly* (Jan. 1982), pp. 37-41.

11. For example, G. V. Kruzhov, "Vklad zaochnyka vuzov," *Vestnik vysshei shkoly* (March 1983), pp. 8-12.

# CULTURE

By the term "culture" in this section of the book we mean "elite" or "high culture" as distinct from "popular culture," or the pastimes, entertainments and hobbies of the mass of ordinary people (often shared of course by the cultural elite). We regret that it has not been possible to include a chapter on Soviet popular culture owing to the dearth of specialists in this field. Had we been able to do so, readers doubtless would have discovered that popular Soviet interest in sports, rock music, betting on the horses, how-to books and escapist films and television programs closely parallels that of people in the West—often to the despair of members of the Soviet cultural elite.

In his survey of the cultural scene Irwin Weil is concerned to present, however briefly, the positive and enduring aspects of Soviet high culture (really, of Soviet Russian high culture). Katerina Clark then focuses on recent trends in Soviet literature, and identifies an essential ambivalence reflective of conflict and uncertainty. Geoffrey Hosking in turn suggests that this ambivalence and uncertainty may well reflect disputes within the country's leadership, and explain how literary works exhibiting these qualities manage to be published despite the heavy censorship. In this pervasive yet secretive, top-down political system, Hosking is suggesting, literature can still provide a kind of forum for debating the great political and moral questions of the times.

# 20 CULTURE

## A Survey of the Cultural Scene

### *Irwin Weil*

Moscow has become a huge urban center, with millions of people spread over vast distances which can entail long bus and subway rides. It is easy to form the impression of a hard, drab accumulation of stone and of unsmiling, hurrying people. Yet those who know and love Moscow find the city a veritable mother-hen, sheltering her chicks under her wings; and a little careful attention soon rewards the observer with startlingly beautiful sights.

Amidst those stone piles, and sometimes hidden by them, lovely churches and buildings dating from the fifteenth century are to be found, buildings exhibiting the warmest and most charming connections of brick, mortar, and wood and combinations of color and shape. The old Novodevichii Convent, for example, is a movingly beautiful sight, especially early in the morning under the slanting rays of the sun. There are also tens of thousands of people who react with an equally startling and arresting sensitivity to wide aspects of the world around them. Their intellectual interests are catholic, whether their work be in the humanities, the sciences, or engineering.

The Soviet cultural scene in many ways runs parallel to the physical and human map of Moscow, so unlike the Petersburg that became Leningrad, with its proud and sublime vistas all on open display—"dusha na rapashku," as the Russians like to say. To those who see it only from the outside, Soviet culture seems to be a juggernaut of harsh ideological assertions, of self-satisfied purveyors of art boasting of quantity, purity of attitude, and the athletic heroism of muscle-bound defenders of the faith. The Russians themselves laugh at this affectation with a Soviet-style anecdote:

*Naive Moscovite*: "Well, comrades, how are things, culturally speaking, in the Tula District?"
*Ministry of Culture Representative*: "Oh, wonderful! In the Tula Writers' Union alone we have over 100 members—that's 100 times better than it was 80 years ago, when we had only one writer in the whole Tula District: Lev Tolstoy."

From the inside, however, Soviet culture looks as different from this standard Western view as does the mother-hen of Moscow from its drab exterior. A vibrancy and joyous energy often produce admirable artistic and cultural results. An outstanding example of this truly Russian phenomenon took place in the spring of 1982: the memorial celebration of the one hundredth anniversary of the birth of Kornei Ivanovich Chukovsky, who died in 1969.

Chukovsky is known in the West among psychologists and linguists for his highly original work on children's language.[1] He is also known, to a lesser degree, for his sparkling children's poetry and his literary criticism. In the Soviet Union, it was impossible to grow up without his rhymes and rhythms on your lips, and Chukovsky's literary work and judgments helped to form more than one generation of writers and critics. His country house at Peredelkino, the writers' colony outside Moscow, was adjacent to a special children's library built and stocked by him. The house was also the gathering place of some of the best creative talent among the Moscow intelligentsia. Like the great nineteenth- and early twentieth-century Russian writers to whose memory and principles he remained faithful, Chukovsky knew how to bring talented people together in an "at home" atmosphere and to elicit from them imaginative literary efforts in both prose and poetry. He was also gifted in dealing with children and in encouraging them to become interested in the arts.

The celebration of Chukovsky's hundredth birthday was an event whose various manifestations involved many of the most noteworthy representatives of Soviet culture. At two of the most important Muscovite gathering places for the intelligentsia, the Library for Foreign Literature and the Central Literary Museum, hundreds of people listened to an evocation of his remarkable personality and a reevaluation of his work and influence. Right after the revolution Chukovsky had participated in Gorky's project to make good translations of the best of world literature available to a large readership; and through his life he worked unstintingly to strengthen Soviet literary culture. His critical eye, moreover, did not spare foreign specialists in Russian literature, as I can testify from personal experience.

Those evenings in honor of Kornei Chukovsky provided excellent insight into the interests and preoccupations of the Soviet intelligentsia.

Writers and critics described in detail the care he took in reviewing their work. Audiences crowded around displays of his writings in both Russian and foreign-language editions. Leading Russian authors gave readings from their own works. In short, these Russians of the 1980s were looking back over 70 years or more and once again drinking in that great tradition of literature and poetry which is the subsistence and patrimony of their language and culture. The tradition is as alive today as it was at the beginning of the century. Contemporary Soviet citizens can spout reams of this poetry by heart, and the editions containing it are sold out as soon as they hit the bookstore counters. Ironically, one can buy such works most easily at the foreign currency stores, and they are always welcome gifts to one's Soviet friends.

Several evenings after the Chukovsky celebration at the Moscow Central Literary Museum a television program devoted to his work and influence was broadcast to an audience of many millions. In addition to the commentary and documentary pictures, interviews with some of the leading figures in Soviet culture touched on many of the issues that Chukovsky had dealt with during his long life. Again, the program provided a vast panorama of the cultural scene over the last four generations of Russian and Soviet history, and the Soviet viewers with whom I watched it expressed both fascination and pride. One's reactions, of course, were inevitably also affected by the knowledge that Kornei Chukovsky's daughter, Lidiia, has been one of the most courageous of the literary dissenters as well as a gifted writer and critic in her own right. Her voice has always defended freedom of speech, attacked literary censorship, and offered sympathy to those who suffered repression.[2]

Many who took part in the Chukovsky anniversary observances themselves make important contributions to Soviet culture, as I indicated. The sponsor of one entire event was Liudmila Gvishiani, the daughter of Aleksei N. Kosygin, the late Soviet prime minister. She supports a great deal of cultural work in Moscow and can take considerable credit for encouraging many truly creative aspects of Soviet culture. The moderator of another event is connected with the Gorky Institute of World Literature in Moscow, a branch of the Soviet Academy of Sciences which enjoys great prestige and influence.

The Gorky Institute has a scholarly staff of several hundred, all of whom are involved in projects of literary theory and criticism as well as in publishing texts important for the understanding of literature. The moderator of the Chukovsky evening is concerned with, among other things, a major Chekhov project. Apart from a new, multi-volume collection of Chekhov's complete works and correspondence (whose chief editor recently attended an international symposium on Russian literature at Northwestern University), there are in preparation several volumes covering Chekhov's influence in many different countries and languages.

These latter volumes will appear in a series called *Literaturnoe nasledstvo (Literary Heritage)*, which has for decades been publishing important materials by and about major authors. A valuable collection of literary sources, the series is typical of the best work done at the Gorky Institute, which strongly encourages Soviet study of, and reaction to, contemporary Western literary criticism and theory. At the same time, the Institute is trying to increase the scope and number of its international symposia involving Soviet and foreign scholars and specialists. Many of its representatives have visited the United States over the last two years, and there is hope that much useful scholarly research will be forthcoming.

Mindful of the Institute's work on Chekhov, considerable interest has been shown in a new production of *The Three Sisters* at the Taganka, one of Moscow's most interesting and controversial theaters. Its director, Yury Liubimov, has staged productions which have become fixtures in Soviet cultural life, including several of Shakespeare's plays as well a dramatization of Bulgakov's *The Master and Margarita*. This outstanding novel, combining the Faust legend, a re-doing of the Gospel of St. Matthew, and a raucous satire on Soviet life in the 1920s, remained "in the drawer" until 26 years after Bulgakov's death. Its publication (1966-1967) was a major event in both Soviet and Western literature, and it has been a favorite rallying-point in Soviet literary circles ever since.[3] Liubimov's dramatization has become a consistently popular staple of the Taganka Theatre, always sold out far in advance.

Predictably, Liubimov's version of Chekhov's *The Three Sisters* is radically different from that created by Stanislavsky and lovingly preserved to this day by the world famous, but by now slightly musty, Moscow Art Theatre. And it set the Moscow theatrical world's teeth on edge. The very walls of the Taganka come down (on hydraulic lifts) for few moments to expose the city itself and its freezing temperatures behind a Russian army band dressed in pre-revolutionary uniforms (the device suggests the sisters' repeated exclamation: "To Moscow, to Moscow!"). Upstage is a tinny cyclorama, with military barrack spigots and iconic representations, against which the actors noisily bang and bump. At center stage is a crude platform of unfinished wood which the actors mount when speaking internal thoughts. Downstage left are the sisters' rooms, and far downstage, with backs to the audience, sit the soldiers of the local garrison. Chekhov's order of lines is changed, masks are pulled out of pockets and worn — some in the form of round "smiling faces." It seems that everything possible is being done to disorient the spectator, comfortably used to the traditional notion of how Chekhov should be produced.

Predictably, again, all hell broke loose. Some critics loved it, others despised it. Many concerned individuals, including literary specialists of the Gorky Institute, expressed their feelings, some of them aggrieved, to Liubimov. I am in no position to attack or defend this interpretation of Chekhov. But I can testify to the intensity of the feelings aroused among both actors and spectators. For them, Chekhov is a living part of their emotional and intellectual lives. Such identification with an important writer is itself characteristic of Soviet cultural life.

Another aspect of the Taganka Theatre which says much about Soviet culture is the corner devoted to the memory of Vladimir Vysotsky, who died in 1980 and is now the object of an extraordinary cult. Vysotsky played Liubimov's Hamlet, among other leading roles, and was also a balladier who in private performances touched on themes of great power and moment to all levels of society: the clumsy pomposity, favoritism and corruption in high places, the miseries of prison camp life (which he had known firsthand), the futility of war, the tribulations of everyday Soviet life. Unfortunately, Vysotsky was a heavy drinker, and the habit hastened his death at the age of 42. All too many Russian artists and writers suffer from this malady — a theme, again, of Vysotsky's lyrics.

Cassette tapes of Vysotsky's private performances are prized among the Soviet intelligentsia, and his earthy poem-songs are widely known. They always provoke lively discussion among listeners: I have sat through many such an evening with Soviet friends, and I know that Vysotsky leaves no one indifferent to what he has to say. In this respect, he is comparable to Bulat Okudzhava, another popular balladier of the 1960s who has turned to writing highly ironical historical novels.[4]

An extremely popular novelist and short-story writer who died recently was Yury Trifonov. Two of his works have been staged at the Taganka: his chilling *House on the Embankment*, a document of betrayal and cowardice during the Stalin purges, and *The Exchange*, whose plot revolves around the imminent death from cancer of the protagonist-narrator's mother. He watches with increasing horror the progress of her disease and the greed of those around them, mostly family and in-laws, who see her approaching death only as a chance to grab her apartment (through the usual official but largely fictitious "exchange") — an apartment being, of course, a most valuable commodity in the Soviet Union.

The growing horror and pain of the protagonist are deftly understated, and thereby emphasized, by Liubimov's theatrical art. The play's irony and sarcasm provide considerable comic possibilities, and the skilled Taganka actors make the most of them. In one memorable scene, a drunken worker blindly bumps into a tree, becomes angry, and works his way into a mighty argument—with the tree; the actor makes the tree come to life with rare talent. At another point, an old actor mimes with his hands the creation of a vegetable garden; he does it so successfully that the spectator can almost smell the tomatoes and cucumbers. The quality of the art and the actors' concentration are truly impressive, and the theatrical and literary issues are sharply focused. Whether Liubimov's and Trifonov's views are excessively gloomy and misanthropic is a question ardently debated among the Taganka audiences, whose awesome seriousness is recognizable to patrons of small, dedicated theater companies around the world.

The same kind of audience can be seen at classical music concerts in Moscow and Leningrad. The two major Muscovite centers of music are the Tchaikovsky Conservatory and the Gnessin State Musical Pegadogical Institute, both located in lovely areas of the city. The Conservatory is near the stately eighteenth-century buildings of Moscow University and the former Manège of the tsar, now devoted to art exhibits. The Gnessin Institute, a haven especially for chamber musicians and practitioners of folk music, is located near the "Arbat" district, in the midst of older mansions. The latter stand in sharp contrast to the modernistic glass, aluminum and steel high-rises of the nearby Kalininskii Prospekt, a contrast that can be seen as symbolic. For while the excellence of the leading Soviet conservatories and musical institutes is unquestioned, one admiring foreigner has observed that within them "the most modern and the most obsolete teaching techniques exist side by side."[5]

Some concerts take place in halls made venerable by generations of great artists, and today's performances are followed and criticized as vehemently as ever. When the late Leonid Kogan, the well known violinist, with his son Pavel conducting, gave a concert that combined German Romantic music and a semi-popular piece in the main hall of the Tchaikovsky Conservatory, I could hear murmurs of shock at the mixture of styles. The reactions to the violin playing and the conducting were as varied as those in any concert hall whose listeners have been brought up on good performances and passionate musical debate. But in this instance, the great tradition of string playing in Russia made the polemics both sharper and more intense.

Russian musical influence has spread throughout the world, including, most emphatically, North America; this fact hangs over the Soviet musical scene almost palpably. Soviet music lovers are well aware that Soviet-born composers, conductors and performers are now located in many foreign music centers, and have made the Russian musical tradition a living presence everywhere. When foreign orchestras and individual performers come to the Soviet Union, they almost always receive a strong response. Listeners are eager to hear what is being done elsewhere and to learn how the Russian tradition has been mixed with others to produce new styles. Thus the New York Philharmonic Orchestra generated tremendous excitement among Soviet musicians and music lovers when it performed in the Soviet Union a few years ago. Soviet concert-goers knew perfectly well how deeply their tradition had influenced the New Yorkers—something that is true of the orchestras of Chicago, Boston, and many other leading American musical centers as well.

It is noteworthy that within the last two decades a small group of avant-garde composers has arisen in the Soviet Union. The best of their output has been judged, in the words of one Western critic, "very good indeed—so good, in fact, that its originality and power far transcend national differences or political ideology."[6] Perhaps the leading figure here is the "polystylistic" Alfred Schnittke, who is being hailed as the greatest Soviet composer since Shostakovich. Some of his works have been performed in the United States, notably by Continuum, the New York-based ensemble. At home the work of Schnittke and his colleagues is heard in well-attended private concerts, and Schnittke's advocacy by the Soviet violinist Gidon Kremer has helped to gain him a loyal public.

Unfortunately, vocal music is not as well represented in the Soviet Union today as it was a generation or two ago. The fabulous art of the traditional Russian bass—of Reizen and Pirogov, not to mention Shaliapin (still a much-loved figure)—has not been maintained, with the possible exception of Boris Shtokolov's mighty renditions. Today's opera companies and choral ensembles can still provide wonderful spectacles and sounds; but they do not have the outstanding voices that once thrilled the musical world. Nor have they been noticeably innovative in their programming—a characteristic, too, of Soviet ballet and dance, where the power of a glorious tradition in technique and training seems to have inhibited further development.

At a more informal musical level, the Western tradition of the chanteuse, full of dusky promise and scintillating personality, has come to the fore. Many of these singers are effective performers. Yet they lack the intensity of that native semi-folk vocal art of an earlier age so well described by Gorky. Nor do they compare, in range or popularity, with the male balladiers mentioned above.

A kind of hiatus currently obtains in Soviet painting and sculpture.

The fierce campaigns against modernism, "formalism" and abstraction-
ism launched by officialdom as recently as 1974 have taken their toll,
and "socialist realism" remains the favored style.[7] On the other hand,
even in officially sponsored exhibitions one finds paintings in which approved themes are handled in entirely individualistic ways, often to the
point of counteracting the simplistic optimism and political piety of the
official canon. Indeed, one can see reflected in countless private experiments, and in the sometimes officially sponsored fiddling with traditional Russian folk and religious themes, an intense interest in the
possibilities of non-representational art. Any exhibition offering even a
hint of novelty is jammed with eager spectators, and foreign exhibitions
are especially crowded.

In recent years, large numbers of people in both the Soviet Union and
the West have become acquainted with those remarkable movements in
early twentieth-century Russian art which are still called the "avant-
garde."[8] Sadly ignored if not repressed for decades in its own country,
despite its associations with the revolution, a major collection of this art
was brought together with its French counterparts and shown first in
Paris in 1979, and then, with alterations, in Moscow in 1981. Hundreds
of the Russian works had never before been seen on public display, and
the effect of the exhibition on the tens of thousands of Soviet citizens
who saw it during its four-month showing is said to have been electrify-
ing. The exhibition's catalogue is now a highly treasured item among the
Soviet intelligentsia, as it is in the West.

Leading modernist painters are sometimes permitted one-man shows,
as was the case with Boris Messerer in October 1981. Moreover, since
1978 a group of 20 or so non-conformist artists have been exhibiting
their works annually in a basement gallery on Malaia Gruzinskaia Street
in Moscow. None of their paintings and collages are accepted for display
anywhere else, and their themes are clearly "unofficial": openly religious
depictions, surrealist and super-realist efforts, symbolic representations
of good and evil, or semi-abstract compositions. That these and other
avant-garde artists can survive and even prosper outside the official
unions, through which so much of Soviet cultural life is controlled, can
be attributed to the discreet patronage of established musicians and
similar cultural figures, certain senior officials, and leading scientists.
The Kurchatov Institute of Atomic Energy, for example, has hosted a
number of private showings of modern Russian art.

Official attitudes aside, the real public for modern or avant-garde art
in the Soviet Union, as in the West, is probably quite limited. Equally if
not more evident is a fond interest in the art of the past—indigenous,
often humble, and decorative. Hundreds if not thousands of gifted,

energetic and dedicated craftsmen are at work in the Soviet Union today, and their sensitivity to and knowledge of the art of former times can be seen in the frescoes, icons and architectural details of the old churches which they have restored all over the country. The respect — even veneration — felt for these artifacts of Russian culture can hardly be exaggerated; indeed, it constitutes a veritable cult, one that parallels a growing devotion to the masterpieces of Old-Russian literature.[9] This is not mere nostalgia but a kind of cultural nationalism, one which on occasion combines with that Soviet interest in Western art and fashion which is the subject of so much more Western comment.

I have concentrated here on only one nationality within the Soviet Union, the Russian. I do so largely, of course, because it is so dominant. Also, I do not know the languages of the other Soviet nationalities and so cannot read their literatures in the original. Yet it should be noted that major works in other languages are usually translated into Russian, and have an all-Soviet appeal. One of the most acclaimed writers in the Soviet Union today is Chingiz Aitmatov, a Kirgiz author of high standing in the Communist Party who in a series of novellas has dealt with the painful themes of Stalinism, social callousness, national identity and the morality of international politics. More on him in the following chapter.

At the same time, theaters in such cities as Riga, Tallinn and Vilnius vigorously uphold the local culture and language (Latvian, Estonian and Lithuanian) while maintaining a high level of polish and sophistication. This is also true of the Rustaveli Theatre of Tbilisi, the capital of the Soviet Republic of Georgia, which has played Brecht in Berlin and Shakespeare in London to critical acclaim. The international reputation of various other Soviet opera and ballet companies, dance and choral ensembles, individual and group instrumentalists, is familiar enough to need no further mention.

Indeed, a review of cultural life in the Soviet Union today prompts one to hope not only that it may freely flourish, but that exchanges between that country and the West, particularly the United States, may be allowed to developed fully. There is much to be learned, and much to be enjoyed, on both sides. □

1. Kornei Chukovsky, *From Two to Five*, trans. Miriam Morton (Berkeley, California: University of California Press, 1963).

2. At least two of her works are available in English: Lidiia Chukovskaia, *The Deserted House*, trans. A.B. Werth (New York: Dutton, 1967) and *Going Under*, trans. Peter M. Weston (London: Barrie & Jenkins, 1972).

3. Mikhail Bulgakov, *The Master and Margarita*, trans. Mirra Ginsburg (New York: Grove Press, 1967); also translated by Michael Glenny, same title (New York: Harper &

Row, 1967). See also A. Colin Wright, *Mikhail Bulgakov: Life and Interpretations* (Toronto: University of Toronto Press, 1978) and Ellendea Proffer, *An International Bibliography of Works by and about Mikhail Bulgakov* (Ann Arbor, Michigan: Ardis, 1976).

4. Bulat Okudzhava, *Nocturne: From the Notes of Lieutenant Amiran Amilakhvari, Retired*, trans. A.W. Bouis (New York: Harper & Row, 1978); Okudzhava, *The Extraordinary Adventures of Secret Agent Shipov in Pursuit of Count Leo Tolstoy, in the Year 1862*, trans. H. Maisner (London: Abelard-Schuman, 1973).

5. Fred Hechinger, quoted in Boris Schwarz, *Music and Musical Life in Soviet Russia, 1917-1970* (New York: Norton, 1973), p. 305.

6. John Von Rhein, "Music," Chicago Tribune (May 23, 1982).

7. On socialist realism in Soviet painting and its background, see Elizabeth Valkenier, *Russian Realist Art* (Ann Arbor, Michigan: Ardis, 1977).

8. See Camilla Gray, *The Russian Experiment in Art: 1863-1922* (New York: Harry N. Abrams, Inc., 1971); A.Z. Rudenstine, ed., *Russian Avant-Garde Art: The George Costakis Collection* (New York: Harry N. Abrams, Inc. 1981).

9. See Serge A. Zenkovsky, ed. and trans., *Medieval Russia's Epics, Chronicles, and Tales* (New York: Dutton, 1974) for literary samples; and Ruth Daniloff, "Restoring a Russian Heritage," *Smithsonian* (March 1983), pp. 64-73 for painting and architecture, with photographs by Rhoda Baer.

# New Trends in Literature

*Katerina Clark*

There has been much speculation about what will happen to Soviet literature in the post-Brezhnev era. Yet much had happened even before his death. Over the past five years or so, and especially since 1980, significant shifts have occurred which might well determine the future.

Most Soviet literary officials and critics, as well as writers of the most varied hues, have been united of late on one point: that the doctrine of "socialist realism," which goes back to Stalin's time, must be changed. In fact, it is thought to be changing already. In a speech to the Seventh Congress of the Writer's Union in 1981 G. Markov, the Union's head, stressed that what was needed was a "mature" version of socialist realism, one better suited to the stage of "mature socialism" which, in its progress toward communism, the Soviet Union has now reached.

Such declarations became especially prevalent around 1980, and appeared in virtually every issue of the main journals of literary theory and criticism, *Voprosy literatury (Problems of Literature)* and *Literaturnoe obozrenie (Literary Review)*. Writers and critics alike seemed to feel the need to project literary progress for the 1980s beyond what was typical of the 1970s. Fastening on works that appeared in 1980, they declared them to be harbingers of the new. It was as if once the new decade had begun, instant panaceas for the ills of the 1970s would follow. Less readily apparent is a consensus on which of the contending "new directions" should be embraced.

In order to see where Soviet literature might be going, we must first know where it has been. The matter is complex but, in essence, it can be said that Soviet literature today is evolving away from the classic pattern reflected, for example, in Galina Nikolaeva's *Battle en Route* (1957), a novel that has frequently been cited by authoritative Soviet literary figures as a model to emulate.

The novel is set in a factory making ball bearings for Soviet tractors. The hero, Bakhirev, is the factory's chief engineer. Bakhirev has become aware that much of the factory's equipment is obsolescent and drastically needs overhauling if the country's tractors are to operate efficiently. When he puts the problem to the factory administrators they object on the ground that an overhaul would be expensive, would lower their production figures, and hence would damage their chances for certain awards.

Bakhirev knows he will lose his job if he pushes the matter too far. But what of the tractors? The precious harvest? The Soviet economy? Bakhirev is married, with children, but his wife does not share his concerns. Worse still, all she really cares about is her social position and material comforts. She even nags him for not going along with the administration. But in the factory a certain young Tina does share Bakhirev's apprehensions, and he finds himself spending more and more time at work talking to Tina about the vast future prospects of ball-bearing factories. The rest is easy to imagine.

One can tell that this book was published after Stalin's death because the author has dispensed with the sense of decorum which earlier caused writers to avoid involving "positive heroes" in adultery. But in most other respects *Battle en Route* meets our expectations of the classic Soviet novel, expectations encapsulated in the phrase "boy meets tractor." Thus the hero battles the most powerful of careerist bureaucrats and even risks his personal future in the name of the socialist tomorrow as represented by the almighty tractor. In this case his campaign against obsolescence is also a metaphor for de-Stalinization. And the hero's love for the tractor is shared by the "girl"—and so boy and girl come to love one another.

In the past, most (but not all) Soviet critics exulted in the inexorability of the hero's progress. But this is far from the case today. Many critics and writers are concerned to update Soviet literature and to give it greater international respectability—all the while ensuring, of course, that it is not contaminated by that official bugbear, "modernism." From their point of view, the award of the Nobel Prize in literature to Gabriel Garcia Marquez in October 1982 was almost as significant as Brezhnev's death one month later.

Marquez has excellent political credentials in Soviet eyes: a Latin American leftist who lives in voluntary political exile from his native Columbia, he frequently visits Cuba and is an opponent of U.S. "imperialism." Such credentials have made it possible for Soviet critics to cite his writings as models for socialist realism to emulate, particularly his most famous novel, *One Hundred Years of Solitude* (1967), which was published in Russian translation in the journal *Inostrannaia literatura (Foreign Literature)* in 1970. The injunction to follow Marquez was a commonplace of criticism even before the Nobel award. In an article of July 1982 the critic Varvara Grigorian remarked: "It is impossible to have a conversation about literature nowadays without mention of Marquez "

Marquez and socialist realism? How can his eroticism and rich, grotesque fantasy have much to do with all those gray and simplistic tales about "boy meets tractor" and "hero achieves plan"? Soviet critics hope that an injection of what they refer to as "Marquez," but which actually embraces the new Latin American novel in general, will make those tales a little less gray and simplistic. They want to enliven and give depth to them by adding a dimension previously frowned upon, that of "fantastic realism."

When Latin American authors talk of their literary approach they usually refer to it as "magical realism." This is not what the Soviet critics have in mind. When they urge "Marquez" on their authors they think not of a full-blooded version of his "magical realism" but rather of using such relatively tame, non-representational forms as expurgated or invented folk legends. Under this rubric, however, some curious works have slipped into print, such as V. Orlov's *Danilov Al'tist* (1980), in which the devil is a leading character.

I suspect, moreover, that some Soviet critics are using "Marquez" as a front for William Faulkner, who has had a much stronger influence on recent Russian writing by people like Valentin Rasputin. But Faulkner, being American and not "leftist," is automatically a dubious candidate for a Soviet literary mentor. Confirming my suspicion is the fact that in recent Soviet literary criticism Faulkner's name is often slipped into the text a discreet paragraph or two after the mandatory mention of Marquez.

Equally curious, while "Marquez" is being used as a sort of shorthand for what is to be *added* to the socialist realist tradition, the name of a U.S. writer, Arthur Hailey, is being used as a label for a suddenly discredited trend. Hailey's well-known novels *Airport, Hotel* and *Wheels*—which combine information about airports, hotels and the motor industry with tales of struggle between good and bad managers and salacious love plots—are also popular in the Soviet Union, where they have circulated in underground editions. (A translation of *Airport* also appeared openly, in *Inostrannaia literatura* in 1971.) Today, the classic Soviet practice of setting fiction in some place of work such as a collective farm, factory or construction site, and of providing object lessons in the way such places should be run, has been branded "Haileyism" and is widely regarded as quaint but outmoded.[1]

Yet the spate of articles calling for more "Marquez" and less "Hailey" cannot be taken as a call for something entirely new. The principles of what is now designated "fantastic realism" informed such novels as Mikhail Bulgakov's *The Master and Margarita* and Chingiz Aitmatov's *The White Steamship*.[2] Many of the major works published in the late 1960s paid little or no attention to their protagonists' working lives. Indeed, the articles advocating this "new direction" probably represent an attempt to legitimate and to secure gains already made in the face of threats that they may be reversed.

The gains I have in mind are those made under Leonid Brezhnev. Between 1964 and 1982 many writers reacted against such conventions as dividing protagonists into "positive" and "negative" characters, with the hero exemplifying the "positive," and structuring each novel as a tale of economic-cum-political achievement. One kind of writing to come out of this reaction was so-called *byt* prose—fiction about everyday life, generally urban—in which the psyches and moral problems of ordinary people are explored without much reference to their work, or even to the Party.

A more extreme version of this reaction is to be found in "village prose," a movement which came to dominate Soviet fiction in the Brezhnev years. "Village prose" writers not only fail to glory in economic and political achievement, but give their works settings remote in either place or time from the mainstream of Soviet life. They seem to vie with one another in finding settings that are cut off from the outside world and in which the traditional peasant way of life is led. There are sometimes quite literally no tractors in the villages of "village prose."

Soviet "village prose" of the Brezhnev era explores questions of alienation, spirituality and even of religion. Its heroes are more concerned with their relations with each other, their inner lives and sense of identity than they are with the cause of material or political progress. Indeed, there is a marked bias against the modern and its trappings such as technology and urban life, and even against the ideal of material progress. Instead, "village prose" writers are to varying degrees attracted by the pre-revolutionary, traditional peasant way of life, and in many instances by Russian Orthodoxy. They sometimes succumb to Russian chauvinism or anti-Semitism.

"Village prose" is closely allied with what might be called the Russian nationalist school of criticism, which was also very visible in certain literary journals during the Brezhnev years. Extreme versions of this kind of criticism are not merely fiercely nationalistic—and therefore usually anti-Western and anti-Semitic—in sentiment; they also reject the literary gains of the twentieth century, demanding that all writing be based on the classics of pre-revolutionary Russian literature.

The prominence enjoyed under Brezhnev by these two consecutive literary movements—"village prose" and "*byt* prose"—is related to the fact that during these years many bright young writers were squeezed out of Soviet literature and, in many cases, into emigration. The writers of experimental urban prose suffered most. Earlier in this century the Russian Formalists explained literary evolution in terms of fathers and sons, and their model is very useful for describing what has happened to Soviet literature since the Khrushchev years (1955-1964).

Under Khrushchev, the "sons"—that is, the younger generation, ostensibly unsullied by the Stalinism of their elders—challenged their literary "fathers." Under Brezhnev, however, the "fathers," as those "sons" of the Khrushchev years who remained in Soviet literature had by then become, simply suppressed the new crop of "sons." They restricted the younger generation's entry into literature so severely that at the Writers' Congress of 1981 only three percent of the delegates were under forty. As critics, moreover, the "fathers" have also been very hard on those representatives of the younger generation who do manage to get into print. In some instances, works have been condemned explicitly as typical of "writers 25 to 35 years old." In other words, in the literary life of a country with an aging leadership there seems to be a widespread prejudice against youth.

Thus the generation that the Formalists identified as the "sons" was disenfranchised. There have been some grass roots attempts, all abortive so far, to rectify this situation. In 1978, for instance, some of the livelier writers of the Khrushchev era joined forces with some of the younger writers and tried, unsuccessfully, to put out an anthology called *Metropol*.[3] Again, in the fall of 1980, one of the contributors to *Metropol*, Evgeny Popov, and some of his colleagues tried to set up a Young Writers' Club to bring out experimental works in small print runs. But the KGB intervened before that enterprise got off the ground.

It is, of course, not mandatory that a writer be under forty in order to be innovative. The irony is that those who remain in Soviet literature are desperately seeking "new directions." This has given rise to all the talk about "Marquez" and also to some, largely unexciting, experiments with the novel form, that being the dominant literary genre in the Soviet Union today. Yet judging by what appears in the more official sources, these critics are really advocating that writers reject "village prose" and start from the earlier or classic paradigm of "boy meets tractor" in

creating a new one. This new paradigm is to express the country's—
or the leadership's—current concerns, which have less to do with brute
industrialization and more with international affairs and internal
cohesion.

Thus the catchwords *globalnost* (of global scope) and *masshtabnost*
(on a large scale), like "a multinational literature" and "the positive
hero," are now standard in Soviet criticism. The terms are directed either
implicitly or explicitly against the trend in "village prose" of setting
works in remote and antiquated places where people of only one ethnic
group live, and of having protagonists of only marginal political and
economic significance.

Often critics attack "village prose" outright, usually labelling it a
literature of nostalgia. One such critic, writing in *Literary Gazette
(Literaturnaia gazeta)* in 1979, declared that while he had no objection.
to writing about peasants as such, more representative peasants should
be chosen as subjects—for instance, the "peasant technician" who sits at
a desk and handles the controls regulating water levels for an entire
district.

It is not just the lack of technology in "village prose" that troubles such
critics, but also the lack of ideology and, conversely, the cult of religion
with its strains of Russian Orthodoxy. The latter is not usually attacked
outright. In his speech to the Seventh Writers' Congress, for example,
Markov alluded to religion only indirectly when lamenting the fact that
"lately people have avoided mention of the positive hero when talking of
a work's protagonists. Instead, they use expressions like 'national
character' and 'a spiritual person.'"

Another important motive in the campaign against "village prose"
(and the related Russian nationalist school of criticism) is the desire to
minimize ethnic divisions and to stress Soviet unity. This is clear in
Markov's speech, where he marvels at the fact that, while Soviet
literature is written in 77 languages, it exhibits great unity. Of course,
this mystical unity is partly a function of Russian cultural hegemony.
Despite the recent reaction against the national school of criticism, there
is little evidence that the powers-that-be want to lessen Russian dominance over minority literature. Thus an article on recent Georgian
literature published in 1982 in the journal *Druzhba narodov (Friendship
of the Peoples)* repeats the stock observation about how much the various peoples of the Soviet Union have in common, and then celebrates
both the great love Russian writers have always had for Georgia—"think
of Pushkin, Lermontov and Pasternak"—and the great love Georgian
writers have always had for Russian literature.

Indeed, in pursuit of a truly multinational literature, editors of Soviet literary periodicals have been instructed to publish more works by authors from the ethnic minorities, but in so doing, to stress the theme of unity. Everyone was particularly gratified, therefore, when the novel *The Call of the Heart*, by Uzbek writer Sharaf Rashidov, came out in Russian translation in 1982. It was described at the time as representing "fiction" by an author of one nationality in which almost all the protagonists are of another."

Nor has recent Soviet fiction contended itself with expanding its "scale" to give more place to the ethnic minorities. Under the rubric of *globalnost* it has also emphasized subjects with foreign settings or involving foreign relations. Most novels on these topics, however, seem to be devoted to establishing the moral bankruptcy, cult of violence and militarism of the West. Today one sees the effects of the intensification of the Cold War in all Soviet literary periodicals. In the Party Central Committee's ruling on literature of July 1982, the role of the writer is defined as "teaching the workers to be ready to defend our revolutionary gains."

One novel often singled out as a model for writing on international themes is Yury Bondarev's *The Choice* (1980).[4] In this novel Bondarev contrasts the traditional Russian extremes on the question of East versus West: Slavophilism, on the one hand, and Westernism on the other. The first holds that Russians should return to their roots and embrace everything Slavic; the second, that the West represents progress and enlightenment and so should be emulated. Yet while Bondarev portrays the Slavophiles of today as well-intentioned but misguided—problems are not solved by trying to set back the clock—there is also something sinister in his depiction of a West saturated with intelligence agents.

The vices of the West are particularly illustrated in the story of the hero's childhood friend, a man who choose to stay in the West after being taken prisoner during World War II but now feels his mistake so acutely that he no longer has any desire to live. His one aim is to return to the Soviet Union to see his mother. This anti-Western theme might be a sign of the times. Bondarev is best known for his 1962 novel, *The Silence*, one of the first works published in the Soviet Union on the theme of a person wrongly arrested and sent to the camps. At the time it functioned as a sort of warm up for Solzhenitsyn's *One Day in the Life of Ivan Denisovich*, which appeared shortly afterward.

The appearance of fiction with a more impressive scale to its subject matter does not mean that "village prose" has been killed off. Nor have most critics condemned it completely. Instead, they call for a literature representing the best of "village prose," in particular its concern for preserving past traditions and culture, while giving modern life and ethnic diversity their due and the deprived reading public its lost "positive heroes."

In large measure, however, "village prose" survives among the ethnic minorities. Journal editors are able to fill their enlarged quotas for non-Russian works by publishing the works of authors from the Baltic Republics or from Georgia and Armenia. Purists complain that this is not the real thing, since "village prose" is essentially about the traditions and culture of the Russians; some purists even insist that in order for a work to be properly so called, it must be written by an Orthodox believer.

Soviet literature today also exhibits an overriding concern with memory. In almost all recent works of fiction the protagonists are musing over their past. Usually they are based on the author's own experiences (although it is not always presented as autobiographical); and memories of the past can serve many purposes. In V. Semin's *The Dam* (1981), for instance, the hero's excursion into the past becomes a pretext for recalling the barbarity of the Americans when they liberated the German prison camp he was detained in during World War II, and how his faith in humanity was later restored when he worked on the construction of a big Soviet dam. A. Chivilikhin's novel of 1980 is actually called *Memory* and is pretentiously subtitled "A Novel-Essay." One of several much-heralded attempts in recent years at innovation in the novel form, it is a rambling historical overview of the fate of the Russians which focuses primarily on the medieval invasion of Genghis Khan. But it also discusses Russian heroism during World War II, and the distortions of historical accounts of Russia's origins perpetrated by Germans who were misguidedly imported by Tsar Peter the Great to run the earliest Russian academic institutions.

In fiction by writers from the ethnic minorities, however, the theme of memory has served as a means for exploring the traditions and national identity of the author's own people. Indeed, such writers have often included historical material that Soviet historians have not been able to publish. And of course the theme of memory has been used by many as an occasion for a new look at the evils of Stalinism.

Thus the theme of memory has been espoused by writers from all sections of the Soviet political spectrum. Yet the excursion into the past has been more than a convenient device for putting forth one's own political viewpoint. Even if only partially and superficially, it has meant that Soviet literature is no longer primarily a literature of *action*; in some measure, it has become a literature of *contemplation*. It is more philosophical, more self-conscious—even meta-literary. Indeed, in some works recollection of the past has become the occasion for a philosophical investigation into the nature of time itself. True, this sort of thing was done better by writers of an older generation. What is new today is not the phenomenon itself, but its popularization.

Questions of time and place, then, are very much in the forefront of the Soviet writer's attention. As the official slogans *globalnost* and *masshtabnost* suggest, there has been reaction against the narrow parameters which characterized so much literature under Brezhnev. But in reacting against these constrictions writers have gone to another extreme, and the typical novel of today is set in a singularly broad range of places and times. The pattern most often found in conservative fiction extends from World War II to the present and covers both the Soviet Union and the West. Increasingly, however, the boundaries are pushed out to include the timeless past of folk legend and the distant future of intergalactic communication.

The best example of a Soviet novel with this new scale and global scope is Chingiz Aitmatov's *The Day Lasts More than a Hundred Years*.[5] It has enjoyed spectacular prominence in Soviet literary circles since its appearance in 1980, and overnight was elevated to the status of a canonical exemplar of socialist realism. It has been hailed as *the* harbinger of the "new directions" for the 1980s.

Aitmatov's novel manages to encompass a vast range in place and time partly because it combines two plot lines. One tells the story of Edigei, a simple Kazakh laborer who works on a railway siding in the Sarozek desert. Edigei's old workmate and mentor, Kazangap, has died, and the plot covers the day or so Edigei spends preparing Kazangap's body and burying it according to the Muslim rituals of his people. Into this plot are woven, through Edigei's recollections and thoughts, incidents from the past under Stalin and Khrushchev as well as some stories that are purportedly legends of the Sarozek people but were almost certainly invented by Aitmatov.

The most central of these legends is that of the cemetery of Ana Beiit, where Edigei is to bury Kazangap. In the old days, legend has it, the Sarozek people were oppressed by invaders (with the conveniently Chinese-sounding name of *Zhuanzhuan*) who used to capture young warriors and submit them to torture. First they would shave their heads and then, from the udders of freshly killed camels, they would fashion caps which fit closely on the young men's heads. The latter would be driven into the desert, and when the heat had contracted their caps they would be in unspeakable agony. Most would die, but the few who survived would be left, zombie-like, with no memory of their past and no knowledge of their identity. The invaders prized these survivors, called them the *mankurt*, and kept them as slaves because they would never rebel.

The cemetery is named after a widowed mother whose only son was subjected to this torture and survived. She risked her life seeking him out and trying to teach him who he was and the name of his dead father. The bewildered son killed his mother at the instigation of his captors, but as she fell her white kerchief turned into a bird which flew over the steppe at night calling out his mother's words: "Remember who you are! What is your name? Your father is Donenbai, Donenbai, Donenbai!" The cemetery was founded on the spot where she died.

The second of Aitmatov's plot lines concerns a joint U.S.-Soviet space mission. The astronauts become aware of a superior civilization on a planet in another galaxy. When they visit the planet the inhabitants suggest an exchange of knowledge with Earth. But the American and Soviet authorities resolve jointly to cut off all further contact by establishing a ring of rockets around the Earth.

The two plot lines are linked by the accident that the Soviet base from which the rockets are launched is very close to Edigei's railway siding. Primarily, however, they and the different narrative levels are connected by a series of symbols and parallels: the *mankurts'* loss of memory in the Edigei story parallels, for example, the ring of rockets in the story of the joint space mission.

*The Day Lasts More than a Hundred Years* is not only extremely popular with Soviet literary officialdom; it has also captured the imagination of the intelligentsia. One reason is that it reflects everything that is in the mainstream of contemporary literature. It has scale and global scope; it interweaves the themes of memory and ethnic identity; it follows Marquez in the "fantastic realism" of the pseudo-legends and echoes Faulkner's *As I Lay Dying* in the story of Kazangap's burial. It contains recollections of Stalinist infamy, homilies on the work ethic, and even a positive hero—one who has so impressed the literary authorities that he is now included in the short list of great positive heroes of all time. Aitmatov's novel is also a splendid example of multinational literature, having been written in Russian by a Kirgiz about the Kazakhs.

To be sure, another reason for the novel's popularity with such a wide range of readers is that it is highly ambivalent. It is possible, for instance, to interpret the science fiction plot in radically different ways. The way most commonly found in Soviet criticism is to see it as a condemnation of U.S. militarism and rapaciousness. Another is to consider it an allegory for the iron curtain, the Berlin Wall or, more generally, for Soviet mind control.

This ambivalence derives largely from the presentation of most key aspects of the novel—its setting, characters and main events—in such a way that they seem to combine the principles of "village prose" with the clichés of old-style, Stalinist socialist realism. In consequence, while some readers see in Edigei a male version of the aging peasant woman who is typical of the heroes in Valentin Rasputin's "village prose," other Soviet crticis have proclaimed him a new Pavel Korchagin, the protagonist in N. Ostrovsky's *How the Steel Was Tempered* (1934) and the quintessential positive hero.

Ambivalence has always been a feature of socialist realism, owing to the tension between a writer's need to pay obeisance to its conventions and to various political mandates and his need to express his own point of view. But the extraordinary ambivalence in *The Day Lasts More than a Hundred Years* is what makes it *the* work of the times. For this is a period of great ambivalence in Soviet literature, a time of change in which the contending "new directions" have not yet been resolved.

The official point of view wants Soviet literature to move back toward the 1950s, the era of positive heroes. A model for fiction would be Galina Nikolaeva's *Battle en Route*, but with more sophistication, "global resonance" and ethnic diversity. Another strong lobby within Soviet literature, however, wants to develop further the formal gains made in the 1970s, replacing "Hailey" with "Marquez." At the same time, the ideologues of "village prose" and the Russian nationalist school of criticism are fighting to regain their dominance. And most writers are exploring questions of identity and authenticity via the themes of memory and time, a quest which may lead to still further developments in writing, whether formally or thematically.

Borrowing the title of Nikolaeva's novel we might say, in sum, that the Soviet literary scene today presents a battle en route. Which trend will triumph remains to be seen. □

1. See further Katerina Clark, "'Boy Meets Tractor' and All That: The Parable Structure of the Soviet Novel," in Richard Freeborn and others, eds., *Russian and Slavic Literature* (Columbus, Ohio: Slavica, 1977), pp. 359-75.

2. Bulgakov's *The Master and Margarita* was first published in the Soviet Union in the journal *Novyi mir (New World)* in 1966-67; see above, Chapter 20 and n. 3. Aitmatov's *The White Steamship* has been published in English translations by Mirra Ginsburg (New York: Crown, 1972) and by T. and G. Feifer (London: Hodder & Staughton, 1972).

3. For more on the *Metropol* affair, see the following chapter.

4. English translation published in *Soviet Literature*, 1981 (Nos. 7, 8, 9).

5. English translation by John French, with Foreword by Katerina Clark (Bloomington, Indiana: Indiana University Press, 1983). In addition to *The White Steamship*, two other works by Aitmatov are available in English: *Farewell Gul'sary!* trans. J. French (London: Hodder & Staughton, 1970) and *The Ascent of Mount Fuji: A Play*, trans. N. Bethell (New York: Farrar, Straus & Giroux, 1975).

# 22

## The Politics of Literature

### *Geoffrey Hosking*

When I went to Moscow recently to study questions of literary policy, my first seminar unexpectedly took place at Sheremetevo Airport. A border guard discovered in my suitcase five copies of my book, *Beyond Socialist Realism*,[1] which I was bringing as gifts. Finding that the authors discussed in it included not only Vasily Shushkin, Valentin Rasputin and Yuri Trifonov—published in the Soviet Union and therefore acceptable—but also Aleksandr Solzhenitsyn and others no longer published there—and hence unacceptable—he challenged me.

> "So," he said, "I see you have written not only about good writers."
> "Is Solzhenitsyn a bad writer?" I asked innocently.
> "No-o-o," he replied, a little hesitantly. "He's not exactly what you'd call a bad writer. But [with more assurance] he's not one of us [*on - ne nash*]."
> "What does that mean—not one of us?"
> At that the guard looked me straight in the eyes and stated categorically: "Solzhenitsyn is an enemy."

In fairness I should add that, after much consultation and several days' delay, I was invited to pick up my books at the airport and take them into Moscow. Nevertheless, the image of the stern border guard, the two tribal cultures and the writer raised to the status of a national security problem haunted me throughout my trip.

It is in no way a new state of affairs. Probably the most widely appreciated fact about contemporary Russian literature is that in its homeland it is controlled by rigid censorship and bureaucracy, and therefore has to seek outlets in publication abroad. Nothing that I am about to say seriously undermines the validity of that fact.

All the same, against that background there are one or two paradoxes. From time to time *inside* the Soviet Union works are published which —not quite unambiguously, but clearly enough to the normally sensitive reader—do seem to contradict some of the most cherished tenets of Marxism-Leninism, or key elements in the officially approved history of the Party and of Soviet society. Valentin Rasputin, for example, in *Farewell to Matyora* (1976), casts doubt on the whole concept of technological progress, and instead proposes as an ideal the old-fashioned outlook and religious beliefs of an old woman. Vasily Belov, in *On the Eve* (1976), implies that the collectivization of agriculture in the early 1930s was a violent and destructive intervention into a peaceful and productive peasant way of life. Yury Trifonov, in *The Old Man* (1978), traces the moral decay of present-day Soviet society to the inhumanity of the Bolsheviks themselves, during and after the Civil War (1918-1920). The most recently published novel of Chingiz Aitmatov, *The Day Lasts More Than a Hundred Years* (1980), discussed at length by Katerina Clark (Chapter 21), accuses both the American and Soviet leaderships of pursuing great power politics of a kind that kills all that is human in man by cutting him off from his past and his traditions.

Soviet critics, of course, interpret these novels somewhat differently, though only, I feel, by ignoring or distorting their essential features. But the important question is: how is it possible to publish in the Soviet Union works which can plausibly be interpreted as I have done?

Katerina Clark suggests that the answer may lie in the very ambivalence—or ambiguity—of these works. But it may also lie in the actual functioning of ideology in Soviet society. What does Marxism-Leninism actually *mean* nowadays? There was a time when the official propagation of the ideology was intended to arouse universal enthusiasm for the tasks of building a future socialist society. Today, as Alexander Zinoviev and others have shown, the regime has to be content with much less. Full-hearted belief can be expected, probably, only from the young and the naive: from everyone else what is exacted is ritual obeisance to the externals of the ideology as symbols of authority.

The inner meaning has changed, too: economic stagnation, ideological super-saturation and the arms race have combined to produce a situation where, in the eyes of most Soviet people, the term "communism" no longer denotes a society of the future but rather a great power bloc of the present. The impetus is no longer toward building what is new, but rather toward defending and perhaps extending what is already held.

This has produced a psychological change: the leaders have become very conservative and militarist in outlook in a way that one might characterize as "great-power chauvinist." It was already partly true in Stalin's time, although at that stage some of the dynamism of economic growth still remained. Under Khrushchev an attempt to return to the idealism of communism's early days was made, but this proved too disturbing for most of the political elite, and Brezhnev allowed a gentle consolidation of the present attitude.

There are two main varieties of this "great-power chauvinism": Russian nationalism and multinational Soviet imperialism. Recent research by two emigre scholars, Alexander Yanov and Mikhail Agursky, has done much to elucidate the two varieties in their relationship to politics and culture, although the two scholars take opposite views of their significance. Yanov regards Russian nationalism as an expansive and dangerous force, while Agursky concludes that it is the multinational imperialists who are more threatening, since they are in alliance with the Soviet "military-industrial complex."[2]

Whichever variety one sees as dominant at any given juncture—and probably both are strong—there are certain tendencies in contemporary Soviet society that must seriously worry anybody concerned about the economic and military strength of the country. There is the growth in corruption and criminality, which undermines the productivity of the economy. There is the trend toward poorer health and shorter life expectancy among the male population which, coupled with very high rates of alcoholism, clearly undermines both the growth and the efficiency of industry (see Chapter 26). There are the environmental problems, which, as we have also seen (Chapter 12), often lead to moderate gains in one sector of the economy—usually the industrial—being heavily outweighed by horrifying losses in another—usually agriculture or fisheries. Also worrying are the demographic developments discussed below by Ralph Clem, which project a continued low birthrate in the European and urban parts of the country in contrast with the high rates in Asia and the Caucasus. This is precisely opposite to the needs of the army and industry, and seems to result from persistent difficulties in housing, income distribution, welfare services and family life.

These, then, are all problems which must worry the leaders of a great power. They have, moreover, a strong moral dimension (family stability, honesty at work, and so on) which official Soviet ideology is ill-equipped to deal with. It is precisely in this area of doubt and bewilderment that, I suggest, literature has established an insecure and vulnerable bridgehead.

In his recent study, *Reform in Soviet Politics,* Thane Gustafson show-

ed that expert opinions tend to be fed into the Soviet political system only when one political faction has an interest in them, or when there is
deadlock and uncertainty.[3] The same may apply to literary works,
where their areas of concern overlap with those of the political leadership, as they probably do when matters such as family morality,
economic probity and the degradation of the environment are at issue.

But good writers tend to take their explorations much further than the
politicians find comfortable. And this is where the heavy bargaining
comes in, a process which is, by all accounts, such a crucial aspect of the
Soviet literary scene. The leading participants in this are the censorship,
the editors of journals and publishing houses, the officials of the Writers'
Union, the Party (in serious cases the Cultural Department of the Central
Committee) and, of course, the writer himself.

The official state censorship organ, *Glavlit*, has an important regula-
tory role. Its job is to prevent unmentionable subjects and people from
appearing in print, or to ensure that they do so only in certain narrowly
defined ways. It is negative censorship. The writer also performs a kind
of censorship on himself when he sits at his desk, calculating what has
the remotest chance of being acceptable, and what is not worth wasting
time over.

The really decisive role, however, belongs to the editors. Editorial
boards are appointed by and are answerable to the Writers' Union, while
in the Writers' Union itself the top appointments are almost certainly in
the *nomenklatura* (appointments list) of the Party Central Committee
(Chapter 4). There is thus a straightforward hierarchy of patronage,
reinforced by the regular visits made by senior editors and Writers'
Union officials to the Central Committee Cultural Department to receive
the latest authoritative directives.

Editors and Union officials, then, are in close touch with the "Party
line," the current campaigns and taboos; and these have a decisive impact on their thinking. Much of what they have to decide, however, does
not belong so much to the realm of politics as to that of literary taste.
Here probably the most important factor is that many editors and virtually all officials are themselves at best second-rate writers. They have
never enjoyed a reputation of their own, and are dependent on official
favor for respectable print runs of their own writings. Their tastes,
especially as they get older (and most of them *are* elderly), tend to be conservative and anti-experimental. They have a natural suspicion of the
young, talented and innovative, whose writings they do not fully understand and whose popular success they resent.

All this induces a stereotyped drabness in official taste which has little
to do with ideology; elderly bureaucrats given a monopoly over culture

in *any* political system might well produce similar results. The tight grip that such men have on the Soviet publishing world is very disheartening for young writers. At the Seventh Writers' Union Congress in 1981, as Katerina Clark mentioned, the proportion of delegates under 40 years of age was just 3 percent.

A few editors, however, have succeeded in assuming a bolder and more creative role. This is important, since it is the editors who convey to the writers the prohibitions of *Glavlit*. It is the editors who discuss with them the necessary rewriting and bargain with them over questions of language, style and taste, as well as over the subtler political implications of what they have written. Solzhenitsyn's autobiography contains long and vivid descriptions of his negotiations with Alexander Tvardovsky, the editor of *Novyi mir* (*New World*).[4] Similar scenes, with less momentous results, are daily reproduced in editorial offices all over the Soviet Union. It is at these sessions that the final product, the published text, takes shape. An editor of honesty, good literary judgment, determination, experience and cunning can make a great difference at this stage.

From this point of view, Tvardovsky was probably the most remarkable editor Soviet literature has ever known. During his stewardship (1950-1954 and 1958-1970) *Novyi mir* published many outspoken works, penetrating in their portrayal of the realities of Soviet society and sometimes disruptive to official ideology in their implications. Solzhenitsyn's evocation of the Stalinist labor camps in *A Day in The Life of Ivan Denisovich* (1962) was only the best known example.[5] Tvardovsky's boldness cost him his position in the end; he was bitterly criticized by some of his more timid colleagues from other journals, and in 1970 had to resign his editorship. The struggle, however, had been a long one. In the course of it some fine works of literature were published, and some first-rate young authors managed to establish themselves.

There has never been a wholly worthy successor to Tvardovsky, at *Novyi mir* or any other journal. Still, since 1970 some journals have managed to establish a reputation for publishing interesting works fairly regularly. The two most notable are *Nash sovremennik* (*Our Contemporary*) and *Druzhba narodov* (*Friendship of the Peoples*). It is probably no coincidence that both of them, to some extent, can be identified with the two varieties of great-power chauvinism I singled out earlier: the first with Russian nationalism, the second with multinational Soviet imperialism. In case of need, that is to say, each journal probably has protectors at the very highest levels of the Party.

In the spring of 1981 I was able to visit the editorial offices of both journals and to discuss with some of the editors their perceptions of their aims and problems. In spite of the different orientations of the two journals, the editors' attitudes had a great deal in common. In both I found a concern for literature as a socially responsible force. While remaining loyal to the political leadership, the editors felt that literature played a very special role since writers could afford to take a longer and more radical view of social problems than could politicians, who by the nature of their trade have to react quickly and offer immediate solutions. Writers, therefore, must sometimes be controversial. "Literature must contribute an element of creative friction," as someone said, "so conflicts are inevitable." Thus, the editors I spoke to were proud of the struggles they had conducted on occasion to get works published in which they believed, though they were not willing to give me a detailed account of their battles with any particular higher authority.

There is in both journals a feeling that the Soviet Union is threatened by a faceless "international technocracy," vaguely identified as American in origin, which undermines people's roots as embodied in their language, folklore, history and traditions. *Nash sovremennik* is, of course, particularly keen to revive elements of Russian national tradition, especially those associated with the village. This has been apparent in their publishing policy for many years. Their authors include the leading exponents of "village prose": Vasily Belov, Valentin Rasputin, Vladimir Soloukhin, Fyodor Abramov, Viktor Astafyev, Vasily Shukshin.

These "village writers" have done the most since the early 1960s to preserve and revive peasant speech and reforge it as a literary language, using it to champion the values of the traditional agricultural way of life. They have seen the patience, slow rhythms, simplicity, self-reliance, and devotion to family and hearth characteristic of rural life as antidotes to the demoralized and anemic lifestyle they discern in the towns. Some have even suggested, rather vaguely but unmistakably, that traditional religion has much to offer modern urban man, uncertain of his identity and without a firm anchor for his moral life.

*Nash sovremennik* has helped to sponsor this revival of interest in religion. As its editors confirmed to me, they were not interested in any particular denomination, but felt that in a world torn from its moorings, a religious outlook could strengthen man's sense of solidarity with his fellows, his self-discipline, his devotion to duty, and his readiness to sacrifice himself for a worthy cause. Indeed, much of what they said seemed to imply that the materialist atheism of the West was a threat to the Soviet way of life! When I asked if their outlook was not contrary to Marxism, they replied that they were opposed to "crude Marxism." Lenin, I thought, must be turning in his mausoleum.

*Druzhba narodov* takes its material from very different sources. Its mission has been to promote awareness of non-Russian cultures. In practice, however, its outlook has much in common with that of *Nash sovremennik*. Much of the best non-Russian literature is of course concerned with the history and traditions of the non-Russian peoples, many of which are rural and often tinged with religious values. In addition, *Druzhba narodov* has promoted some of the best Russian writing of recent years, notably the later novels of Yury Trifonov, who, though not himself a believer, was strongly influenced by the Christian personalism of Dostoevsky.

To return to the four novels I mentioned at the beginning of this chapter: Rasputin's was published in *Nash sovremennik*, Trifonov's in *Druzhba narodov*, and Aitmatov's in *Novyi Mir*. Belov published early chapters from his in the northern provincial journal *Sever* (*The North*), and the complete novel (apparently much censored) with the publishing house *Sovremennik*, which has recently promoted a large body of "village prose." From the evidence they offer, it appears to be sometimes possible for an established author, backed by a strong and experienced editor, to publish works that implicitly conflict to some extent with the official ideology. This probably occurs, however, only after a long struggle, often with severe damage to the text on the way, and provided certain conditions pertain:
  • The style and language of the work must not be too innovative, nor too obscure, since this would arouse suspicions that the author was trying to hoodwink the censorship, and would in any case offend the taste of responsible literary bureaucrats.
  • The work must have *some* positive outlook: nihilist, absurdist works or those which disclaim any moral stance are not generally acceptable.
  • Divergence from official ideology must not be too wide or too clearly stated. Thus religious values in general may be evoked as a moral or social force, but the preaching of any particular creed, or any sustained philosophical discussion of religion, would be unacceptable. In general, implication is preferred to direct statement.
  • Similarly, while it is sometimes possible to allude to sufferings imposed by the Soviet government on its own people, no consistent historical analysis is possible. This is doubtless why historians have always feared to tread where novelists have sometimes gingerly tiptoed .
This still leaves fairly narrow boundaries for permissible literature. The list is long of those writers who have, deliberately or involuntarily, stepped across them and thereby lost their native audience—and, in many cases, eventually their homeland as well. By now it includes most

of the major names, at least in prose fiction, of the 1950s and 1960s. They all made their name at a time when young talent was being actively sought, during the post-Stalin "thaws." This is not happening today. In fact, it is probably more difficult now than it has ever been for a young writer to establish himself in the Soviet Union.

To tackle this problem, Vasily Aksyonov, himself the leading "youth" writer of the early 1960s, joined forces in 1978 with two representatives of the current younger generation, Evgeny Popov and Viktor Erofeev, both in their early thirties. Their idea was to bring out an anthology, to be titled *Metropol*, in which writings of that younger generation would appear with a few pieces by more established authors. A key element of the enterprise was that the authors should edit the work themselves — bypassing the complex and often harmful maneuvering already described — and present a complete text ready for printing, to be published unchanged. The plan fell through when the Writers' Union prevented publication. A copy prudently sent out in advance to the West, however, was published there. Popov and Erofeev were expelled from the Union — or more accurately, its secretariat vetoed their acceptance, which had recently been voted by the Moscow branch. Aksyonov subsequently emigrated, declaring that he could see no future for himself as a writer in the Soviet Union.[6]

*Metropol* was a test case. As far as an outsider can judge, some of the items in it could have been published by a strong and experienced Soviet editor through the normal channels. Others would probably have been disqualified because of their emphasis on sexual or religious experience, or because of their experimental language. The clearest philosophical statement in the collection is an article by Viktor Trostnikov, who argues that developments in the natural sciences in the twentieth century tend to refute the materialist and atheist understanding of the world, and to provide evidence for an idealist or religious outlook. Trostnikov's thesis would probably find a lot of sympathy among some writers publishing regularly in the Soviet Union, but its arguments are too extended and unambiguous for his piece ever to have been acceptable to a Soviet editor.

Probably, however, the most objectionable feature about *Metropol* to the literary bureaucrats was simply that young and virtually unknown authors were seeking to avoid the established publishing procedures.

Overall, therefore, it is difficult to be very optimistic about the future of Soviet literature, or at any rate that part of it which is actually published in its homeland. Established writers, supported by determined editors, can still use the major concerns, disputes and uncertainties of the Party leadership to publish interesting and probing works of high quality. But the struggle to do so is always exhausting, usually damaging and sometimes unavailing. The emerging talents of the Khrushchev "thaw" are now older, and publishing either in exile or less and less at home. Three of them—Yury Kazakov, Shukshin and Trifonov—have died prematurely in recent years. Up-and-coming writers who might replace them have either to conform to the grey orthodoxy of the establishment, or take the risk of bringing out their first major publications abroad, which of course can easily lead to permanent blacklisting at home.

There are more sinister signs too. When Georgy Vladimov, whose *Faithful Ruslan* is one of the outstanding novels of recent years, resigned in exasperation from the Writers' Union in 1977, he called the organization a "police station." That may indeed be one of its functions. In autumn 1980, Evgeny Popov and some of his colleagues tried to set up a Young Writers' Club, to bring out experimental works in small print runs. On the very day that he handed in the statutes of the proposed club at the Writers' Union he was detained in the street and questioned by the KGB. At the same time, the apartments of all the participants were searched. One of them, Evgeny Kozlovsky, was subsequently arrested and apparently persuaded to dissociate himself from his writings.

Perhaps, in fact, my little "seminar" at Sheremetevo Airport really was the most significant event of my trip. But, being an optimist, I continue to hope that it is the "creative friction" that will prevail. □

**1.** Geoffrey Hosking, *Beyond Socialist Realism: Soviet Fiction since Ivan Denisovich* (New York: Holmes and Meier, 1980).

**2.** Alexander Yanov, *The Russian New Right: Right-Wing Ideologies in the Contemporary USSR,* trans. Stephen B. Dunn (Berkeley, California: Institute of International Studies, University of California, 1978); Mikhail Agursky, *The Soviet Military-Industrial Complex* (Jerusalem: Magnes Press, Hebrew University, 1980.)

**3.** Thane Gustafson, *Reform in Soviet Politics: Lessons of Recent Policies on Land and Water* (Cambridge and New York: Cambridge University Press, 1981).

**4.** Aleksandr Solzenitsyn, *The Oak and the Calf: Sketches of a Literary Life in the Soviet Union,* trans. H. Willetts (New York: Harper and Row, 1980).

**5.** The English translation by Max Hayward and Ronald Hingley (New York: Praeger, 1966) is considered the best.

**6.** V. Aksyonov and others, *Metropol: Literaturnyi almanakh* (Ann Arbor, Michigan: Ardis, 1979). An English language edition has also appeared: Aksyonov, *Metropol: Literary Almanac* (New York: W.W. Norton and Co., 1983); see the informative reviewby Helen Muchnic, New York Times *Book Review* (Feb. 27, 1983), pp. 1, 32-33.

SOCIETY

The authors of this final section discuss various of the more urgent questions raised by a survey of Soviet society today. Ralph S. Clem, in describing its complex ethnic structure, points out the many problems it has in common with other multi-ethnic societies, and reaches the perhaps surprising conclusion that on the whole Soviet rule has strengthened the position of the ethnic minorities. The current state of religion is the subject of Paul A. Lucey's essay, which like the previous chapter abounds in facts not readily available elsewhere. Readers may again be surprised to learn that at least 30 percent of the Soviet population are practicing believers—not as high a proportion as in the United States, to be sure, but more than in many other Western societies. And Mary Ellen Fischer raises "the woman question": not just the legal rights and status of Soviet women, but the actualities of their situation with respect to both the unfulfilled promises of the past and their future prospects.

Lastly, David E. Powell reminds us of the traumatic history of Soviet society, points to the generally beneficial nature, until recently, of social change in the Soviet Union, and expands on certain ominous developments in Soviet society today. His essay may be read as a detailed summary of points raised in various earlier chapters. The picture to emerge is one of a troubled society, its heroic—and tragic—age behind it, its future uncertain. But Powell also notes that much of what he discusses is endemic in modern life. It is right that this book should end with a reminder of our common humanity.

# 23

## SOCIETY

## Ethnicity

*Ralph S. Clem*

On April 14, 1978, several thousand people took to the streets of Tbilisi, the capital of the Georgian Republic of the Soviet Union, in protest against changes in the Republic's constitution which would have downgraded the official status of the Georgian language. The next day, the authorities cancelled the proposed revisions and restored the indigenous tongue to its privileged position.[1] The significance of this event, probably not fully appreciated in the West, lies in its dramatic illustration of the salient aspect of contemporary Soviet reality: that the Soviet Union is an ethnically diverse state, one in which all of the problems common to multi-ethnic countries manifest themselves. If one wishes to understand the forces shaping Soviet society, therefore, the nature and role of ethnicity is a prime consideration.

The Soviet Union is one of the world's most ethnically heterogeneous countries in terms both of the number of ethnic groups and of their respective socio-cultural characteristics.[2] The population of the country comprises some 100 separate ethnic groups — or nationalities, in Soviet parlance — among which is to be found an extraordinary variety of languages, religions, phenotypes and the other attributes, tangible and intangible, of ethnic identity. The Russians are by far the largest such group numerically, accounting for just over half the country's population. Minority groups range from several tens of millions to several thousands (see table).

This remarkable assemblage of peoples is the result of a historical process of territorial expansion which lasted for about four centuries. During this period the Russians moved out in all directions from their ethnic hearth in the northwestern part of what is today the Soviet Union to take over neighboring lands inhabited by non-Russians. The Empire of the

## Population of Major Soviet Ethnic Groups

| Ethnic group: | Population (in thousands) | | | Average annual growth rate (in percent) | | Percent of total Soviet population | | |
|---|---|---|---|---|---|---|---|---|
| | 1959 | 1970 | 1979 | 1959-1970 | 1970-1979 | 1959 | 1970 | 1979 |
| Russians | 114,114 | 129,015 | 137,397 | 1.1 | .7 | 54.65 | 53.37 | 52.42 |
| Ukrainians | 37,253 | 40,753 | 42,347 | .8 | .4 | 17.84 | 16.86 | 16.16 |
| Uzbeks | 6,015 | 9,195 | 12,456 | 3.9 | 3.4 | 2.88 | 3.80 | 4.75 |
| Belorussians | 7,913 | 9,052 | 9,463 | 1.2 | .5 | 3.78 | 3.74 | 3.16 |
| Kazakhs | 3,622 | 5,299 | 6,556 | 3.5 | 2.4 | 1.73 | 2.19 | 2.50 |
| Azerbaidzhanis | 2,940 | 4,380 | 5,477 | 3.7 | 2.5 | 1.41 | 1.81 | 2.08 |
| Armenians | 2,787 | 3,559 | 4,151 | 2.2 | 1.7 | 1.33 | 1.47 | 1.58 |
| Georgians | 2,692 | 3,245 | 3,571 | 1.7 | 1.1 | 1.29 | 1.34 | 1.36 |
| Moldavians | 2,214 | 2,698 | 2,968 | 1.8 | 1.1 | 1.06 | 1.12 | 1.13 |
| Tadzhiks | 1,397 | 2,136 | 2,898 | 3.9 | 3.4 | .67 | .88 | 1.11 |
| Lithuanians | 2,326 | 2,665 | 2,851 | 1.2 | .8 | 1.11 | 1.10 | 1.09 |
| Turkmens | 1,002 | 1,525 | 2,028 | 3.9 | 3.2 | .48 | .63 | .77 |
| Germans | 1,620 | 1,846 | 1,936 | 1.2 | .5 | .78 | .76 | .74 |
| Kirgiz | 969 | 1,452 | 1,906 | 3.7 | 3.1 | .46 | .60 | .74 |
| Jews | 2,268 | 2,151 | 1,811 | - .5 | -1.6 | 1.09 | .89 | .69 |
| Chuvash | 1,470 | 1,694 | 1,751 | 1.3 | .4 | .70 | .70 | .67 |
| Latvians | 1,400 | 1,430 | 1,439 | .2 | .1 | .67 | .59 | .55 |
| Bashkirs | 989 | 1,240 | 1,371 | 2.1 | 1.1 | .47 | .51 | .52 |
| Mordvinians | 1,285 | 1,263 | 1,192 | - .2 | - .6 | .62 | .52 | .45 |
| Poles | 1,380 | 1,167 | 1,151 | - 1.3 | - .1 | .66 | .48 | .44 |
| Estonians | 989 | 1,007 | 1,020 | .2 | .1 | .67 | .42 | .39 |

| | | | | | | | | |
|---|---|---|---|---|---|---|---|---|
| Chechens | 419 | 613 | 756 | 3.5 | 2.4 | .20 | .25 | .29 |
| Udmurts | 625 | 704 | 714 | 1.1 | .2 | .30 | .29 | .27 |
| Mari | 504 | 599 | 622 | 1.6 | .4 | .24 | .25 | .24 |
| Ossetians | 413 | 488 | 542 | 1.5 | 1.2 | .20 | .20 | .21 |
| Avars | 270 | 396 | 483 | 3.5 | 2.2 | .13 | .16 | .18 |
| Komi[a] | 431 | 475 | 478 | .9 | .1 | .21 | .20 | .18 |
| Koreans | 314 | 358 | 389 | 1.2 | .9 | .15 | .15 | .15 |
| Lezgins | 223 | 324 | 383 | 3.5 | 1.9 | .11 | .13 | .15 |
| Bulgarians | 324 | 351 | 361 | .7 | .3 | .16 | .15 | .14 |
| Buryats | 253 | 315 | 353 | 2.0 | 1.3 | .12 | .13 | .13 |
| Greeks | 309 | 337 | 344 | .8 | .2 | .15 | .14 | .13 |
| Yakuts | 233[b] | 296 | 328 | 2.2 | 1.1 | .11 | .12 | .13 |
| Kabardinians | 204 | 280 | 322 | 2.9 | 1.6 | .10 | .12 | .12 |
| Karakalpaks | 173 | 236 | 303 | 2.9 | 2.8 | .08 | .10 | .12 |
| Dargins | 158 | 231 | 287 | 3.5 | 2.4 | .08 | .10 | .11 |
| Kumyks | 135 | 189 | 228 | 3.1 | 2.1 | .06 | .08 | .09 |
| Uyghurs | 95 | 173 | 211 | 5.6 | 2.2 | .05 | .07 | .08 |
| Gypsies | 132 | 175 | 209 | 2.6 | 2.0 | .06 | .07 | .08 |
| Ingush | 106 | 158 | 186 | 3.7 | 1.8 | .05 | .07 | .07 |
| Gagauz | 124 | 157 | 173 | 2.2 | 1.1 | .06 | .06 | .07 |
| Hungarians | 155 | 166 | 171 | .6 | .3 | .07 | .07 | .07 |
| Tuvinians | 100 | 139 | 166 | 3.0 | 2.0 | .05 | .06 | .06 |
| Kalmyks | 106 | 137 | 147 | 2.4 | .8 | .05 | .06 | .06 |
| Karelians | 167 | 146 | 138 | −1.1 | −.6 | .08 | .06 | .05 |
| Karachay | 81 | 113 | 131 | 3.1 | 1.7 | .04 | .04 | .05 |
| Romanians | 106 | 119 | 129 | 1.1 | .9 | .05 | .05 | .05 |
| Kurds | 59 | 89 | 116 | 3.8 | 3.0 | .03 | .04 | .04 |
| Adye | 80 | 100 | 109 | 2.0 | .0 | .04 | .04 | .04 |
| Laks | 64 | 86 | 100 | 2.7 | 1.7 | .03 | .04 | .04 |

Sources: 1959 and 1970 figures from USSR, Tsentral'noe Statisticheskoe Upravlenie, *Itogi Vsesoiuznoi Perepisi Naseleniia 1970 goda* (Moscow: Statistika, 1973),IV, pp. 9-11; 1979 figures from USSR, Tsentral'noe Statisticheskoe Upravlenie, *Naselenie SSSR* (Moscow: Politicheskaia Literatura, 1980), pp. 23-26.

[a]Figure for Komi includes Komi-Permyaki.

[b]The number of Yakuts was reported as 236,655 in the 1959 Census itself.

last century was formed, in other words, through the addition of non-Russian territory to the Russian core; and the present Soviet state is, geographically, almost identical to its tsarist predecessor.

Two key elements of the present ethnic situation derive from the manner in which the state took shape spatially. First, it is generally the case that the periphery of the Soviet Union is ethnically non-Russian territory, while the Russian homeland is geographically the center, a situation fraught with obvious geopolitical significance. Non-Russian lands extend in a vast arc from the shores of the Baltic Sea in the northwest (Estonia, Latvia, Lithuania); south along the western border (Belorussia, Ukraine, Moldavia); east across the Caucasus (Armenia, Georgia, Azerbaidzhan); on to Central Asia (the areas inhabited by Turkmen, Uzbeks, Tadzhiks, and Kirgiz) and the Kazakh steppe; and, finally, across Asia to the Pacific Ocean (homelands of the Buryats, Tuvinians, Altays, Khakas and other peoples). Sharpening this Russian/non-Russian, center/periphery dichotomy are several irredentist situations in which members of the same ethnic group live on both sides of the Soviet border, as in the case of the Finnish Karelians, much of whose homeland was incorporated into the Soviet Union in World War II.

Second, in spite of the proliferation of ethnic Russians in all regions of the country, the other Soviet peoples are still usually concentrated in their ancestral homelands. Thus ethnicity, in the Soviet context, has a territorial aspect which differentiates it in some degree from multi-ethnic societies which evolved through immigration. Furthermore, the Soviet Union is structured administratively as a federation of 15 nominally independent units (Union Republics), each of which is officially the homeland of a major national group. Smaller nationalities, and some of the larger ethnic groups with homelands in the interior (where even nominal independence would be an obvious fiction), are recognized administratively by lower-level units of various types. All told, there are 53 ethnically defined political-administrative units in the Soviet Union, representing over half of all Soviet national groups.

Given this complex ethnic structure, it is imperative to investigate ethnicity with respect to Soviet history, contemporary reality, and the future of the "Union" itself. Unfortunately, in spite of the increasing number of relevant works appearing in the Soviet Union and in the West, and even though the best of them are insightful and factually informative, our understanding of Soviet society in general and of ethnicity in particular has been hampered by an approach to societal phenomena in that country which regards them as basically unique. This particularistic approach, it should be stressed, has generally been adhered to on both sides of the ideological divide.

Thus Soviet scholars almost always adhere to the Marxist view that social dynamics—including ethnic group relations—are determined by the nature of the specific economic system, and therefore maintain that societies based on a socialist economy will be inherently different from capitalist societies. Any cross-system similarities in social trends are dismissed by Soviet scholars as superficial and ephemeral.

In the West, on the other hand, comparative research in the social sciences has long been hampered by an unscientific tradition which holds that societal traits are unique to time and place, and not amenable to broad generalizations because of cultural conditioning and human unpredictability. Moreover, as Robert Lewis has noted, Western scholars have attributed a uniqueness to Soviet society on the assumption that a "totalitarian" state is capable of decisively controlling basic social processes.[3] If a government could actually regulate, with even moderate success, such aspects of human behavior as migration, then a fundamental difference would indeed exist between totalitarian states and those in the West where social trends are, in effect, the summation of myriad individual actions. A difference of that kind would then rule out the use of models derived from Western experience in explaining social change in the Soviet Union.

Partly as a consequence of this attitude we in the West have tended to impute to Soviet society a distinctiveness that is not usually warranted by the facts. It seems clear enough that, so far as ethnicity is concerned, today's Soviet Union has much more in common with other multi-ethnic societies than not. If we consider the ethnically-related troubles in such Western states as Belgium, Canada, Spain, and the United States, it will come as no surprise that bilingualism, assimilation, ethnic intermarriage, affirmative action, regional autonomy, a shifting composition of the population along ethnic lines, and the geographical mixing of ethnic groups through migration are all contentious issues in the multi-ethnic Soviet Union as well.

Language is perhaps the most sensitive of these issues, especially the role and status of the official *lingua franca*, Russian, in relation to the various non-Russian tongues. The importance of this issue derives in part from the overtly ethno-symbolic quality of language, in part from the belief among scholars, both Western and Soviet, that the increasingly widespread use of Russian by non-Russians presages a loss of ethnic identity—or ethnic assimilation. And the most contentious aspect of the issue concerns the use of Russian in education, whether as the medium of instruction or as the object of separate study.

Following the advent of Soviet rule, the network of indigenous language schools in the various national homelands was greatly expanded. Yet considerable variation exists today in the degree to which the non-Russian tongues are in fact an integral part of the school system. The use of non-Russian languages as the medium of instruction differs from group to group, with some nationalities granted much more extensive rights than others. These rights are tied to the ranking of the ethnic territories in the federal hierarchy. Students who are members of numerically larger ethnic groups can receive native language instruction throughout secondary school and, in some cases, at the university as well (although the selection of courses available in the vernacular may be limited). Those from smaller nationalities may only be able to attend school in their own language in the primary grades, if that.[4]

Another facet of this question is the choice available to parents. Schools in which Russian is the medium of instruction have been established in all of the non-Russian ethno-territories in addition to native-language schools, leaving parents of any nationality the choice of sending their children to either type of school. Until 1958, however, children were required to study Russian in the native-language schools and the local language in the Russian-language schools. Then the Soviet government promulgated a set of educational reforms, one of which made the study of languages other than the medium of instruction voluntary rather than mandatory. This led to some hostility and resistance among several of the largest non-Russian ethnic groups, apparently out of fear that non-Russian students in Russian-language schools would abandon non-Russian language courses. This move was also seen by some in the West as further evidence that the Soviet authorities were attempting to accelerate the process of ethnic homogenization, or Russification.[5]

If the Soviet government has been actively promoting the formal adoption of Russian as one's "native tongue" by non-Russians, it has not had much apparent success. The 1979 Soviet census revealed that only about 13 percent of the non-Russian population considered Russian their native tongue; the comparable figure was 10.8 percent in 1959 and 11.5 percent in 1970. At the same time, 49 percent of all non-Russians said that they had a fluent command of Russian as a second language, which represents a major increase, even since 1970, when the comparable figure was 37 percent. These and other linguistic data indicate a growing trend toward bilingualism among the non-Russian ethnic minorities. The number of Russians who speak another language remains, however, quite small.

Brian Silver has suggested that whereas the influence of social change (urbanization, higher levels of education, a greater frequency of interethnic contact) has had the effect of promoting the use of Russian, reten-

tion of the non-Russian tongues has been perpetuated by maintenance of
the native-language schools and by extensive use of these languages in
the media.[6] In short, allowing for differences among nationalities and
especially between generations (today's young people tend to have a
higher level of Russian fluency and to be less faithful to their native
tongue), the ethnic minorities certainly are not yet disappearing
linguistically.

Another way of judging the extent to which ethnic homogenization
has taken place in the Soviet Union is to look at the frequency of intermarriage. Given the taboos generally associated with this subject, it is
not surprising that among the non-Russian peoples of the Soviet Union
there is a consistently high level of in-group marriage (endogamy). A
recent major work, based on 1969 data from 14 of the larger non-
Russian nationalities, shows that in no case did the level of those marrying endogamously drop below 82 percent, and that for nine of the 14
groups the percentage of endogamous marriages was over 92.[7] Even
when demographic and socio-cultural factors are taken into account, the
impression remains that ethnic attachments are sufficiently strong to
condition significantly the choice of a marriage partner—this in spite of
the fact that the Soviet government views exogamy as "progressive."

Inasmuch as linguistic Russification and the incidence of exogamy
have been relatively limited in scope, we may suppose that ethnic
reidentification, or assimilation, has been similarly insignificant. While
recognizing that it is extremely difficult to measure assimilation empirically, one study put the total number of non-Russians who from
1926 to 1970 assumed a Russian identity at between four and six
million, or about 2 percent of the 1970 population.[8] The vast majority
of those assimilated were Ukrainians and Belorussians, who are linguistically and culturally akin to the Russians. A few other groups—Karelians, Mordvinians, Germans and Jews among them—accounted for
almost all of the balance. Among most Soviet ethnic groups, therefore,
assimilation is virtually unknown.

Sociologist Daniel Bell points to several key aspects of ethnicity which
account for its salience and persistence in the contemporary world and
which are directly relevant to the Soviet situation.[9] The first of these is
the politicization of ethnicity, wherein the proliferation of the power of
the state forces people to rely on ethnic groups as a means of bringing
pressure to bear on the system. The Soviet "revolution from above"
made it obvious to all where the center of power was, and established
the state as the focus for any claims to be made by ethnic groups. As
Glazer and Moynihan put it, the Soviet state is obviously "the direct
arbiter of economic well-being."[10] The ethnic group turns out to be an

ideal vehicle for exacting concessions from the state, as Bell noted, because it combines an interest-group function with an affective tie. Furthermore, the Soviet regime has done much to legitimate this approach, since it insists on labelling individuals ethnically and has acted (perhaps not always deliberately) to stimulate ethnic awareness in a variety of ways.

By far the most important sanctioning of ethnicity in the Soviet Union lies in the very political structure of the state. The creation of the Union of Soviet Socialist Republics as a federation of ethnic territories has been viewed as a clever solution to the problem of disintegration inherent in multi-ethnic countries, a problem of immediate concern in the early years of Soviet power.[11] Ethnic autonomy, as represented in the elaborate treaty arrangements binding the ethnic units to the Union, was plainly a tactical political concession, probably thought to be temporary. Yet by formalizing the ethnic configuration of the state, Lenin and his successors provided what turned out to be a lasting, legitimate focus of national aspirations. It could be argued, then, that what was viewed by some as a shrewd maneuver and a fraud has instead proved to be a means whereby ethnic group interests, such as education and native language rights, can be safeguarded and appropriate demands made on the state.[12]

Moreover, because the ethno-territorial link was and is legally explicit, the regions have become the instruments for attaining the central goal of Soviet policy toward the nationalities: the approximate equalization of levels of socio-economic development among them. The government has had some notable successes in this respect, in education and public health, for instance. But three interconnected factors have impeded further progress and are likely to continue to do so.

• Like most countries, the Soviet Union has its economic "problem regions." Owing to the geographically unequal distribution of natural resources, the exigencies of war and strategic considerations, and the pressing need to optimize scarce investment capital, some areas remain relatively backward.[13] Since ethnic groups are usually found mainly in their respective homelands, those groups inhabiting the backward regions will be relatively disadvantaged.

• A second reason for the failure to close the inter-ethnic development gap has been the proliferation of Russians throughout the Soviet Union. Unfavorable economic and social conditions, particularly in the rural areas of their own ethnic territory, provided the impetus for the out-migration of millions of Russians to other parts of the country, including the non-Russian lands, where their number rose from 6.2 million in 1926 to 23.9 million in 1979. The vast majority of these Russian migrants settled in urban areas and in many instances took the better jobs, thereby foreclosing opportunities for upward mobility by the local inhabitants. Once a Russian presence is established it takes on an inertial character, since a large Russian population in a non-Russian area provides the linguistic and cultural atmosphere attractive to other Russian migrants.

• The third and potentially most troublesome factor is the striking inter-ethnic variation in population growth (see table). Broadly speaking, the Baltic and Slavic peoples of the Soviet Union—the Estonians, Latvians, Lithuanians, Belorussians, Ukrainians and, most notably, the Russians—are characterized by low rates of growth, while the ethnic groups of Central Asia (Uzbeks, Tadzhiks, Kirgiz, Turkmen, Kazakhs), like certain nationalities of the Caucasus region, are increasing at a phenomenal rate. Most of the peoples of the Volga-Urals area (for example, Udmurts, Tatars, Bashkirs) and two of the largest Caucasian nationalities (Armenians and Georgians) are intermediate in population growth rates.

These different rates of growth are affecting the ethnic balance of the total Soviet population. A shift is clearly taking place toward the rapidly growing Central Asian and Caucasian nationalities and away from the slowly growing or even numerically decreasing European (Baltic and Slavic) peoples. However, because the latter still comprise such a large proportion of the total population, and because demographic trends typically take several generations to achieve real results, the much heralded change in the Soviet ethnic balance will be slow, and care should be taken not to exaggerate its pace. In 1959, the main European groups accounted for 78.5 percent of the Soviet population, while the major Central Asian nationalities amounted to 6.2 percent of the total. By 1979 the figures were 74.2 percent and 9.9 percent respectively. Similarly, great and perhaps undeserved significance has been attached to the relative decline of the Russians over the same period, from 54.7 percent of the total Soviet population to 52.4 percent.

In sum, the long-term implications of any changes in the ethnic balance of the Soviet population do not warrant use of the term "crisis," which has been employed in the Western media.[14] For one thing, the rapidity of change has been consistently overestimated. Estimates that by the year 2000 one of every three Soviet citizens will be from one of the Muslim ethnic groups are highly improbable: something on the order of 20 percent seems more likely. The latest Soviet census (1979) revealed that a major deceleration in the rate of increase among the faster-growing nationalities is under way (see table), and fertility data—though sketchy—appear to confirm this. Still, the spatial variation in population growth means that virtually all new increments to the Soviet work force will be in Central Asia and the Caucasus.[15] And this will in turn complicate future economic decisions, as planners will be forced to choose between areas where labor is available and areas where other fac-tors—natural resources, transportation, return on investment—are more favorable.

Alternatively, it is possible that large-scale migration will take place from labor-surplus areas in Central Asia to labor-deficient regions like Siberia and parts of Soviet Europe.[16] Yet if the interregional supply of and demand for labor were balanced through such migration, the social and political costs could outweigh the economic benefits. In other societies ethnic mixing has often led to heightened tensions and frequent-ly to violence, and there is no reason to believe that the Soviet Union would be immune to such conflict.

Moreover, as the share of the population accounted for by the non-European ethnic groups continues to rise, the Soviet leadership will need to decide to what extent it should foster the further integration of these nationalities in the army, the Party, and the modern sectors of the economy. Affirmative action schemes, which elsewhere have created dis-cord, as individuals either seek advantage or attempt to maintain it through membership in an ethnic group, are bound further to divide Soviet society along ethnic lines. Not much is known about any such policies in force today. But in the 1960s, apparently, the Soviet govern-ment implemented some kind of an ethnic quota system to raise the per-centage of previously disadvantaged nationalities in higher education. The quotas were not well received by "achiever groups" which had been proportionately over-represented, and contributed to the rise of the Jewish dissident movement and the resurgence of Russian nationalism.

After some 65 years of Soviet rule, the economic and social develop-ment fostered by the regime has for the most part strengthened the posi-tion of the ethnic minorities. In particular, modernization has produced educated, urbanized and politically mobilized non-Russian elites. In the future, these elites, working through the federal structure, may very well be able to pursue ethnic issues and to secure additional benefits for their regions. So long as such pressures are couched in acceptable terms and do not threaten the survival of the state itself, it would appear highly unlikely that the harsh measures employed during the Stalin era could now be invoked against them. Nor is it probable that a diversionary appeal to ideology or to the need to make sacrifices for the sake of future generations would succeed today.

In this regard the Soviet Union faces challenges similar, if not identical, to those which confront most multi-ethnic countries. This is not to say that issues like bilingualism, regional autonomy, and socio-economic equality are unimportant, but rather that they are both critical *and* typical of such countries. Thus viewed, we can say that a major question in coming decades will concern the ability of the Soviet leadership to adapt to changing conditions and to satisfy ethnic group interests while maintaining the basic integrity of the system. As in Canada, Yugoslavia, Belgium, Nigeria, the United States and a host of other multi-ethnic societies, the course of events in the Soviet Union will depend to a considerable degree on the ways in which ethnic minority demands are dealt with. If such problems are handled in a sensitive and reasonable fashion, change will be evolutionary rather than revolutionary. □

1. Craig R. Whitney, "Soviet Georgians Take to Streets to Save Their Language," New York Times (April 15, 1978).

2. For details see Ralph S. Clem, "Russians and Others: Ethnic Tensions in the Soviet Union," *Focus*, XXXI, 1 (1980).

3. Robert A. Lewis, "Comparative Demographic Research and the USSR," paper presented at the Conference on Russian and Soviet Demography, Princeton University, July 1974.

4. Brian D. Silver, "The Status of National Minority Languages in Soviet Education: An Assessment of Recent Changes," *Soviet Studies*, XXVI, 1 (1974), pp. 28-40.

5. Yaroslav Bilinsky, "The Soviet Education Laws of 1958-59 and Soviet Nationality Policy," *Soviet Studies*, XIV, 2 (1962), pp. 138-57.

6. Brian D. Silver, "Bilingualism and Maintenance of the Mother Tongue in Soviet Central Asia," *Slavic Review*, XXXV, 3 (1976), pp. 406-23; see also Roman Szporluk, "West Ukraine and West Belorussia: Historical Tradition, Social Communication, and Linguistic Assimilation," *Soviet Studies*, XXXI, 1 (1979), pp. 76-98.

7. L.V. Chuiko, *Braki i razvody* (Moscow: Statistika, 1975).

8. Robert A. Lewis, Richard H. Rowland, Ralph S. Clem, *Nationality and Population Change in Russia and the USSR* (New York: Praeger, 1976), pp. 282-87.

9. Daniel Bell, "Ethnicity and Social Change," in *Ethnicity: Theory and Experience*, edited by Nathan Glazer and Daniel P. Moynihan (Cambridge, Massachusetts: Harvard University Press, 1975), pp. 141-74.

10. Nathan Glazer and Daniel P. Moynihan, "Introduction," in *Ethnicity: Theory and Experience*, pp. 1-26.

11. Richard Pipes, *The Formation of the Soviet Union* (New York: Atheneum, 1968).

12. Teresa Rakowska-Harmstone, "The Dialectics of Nationalism in the USSR," *Problems of Communism*, XXIII, 3 (1974), pp. 1-22.

13. I.S. Koropeckyj, "Equalization of Regional Development in Socialist Countries," *Economic Development and Cultural Change*, XXI, 1 (1972), pp. 68-86. See also I.S. Koropeckyj and G.E. Schroeder, eds., *Economics of Soviet Regions* (New York: Pergamon, 1981).

14. For example, Herbert E. Meyer, "The Coming Soviet Ethnic Crisis," *Fortune* (Aug. 14, 1978), pp. 156-65.

15. Ralph S. Clem, "Regional Patterns of Population Change in the Soviet Union, 1959-1979," *Geographical Review*, LXX, 2 (1980), pp. 137-56.

16. Lewis, Rowland, Clem, *Nationality and Population Change*, pp. 354-81.

# 24

## Religion

*Paul A. Lucey*

As recent events in Poland have illustrated, it is impossible to understand the social development of Eastern Europe without taking into account the religious factor. The importance of this factor varies greatly from country to country, yet nowhere is it without significance. In the Soviet Union, the political subservience of its leadership means that the Orthodox Church plays a totally different role from that of the Catholic Church in Poland. Still, deep in the bosom of Soviet rural—and sometimes even urban—society, religion is the dominating factor in the lives of tens of millions of people. Its resilience in the face of varying forms and degrees of persecution has been remarkable.

Following the revolution in 1917 the Bolshevik government moved to nationalize all property belonging to religious organizations, to end their philanthropic and educational activities and to curtail their political influence. During the ensuing Civil War and in the early 1920s, churchmen declaring themselves opponents of the new regime or resisting the implementation of its program were dealt with summarily as counterrevolutionaries. When it was possible to affect the course of internal church affairs, by playing favorites or by directly manipulating clergy sympathetic to Soviet power, the regime did not hesitate to do so.

But as the political and military situation became more stable, open clashes between the state and the largest religious organization in the country, the Russian Orthodox Church, were less frequent. In 1925 the Russian Patriarch, Tikhon, elected by a church council in 1917, declared his loyalty to the Soviet government. A kind of peace between church and state was achieved even while the state conducted anti-religious propaganda on a large scale. During the 1920s Soviet religious policy actually favored the small but rapidly growing Protestant "sectarians" who had

293

been suppressed under the old regime. That Jewish religious life declined was due as much perhaps to the promotion of a distinctly secular Yiddish culture as to the zealous atheism of the Communist Party's "Jewish Section." At the same time, Soviet religious policy during this decade was tolerant of Islamic institutions. Islamic schools, courts and clerical land holdings were still widespread in Central Asia as late as 1928.

The emergence of Stalin's dictatorship was accompanied by more drastically severe policies against all religions. The 1929 Law on Religious Associations prohibited virtually all religious activity other than worship on state-licensed premises, and simplified the mechanism for dissolving "unwanted" religious associations. Nor was the assault on religion limited to such formal methods. Not only the churches as institutions, but believers as individuals were subjected to intense persecution throughout the 1930s. By the outbreak of World War II, tens of thousands of clergy and probably several million believers had been arrested; all monasteries, seminaries and most places of worship had been forcibly closed; and centralized ecclesiastical administration had ceased.

The war brought a respite, however, as the regime sought to enlist in the defense effort any institution capable of inspiring traditional patriotism. Not long after the German attack in June 1941, Stalin allowed the few remaining Russian Orthodox bishops to begin rebuilding; and by the war's end, some 18,000 Orthodox parishes had been reconstituted, seminaries and monasteries were being re-opened, and the patriarchal office, empty since Tikhon's death in 1925, was occupied by the newly elected Patriarch Sergei.

The new policy did not affect all religions equally. While the Evangelical Christians, the Baptists, the Georgian Orthodox Church and the Armenian Apostolic Church all enjoyed a renaissance, the Eastern-rite Catholics of the Ukraine, the Ukrainian and Byelorussian autocephalous Orthodox Churches and the Jews did not. By 1946 all the autocephalous Orthodox Churches except Georgia's had been forcibly merged with the Russian Orthodox Church. The four-million-strong Church of the Ukraine was abolished and its parishes, too, were absorbed.

The Jewish community, decimated by the Nazi occupation, was driven by Stalin's anti-Semitic postwar policies even closer to extinction. Islam enjoyed some of the benefits of the new policy — the reopening of many of its mosques and reduction of anti-Islamic propaganda — but was not allowed to resume its position of cultural and civil prominence in the Central Asian republics. Finally, religious communities (mostly Christian) in the newly-annexed Baltic states were subjected to the kind of revolutionary terror which the other churches had experienced in the years after 1917.

This policy of limited and selective toleration of organized religion lasted only until the late 1950s. From 1959 to 1964 the Khrushchev regime conducted a virulent anti-religious campaign which brought about the closure of over half the remaining places of worship and a number of seminaries and monasteries. The Moscow Patriarchate, the All-Union Council of Evangelical Christians and Baptists, and the leading bodies of the other religious communities were forced to adopt measures restricting the activities of parishes and congregations even further than required by the 1929 Law on Religious Associations. Church leaders who resisted these measures were arrested on trumped-up financial or other criminal charges.

Khrushchev's anti-religious policies have been much moderated since his fall in 1964. While anti-religious propaganda under Brezhnev remained an important feature of the "ideological training" conducted in schools, universities, factories and in the media, instances of arbitrary administrative action against religious groups were less common. Few of the losses sustained during the Khrushchev persecution have been made good, however. Indeed there appears to have been a further net decline in the number of places of worship since 1964, and known believers are still subject to discrimination in education and employment. On the positive side, a 1975 revision of the Law on Religious Associations virtually restored the right of legal entity to religious organizations, and in the late 1970s, religious communities that operated seminaries or gave correspondence courses were allowed to increase their annual intake.

What is the situation today of the major religious communities in the Soviet Union? Certainly the largest and most important is the Orthodox Church.[1] With something like 50 million faithful in 68 dioceses in the Soviet Union, it still claims the allegiance of more than one-fourth of the Slavic population.[2] The Moscow Patriarchate, the administrative center of the Church, has an annual budget on the order of 300 million rubles ($450 million). As the largest single member-church of the World Council of Churches, the Orthodox Church of the Soviet Union maintains a full program of international contacts and in 1982 opened a multi-million-ruble reception center in downtown Moscow to facilitate this activity. The Church is the only non-communist institution of its size to be officially recognized by the State.

Nevertheless, it would be a mistake to think that the Orthodox Church enjoys anything like a privileged relationship with the Soviet regime—apart from being offered, on occasion, a special platform to endorse Soviet foreign policy. Orthodox believers are just as likely to suffer discrimination as are members of other religions. The right to worship, the most important religious freedom for Orthodox believers, is in practice denied to many millions owing to government restrictions on the number of open churches in the Soviet Union. There are fewer than 7,000 "working" Russian Orthodox churches today. This compares very unfavorably with a country like Romania, for instance, where 17 million Orthodox believers have over 10,000 places of worship.

Official figures suggest there are now perhaps 6,500 registered Orthodox priests in the Soviet Union (9,100 in Romania). This represents some improvement since the mid-1970s, when several bishops openly expressed alarm at the shortage of priests, but it is still necessary to assign monks and ostensibly retired priests to active duty in the parishes. Enrollment at the Church's three seminaries—in Zagorsk (near Moscow), Leningrad and Odessa—and two theological academies—in Zagorsk and Leningrad—has risen over the last four years. Between 1,800 and 2,000 young men, including correspondence students, are currently being trained as priests.

Orthodox monasticism has been drastically curtailed in the last 60 years. There were 1,023 monasteries and convents functioning in 1917; today only six monasteries and ten convents remain. These institutions had some 1,200 members in 1976. Underground monasticism is thought to be extensive, but there are, perforce, no reliable statistics.

The Moscow Patriarchate produces a monthly journal in English, French and German as well as Russian, but probably only about 20,000 copies of each Russian issue are printed and a large proportion of these are exported. The Church does not have its own printing presses, but, like other organizations, it must arrange to have its printing done on state-owned presses. Besides its journal, the Patriarchate is permitted to publish an annual calendar, a theology series, various service books, limited and infrequent editions of the Bible, and publications for special events.

Prospects for the future of the Orthodox Church in the Soviet Union are mixed. A policy of outward subservience to the government's domestic and foreign policies has secured for it the resources necessary to sustain the level of activity to which it was reduced by the Khrushchev anti-religious campaign in the 1960s. But during the Brezhnev years an implicit challenge to the Church leadership came from the religious wing of the dissident movement. Human rights monitoring groups have documented numerous violations of religious and other civil rights and have called on the Moscow Patriarchate to defend believers in conflict with state authorities. The Orthodox leadership has sought to avoid public involvement in specific cases, but when pressed, has supported official charges against individual believers. There is some evidence that Church leaders have privately sought more lenient sentences for several convicted religious dissidents.

From comments in the Soviet press and from official and unofficial sources it is increasingly evident that the young and the educated are finding in the Orthodox tradition a treasury of Russian national culture and a personal, non-Marxist system of ethics. This suggests that the Church leadership may face increased pressure to assume a more independent role in the social and political, as well as the spiritual, life of the country.

Protestantism has a long history in two of the Baltic republics, Latvia and Estonia, where the Evangelical Lutheran Church remains loosely associated with Latvian and Estonian national identity. Lutheran seminaries in Riga and Tallinn train perhaps a dozen pastors each year. Fewer than 200 registered pastors must serve over 350 congregations with a combined membership of roughly 600,000.

Since the nineteenth century there have been active and expanding communities of Baptists, Evangelical Christians and Pentecostals in the territory of the present-day Soviet Union. While reliable statistics are hard to come by, it is probable that there are at least 520,000 baptized adult members of these denominations scattered throughout the Soviet Union, with the greatest concentration in the Ukraine. Taken together with children and unbaptized adherents, this represents at least one million people in 5,000 to 8,000 congregations.[3]

The All-Union Council of Evangelical Christians and Baptists is the officially recognized umbrella organization of these denominations. The Council has existed since 1944, when Stalin imposed on Baptists and Evangelical Christians a unity they had been unable to achieve freely. The Union's current baptized membership is perhaps 350,000, including some 30,000 Pentecostals and an equal number of Mennonites.[4] From its headquarters in Moscow's Baptist church the All-Union Council publishes a journal, *Herald of the Brethren (Bratsky vestnik)*, and runs a theological correspondence course which some 300 students have completed since its inception in 1968. Current enrollment for the three-year course is just over 100. There have been negotiations with authorities about opening a seminary, but there is no indication that this will be permitted.

Other Protestants in the Soviet Union are organized under the Council of Churches of Evangelical Christians and Baptists, consisting of congregations which are not legally registered with the state and have rejected the All-Union Council leadership because of its cooperation with the state. Originally a reform movement within the All-Union Council, the

Council of Churches of Evangelical Christians and Baptists has no official status, and its leadership has periodically been decimated by arrests. Despite this, it is thought to have a present baptized membership of close to 100,000 in perhaps 2,000 congregations. Moreover, the organization has the most impressive underground printing operation in the Soviet Union, having produced well over half a million pieces of religious literature since 1971. The Council of Churches is, after the emigration movement among Soviet Jews, the largest dissident movement in the Soviet Union. And if its renown abroad has not been as great as that of the Jewish emigration movement, it has forced Soviet authorities to make substantial concessions.

Two churches closely associated with nationality in their respective republics are the Georgian Orthodox and Armenian Apostolic—or Gregorian. --Churches.

The Georgian Orthodox Church has its own patriarch and thus constitutes an independent sister church of the Russian Orthodox. The current Georgian Patriarch, Ilya II, has done much to restore his Church's fortunes since he succeeded the corrupt and enfeebled David V in 1977. Most notable has been his effort to restore diocesan administration. Nine of 15 sees were vacant at the time of Ilya's election; now only three remain empty. The Georgian Patriarchate publishes a journal and calendar, but has had great difficulties in disseminating other religious literature.

The Georgian Church's most serious problem is the lack of registered churches and priests. Of some 2,000 churches and chapels functioning before the Revolution, there remain only about 40 "working" Georgian Orthodox churches. There are something over a hundred registered priests, 40 to 50 nuns in four convents and a smaller number of monks in the two monasteries (there were 27 in 1917) which were reopened in the late 1970s. The seminary in Mtskheta, the ancient Georgian capital, has an enrollment of about 25.

It is thought that something like two-thirds of the Georgian population, or roughly three million people, remain regular worshipers. And, as in other parts of the Soviet Union, a notable proportion of young people are showing a renewed interest.

The Armenian Apostolic Church is widely regarded as enjoying the greatest degree of freedom of any religious body in the Soviet Union. The Supreme Patriarch-Catholicos of All Armenians, Vazgen I, has authority over five dioceses in the Soviet Union, only three of which are in Armenia proper. The center of Armenian Christianity is the Patriarchal Cathedral at Echmiadzin, where four of six surviving monasteries

and the Theological Seminary are also located. In 1978 seminary enrollment was reported to be 56, so it appears that new priests are being
trained at a rate sufficient to maintain the present total of roughly 130.

There are some 40 working churches in Armenia (1,450 in 1917),
and it seems most unlikely that this is enough, since at least 60 percent of
the 3.5 million Armenians living in Armenia or neighboring Soviet republics remain practicing believers. Some 70 percent of newborn infants
are baptized. This says much for the strength of Armenian nationalism,
of which the Church is a vital element. A revival of religious interest
among young people has been gaining strength in recent years. Uniquely
among religious communities in the Soviet Union, the Armenian Church
possesses its own printing facilities, as is evident in the well-stocked book
stalls found in Armenian churches.

There are about three million Latin-rite Catholics in the Soviet Union,
of whom the majority are in the Lithuanian republic. It is widely assumed that 75 percent of the Lithuanian population remains loyal to this
church. Indeed, the Catholic faith and national identity are as closely
related in Lithuania as they are in neighboring Poland. Like the Poles,
Lithuanian Catholics have shown themselves to be remarkably resolute
in resisting the anti-religious policies of the Communist government. But
unlike Poland, Lithuania was fully incorporated into the Soviet Union at
the end of World War II, and its Catholic Church has had to endure
more brutal anti-religious policies than any employed in Poland.

The Lithuanian episcopate has been much weakened since the advent
of Soviet rule. Though the Pope appointed two bishops in 1982, two of
six dioceses are still run by administrators. Bishop Julijonas
Steponavičius, who is believed to be a Cardinal, has been in exile since
Khrushchev's anti-religious campaign.

There are, to be sure, some 628 working Catholic churches in
Lithuania, only 80 fewer than existed in 1940 when the country was annexed (more than 500 chapels and other non-parish churches were closed.) Yet something like 100 parishes are without priests. Today there are
fewer than 700 Catholic priests in the country (1,450 in 1940) and nearly one-quarter of these are over 70 years old. All monastic orders were
abolished in 1947, and the single surviving seminary, in Kaunas, had until quite recently produced only a handful of graduates each year. The
state authorities have allowed the seminary to increase its enrollment
since 1975, so that the current number may be between 70 and 100.[5]

The Lithuanian clergy and faithful have responded to anti-religious
pressures with both public resistance and clandestine initiatives.[6] Since
1972 more than half the Catholic clergy and well over 200,000 laymen

have signed petitions and appeals protesting Soviet policy against their church. A clandestine seminary seems to have been functioning since the early 1970s, and by 1979 some 19 of its graduates had been ordained. A Soviet source confirms the existence of clandestine convents that in 1976 housed some 1,500 nuns.

Perhaps the most beleaguered of the officially recognized religious communities in the Soviet Union are the Jews. According to the 1979 census, assimilation and emigration have reduced the Jewish population to 1,811,000, about 88 percent of whom live in the western regions. Soviet sources indicate that only between 1 and 3 percent practice their faith, although the figure is somewhat higher in the Baltic Republics. Jews living in the Caucasian Republics and in Central Asia are more religious; perhaps 20 percent are practicing.

In sum, there may be 60,000 to 100,000 observant Jews in the Soviet Union today, for whom the rabbi of Moscow's Arkhipov Street Synagogue and his assistant act as spokesmen. At the same time, there are between 50 and 60 open synagogues (as against some 6,000 in 1917) and an indeterminate number of smaller "prayer houses." Of the synagogues, approximately half are in Central Asia and the Caucasus.

The Soviet Union today has no more than a handful of trained rabbis. Certainly, most synagogues do not have one. The tiny, ill-equipped yeshiva (school) attached to Moscow's Choral Synagogue, with a current enrollment of five, cannot replace the rabbis who have retired or died during the last decade. Recently some half-dozen young Jews have been allowed to study at yeshivas in Budapest and New York. These programs are clearly insufficient to replenish the rabbinate in the Soviet Union.

Jewish religious literature has been virtually impossible to obtain for decades. The Moscow and Leningrad synagogues do publish calendars, but since the 1920s three editions of a prayer book and one edition of the Pentateuch comprise the sum total of Jewish religious literature printed in the Soviet Union.

Prospects for the survival of Jewish secular culture—of the Jewish "nationality," as it is officially described—are generally considered bleak. State-encouraged anti-Semitism will doubtless deter many from identifying with Judaism. But throughout the 1970s thousands of European Jews from precisely the most secularized strata of the population cultivated a sense of their Jewishness. And with the likelihood of greatly reduced emigration in the 1980s, the Jewish cultural renaissance, stimulated by the emigration movement, may well develop a more religious direction.

The picture is somewhat different with respect to Islam. The largest and most important of its four "Spiritual Directorates" is that of Central Asia and Kazakhstan, with headquarters in Tashkent. Currently Mufti Shamsutdinkhan Babakhan is its president. The Spiritual Directorate of Muslims in Russia and Siberia, with headquarters in Ufa, is responsible for Islamic communities in the Tatar and Bashkir Autonomous Republics. Since 1980 its president has been Mufti Talgat Taziev. The Spiritual Directorate of the North Caucasus and Dagestan has head-quarters in Makhach-Kala (Dagestan Autonomous Republic), with Mufti Mahmud Gekkiev as its president; and the Muslim Spiritual Directorate of Transcaucasia, centered in Baku, is responsible for the predominantly Shi'ite Muslims of Azerbaidzhan and the neighboring republics. Its president since 1980 has been Sheikh Hadji Ali Shukur Pasha, who is Shi'ite; the vice-president is, as a rule, a Sunni, in deference to the large Sunni minority in the Caucasus.

These Spiritual Directorates conform roughly to the old tsarist government's system for supervising Muslim affairs. The great majority of Soviet Muslims are of the Sunni rite, which does not favor centralized ecclesiastical administration. But as with the Baptists and Evangelical Christians, in the mid-1940s the Soviet government's interest in centrally organized religious life superseded any objections the believers might have had. And, again like the Evangelical Christians and Baptists, Islamic activity in the Soviet Union is bifurcated into the officially recognized and the clandestine.

The face of "official" Islam in the Soviet Union is in some respects a sad one. Of some 26,000 mosques in use at the time of the Revolution, only some 400 to 450 are believed to be functioning today. An army of some 45,000 mullahs has been reduced to fewer than 2,000. There are only two medressehs (seminaries), one in Tashkent and one in Bukhara, graduating no more than 15 to 20 students each year. Islamic religious literature is extremely scarce: only five small editions of the Koran since World War II. Yet, in spite of these deprivations the officially recognized leadership of the Islamic community is perhaps the most abject in its support of Soviet propaganda regarding religious freedom.

Nevertheless, it has been plausibly argued that the Muslim leadership has gained rather more from its cooperation with the authorities than the authorities have themselves. Muslims have won some significant concessions in recent years: the opening of some 30 new mosques since 1975, an edition of the Koran in 1977 and the opening in 1971 of a higher theological course at the Tashkent medresseh. The standard of theological education for the officially recognized mullahs has risen dramatically over the last 15 years, largely as a result of the new course. But it can also be argued that it has been in the Soviet regime's own interest to provide a small number of politically reliable Muslim clerics to make a favorable impression on Muslims from abroad.

Parallel to the official Islamic establishment there appears to be a sizable "unofficial" Islam. Unregistered mullahs and religious activists belonging to Sufi brotherhoods (clandestine and highly disciplined religious orders) support themselves by religious ministrations to the faithful in areas where the services of registered mullahs are either unavailable or unwanted. The Sufi orders espouse an extremely conservative brand of Islam, considered to be fanatical and "anti-Soviet" by the authorities. Indeed, the most prominent of these orders have a history of resistance to Russian and now Soviet power. It is not known how many unregistered mullahs exist, but it is safe to assume that in many rural areas they are more active, and possibly more visible, than representatives of official Islam.

According to the 1979 census, as we saw in the preceding chapter, some 43 million people in the Soviet Union belong to traditionally Muslim ethnic groups—Uzbeks, Kazakhs, Tatars, Azeris, Tadzhiks, Turkmen, Bashkirs and two or three dozen smaller nationalities. This represents an increase of more than 100 percent since 1959, bringing the proportion of ethnic Muslims in the Soviet population to 16.5 percent.

The extent to which these ethnic groups remain distinctly Muslim is of immediate concern to the Soviet authorities. Official statistics suggest that allegiance to Islam remains high in areas where the clandestine Sufi brotherhoods are active. Some 80 percent of the ethnic Muslims in these areas still perform or have performed Muslim rites of passage. One mufti told a British journalist in 1979 that contrary to standard Soviet medical practices, more than 90 percent of newborn males in his republic were circumcised; he also said that the great majority of his compatriots were buried according to Muslim custom. The resistance of ethnic Muslims to intermarriage is even more striking.

For 60 years the state has encouraged in its Muslim territories a secular nationalism at the expense of Islam, so as to facilitate social and cultural integration into the Soviet Union. Obviously, widespread popular identification with Islam retards this process. Furthermore, the remarkable vitality of the clandestine and fundamentalist Sufi brotherhoods presents the possibility, however distant, of an Islamic revival which could have both anti-Soviet and anti-Russian overtones.

In conclusion, it is probable that not less than 30 percent of the Soviet population remain practicing believers. In the non-Russian republics, where religion and national or ethnic consciousness are closely related, the percentage is generally higher; and all of these religious communities report a significant increase in the interest shown by educated, urban young people over the last decade.

The resilience of Islamic belief, coupled with the demographic dynamism of the ethnic Muslims, poses complex political and economic problems in the long run. Throughout the Soviet Union the Evangelical Christians and Baptists are active missionaries, and the various dissenters are determined to conduct their activities without regard to government restrictions.

The Orthodox Church, on the other hand, appears to be a sleeping giant. Nevertheless, this body, too, by its very presence in society, exercises a kind of influence. Since Khrushchev's fall its appeal to the young and the educated has steadily increased, and to the extent that the Orthodox Church becomes identified with Russian national feeling, this process can only accelerate. It is most unlikely, however, that the Soviet regime could ever accommodate itself to a Russian nationalism based on the faith which for 60 years it has sought to eradicate. □

1. See report of Vasily Furov, deputy chairman of the State Council for Religious Affairs, in *Vestnik russkogo khristianskogo dvizheniia*, 130 (1979), pp. 275-344.

2. Figures from William C. Fletcher, *Soviet Believers* (Lawrence, Kansas: Regents Press, 1981).

3. Walter Sawatsky, *Soviet Evangelicals since World War II* (Kitchener, Ontario/Scottsdale, Pennsylvania: Herald Press, 1981).

4. Besides the roughly 30,000 Pentecostals in the All-Union Council there are about 70,000 in either autonomously registered or unregistered congregations.

5. There is also a much smaller seminary in Riga which trains priests for Latvia's 200,000 Catholics and for scattered Catholic parishes in Central Asia.

6. See Michael Bourdeaux, *Land of Crosses: The Struggle for Religious Freedom in Lithuania, 1938-78* (Chumleigh, Devon: Augustine Publishers, 1979).

7. Alexandre Bennigsen and Chantal Lemercier-Quelquejay, *Les Musulmans oubliés* (Paris: François Maspero, 1981).

# 25

# Women

*Mary Ellen Fischer*

A chicken is not a bird; a woman is not a human being. — Russian proverb.

The first class oppression coincides with that of the female sex by the male. — Engels, *The Woman Question*.

Women . . . should all know what the proletarian dictatorship will mean to them — complete equality of rights with men, both legal and in practice, in the family, the state, and in society. — Lenin, *The Emancipation of Women*.

We hate the bourgeois family, but . . . the main kernel of society . . . is the family. — Lunacharsky, circa 1926.[1]

A clearly stated goal of the Bolshevik revolution was the elimination of the subordinate status of women in Russia. Marx and Engels had recognized and denounced the oppression of women in bourgeois society; Lenin promised that his revolution would establish a new society in which women would achieve equal status with men.

The 1917 revolution brought profound changes in the political and economic organization of Russia, and also in the ideological assumptions of that society, but the record of the revolutionaries in achieving their various goals is mixed. Not all of the promises have been fulfilled, and this is certainly true for what Engels termed "the woman question." The revolution quickly brought legal equality to Russian women, but the struggle of these women to attain social and economic equality with their male comrades in both public and private life has been more prolonged and less successful. Indeed, visible in the Soviet Union today are many of

305

the differences between male and female patterns of political and economic participation that can be found in societies without such a strong ideological commitment to the equality of women.

There can be no doubt that the situation of women has improved since 1917. Their legal and socio-economic status before the revolution was miserable at all levels of society. In peasant families the division of labor by sex did make the wife an important contributor to the economic well-being of the household. At the same time, however, the separation of roles produced double standards of behavior in which men were expected to drink, smoke, swear, engage in extra-marital sex and use their fists freely against other men and against their wives. None of these activities was permissible for women, who were expected to show "subordination, obedience, and a slavish devotion" and to forgive a beating since it was "the nature of men" to be "hot-tempered." In Russian peasant society, wife-beating demonstrated masculinity, while overt affection was considered abnormal.[2]

In pre-revolutionary Russia upper-class women in some ways fared worse than did peasant women, since the greater economic resources of the family meant that they could be completely segregated from the outside world. In the seventeenth century the seclusion of such women was a matter of family honor. The husband's horsewhip, used in the "training" of the wife, hung by custom at the head of the bed. Eighteenth-century reforms brought some improvements, but nineteenth-century lithographs still depict the public punishment of noblewomen by flogging.[3] The despotism of the tsar over his subjects, based on divine right, was mirrored in the husband's power over his wife and children. The 1836 Code of Russian Laws stipulated that "the woman must obey her husband, reside with him in love, respect, and unlimited obedience, and offer him every pleasantness . . . as the ruler of the household." A Russian woman did have certain property and inheritance rights denied to her West European counterpart, but the fact remains that a woman in tsarist Russia had few civil rights: without the express permission of her father, and after marriage her husband, she could not work, study, trade or travel.[4]

Nineteenth-century polemics between Russian conservatives who wished to preserve the traditions of Russian society and reformers hoping to bring about political and economic change reveal a contrast in the attitudes of these men toward the roles of women. Because the confinement of women to the home was considered by many necessary to the preservation of indigenous Russian values, conservative politicians tended to advocate restrictions against women's access to education or to a wider role in society. But male reformers tended to advocate change in the status of women, particularly if they had themselves been influenced by Western concepts of social change, progress and even romantic love. Around 1840, the writer Mikhail Lermontov asked, "To love . . . but whom? . . . In love there must be equality in physical and in moral feeling." The only solution to this search for "love" was to find an intelligent woman and educate her, for until the late 1850s secondary education was available only to a tiny number of upper-class women. And that education focused on subjects such as music, needlework or French, with the goal of providing a pleasant home environment for their future husbands.[5]

There was no higher or professional education for women in Russia until the 1870s. Then, after Tsar Alexander II was assassinated in 1881 and a young woman was found to be one of the assassins, even those recent concessions to women were rescinded. Conservatives were reinforced in their fears: women let out of the home endangered the political and moral fabric of society. Higher education once more was closed to women, and the employment of middle- or upper-class women remained limited to the private economy, usually in homes as teachers or governesses. Just as the moderate reform movement in Russia, frustrated by repeated failures and persecution, became a radical revolutionary movement, so the women's movement became radicalized. Many women, in fact, joined the wider movement for political revolution and the destruction of the tsarist regime.

After 1890 Marxism became prominent in Russia as an ideology of revolution and in 1917, under Lenin's leadership, the Bolshevik faction of the Social Democratic Party emerged as the dominant radical force. Women revolutionaries were attracted to the writings of Marx and Engels for their analysis of sexual as well as class oppression. Engels in particular detailed the double oppression of women under capitalism: they were exploited as cheap labor in mills, mines and factories, where they worked under terrible conditions, and were treated as possessions and instruments of production by their husbands. Under socialism, Engels had promised, women would be liberated from both forms of bondage.

Lenin continued this emphasis on women's liberation, declaring that "we have to win over the millions of working women in town and country. . . . There can be no real mass movement without the women."[6] Lenin was a political pragmatist with a genius for sensing the issue that would evoke a positive response in his audience. He was also an elitist in his certainty that he alone knew what was right for Russia and that the Bolshevik Party under his leadership was the instrument for establishing a new society. Since that society would bring the liberation of both men and women, Lenin did not scruple to make promises and to use whatever slogans and arguments were necessary to persuade different social groups to support him in his goals. The first need, he believed, was the political revolution to destroy the old regime; then would come, inevitably, the end of oppression based on class or sex.

In the three years following the Bolshevik seizure of power, many laws were passed to improve the status of women. They were granted full legal equality with men, mutual consent was required for marriage, and women were allowed the right to keep their own names and to obtain an abortion or a divorce on request. The Party also announced its intention of freeing women from household work by providing communal facilities for such traditional burdens as childcare, laundry and cooking. Women would be expected to do the work in these communal facilities—but it would be for wages, making it productive labor in the Marxist sense.

Finally, an organization was formed specifically for women: the *Zhenotdel* (Women's Department). Women were taught to read, to care for themselves and to participate in the new socialist society; their rights were explained and their expectations raised. As early as 1923, however, a Party resolution condemned the *Zhenotdel* for "feminist deviationism," for turning people away from the class struggle. The next year the organization was criticized for excessive complaints about material conditions harmful to women. The most outspoken feminist within the Party leadership, Aleksandra Kollontai, was "banished" to diplomatic service in Norway.[7] By 1928 "feminism" was declared to be anti-Marxist, an attempt to convert the class struggle to a sex struggle. Somehow in that first post-revolutionary decade the two struggles had become separated.

Lenin had some blind spots, especially when it came to the oppression of Soviet women. For example, he usually ignored the basic conflict of interest between men and women communists. He did not appear to realize that men would have to relinquish certain privileges for women to gain equality, or that men would probably be reluctant to give up these privileges. He did recognize that many loyal Bolshevik men did not accept women's equality, and that some "educational" work was needed to "root out the old slaveowner" point of view even within the Party. One incident illustrates the difficulty: in 1918 the new Workers' Soviet (Council) of the town of Vladimir decreed that henceforth every woman over 18 would become the property of the state and be required to register at a central bureau of free love. In the interest of the state, men aged 19 to 50 could choose one registered woman a month, without her consent, and the children of these unions would become state property. The decree was quickly rescinded by the Bolshevik leadership, but less public forms of oppression continued. Particularly difficult was the situation of women in traditionally Moslem areas, where violence against *Zhenotdel* workers was not unusual.[8]

Another important factor in gradually reducing the drive for women's equality was the devastated economy. Marx had predicted that socialism would come first to a highly industrialized society, one that had achieved the means to abolish economic scarcity. There would be plenty for everyone, and inequalities—based on class or sex—would disappear. In fact, the revolution took place in a semi-industrialized country badly weakened by World War I, and was followed by three years of civil war in which the Bolsheviks had to fight for survival before they could worry about their revolutionary goals. The socialist revolution occurred at a time of extreme economic scarcity—just the reverse of Marx's prediction—and the egalitarian goals of the revolutionaries began to evaporate. The economy in 1921 needed experts, technicians and specialists. To gain their cooperation the state had to pay them higher wages than were paid to unskilled workers. Wage stratification brought with it social stratification, and a political and social system that was not egalitarian.

Later, the pressure of reconstruction would turn into the pressures of economic growth. The Bolsheviks, after all, were committed not only to equality but also to a program of industrial development. Indeed, Lenin had found it necessary almost immediately to restore both the hierarchy of command in the armed forces and one-person management in the factories, having concluded that just as councils of soldiers could not fight a war effectively, so councils of workers could not manage high rates of production. When women began to compete for the favored jobs, male factory workers objected to their employment in any but their traditional capacities. So women were temporarily held back to prevent trouble and economic slowdown.

Then the post-revolutionary legal changes affecting the family and family life were brought into question. The easy divorce laws, along with shifts in the living patterns and consciousness of men and women, were contributing to the breakup of many marriages. Easy abortion combined with economic difficulties had brought down the birthrate at a time when the Party wished to encourage population growth in order to replace the losses of war and famine. As revolutionaries, Marxists had condemned the bourgeois family as a reactionary institution, but as rulers, most Marxists had come to believe that the family was necessary for the stability of the new society. Commissar of Education A.V. Lunacharsky, in the mid-1920s, expressed the dilemma: "We hate the bourgeois family, but . . . the main kernel of society . . . is the family."

After 1928 the rapid development of heavy industry was given priority, as was a stable family and social system—to produce an efficient labor force. As a result, the laws affecting women and the family began to change again, culminating in a decree of 1936 making abortion illegal and divorce very difficult.[9] The gradual decline in revolutionary fervor throughout the 1920s saw the egalitarian goals of the old Bolsheviks lose out to the need for hierarchical social and economic organization in the army, the factory and even the home.

Another set of factors contributed substantially to the Bolsheviks' failure to fulfill their promises to women. Lenin, like most of his male colleagues, never fully realized the extent of women's oppression *outside* the workplace. Therefore, he concentrated on institutional and economic reforms such as equality in law and in education. At home he assumed that women would be freed from housework and childcare by "a reallocation of familial and societal functions . . . from the individual household to the sòcial collective."[10] In other words, roles *within* the home would not change; men would not begin to share those responsibilities. Instead, the drudgery would be eased by communal kitchens, public dining rooms and laundries, crèches, kindergartens and children's homes. Male privilege in the home was never confronted directly.

The provision of communal facilities to liberate women, however, turned out to be prohibitively expensive for the new revolutionary society. Even the new work laws limiting hours or providing maternity leave or childcare were regarded as impractical, and frequently were not implemented in the ruined economy. Here also the pressures arising from economic devastation turned into pressures for rapid development. Under Stalin priority was given to development goals rather than current consumption. This made the women's triple burden of job, home and family still heavier, for it was home appliances and social services that remained among the most neglected and backward sectors of the Soviet economy.

As Marx might have predicted, economic scarcity has been crucial in the evolution of Soviet society and of the role of women in that society. Yet there is no doubt that the Soviet government has achieved tremendous gains for its population in living standards as well as national power, and that Soviet women have shared in these gains in two important ways. First, their legal equality with men has not been rescinded or questioned. Second, they have been mobilized into the labor force at rates unequaled by any other industrial society: Soviet women make up just over 51 percent of the labor force and 85 percent of Soviet women are employed full time.[11] This has meant greater female participation not only in skilled and technical occupations and in the professions than is usual elsewhere, but also in heavy, unskilled, physical labor for industry and agriculture. For the Soviet Union throughout its history has known not only shortages of labor, but also of *man*power—a demographic imbalance brought on by huge losses in both World Wars. Thus, there has been continuous pressure on women to work as well as some room for them at the top. The ideological assumption that women would achieve liberation by employment outside the home has been reinforced by economic necessity.

Yet despite significant shifts in the status of Soviet women, their economic roles reflect patterns present in societies without such a strong ideological commitment to sexual equality. One such pattern is the concentration of women in economic sectors where they are assumed to have special skills or qualifications: the food and textile industries, for example, or education, or social services. Such sectoral segregation in the Soviet Union actually seems to be increasing, perhaps partly as a result of the improving demographic balance and the reappearance of males to fill their traditional occupations. In 1959, for example, only 33 percent of women were employed in "women's" sectors, but by 1970 the figure had climbed to 55 percent.[12]

Another pattern involves "professional takeover": as more women move into a particular profession or occupation, it becomes stereotyped as "women's work." Soviet medicine, where 69 percent of doctors are women, is a dramatic example of this process. But the prestige, power and financial rewards associated with such sectors usually are reduced as women enter them. The causal relationship is often unclear: does a profession decline in desirability because women move in, or do men move out because it has become less rewarding or attractive for some other reason? Whatever the cause, Soviet women clearly are concentrated in sectors with lower prestige and financial reward.

A similar case is the pattern of salaries among categories of workers within a specific sector. The sector with the highest proportion of women—skilled non-manual workers—is at the middle range in educational level but at the bottom in income. Even skilled manual workers are better paid. The average Soviet woman earns about 65 percent as much as the average Soviet male.[13] This is slightly higher than the comparable U.S. figure, but it is not equality.

Finally, in explaining the relatively low income of women in a system which guarantees equal pay for equal work, we must consider the vertical segregation within sectors of the Soviet economy. Women are clustered at the bottom. In agriculture, for example, where women make up over half the labor force, there is a clear division of labor: men operate the machines, women work with their hands. Men are the directors, bookkeepers, tractor and combine drivers and irrigators; women are the field-team leaders and members, the cattle and poultry workers, the vegetable- and melon-growers and the non-specialized workers. Only during World War II did women constitute as much as 14.2 percent of farm directors; by 1961 the figure was back to the pre-war proportion of less than 2 percent; by 1975, 1.5 percent. The situation in industry is comparable: in 1975 women made up 65 percent of the age cohort of industrial administrators, but only 9 percent of directors were female and these were concentrated in textiles or food processing.[14]

In the professions, the same pattern emerges. As responsibility, status and pay go up the proportion of women goes down. One Soviet source complained, for example, that "while men comprise 15 percent of all medical personnel, they are 50 percent of all chief physicians and executives of medical institutions." In science and scholarship, women have formed a rather stable share of the total number of specialists, ranging from 36 percent in 1950 to 40 percent in 1975. But they make up 50 percent of junior research associates, 24 percent of senior researchers, 22 percent of associate professors, and only 10 percent of full professors. In 1977 there were 14 women in the 749-member Academy of Sciences: three were full members; 11 were corresponding members.[15]

The pattern of women's economic participation in the Soviet Union thus resembles that found in other industrial societies in some respects: horizontal and vertical segregation with negative impact on status, responsibility and income. Political participation is even more limited. As a rule, the proportion of women varies inversely with the power of the office or legislative body. For example, women delegates make up between 44 and 48 percent of the delegates to local soviets, while the proportion drops close to 30 percent in the Supreme Soviet. Among the delegates to the latter, moreover, women are less likely to be Party members, they hold less important posts in their occupations, and they show more rapid turnover rates within the body. All these factors militate against their playing an influential role. In addition, as Mark Beissinger shows, these legislative bodies are not seats of power in the Soviet system, since the Party organs make policy decisions and then use the Soviets to ratify these policies and to discuss methods of implementation (see Chapter 4).

Real power lies in the Party, and here we find few women. Since the early 1960s efforts to recruit women into the Communist Party have intensified, and the female proportion of total membership is now about

27 percent. (The figure was 8 percent in 1922.) But if we examine age cohorts, we discover that 14.1 percent of all Soviet males over 18 are members, as against 3.7 percent of all females over 18. This discrepancy is not a function of educational lag, because the ratio remains the same for those who have completed higher education. As many as one-third of the first secretaries of primary Party organizations are women, but the proportion drops sharply in higher positions. For example, less than 4 percent of urban, district or regional Party secretaries are female. Since 1918 the proportion of women in the Central Committee has never exceeded 4.2 percent. Even that low figure does not reflect the true situation in the Central Committee, since about a third of the women are there for honorary or titular reasons—the cosmonaut Tereshkova, for example. (Men are also there for such reasons, of course, but in much smaller proportion.)

At the top of the Party and state hierarchies women have been almost totally absent. The one female member of the central Secretariat in the post-World War II era was Ekaterina Furtseva, who was also Minister of Culture when she died in 1974 and the only woman ever to serve—for three years—in the all-powerful Party Politburo. A minister of health in the 1950s was the only other woman ever to serve in the Council of Ministers. Aleksandra Kollanti remains the only woman ever to serve as a Soviet ambassador. Vertical segregation in the political system is matched by horizontal or occupational segregation. Women officials usually deal with health, culture, social security, light industry and consumer services rather than the armed forces, foreign or Party affairs, heavy industry or internal security. Real political power remains firmly in the grip of men.[16]

Marx and Engels, and even Lenin, assumed that work outside the home in "productive" labor would liberate women from their subservient position in bourgeois society. Soviet women have not only the right but the duty to work side by side with men. Yet the issue of oppression in the home or the possibility of shifting sex roles within the family has never been directly confronted by the Party leaders. And the triple burden—job, home, family—has prevented women from competing effectively with their male colleagues for political or economic promotion. Their lower performance, in turn, has reinforced lower expectations of these women, expectations held by themselves as well as by the men supervising or competing with them. This has resulted in the patterns of political and economic participation so familiar to scholars studying women in other societies.

The prognosis for Soviet women is not clear. One important factor, however, contributes to pessimism: the demographic imbalance has largely been rectified, and while it is socially advantageous to have equal numbers of males and females in the younger and middle-aged cohorts, this could also mean that there will be less room for women at the top (or as students in educational institutions leading to prestigious occupations). In general, Soviet officials have not shown the commitment to the equality of women which would give women good jobs when they are competing with men. On the other hand, women's awareness of exploitation has been growing in recent years. And if a major shift toward shared sex roles within the home has never been considered by most Soviet citizens, male or female, the Soviet media did begin to discuss the problem during the Brezhnev era.[17]

There seem to be three major orientations among Soviet analysts regarding the proper policies to be adopted on "the Woman Question." One, with the smallest number of advocates, would encourage a better sharing of household work within the family. A second would emphasize the provision of communal facilities and consumer goods in gradually improving the lives of women. The third reflects another demographic problem facing Soviet society: the low birthrate, particularly among the Russian population. Analysts concerned with higher population growth stress the need to increase maternity leave—currently one year at 30 to 40 percent of salary—as well as subsidies, and perhaps even to offer women the option of quitting the labor force altogether to raise their children. This would reinforce sex role differentiation and intensify inequalities in the labor market, but it would give many women a choice not now available to them: staying home.

None of these three policy orientations would be clearly superior in fulfilling the Party's priorities of increasing both the birthrate and economic production. The first might raise the quality of women's participation in the labor force, but it might reduce men's productivity without increasing the birthrate. The second might increase women's productivity but would be very expensive and might not bring more rapid population growth; the record in other industrial societies which have tried it does not promise a higher birthrate along with higher living standards. The third option would reduce the number of working women and would be ideologically unpalatable to a large proportion of Soviet women who have come to believe strongly in a career as a prerequisite to liberation. Yet it is the one most likely to increase the birthrate.

Brezhnev managed to postpone any major decision on this issue during his lifetime. The possibilities were widely discussed, however, and the new Soviet leadership will have to take a stand in the near future. Although the outcome of the debate is unpredictable, it is likely that Party choices in this area will affect the lives of more Soviet citizens more profoundly than any other matter of internal policy awaiting decision at the top. Meanwhile the wide range of opinion on the subject among Soviet citizens can be seen from the following quotations, culled from letters and articles in the Soviet press:[18]

> Free a woman from the kitchen and you give her the freedom of a silly hen. Who needs such a woman? Woman is supposed to adorn the hearth just as flowers adorn the meadow.

> Girls, for all your equality with us men, stay feminine, gentle, and weak (in the best, Marxist sense of this concept).

> The shop class teaches men's work. Girls have home economics, but men must be men.

> [Outside work] is the most important and primary condition for our liberation from the authority of men and is the guarantee of our independence, our sense of our own value and freedom.

> Under the new order of things, the kitchen will belong to anyone who wants to eat.

> I doubt that I will ever marry again. Why should I? Having a husband is like having another baby in the apartment. □

1. Jessica Smith, *Woman in Soviet Russia* (New York: Vanguard Press, 1928), p. 4; Frederick Engels, *Origin of the Family*, excerpted in *The Woman Question* (New York: International Publishers, 1951), p. 21; V. I. Lenin, *The Emancipation of Women* (New York: International Publishers, 1934), p. 113; Lunacharsky as quoted in Smith, p. 92.

2. See H. Kent Geiger, *The Family in Soviet Russia* (Cambridge, Massachusetts: Harvard University Press, 1958), pp. 217-18 or David and Vera Mace, *The Soviet Family* (Garden City, New York: Doubleday, 1963). Recent scholarship on the topic is surveyed in David L. Ransel, ed., *The Family in Imperial Russia: New Lines of Historical Research* (Urbana, Illinois: University of Illinois Press, 1978).

3. Janet Wertzner Salaff and Judith Merkle, "Women in Revolution," *Berkeley Journal of Sociology*, 15 (1970), p. 3; Dorothy Atkinson, "Society and the Sexes in the Russian Past," in Dorothy Atkinson, Alexander Dallin and Gail Lapidus, eds., *Women in Russia* (Stanford, California: Stanford University Press, 1977), p. 17.

4. Richard Stites, *The Women's Liberation Movement in Russia: Feminism, Nihilism, and Bolshevism, 1860-1930* (Princeton, New Jersey: Princeton University Press, 1978), pp. 4-7. This is the basic study of the subject.

5. For the Lermontov quotation, see Salaff and Merkle, "Women in Revolution"; more generally, see Stites, *Women's Liberation*, Chaps. 1-2.

6. Lenin, *The Emancipation of Women*, p. 110. On the radicalization of the women's movement during the nineteenth century, see Stites, *Women's Liberation*.

7. Two recent biographies of Kollontai document her early contributions and eventual disgrace: Barbara Evans Clements, *Bolshevik Feminist: The Life of Aleksandra Kollontai* (Bloomington, Indiana: Indiana University Press, 1979); Beatrice Farnsworth, *Aleksandra Kollontai: Socialism, Feminism, and the Bolshevik Revolution* (Stanford, California: Stanford University Press, 1980).

8. On the Workers' Soviet of Vladimir, see Salaff and Merkle, "Women and Revolution." On the status of Moslem women in the Soviet Union, see Gregory Massell, *The Surrogate Proletariat: Moslem Women and Revolutionary Strategies in Soviet Central Asia, 1919-1929* (Princeton, New Jersey: Princeton University Press, 1974).

9. In the post-Stalin period, abortions once again became the primary method of birth control in the Soviet Union. For a recent discussion of this issue see Alastair McAuley, *Women's Work and Wages in the Soviet Union* (London: Allen and Unwin, 1981), pp. 203-5.

10. Gail Warshofsky Lapidus, *Women in Soviet Society: Equality, Development, and Social Change* (Berkeley, California: University of California Press, 1978), p. 55.

11. Gail Warshofsky Lapidus, ed., *Women, Work, and Family in the Soviet Union* (Armonk, New York: M. E. Sharpe, 1982), p. x. This volume contains translations of current Soviet articles on these topics.

12. Lapidus, *Women in Society*, p. 174.

13. McAuley, *Women's Work*, p. 206, estimates 60 to 65 percent in the 1970s; Lapidus, *Women and Family*, p. xxi, estimates 65 to 70 percent. See also Lapidus, *Women in Society*, pp. 190-94.

14. Lapidus, *Women in Society*, pp. 178-83. See also McAuley, *Women's Work*; and Michael Paul Sacks, *Women's Work in Soviet Russia: Continuity in the Midst of Change* (New York: Praeger, 1976).

15. Lapidus, *Women in Society*, pp. 188-89. The Soviet source referred to is M. Sonin, writing in *Literaturnaia gazeta* (April 16, 1969).

16. On women's participation in the political process, see Lapidus, *Women in Society*, Chap. 6. For the sectoral concentration of female political officials see Joel C. Moses, "Indoctrination as a Female Political Role in the Soviet Union," *Comparative Politics*, 8 (July 1976), pp. 525-47 and his *The Politics of Female Labor in the Soviet Union* (Ithaca, New York: Cornell University, Center for International Studies, Western Societies Program, Occasional Paper No. 10, 1978). For more recent figures, see Anthony Austen, "Kiev Woman Rises in Party Job but Not All the Way," New York Times (March 6, 1981); Nicholas Daniloff, "No Equality for Russia's Women," Chicago Tribune (June 30, 1982).

17. Thus two studies by Soviet scholars reported in the media in 1982 showed that in addition to a full-time job outside the home the average Soviet woman spends 25 to 28 hours per week cooking, cleaning house, doing the laundry, and shopping—compared to four to six hours for the average man. On this and other social and economic problems with special implications for Soviet women, see *Current Digest of the Soviet Press*, 34 (issues for June 9, Aug. 25, Sept. 29, Nov. 3, Dec. 1, Dec. 15, Dec. 29, 1982).

18. Quotations from *Literaturnaia gazeta*, especially the essay by Larisa Kuznetsova, "Whose Job Is in the Kitchen?" (July 12, 1967), translated in *Current Digest of the Soviet Press*, 19, No. 33; *Komsomol'skaia pravda*, "We Ask our Men" (May 27, 1966) and letters about manners (Dec. 8, 1967), in *Current Digest* . . . , 17, No. 29 and 19, No. 1; also Daniloff, "No Equality." For references to these and other articles, I am indebted to an unpublished paper by Marilyn Power Goldberg, "Women in the Soviet Economy."

# 26

## A Troubled Society

### David E. Powell

For most of the twentieth century Russian and Soviet society has experienced intense turmoil. World War I was an enormous cataclysm, and not only because millions of Russians were killed, wounded or captured in this meaningless crusade. The conflict meant the forcible uprooting of millions of peasants; it produced destruction and devastation on a vast scale; and it led to peasant land seizures in the countryside and bread riots in the cities. Finally, it brought about the fall of the Russian monarchy and then of the Provisional Government which had replaced it.

The "Great October Socialist Revolution" of 1917, foreign invasion and the Civil War were followed by a famine which took more than two million lives and left the rest of the population exhausted and terrified. Although the New Economic Policy of the 1920s provided a brief respite, the population continued to experience other forms of pressure and disruption. The secret police, the Party and the *Komsomol* (the Party's youth affiliate) carried out a campaign of terror against organized religion. More generally, the authorities initiated a wide-ranging program of undermining traditional loyalties and relationships. Church and state were separated, as were church and school; women were "liberated" (see Chapter 25) to pursue their own educational, family and career objectives; and children were encouraged to identify with the new "progressive" regime rather than remain in thrall to "backward" parental authority.

The late 1920s witnessed the beginning of what some have termed the *real* Russian revolution, the so-called "revolution from above" which Stalin imposed on the masses. As Stephen F. Cohen and other of my colleagues have noted, Stalin's policies entailed collectivization o-agriculture (the establishment of collective and state farms), rapid industrialization, and the introduction of Five-Year Plans with their all-but-impossible quotas and demands for "labor discipline."

Exceedingly high rates of investment, low wages, crowded housing and an assembly-line speed-up took a heavy toll on ordinary citizens, but the regime was unremitting and remorseless. In 1931, the head of the Institute for the Protection of Labor denounced as anti-Soviet the "fatigue theory" or "protective fatigue theory," that is, the notion that the feeling of weariness is a "warning signal indicating that further exertion may have consequences harmful to the human organism." Anyone who argued otherwise was to be unmasked and declared a "class enemy"—not just scientifically incorrect, but politically subversive.[1] A 1932 law stipulated that anyone who failed to appear for work without a valid reason could be dismissed, deprived of the right to use a ration card and evicted from the apartment that had been allocated by the enterprise.[2]

At the same time, the apparatus of terror was turned into an instrument designed to atomize society. Informers, spies, incessant propaganda about "the class enemy" and the need to "intensify the class struggle" made it all but impossible for people to speak candidly, to joke or even to relax. Officials called for eternal vigilance and society had no choice but to accept their admonitions. The implications for relations within the family, between friends, and among fellow-workers were devastating. The very authorities who sang the praises of "collectivism" were, of course, doing their best to destroy the ties that had linked society for centuries. For a time—but not forever—they were extraordinarily successful.

The constant fear of arbitrary arrest, incarceration, execution or banishment to the camps did not end with the outbreak of World War II. The seizure and absorption of eastern Poland in 1939, and of the Baltic states in 1940, were accompanied by large-scale arrests and deportations. After the German invasion of the Soviet Union in 1941, Stalin ordered the forcible deportation of several million Volga Germans, Crimean Tatars, Chechen, Ingushi, Karachai and other minority nationalities from their homelands inside the Soviet Union—the Volga Germans in 1941, the others in 1943 to 1944. Most were hauled off in boxcars and resettled in Kazakhstan, Central Asia and Siberia. Thousands of these unfortunate individuals, regarded by Stalin as a potential "fifth column" ready to collaborate with the invader, perished en route to their new homes.

The war itself and its effects on Soviet society probably cannot be comprehended by an outsider. Some 20 million Soviet citizens died as a result of the German invasion, either in battle or from starvation or disease.

But World War II wound up reinforcing powerful feelings of national pride and patriotism that the Soviet regime was desperately anxious to foster. Thus, even though Marx and Engels had taught that "working-men of the world" had no country, Stalin encouraged his countrymen to see the conflict with Germany as "The Great Patriotic War" or "The Great War for the Motherland." Many of the controls which had been placed on the various churches were relaxed, and official propaganda likened the struggle against the Nazis to earlier battles to cast out other cruel invaders. There was an enormous upsurge of patriotic feeling, a willingness to sacrifice, and an identification of personal goals and feelings with those of the Soviet state. Society, in a sense, was reconstituted under the terrifying pressure of war.

The postwar years witnessed a return to many of the policies that had stifled Soviet society in the 1930s. The need to reconstruct the country's industrial base as quickly as possible meant housing that was as shabby as it was crowded and consumer goods that were limited in quantity and of poor quality.

Minimal attention was given to developing the agricultural sector and improving the people's diet. Long hours of hard work without commensurate rewards inevitably gave rise to low labor productivity, spoiled and defective goods, and to a labor force that made a mockery of the propaganda image of smiling men and women enthusiastically setting new production records. The situation in the countryside was, if anything, worse: an irrational system of incentives and rewards, along with a shocking lack of investment capital, kept the collective farm system and the population that worked it backward and miserable.

Not until Stalin's death in 1953 could the authorities begin to improve their ties with society. They did so in ways that were both dramatic and subtle. Perhaps most important was the elimination of mass terror: Lavrenty Beria and other secret police officials were arrested and shot as "enemies of the people," and millions of ordinary men and women were released from labor camps. Promising "a return to Leninist norms of socialist legality," the Communist Party reasserted its control over all social and economic institutions, and in large measure removed the arbitrariness that had prevailed under Stalin.

There was also a major effort to raise the standard of living, to reduce the differences between "mental and physical labor," and to bring the quality of life in rural areas up to that of urban residents. These policies were implemented by improving the quantity and quality of health care, offering better educational opportunities and higher wages, and providing more consumer goods. A massive program of housing construction was undertaken, minimum wage and old-age pensions were increased, and vastly greater attention was devoted to a variety of other social welfare programs. All of these measures, it would appear, were designed to demonstrate the regime's solicitude for the masses and, to use John F. Kennedy's famous phrase, "to get this country moving again." At a further remove, the new approach may well have involved an attempt to prove what the Communist Party leadership had long claimed: "The Party and the people are one!"

Until fairly recently, social change in the Soviet Union was uniformly beneficial to the ordinary citizen, in both the standard of living and the quality of life. Before the revolution, life expectancy among women in Russia was 33; today it is 74. Among men, the figure rose from 31 to a high of 66 in the mid-1960s. A similar development can be traced for infant mortality. According to official data, in 1913 more than one out of every four children (268.6 per 1,000 live births) died before the age of one. By 1971, that figure had fallen to 22.9, an astonishing improvement in little more than half a century.[3]

In the main, both the increase in life expectancy and the drop in infant mortality can be attributed to successful efforts in public health and sanitation. The authorities brought under control many of the life-threatening diseases that had affected infants and young children, and they did away completely with epidemics and certain debilitating illnesses. They trained more physicians and built more hospitals and clinics than their counterparts anywhere else did, and they have introduced an elaborate program of prevention and early detection. Despite continuing problems—rural-urban differences, technological backwardness, shortages of medicines and equipment, the generally low quality of medical care and so on—the overall improvement in public health represents one of the truly extraordinary accomplishments of the Soviet regime.

Increasing degrees of freedom, prosperity and "modernity" are, however, by no means incompatible with retrograde social developments. As the U.S. experience with environmental pollution, drug abuse, youth alienation and vandalism suggests, less rigid social control in a time of expanding prosperity can give rise to various threats to the social order. Recent years in the Soviet Union have witnessed an increase in infant mortality along with a drop in male life expectancy. While the precise dimensions of these shifts cannot be ascertained from published sources—the Soviet statistical authorities responded to these developments by deciding not to release additional information—we do know that the situation continues to be highly unsettling to the regime.

Before the ban on information, the principal Soviet statistical handbook revealed that male life expectancy had fallen from 66 to 64, and that infant mortality had increased from 22.9 per 1,000 live births in 1971 to 27.9 in 1974. The continued silence strongly suggests that conditions continue to deteriorate—or at least have not improved.

Other demographic developments are of a more common nature. Thus, the Soviet population, like that of most other advanced industrial societies, has been growing older. The number of persons of pension age (55 and above for women, 60 and above for men) increases with each passing year. On the eve of World War II, approximately 9 percent of the population were eligible for retirement, but by 1959 the proportion had increased to 12 percent. The 1970 census revealed that the figure had risen to 15 percent, and even though the necessary data from the 1979 census have not been published, Soviet experts put the figure at 15.5 percent today. One out of every 15 individuals in 1939 was 60 or older; the proportion today is one of eight.[4]

The "graying" of the Soviet population has important implications for the country's manpower situation. Inasmuch as the process is expected to continue for the next several decades at least, prospects for continued economic development may well be severely threatened. While greater numbers of pensioners will place increased burdens on the planners' resources, lower birth rates will deprive the economy of badly needed workers for industry, construction and agriculture. Young people are waiting longer before marrying, and married couples are deferring still further the decision to have a child. As a rule, those who do have children have fewer than their parents did and this trend will probably continue. In fact, given the dramatic decline in marriage rates and the equally striking increase in divorce rates, it is clear that the population will continue to expand at a slow pace.[5]

The rate of growth of the Soviet labor force has fallen even more sharply and promises to continue to do so. According to two U.S. government specialists, the rate of expansion during the period of 1970 to 1990 will be only one-third of that which prevailed between 1950 and 1970. Central Intelligence Agency analysts predict that annual increments to the Soviet working age population will average less than 500,000 during the 1980s; the average figure for the most recent Five-Year Plan (1976-1980) was 2,029,000 persons per year.[6]

As recently as 1950, more than one-fourth of the Soviet population was not involved in "social production" or full-time study; today, the figure is a mere 5 percent. In the past, additions to the work force could be secured by recruiting women who were engaged in household work or rural dwellers who devoted their time to farming their private plots, but these "reserves" have essentially disappeared. Further, the relatively small 1960s generation who will be entering the 1980s labor force will be unable to replace the much larger 1920s generation who will be leaving it.

In an effort to cope with this situation, the authorities have moved in several directions. First, the Soviet educational system has been modified: the proportion of general secondary school graduates admitted to institutions of higher learning has declined and vocational training in the secondary schools has been expanded. Second, more resources have been channeled into pre-school (or day-care) institutions, so that today 43.3 percent of all children under the age of seven are enrolled in nurseries or kindergartens. Third, the regime has been increasing its use of child labor. According to the newspaper *Ekonomicheskaia gazeta*, ten million school children were responsible for production valued at 400 million rubles (approximately $560 million at the then official rate of exchange) in 1977 alone.[7]

Efforts have also been made to utilize older men and women in the Soviet work force. Planners have been recruiting retirees and encouraging workers who are approaching pension age to remain on the job. In 1965, only 12 percent of all pensioners living in the Russian Republic had jobs, but a decade later the percentage had doubled. In 1977, some 24 percent of all people of retirement age were employed in the public sector; today, the figure is 30 percent, which means that seven million men and women eligible for pensions have decided to stay at work. When asked, most of these individuals mention financial need; but almost as many say they want to maintain ties with their fellow workers, feel that they are doing something useful with their lives, or cite similar motives. Because wages have gone up far more rapidly than pensions, it is likely that this trend will continue.

Since Stalin's death, Soviet citizens have been permitted and even encouraged to seek employment opportunities that suit their needs. As a result, they have become increasingly sophisticated and demanding about where they are willing to work. Although there is nothing inherently harmful about men and women changing jobs — in a number of respects this is a healthy process for both the individual and the system — so many workers (approximately 22 percent) are doing so that labor turn over has become rather troublesome to Soviet planners.

When workers from factories or areas with a manpower surplus move to enterprises or localities suffering a labor shortage, the result is a gain for all. People attracted by higher wages or other inducements to new enterprises and construction projects, especially those in remote areas, can be put to especially good use. In addition, recent efforts to release "superfluous workers" from some enterprises have contributed to a more rational distribution of the labor force.

But there is widespread agreement that the level of job turnover in the Soviet Union today is not within acceptable limits. Soviet specialists have termed it "harmful" and say that it is "not justified by any objective need." They term it "a barrier to the progress of society," "a disease" and "a social evil which requires opposition on a joint and organized basis." The data they cite clearly indicate that the large numbers of workers quitting their jobs create economic problems for the enterprises they leave, for those they join, and for themselves and their families.

Thus according to Soviet estimates, between 40 and 75 percent of those who change their place of work also change their occupation. Money initially spent for specialized training is therefore wasted, and new funds are required for retraining. Moreover, low morale and high labor turnover contribute to on-the-job injuries, introduce uncertainties into the housing market, cause a deterioration in "the psychological climate of work collectives" and lead to violations of "labor and social discipline." Sample surveys indicate that most violators of labor discipline have held a given job for only a brief time; they also suggest that some 75 to 80 percent of the workers who do not fulfill their production quotas have worked at their jobs for less than a year. One study found that fully 60 percent of all defective goods produced at a particular enterprise were the work of individuals who had been employed there for less than a year.

In an effort to curb high rates of turnover, the Soviet authorities have tried to reward more conscientious workers and to punish "slackers" and "rolling stones." In the past decade, however, a number of Soviet sociologists and industrial psychologists have pointed out that the lack of industrial democracy—Soviet workers have virtually no influence over their wages, hours or working conditions—has given rise to feelings of powerlessness. Such feelings in turn present a major barrier to job satisfaction and to raising productivity. The specialists argue that industrial morale will improve only if a more democratic "microclimate" is established at individual enterprises—if, that is, "everybody, regardless of his position, feels that he is significant and necessary." Some have urged that workers be permitted, even encouraged, to acquire a sense of ownership, and have called for their participation in industrial planning and management. Such an approach would involve bringing ordinary workers into the decision-making process in individual shops and factories, thus encouraging personnel at all levels to help eliminate production bottlenecks and to participate in the setting of work norms and wage rates.

However laudable these proposals are, and whether or not they could help raise the level of job satisfaction and so increase labor productivity, it is highly unlikely that there will be anything more than cosmetic change in this sphere. Just as Marx observed a century ago that "no ruling class ever voluntarily gives up state power," the State Planning Committee, the Communist Party and the managerial elite are hardly likely to give up their control over the labor force. Furthermore, the Yugoslav experience with workers' councils, as well as the more recent Polish experience with the independent trade union, Solidarity, cannot help but reinforce the determination of Soviet officials to cling tenaciously to their power.

The post-Stalin relaxation of controls on population movement has resulted in large-scale voluntary shifts of people from the countryside to the cities and from one area of the country to another. According to official data, 62 percent of the population now live in urban areas—although the Soviet conception of "urban areas" and "urban-type settlements" entails a much less concentrated pattern of residence than is normal elsewhere. Still, a massive exodus from the villages has undeniably occurred, an exodus that until very recently showed no signs of slowing.

Annually for the past 20 years or more some 1.5 to 2.0 million rural dwellers have migrated to the cities. The movement was not spontaneous or unexpected; indeed, it resulted primarily from official policy. Committed to a program of industrial development that required the skills of a large, urban labor force, and perhaps sharing the contempt of Marx and Engels for "the idiocy of rural life," the government had actively encouraged peasants and their children to leave the countryside. Until a decade or so ago, the authorities welcomed urbanization, viewing it as a prerequisite for industrialization and economic development as well as a means of increasing social mobility and bringing "backward" citizens into the socioeconomic mainstream. Now, however, they are reassessing their unqualified endorsement of the process and eventually may place rigid restrictions on this movement.

Rural-urban migration is primarily a movement of teenagers and those in their twenties and early thirties. In the main, it is "the best and the brightest," the young people with energy, ambition and skills who abandon the farm and make their way to the city. Machine operators (tractor drivers, truck drivers, combine operators, among others) as well as members of the rural intelligentsia (schoolteachers, librarians, agronomists or economists) are especially anxious to leave. Those who go to the countryside on obligatory assignments after finishing their education in the city generally leave as soon as their period of required service is up.

In a classic study of Soviet migrants and potential migrants, T. I. Zaslavskaia found that most respondents pointed to the quality of life in the city as the primary inducement to leave home.[8] In particular, they cited the diversity of the urban environment, better working conditions, more interesting and remunerative jobs, more and better services, and better opportunities to continue their own education or that of their children. Zaslavskaia was bold enough to add that younger men and women not only found farm work uninteresting but also were frustrated because they were not "masters of the land." Yet if the point is well taken, it is difficult to believe that the system of socialized agriculture will soon be abandoned. Collectivization was introduced for *political* rather than economic reasons, and the same factors that mandate Party control over industry ensure that socialized agriculture will persist for the foreseeable future.

The Soviet authorities still view the rural exodus as "a historically legitimate, progressive process," one required by "the objective laws of social development." Yet officials and specialists alike are becoming increasingly uneasy with some of its consequences. There are four major areas of concern.

• Rural dwellers tend to move to the city from precisely those areas (Siberia and the Urals) which already suffer from manpower shortages, while villagers in areas of surplus manpower (Central Asia, Moldavia and the Caucasus) have been the most reluctant to leave for the cities. Few individuals, whether peasants or urban residents, are anxious to move to the energy-producing areas of Siberia or to the Sino-Soviet border.

• People who reach the city tend to marry later and to have smaller families than those who remain in the village. There has also been a sharp decline in rural birth rates, largely because of the departure of men and women in their twenties and early thirties. In view of the labor shortage, official concern is clearly warranted.

• The enormous influx of rural folk into Soviet cities has led to or exacerbated a wide array of urban problems, ranging from crowded nousing, crime and delinquency to emotional disorders and marital instability. Statistics on crime and delinquency in the Soviet Union continue to be a state secret (as they have been since 1927), but increasingly frequent and pointed press coverage of such matters strongly suggests that anti-social behavior among the young is getting out of hand.

• Finally, uncontrolled rural out-migration has been found to be "in conflict with the needs of agricultural production." The most competent and promising youngsters abandon the land, leaving the farms to older less skilled and less productive workers. Soviet studies showing a decrease in the rural population generally have revealed an even sharper drop among those of working age. In fact, most research actually underestimates the disparity between young and old, since persons listed as "able-bodied workers" on some collective farms include women whose husbands work at nearby enterprises. These women remain on the farms to cultivate their private plots for family needs, contributing little to the collective's effort.

While we have been here looking primarily at the social aspects of rural-urban migration, the phenomenon is of even greater importance economically, as D. Gale Johnson indicates (Chapter 16).

Over the past several decades, there has been a dramatic increase in alcohol consumption almost everywhere in the Soviet Union and among almost all population groups. Soviet sources acknowledge that between 1940 and 1980, when the country's population increased by some 36 percent, sales of alcoholic beverages (corrected for price changes) increased almost eightfold. From 1970 to 1980, when the population grew by 9 percent, alcohol sales rose by 77 percent. These figures indicate that current levels of alcohol consumption are more than just a modern version of the traditional Russian "drinking problem." Indeed, according to U.S. economist Vladimir Treml, the Soviet Union now ranks first in the world in consumption of distilled spirits. Treml has found that total *per capita* consumption of all alcoholic beverages has been increasing by 5.6 percent annually over the past 20 years.[9]

An increase in consumption levels, even of this magnitude, does not necessarily imply a commensurate increase in alcohol abuse or alcoholism. Yet there has, in fact, been an enormous increase in problem drinking. A professor at the Academy of the Ministry of Internal Affairs reported in 1980 that 37 percent of the country's male workers "abuse" alcoholic beverages, and other Soviet analysts have expressed dismay at the rapid growth of alcohol-related crime, motor vehicle accidents, on-the-job injuries, birth defects and similar misfortunes.

According to Boris M. Segal, a physician who carried out a large-scale study of the drinking habits of the Soviet population in the 1960s, the highest incidence of drinking and alcoholism occurred in the Russian Republic. There, 91 percent of the adult population were "drinkers" (that is, not abstainers), while 11 percent of the population over the age of 15 and 13 percent of those over 21 could be classified as alcoholics. The other two Slavic republics, Belorussia and the Ukraine, showed rates of alcoholism almost as high, while the three Baltic republics (Estonia, Latvia and Lithuania) ranked fourth, fifth and sixth.

Throughout the country as a whole, Segal's data indicated, 44 percent of citizens 15 years of age or older drank, in contrast to 95 percent of those of Russian nationality. In regions of high wine consumption, primarily the Caucasus and Moldavia, there was a striking discrepancy between "the relatively high incidence of drinking and the relatively low incidence of alcoholism." The lowest figures for drinking and alcoholism were found among Jews and among Moslems residing in the Central Asian republics.[10]

Alcohol abuse is particularly widespread among poorly educated and relatively unskilled urban blue-collar workers, although other groups are by no means immune. In recent years, in fact, the incidence of both drinking and problem drinking has risen in all social strata. But what seems to be especially troublesome to the authorities is the growing problem of alcohol abuse among women and teenagers. Scientists, scholars, journalists and public health law enforcement officials have expressed genuine alarm at this phenomenon, arguing that problem drinking poses a grave threat to society and to the economy.

In the Soviet Union today, alcoholism and associated diseases are the third leading cause of death; only cardiovascular diseases and cancer rank higher. In fact, given the close correlation between heavy drinking on the one hand and cardiovascular problems and cancer on the other, many specialists are inclined to place alcoholism first.

There is perhaps even more concern about the link between alcoholism and birth defects. The dramatic rise in alcoholism among women—far more rapid than among men—has been accompanied by increasing numbers of miscarriages, premature births, small babies and brain-damaged children. Medical journals and the popular press note that among the offspring of female alcoholics there is a higher incidence of infant mortality, mental retardation and a variety of serious physical defects.

Many other ills are associated with alcohol abuse in the Soviet Union. For example, approximately half of all divorces are attributed to drinking problems: in study after study, drunkenness is cited more than any other factor as a reason for the wife initiating divorce proceedings. Suicide, too, is often linked with alcohol. Soviet researchers have determined that more than half of all men and women who take their own lives are not sober when they do so, and one investigation found that almost half of those who committed or attempted suicide were alcoholics.[11]

The consumption of alcoholic beverages is closely associated with crime and delinquency. Data from the 1920s indicate that 23 to 25 percent of persons convicted of crimes were drunk when they committed the

act; today, approximately half—estimates range from 45 to 63 percent—of all crimes are committed by people who are intoxicated. Certain categories of criminal behavior are especially strongly correlated
with drunkenness. Some 60 percent of all thefts and more than 80 percent of all robberies are attributed to intoxicated individuals. Figures for
crimes against the person conform to this pattern: 74 percent of all
premeditated murders, 76 percent of all rapes and more than 90 percent
of all acts of "hooliganism" (a highly elastic term which covers behavior
ranging from "disturbing the peace" to "assault" and "assault and battery") are the acts of people who were drunk at the time.[12]

It is unclear whether the Soviet authorities can prevent the situation
from getting worse. They have raised the price of alcoholic beverages repeatedly; reduced the number of retail liquor outlets; introduced a wide
array of criminal and civil penalties; disseminated anti-alcohol propaganda in the mass media, at schools and at workplaces; and have tried
in many other ways to curb the people's desire to drink. But none of
these measures has been successful, and even some sort of "dry law"
would be unlikely to do the job. The existing problem of illicitly
manufactured liquor would only grow worse, and in turn lead to public
health and law enforcement difficulties that the regime prefers not to
face. Besides, the sale of alcoholic beverages is highly remunerative, providing the single largest source of budgetary revenue for the state.

Turmoil has marked Russian and Soviet society since the beginning of
the century. Before the Bolshevik coup, most of this turmoil consisted of
anomalies—disruptive incidents and episodes that appeared against a
backdrop of conservative institutions and processes. By contrast, the
Communist Party has deliberately sought since 1917 to engineer a social
and economic transformation, and to this end has consciously revolu-
tionized the country.

As the years have gone by, however, and as the regime has consoli-
dated itself, it has been increasingly inclined to pursue conservative
rather than radical policies. The authorities reward hard work and obedience, while punishing those who deviate from prescribed norms. Personal values and behaviors are also, in the main, highly conventional.
Children go to school, are taught to be respectful toward their elders,
and to seek good grades, admission to an institution of higher learning
and a comfortable white-collar job. Adults tend to be highly family-
oriented, anxious to obtain a better apartment, a new car, a country
*dacha* or various other consumer goods that are in short supply.

Although the shortage of consumer goods has led to widespread corruption and a flourishing black market, it would seem that most people

in the Soviet Union live out their lives either in a state of "quiet des peration" or in pursuit of their personal ambitions. And in this, it would seem, they behave much as do their counterparts in other countries. □

1. *Pravda* (May 21, 1931), cited in Solomon M. Schwarz, *Labor in the Soviet Union* (New York: Frederick A. Praeger, 1951), pp. 281-82.
2. Robert Conquest, ed., *Industrial Workers in the U.S.S.R.* (New York: Frederick A. Praeger, 1967), p. 99.
3. *Narodnoe khoziaistvo SSSR v 1973 g.* (Moscow: Statistika, 1974), p. 43; Murray Feshbach and Stephen Rapawy, "Soviet Population and Manpower Trends and Policies," *The Soviet Economy in a New Perspective*, Joint Economic Committee, U.S. Congress (Washington, D.C.: U.S. Government Printing Office, 1976); Christopher Davis and Murray Feshbach, *Rising Infant Mortality in the USSR in the 1970s*, U.S. Bureau of the Census, Series P-95, No. 74 (Washington, D.C.: U.S. Government Printing Office, Sept. 1980).
4. Stephen Sternheimer, "The Graying of the Soviet Union: Labor and Welfare Issues for the Post-Brezhnev Era," *Problems of Communism*, XXXI, 5 (Sept.-Oct. 1982).
5. *Politicheskoe samoobrazovanie*, 8 (1981). The rate of population increase was 1.78 percent in 1960; by 1980, it had fallen to 0.79 percent. The number of births per 1,000 women aged 15 to 49 fell from 139.5 in 1938-1939 to 88.7 in 1958-1959; by 1978-1979, it was only 69.9. For official Soviet figures indicating that one of every three marriages ends in divorce, see *Vestnik statistiki*, 12 (1981), p. 63.
6. Feshbach and Rapawy, "Soviet Population"; also *USSR: Some Implications of Demographic Trends for Economic Policies*, ER 7-10012 (Jan. 1977), p. 3.
7. *Ekonomicheskaia gazeta*, 20 (1978), p. 17.
8. T.I. Zaslavskaia ed., *Migratsiia sel'skogo naseleniia* (Moscow: Mysl', 1970).
9. Vladimir G. Treml, *Alcohol in the USSR* (Durham, North Carolina: Duke University Press, 1982).
10. Boris M. Segal, "Drinking Patterns and Alcoholism in Soviet and American Societies: A Multidisciplinary Comparison," in Samuel A. Corson, ed., *Psychiatry and Psychology in the USSR* (New York: Plenum Press, 1976), pp. 189-90.
11. *Molodoi kommunist*, 9 (1975), p. 102; S.M. Livshits and V.A. Iavorskii, *Sotsial'nye i klinicheskie problemy alkogolizma* (Kiev, 1975), p. 89, cited in S.S. Iatsenko, *Ugolovno-pravovaia bor'ba s p'ianstvom i alkogolizmom* (Kiev, 1977), p. 8.
12. The most comprehensive study of the relationship between alcohol and crime is Iu. M. Tkachevskii, *Pravovye mery bor'by s p'ianstvom* (Moscow, 1974).

# Further Reading Suggestions

These suggestions are confined to books published in English in the last few years. Every title listed contains numerous further suggestions.

Three books similar in coverage to this one, but more detailed, specialized and/or extensive in their treatment, are: Stephen F. Cohen, Alexander Rabinowitch and Robert Sharlet, editors, *The Soviet Union since Stalin* (Bloomington, Indiana: Indiana University Press, 1980); Archie Brown and Michael Kaser, editors, *Soviet Policy for the 1980s* (Indiana University Press, 1982); and Robert F. Byrnes, editor, *After Brezhnev: Sources of Soviet Conduct in the 1980s* (Indiana, 1983).

A good source of information on all aspects of the subject is Archie Brown, John Fennell, Michael Kaser and H.T. Willetts, editors, *The Cambridge Encyclopedia of Russia and the Soviet Union* (Cambridge and New York: Cambridge University Press, 1982).

## HISTORY

Nicholas V. Riasanovsky, *A History of Russia*, 3rd edition (Oxford and New York: Oxford University Press, 1977) remains the best single-volume textbook of the whole of Russian history, including the Soviet period (to 1976).

Three textbooks covering Soviet history (with some pre-revolutionary background) are: Adam B. Ulam, *A History of Soviet Russia* (New York: Praeger, 1976; new edition in preparation); Donald W. Treadgold, *Twentieth Century Russia*, 5th edition (Chicago: Rand McNally, 1981); and Martin McCauley, *The Soviet Union since 1917* (London and New York: Longman, 1981). Basil Dmytryshyn, *USSR: A Concise*

*History*, 3rd edition (Charles Scribner's Sons, 1978), though tedious, contains a valuable appendix of documents, including complete texts of Nikita Khrushchev's speech of 1956 denouncing Stalin and the 1977 Soviet or "Brezhnev" constitution.

The best single study of the early formative years of the Soviet Union is Sheila Fitzpatrick, *The Russian Revolution* (Oxford and New York: Oxford University Press, 1983): short, to the point and well written.

## POLITICS

Merle Fainsod, *How Russia Is Ruled* (Cambridge, Massachusetts: Harvard University Press, 1963) has been revised by Jerry F. Hough and published under the title *How the Soviet Union Is Governed* (Harvard, 1979). The change in title as well as Hough's extensive revisions of the text indicate how much perceptions of Soviet politics have changed since Fainsod's classic first appeared (1953), the "totalitarian" model of the 1950s now giving way to a more complex, less monolithic one. H. Gordon Skilling and Franklyn Griffiths, editors, *Interest Groups in Soviet Politics* (Princeton, New Jersey: Princeton University Press, 1971) remains a basic work, as does John N. Hazard, *The Soviet System of Government*, 5th edition, revised (Chicago: The University of Chicago Press, 1980), which is legal-administrative in approach and contains a valuable appendix of documents.

For more recent developments, see Jerry F. Hough, *Soviet Leadership in Transition* (Washington, D.C.: The Brookings Institution, 1980); Seweryn Bialer, *Stalin's Successors: Leadership, Stability, and Change in the Soviet Union* (Cambridge and New York: Cambridge University Press, 1980), which is more solid; and, more speculative, George W. Breslauer, *Khrushchev and Brezhnev as Leaders: Building Authority in Soviet Politics* (London and Boston: George Allen & Unwin, 1982).

On foreign policy, Adam B. Ulam, *Expansion and Coexistence: the History of Soviet Foreign Policy, 1917-1973* (New York: Praeger, 1974) is a standard work, now supplemented by his *Dangerous Relations: The Soviet Union in World Politics, 1970-1982* (Oxford and New York: Oxford University Press, 1983). For more specialized studies, see Erik P. Hoffmann and Frederic J. Fleron, editors, *The Conduct of Soviet Foreign Policy*, 2nd edition (New York: Aldine, 1980); Seweryn Bialer, editor, *The Domestic Context of Soviet Foreign Policy* (Boulder, Colorado: Westview Press, 1981); Alexander L. George, editor, *Managing U.S.-Soviet Rivalry* (Westview Press, 1983); and David Holloway, *The*

*Soviet Union and the Arms Race* (New Haven, Connecticut: Yale University Press, 1983).

## THE ARMED FORCES

Harriet Fast Scott and William F. Scott, *The Armed Forces of the USSR* (Boulder, Colorado: Westview Press, 1979) is the basic work, to be supplemented by David R. Jones, editor, *The Soviet Armed Forces Review Annual*, now in its sixth volume (Gulf Breeze, Florida: Academic International Press, 1982).

More specialized works include Timothy J. Colton, *Commissars, Commanders, and Civilian Authority: the Structure of Soviet Military Politics* (Cambridge, Massachusetts: Harvard University Press, 1979) and Derek Leebaert, editor, *Soviet Military Thinking* (London and Boston: George Allen & Unwin, 1981).

Two excellent studies of the relationships between Soviet military power and Soviet diplomacy are Stephen S. Kaplan and others, *Diplomacy of Power: Soviet Armed Forces as a Political Instrument* (Washington, D.C.: The Brookings Institution, 1981) and David Holloway, *The Soviet Union and the Arms Race* (New Haven: Yale University Press, 1983).

Andrew Cockburn, *The Threat: Inside the Soviet Military Machine* (New York: Random House, 1983), an extremely negative account based on conversations with Soviet emigres and U.S. intelligence sources, is essentially a polemic against the equally hyperbolic image of a ruthlessly efficient Soviet military "machine" as presented, for instance, in Viktor Suvorov, *Inside the Soviet Army* (New York: MacMillan, 1983); Suvorov is the pen name of an ex-Soviet army captain now living in England.

## THE PHYSICAL CONTEXT

Recent geographical studies of the Soviet Union include: John C. Dewdney, *A Geography of the Soviet Union*, 3rd edition (Oxford and New York: Pergamon Press, 1979); Dewdney, *USSR in Maps* (New York: Holmes and Meier, 1982); and Leslie Symons, editor, *The Soviet Union: a Systematic Geography* (Totowa, New Jersey: Barnes & Noble, 1983), which is compact, well illustrated, and provides numerous suggestions for further reading.

On Soviet economic development and its impact on the environment, see Leslie Dienes and Theodore Shabad, *The Soviet Energy System: Resource Use and Policies* (New York: John Wiley & Sons, 1979); Thane Gustafson, *Reform in Soviet Politics: Lessons of Recent Policies on Land and Water* (Cambridge and New York: Cambridge University Press, 1981); Robert G. Jensen, Theodore Shabad and Arthur W. Wright, editors, *Soviet Natural Resources in the World Economy* (Chicago: University of Chicago Press, 1983); and Boris Komarov, *The Destruction of Nature in the Soviet Union* (White Plains, New York: M.E. Sharpe, 1980). The last is a sensational work, smuggled out of the Soviet Union, which, if even half true, amounts to a devastating indictment of environmental management in the Soviet Union.

For helpful introductory guides to the literature on Soviet architecture and urban planning (not plentiful in English), see Anatole Senkevitch, *Soviet Architecture, 1917-62: a Bibliographical Guide to Source Material* (Charlottesville, Virginia: University Press of Virginia, 1974) and Paul M. White, *Soviet Urban and Regional Planning* (New York: St. Martin's Press, 1980). For the whole history of Russian and Soviet architecture, see William C. Brumfield, *Gold in Azure: One Thousand Years of Russian Architecture* (Boston: David R. Godine, 1983), which is beautifully illustrated with the author's own photographs.

## THE ECONOMY

A good brief introduction is Franklyn D. Holzman, *The Soviet Economy Past, Present and Future* (New York: Foreign Policy Association Headline Series No. 260, 1982). Longer, but still intended for the lay reader, are James R. Millar, *The ABCs of Soviet Socialism* (Urbana and Chicago: University of Illinois Press, 1981) and, more topical, Marshall I. Goldman, *USSR in Crisis: The Failure of an Economic System* (New York: W.W. Norton, 1983).

Raymond Hutchings, *Soviet Economic Development*, 2nd edition (New York: New York University Press, 1982) is a useful textbook, as is Paul R. Gregory and Robert C. Stuart, *Soviet Economic Structure and Performance*, 2nd edition (New York: Harper & Row, 1981), with extensive bibliography.

Abram Bergson and Herbert S. Levine, editors, *The Soviet Economy: Toward the Year 2000* (London and Boston: George Allen & Unwin, 1983) contains up-to-date appraisals by 15 experts of Soviet technological development, population trends, agricultural and industrial production, consumption patterns, and related political factors. See also the collection edited by Morris Bornstein, *The Soviet Economy:*

*Continuity and Change* (Boulder, Colorado: Westview Press, 1981).

Alec Nove, *An Economic History of the USSR*, revised edition (London and New York: Penguin Books, 1982) is the standard work in its field. Laurence T. Caldwell and William Diebold, Jr., *Soviet-American Relations in the 1980s: Superpower Politics and East-West Trade* (New York: McGraw-Hill, 1980) is a specialized work of obvious interest.

## SCIENCE & TECHNOLOGY

Bruce Parrott, *Politics and Technology in the Soviet Union* (Cambridge, Massachusetts: MIT Press, 1983) studies Soviet "technological strategy" since the late 1920s in both its theoretical and its organizational aspects, and concludes that in the years ahead "technological progress will become an even more critical issue for Soviet foreign and domestic policymakers." Soviet policy in relation to environmental and agricultural issues, both to some degree matters of technological development, is the theme of Thane Gustafson, *Reform in Soviet Politics: Lessons of Recent Policies on Land and Water* (Cambridge and New York: Cambridge University Press, 1981). See also Robert W. Campbell, *Soviet Energy Technologies: Planning, Policy, Research and Development* (Bloomington, Indiana: Indiana University Press, 1980) and Philip Hanson, *Trade and Technology in Soviet-Western Relations* (New York: Columbia University Press, 1981).

For a more theoretically oriented work, see Loren R. Graham, *Science and Philosophy in the Soviet Union* (New York: Knopf, 1972); and for a variety of approaches and themes, Linda L. Lubrano and Susan Grosse Solomon, editors, *The Social Context of Soviet Science* (Boulder, Colorado: Westview Press, 1980).

On education, Mervyn Matthews, *Education in the Soviet Union: Policies and Institutions since Stalin* (London and Boston: George Allen & Unwin, 1982) is a good place to start; and Nigel Grant, *Soviet Education*, 4th edition (London and New York: Penguin Books, 1979)—briefer, more general—is still worthwhile.

## CULTURE

Two outstanding books on Soviet literature are Geoffrey Hosking, *Beyond Socialist Realism: Soviet Fiction since Ivan Denisovich* (New York: Holmes and Meier, 1980) and Katerina Clark, *The Soviet Novel: History as Ritual* (Chicago: University of Chicago Press, 1981). For more background, see Rufus W. Mathewson, *The Positive Hero in Russian Literature*, 2nd edition (Stanford, California: Stanford University Press, 1975); Vera Dunham, *In Stalin's Time: Middle Class Values in Soviet Fiction* (Cambridge and New York: Cambridge University Press, 1976); and Richard Freeborn, *The Russian Revolutionary Novel: Turgenev to Pasternak* (Cambridge University Press, 1982).

For the theater, see Harold B. Segel, *Twentieth-Century Russian Drama from Gorky to the Present* (New York: Columbia University Press, 1979); and, for three translated plays (by Mayakovsky, Babel, and Schwartz), Michael Glenny, editor, *The Golden Age of Soviet Theatre* (London and New York: Penguin Books, 1981).

Boris Schwarz, *Music and Musical Life in Soviet Russia* (Bloomington, Indiana: Indiana University Press, 1983) is the authoritative work in this field.

The Soviet cinema is more completely — because more easily — controlled than any other art form in the Soviet Union; it therefore remains much less reflective of popular tastes than of the purposes of the political elite (and, sometimes, of the interests of the cultural elite). See Richard Taylor, *The Politics of the Soviet Cinema, 1917-1929* (Cambridge and New York: Cambridge University Press, 1979) and Mira Liehm and Antonin J. Liehm, *The Most Important Art: Soviet and East European Film after 1945* (Berkeley, California: University of California Press, 1980). "The most important art" is a quotation from Lenin and provides an ideological justification for political control of the Soviet cinema.

S. Frederick Starr, *Red and Hot: the Fate of Jazz in the Soviet Union* (Oxford and New York: Oxford University Press, 1983), a pioneering work in its field, is as close as we have come to a history of Soviet popular culture. James Riordan, *Sport in Soviet Society* (Cambridge and New York: Cambridge University Press, 1980) is also a pioneering study of an important subject, as is Ellen Propper Mickiewicz, *Media and the Russian Public* (New York: Praeger, 1981).

## SOCIETY

On population trends, see Robert A. Lewis, Richard H. Rowland and Ralph S. Clem, *Nationality and Population Change in Russia and the USSR* (New York: Praeger, 1976); John Besmeres, *Socialist Population Politics* (White Plains, New York: M.E. Sharpe, 1980); and Michael Rywkin, *Moscow's Muslim Challenge: Soviet Central Asia* (Armonk, New York: M.E. Sharpe, 1982).

On religion, William C. Fletcher, *Soviet Believers* (Lawrence, Kansas:

Regents Press, 1981) is the most recent general work; and on women, Gail Warshofsky Lapidus, *Women in Soviet Society: Equality, Development, and Social Change* (Berkeley, California: University of California Press, 1978) is now standard. But see also Lapidus, editor, *Women, Work, and Family in the Soviet Union* (Armonk, New York: M.E. Sharpe, 1982).

On Soviet society more generally, David Lane, *Politics and Society in the USSR*, revised edition (New York: New York University Press, 1978) is a useful source of data and further reading suggestions. Also of interest are Mervyn Matthews, *Privilege in the Soviet Union: a Study of Elite Life-Styles under Communism* (London and Boston: George Allen & Unwin, 1978) and Jenny Brine, Maureen Perrie and Andrew Sutton, editors, *Home, School, and Leisure in the Soviet Union* (Allen & Unwin, 1980).

Two first-hand depictions of Soviet life by U.S. journalists remain outstanding books of their kind: Hedrick Smith, *The Russians* (New York: Quadrangle, 1976) and Robert G. Kaiser, *Russia: The People and the Power* (New York: Atheneum, 1976), both available in more recent paperback editions.

Paul Hollander, *Soviet and American Society: a Comparison* (Chicago: University of Chicago Press, 1978) is a wide-ranging work of great interest.

# A Note for Tourists

Travelling both to and within the Soviet Union has become relatively easy for American and other Western tourists. Given the distances involved, the differing customs, the language barrier and, above all, the Soviet way of organizing things, it is best to go with a group—at least for the first time. It is also much cheaper.

Group tours are arranged by travel companies (American Express, Lindblad, Finnair and others), by various private organizations (college alumni associations; friends of art museums; church, fraternal and professional societies) and by such agencies as the Travel Department of the Chicago Council on Foreign Relations (116 S. Michigan Avenue, 60603) or the Citizen Exchange Council in New York (18 East 41st Street, 10017). Or they can be arranged directly with Intourist, the Soviet bureau responsible for foreign tourism in the Soviet Union (its office in the United States is at 630 Fifth Avenue, New York 10020). Any reputable travel agent can also provide information. And students should be aware of the special opportunities for longer stays and language study available to them (contact the study-abroad or Russian—or Slavic—department of your own school or of the nearest large university).

Meanwhile, tourists with firm arrangements or even would-be tourists might want to consult various of the practical guidebooks available at any good-sized bookstore, the most comprehensive of which is Victor and Jennifer Louis, *The Complete Guide to the Soviet Union* (New York: St. Martin's Press), which is periodically updated. Tourists with an interest in history might also consult the classic *Baedeker's Russia* of 1914, which was reprinted in 1971 by George Allen & Unwin (London and Boston) and is soon to be printed again.

# Authors

*Harley D. Balzer*, currently an American Historical Association Congressional Fellow in Washington, D.C., was formerly a Research Fellow in the Program in Science, Technology and Society at the Massachusetts Institute of Technology.

*Mark R. Beissinger* is Assistant Professor of Government, Harvard University.

*William C. Brumfield* teaches Russian art and architectural history as well as Russian language and literature at Tulane University in New Orleans.

*John E. Carlson* is the pen name of a longtime student of the Soviet Union.

*Katerina Clark*, from Australia, teaches Soviet literature in the Slavic Department at Indiana University.

*Ralph S. Clem* teaches Soviet geography at Florida International University in Miami.

*Stephen F. Cohen* is Professor of Politics and Director of the Russian Studies Program at Princeton University.

*James Cracraft*, a Research Fellow at the Russian Research Center, Harvard University, from 1979 to 1983, is currently Professor of History, University of Illinois at Chicago.

*Alexander Dallin* is Professor of History and Political Science at Stanford University and Chairman of the International Relations Program there.

*Mary Ellen Fischer* is Professor of Government at Skidmore College, Saratoga Springs, New York, where she teaches courses in women's studies and in Soviet and East European politics.

*Marshall I. Goldman* is Professor of Economics at Wellesley College and Associate Director of the Russian Research Center, Harvard University.

*Loren R. Graham* is Professor in the Program in Science, Technology and Society at the Massachusetts Institute of Technology.

*Chauncy D. Harris* is Samuel N. Harper Distinguished Service Professor of Geography and Director of the Center for International Studies at the University of Chicago.

*Geoffrey Hosking* teaches Soviet politics and literature at the University of Essex, Colchester, England.

*D. Gale Johnson* is Eliakim Hastings Moore Distinguished Service Professor and Chairman of the Department of Economics at the University of Chicago.

*David R. Jones* is Director of the Russian Micro-Project at Dalhousie University, Nova Scotia.

*John M. Kramer* is Associate Professor of Political Science and Director of the Program in International Affairs at Mary Washington College, Fredericksburg, Virginia.

*Vladimir Z. Kresin*, trained as a physicist in Moscow, left the Soviet Union in 1979, and is now a staff scientist in the Materials and Molecular Research Division, Lawrence Berkeley Laboratory, University of California.

*Paul A. Lucey*, currently a law student at the University of Wisconsin, was formerly on the staff of Keston College, England, a research institute devoted to the study of religion in the Soviet Union and Eastern Europe.

*James R. Millar* is Professor of Economics at the University of Illinois,

Urbana-Champaign, and is currently also directing the Soviet Interview Project, an extensive study of Soviet life based on interviews with thousands of recent Soviet emigres.

*Eugenia V. Osgood* is a Research Analyst in Soviet affairs at the Library of Congress.

*David E. Powell* is a Lecturer in the Department of Government at Harvard University.

*Joshua Rubenstein* is Northeast Regional Director, Amnesty International, U.S.A.

*Mikhail Tsypkin* is a doctoral candidate and Tutor in the Department of Government at Harvard University. He is a graduate of Moscow State University and held a reserve commission in the Soviet Army before emigrating to the United States in 1977.

*Nina Tumarkin* is Associate Professor of History at Wellesley College.

*Irwin Weil* is Professor of Russian at Northwestern University.

# Index